D1480911

Substance, Force, and the Possibility of Knowledge

Substance, Force, and the Possibility of Knowledge

On Kant's Philosophy of Material Nature

Jeffrey Edwards

UNIVERSITY OF CALIFORNIA PRESS

Berkeley / Los Angeles / London

University of California Press
Berkeley and Los Angeles, California

University of California Press, Ltd.
London, England

© 2000 by the Regents of the University of California

Library of Congress Cataloging-in-Publication Data

Edwards, Jeffrey, 1951–.
 Substance, force, and the possibility of knowledge : on Kant's
philosophy of material nature / Jeffrey Edwards.
   p.   cm.
 Includes bibliographical references and index.
 ISBN 0-520-21847-7 (alk. paper)
   1. Kant, Immanuel, 1724–1804–Contributions in philosophy of
nature.   2. Philosophy of nature.   I. Title.
b2799.n37e38   2000
193—dc21   99-30435
                                                                CIP

Manufactured in the United States of America

08 07 06 05 04 03 02 01 00 99
10 9 8 7 6 5 4 3 2 1

To the memory of Ted Edwards,
my father

Contents

Note on Sources and Translations   ix

Preface   xi

Acknowledgments   xiii

Introduction: The Problem
of Material Transcendental
Conditions in Kant's Theory
of A Priori Knowledge   I

PART I: DYNAMICAL COMMMUNITY,
INFLUENCES, AND MATTER
EVERYWHERE   II

I
The Transcendental Principle of Community
and Its Proof   13

2
Problems in the Third Analogy   23

3
Influence, Matter, and Force in the Transcendental
Analytic and the Metaphysical Foundations of Mechanics   48

PART II: THE HISTORICAL BACKGROUND
TO KANT'S CRITICAL THEORY OF
DYNAMICAL COMMUNITY   61

4
Substance and Substantial Force in Leibniz and Wolff   63

5
Dynamical Community, Physical Influence, and Universal
Harmony in the Development of Kant's Metaphysics   73

PART III: DYNAMICAL AETHER IN KANT'S
PHILOSOPHY OF NATURE   93

6
Corpuscular and Dynamical Theories of Matter
in Seventeenth- and Eighteenth-Century
Natural Philosophy   95

7
The Theory of Physical Aether in Kant's Philosophy
of Nature   112

PART IV: THE THEORY OF DYNAMICAL
COMMUNITY AND THE IDEA OF A
TRANSCENDENTAL DYNAMICS   145

8
The Third Analogy and the *Opus Postumum*   147

9
Kant's Transcendental Theory: Heterodox
Considerations on Its History   167

Notes   193

Bibliography   255

Index   265

Note on Sources and Translations

Kant is generally cited according to volume, page, and line numbers of *Kants gesammelte Schriften* (the "Academy Edition"). Excepted are references to the *Critique of Pure Reason* and Kant's Reflections on Metaphysics (*Reflexionen zur Metaphysik*) (published in volumes 17 and 18 of the Academy Edition). Citations from the *Critique* in the main text are located by the pagination of the 1781 Edition (A) and/or the 1787 Edition (B). Apart from chapter 1, only the B references are given when A runs concurrently with B. In the notes, passages from the *Critique* are cited by page and line numbers of volumes 3 and 4 of the Academy Edition. The Reflections on Metaphysics are normally cited according to the number of the given Reflection. But in longer Reflections specific passages are pinpointed with reference to page and line numbers of volumes 17 and 18 of the Academy Edition.

For writers other than Kant, I have used an author-title system of citation in conjunction with an author-date system. Names are keyed to two alphabetically arranged lists of authors' works (Primary Sources; Secondary Literature) in the bibliography at the end of the book. Works listed under primary sources are generally cited in the endnotes by authors' names, abbreviated titles, volumes (if necessary), and page numbers (e.g., Gassendi, *Animadversiones* 32; Schelling, *Werke,* I 495). Secondary literature is cited by authors' names, publication dates, volumes (if necessary), and page numbers of the corresponding entries in the relevant list (e.g., Strawson 1966, 116; Adickes 1924–25, I 148–149). Wherever feasible, passages from primary sources are located according to standard methods. (Aristotle, for instance, is cited according to the page, column and line numbers of the Bekker edition of the Greek text.)

Works by Leibniz and Wolff are cited as follows:

Leibniz:

GM   *Mathematische Schriften* (ed. Gerhardt)

GP   *Die philosophischen Schriften von Gottfried Wilhelm Leibniz* (ed. Gerhardt)

Wolff:

Cos. gen.   *Cosmologia generalis*

Dt. Met.   *Vernünfftige Gedancken von Gott, der Welt, und der Seele des Menschen* (= *Deutsche Metaphysik*)

Ont.   *Philosophia prima, sive Ontologia*

Psych. rat.   *Psychologia rationalis*

Theol. nat.   *Theologia naturalis*

All translations from German, Latin, and French are my own unless otherwise indicated, though I have consulted works contained in the volumes documented in the list of translations at the end of the bibliography. My aim has been to provide fully literal translations that respect as much as possible the syntax and propositional content of the original sentences.

Preface

This book is the fruit of some twenty years of reflection on the implications of Kant's late philosophy. By Kant's late philosophy I mean mainly the contents of the collection of manuscripts that scholars customarily refer to as the *Opus postumum*. In the history of twentieth-century scholarship, commentators have often responded in one of two ways to the approach, or approaches, to the question of knowledge and objective experience in the *Opus postumum*. Some have denied that Kant's late work on the possibility conditions of our experience of objects is fundamentally inconsistent with the standard view of the nature and limits of a priori knowledge expressed in the major writings of Kant's critical philosophy—above all, in the *Critique of Pure Reason*. Others have admitted that the *Opus postumum* contains much that is incompatible with the standard view, but they have attributed this to Kant's old-age mental ineptitude.

Initially, I took the first way of responding to the *Opus postumum*. But increasing textual familiarity with the Kant's late work showed this path to be implausible. As to the charge of ineptitude, three points must be made directly at the outset: First, it is simply not true that the principal arguments of the *Opus postumum* demonstrate Kant's presumed weakness. Second, even if they did, it would prove nothing more than that even a debilitated Kant is philosophically interesting—indeed, perhaps considerably more interesting than those who reject out of hand the notion that what Kant offers in the *Opus postumum* could be crucial to his account of human knowledge. This brings us to the final point, which is by far the most important of the three at issue. It is that the transcendental theoretic approach to the possibility conditions of experience that underlies the *Opus postumum* is also found in the *Critique of Pure Reason*. To be sure, that approach is not compatible with Kant's standard view of the character of our a priori knowledge of nature. Yet it does inform his thinking in a pivotal text from the first *Critique,* namely, the Third Analogy of Experience.

To say this is *not* to maintain that we should interpret the *Critique of Pure Reason* from the point of view of what takes place in the *Opus postumum.* Quite the contrary: we must seek to understand Kant's late philosophy in light of the arguments contained in a key part of the classic foundational work of Kant's critical philosophy. To clarify these arguments, though, we must investigate the origins of the Third Analogy of Experience in Kant's precritical metaphysics. In doing this, we must also explain how the Third Analogy relates to Kant's philosophy of material nature.

What follows is one attempt to complete these tasks. It is worth noting here that my investigations show how deeply Kant's theory of knowledge remains anchored in the central concerns of Leibnizian metaphysics. These investigations show, too, the extent to which the problem of Spinozism serves as the touchstone for Kant's endeavor to specify conclusively his conceptions of transcendental idealism and transcendental philosophy.

Acknowledgments

The research on which this book is based goes back to my doctoral work at the University of Marburg, where I wrote my dissertation under the guidance of Burkhard Tuschling. My debt to Tuschling's work on Kant and modern philosophy in general will be quite apparent, especially from part four below. Not the least of what I have from Tuschling is the firm judgment that there is a great deal more to Kant's philosophy than is commonly accepted—that there are dimensions of Kant's thought which we have not yet begun to open up properly.

Kenneth R. Westphal's work has also been very significant for my interpretations of Kant's texts and the sources from the history of physics, as will be evident from the endnotes. In addition, Westphal's extraordinarily extensive and acute critical comments have highlighted passages and sections in the manuscript that were in need of fundamental revision. My thanks for his insistence on clarity and rigor in the presentation of my arguments.

I thank as well Edward Casey for his support and friendship during the years in which I have worked on the project. Manfred Baum and Eckart Förster have been steady sources of encouragement to me from the time when I returned from Germany to begin an academic career in the United States.

To Edward Dimendberg and Laura Pasquale, many thanks for seeing the manuscript through the review process at University of California Press. Diana Feinberg and Jean McAneny have provided invaluable guidance in bringing the book through production. Charles Dibble has edited the book with meticulous care. Any remaining stylistic oddities are my own responsibility.

I would like to take this opportunity to express my gratitude to J. B. Schneewind. The subject matter of the book at hand precludes that his influence on my thinking will be obvious. Yet his work on modern moral philosophy has been of great importance for the way in which I have approached the historical source materials treated below. This pertains not only to his vigilance against anachronistic interpretation, but also to his insistence on the philosophic fruitfulness of seventeenth- and eighteenth-century controversies.

At this juncture, it is customary to thank one's long-suffering spouse for her or his patience, forbearance, and good humor. Mine—Allegra De Laurentiis—has indeed endured and forborne much while I have worked on this book. But she certainly does not want to be known for doing so patiently. Still, her sense of humor is in no small part responsible for bringing the project to its completion. I am grateful to her for that, and for everything else.

The Problem of Material Transcendental Conditions in Kant's Theory of A Priori Knowledge

The line of inquiry pursued in this book starts with a most intriguing feature of the Third Analogy of Experience. At A212–214 and B253–261 of the *Critique of Pure Reason,* Kant puts forward a strictly a priori argument refuting the notion that substances could be empirically known to coexist if space were empty of *influences, light,* and *matter.* The relationship between these three elements of the field of appearances is not fully explained in the Third Analogy. But Kant's argument against empty space is clearly meant to demonstrate at least two things: (1) Our experience of coexistent objects depends on there being thoroughgoing continuity in the reciprocal action of all perceivable substances. (2) This thoroughgoing continuity is possible only if space presents us with an all-inclusive or universal dynamical plenum, i.e., a continuum of transeunt causal influences between material objects that encompasses the entire field of outer perception.[1] The implication is that there is a material condition that is also an a priori necessary condition of our experience and knowledge of an objective world.

It is astonishing that such an epistemic condition is treated in the Third Analogy—or anywhere in the *Critique of Pure Reason.* Its presence calls into question Kant's view of what can be accomplished by means of a priori argument in the context of transcendental critique.[2] Insofar as it demonstrates the existence of the dynamical plenum as an a priori necessary condition of experience, the argument against empty space establishes this as a *material* transcendental condition. The proof of dynamically non-empty space thus transgresses the limits that

Kant otherwise places on transcendental arguments in the Transcendental Analytic of his first *Critique*. These arguments are supposed to prove conditions for the possibility of experience in keeping with the tenet that the "understanding can never accomplish a priori anything more than to anticipate the *form* of a possible experience in general" (A246/B303). Besides restricting our theoretical knowledge to appearances, this central tenet of the Transcendental Analytic limits pure a priori knowledge of sensible nature to the formal structure of our experience of objects. Since every content, or material, of this kind of experience is given to us on the occasion of actual experience, it is not subject to a priori determination as an objective feature of the field of appearances; and it does not furnish a material condition that any transcendental argument could establish as an a priori necessary condition of our experience of objects in general.[3] Kant's transcendental arguments are therefore based on the idea that the a priori determinable conditions of our possible experience of objects are purely *formal* conditions. Only formal conditions qualify as candidates for transcendental conditions of experience.

Transcendental critique uncovers these formal conditions on the supposition that objects of the senses must "conform to the constitution of our faculty of intuition" (BXVII), and that our perceptual knowledge of these objects rests on rules of the understanding that "find expression in a priori *concepts* to which all objects of experience necessarily conform, and with which they necessarily agree" (BXVII–XVIII).[4] The formal conditions of our experience of objects that transcendental critique reveals are therefore fundamental subjective conditions of objectively valid cognition. They are obtained through analysis of the a priori specifiable functions of pure understanding in relation to the formal conditions of sensibility. By establishing the epistemic necessity of a non-subjective and material condition, the Third Analogy's argument against empty space is incompatible with this "formalism" of understanding and intuition on the basis of which Kant claims to construct his theory of our a priori knowledge of sensible nature.[5]

In view of this incompatibility, we must inquire more precisely into how the procedure of transcendental argumentation in the Third Analogy might be made to fit Kant's conception of transcendental knowledge in the *Critique of Pure Reason*.[6] We are entitled to call knowledge transcendental only if it is "concerned not so much with objects as it is with the mode of our cognition of objects insofar as this is to be possible a priori" (B25). Since Kant insists that the investigation of the mode of our possible a priori cognition of objects must establish purely formal conditions of objective experience, it follows from his account of transcendental knowledge that no particular perceptual content of our cognition of objects can, *qua* material, be subject to a priori determination beyond the most general determination of its conformity to those formal conditions. It is far from evident that this implication can allow for an a priori argument that demonstrates the existence of a dynamical plenum in space. But perhaps there is a way to make room for such a procedure.

At one juncture in the *Critique of Pure Reason,* Kant does in a certain sense qualify his position regarding the material perceptual content (or contents) of objective cognition. When proving the principle of the Anticipations of Perception, he grants our capacity to determine a priori that every "real of sensation" (B208) and "matter of perception" (B209) must have an intensive magnitude or degree. But he is also quite explicit that we can exercise this capacity "without a particular sensation having to be given" (B209). Moreover, he is careful to show that the perceptual content here in question is not itself an *objective* content with respect to appearances. Although all appearances, as empirically knowable objects of perception, contain the real of sensation, this sensuous content or matter is a "merely subjective representation" (B207). It is a representation from which one can, as a subject, become conscious of being affected. Yet when taken in isolation from the other conditions of possible objective experience, it has no reference to an object of perception, since "sensation is in itself not at all an objective representation, and neither the intuition of space nor that of time is to be encountered in it" (B208).[7]

Thus, we can indeed know a priori that any matter corresponding to sensation must have an intensive magnitude and that appearances or objects of perception must be attributed such a magnitude insofar as the real of sensation is referred to them.[8] This does not mean, however, that any given object of perception is subject to a priori determination in terms of its *particular* material content, or that such an object can be proved to exist a priori as part of the field of appearances. It may seem that precisely these restrictions ought to apply to what Kant purports to establish by means of the Third Analogy's argument against empty space. The argument is not an argument for any particular material content of our experience of objects, since the dynamical plenum cannot itself be perceived in the way that empirically knowable coexistent objects can be perceived. Nor does Kant's argument prove a priori the existence of any of these objects.

Nonetheless, it is supposed to prove the existence of the dynamical plenum as a transcendental condition. And such a condition is inseparable from the objective perceptual contents of the spatial field of outer appearances, since it presents us with a continuum of transeunt influences between all empirically knowable objects in space. Even if it is not anything like a particular empirically knowable object, it is still a material and non-subjective transcendental condition for our cognition of outer appearances as coexistent objects. No condition like this can be a merely subjective representation like the real of sensation.[9]

Kant's analysis of sensation in the Anticipations of Perception therefore cannot be employed to integrate the Third Analogy's deductive procedure with his account of transcendental knowledge. Given that, however, then either Kant's formalistic understanding of his transcendental theory of experience must be open to radical reinterpretation or else a part of this theory militates against that understanding. In any event, the interpretation of Kant's theory of our a priori knowledge of sensible nature must be inadequate if it relies exclusively on Kant's official statements that the a priori specifiable possibility conditions of objective experience can only be formal and subjective conditions.

These conclusions pertain specifically to the Transcendental Analytic of the *Critique of Pure Reason*. But they bear indirectly upon the connection between Kant's transcendental theory and his metaphysics of material or corporeal nature. To see why, we first need to understand how Kant views the relationship between his transcendental principles and the principles and laws of nature during the 1780s.

In the most general sense, Kant's metaphysics of nature shows how all empirical laws "stand under" (B165) the categories and constitutive principles of our a priori knowledge of objects. Kant holds that the understanding is the "source of nature's formal unity" (A127) insofar as the system of principles of pure understanding presents principles of the unity of experience that are also "transcendental laws of nature" (B263). Principles of pure understanding qualify as laws of nature because of the fact that "nature (regarded merely as nature in general) depends (as *natura formaliter spectata*) on the categories as the original ground of its necessary lawfulness" (B165).[10] Empirical laws cannot simply be derived from the transcendental laws of nature's formal unity and necessary lawfulness since they "concern appearances that are determined empirically" (B165). Yet even if experience is required for us to become acquainted with particular empirical laws, these laws presuppose the objective validity of the a priori principles of pure understanding that "alone instruct us about experience in general and about what can be known as an object of that experience" (B165). All empirical laws are necessarily grounded by the system of the transcendental laws of nature even if they are not yielded by these laws as principles of the unity of experience.[11]

In a more specific sense, Kant's metaphysics of nature shows how the fundamental principles and laws of physics are grounded by the principles of pure understanding when these transcendental laws are applied to objects in space by means of the "complete analysis of the concept of matter in general" (4:472.5). This analytic procedure generates the system of principles at issue in the *Metaphysical Foundations of Natural Science* of 1786.[12] The concept of matter in general is an empirical concept. But it is "given in such a way that, besides what lies in this concept, no other empirical principle is needed for knowing things" (4:470.1–4). Consequently, the basic principles and laws of physics can be determined exhaustively if the determinations of the concept of matter in general are articulated completely. Moreover, they can be established as *a priori* principles if it can be shown that these determinations correspond directly to what the principles of pure understanding require as transcendental laws of nature's formal unity.[13] Kant carries out both of these tasks by demonstrating that the categorial functions that give rise to the principles of pure understanding are the same as those that enable us to articulate completely the determinations of the empirical concept of matter in question.[14] He thus constructs his system of the metaphysically foundational principles and laws of physics by specifying a priori an empirical concept according to the table of categories.[15] This procedure of specification enables him to determine the actual ways in which particular empirical laws of physics are grounded by transcendental laws of nature.[16]

It is in the *Metaphysical Foundations* of 1786 that Kant explicates the concept of a universal dynamical plenum. He also establishes there, by means of an argument against empty space, the legitimacy of using this concept in physical explanation. He maintains that matter, regarded dynamically, is something constituted through the interplay of original attractive and repulsive forces. He argues that since matter fills space continuously by virtue of these forces' action, there is no need to assume empty space in order to explain the formation and the physical properties of observable bodies.[17] His argument against empty space leads ultimately to the hypothesis that there is a kind of cosmic matter that, though not directly perceivable, fills continuously the space between all

empirically identifiable bodies.[18] Thus, for the purposes of metaphysically well-founded physical explanation, he entertains the notion that
there may be a universal material continuum constituted through the
interplay of forces.

The parallels between Kant's metaphysical argument against empty
space in the *Metaphysical Foundations* and the transcendental argument
of the Third Analogy are striking. Yet the arguments obviously are not
the same. The metaphysical argument is intended to establish merely
the permissibility of the physical hypothesis that a universal material
continuum of forces exists; it is not supposed to prove the existence of
such a dynamical plenum as an a priori necessary condition of objective
experience and knowledge. Furthermore, the two arguments cannot be
linked simply by assuming that the Third Analogy's dynamical plenum
is a material continuum of forces. In the *Metaphysical Foundations*, Kant
derives and justifies the concept of this kind of continuum by means of
the a priori specification of an *empirical* concept. In the context of his
transcendental theory, however, no concept of an a priori necessary
or transcendental condition of experience is supposed to be obtainable
this way. No analysis of an empirical concept can lead to the acquisition
and deduction of the concept of any transcendental condition. If it did,
Kant would lack the theoretical basis for drawing a distinction between
the transcendental laws of nature's purely formal unity and all other laws
of nature.[19]

Nonetheless, the Third Analogy's concept of a dynamical plenum is
not intelligible except in terms of the *type* of concept of a material continuum that Kant employs in the *Metaphysical Foundations*. Moreover,
the Third Analogy's argument against empty space presupposes that a
universal dynamical plenum can only be a continuum of the original
forces of matter. Although this presupposition does undermine the entire basis for the distinction between the transcendental part of the metaphysics of nature and the foundational principles and laws of physics,
Kant is in fact constrained to accept it. Otherwise, his transcendental
theory cannot deliver an account of substance as appearance that offers
a viable alternative to the Leibnizian monadological theory of substance.[20] As we shall see, the correct appraisal of Kant's concern to provide this alternative is indispensable for interpreting properly the Third
Analogy. It is also crucial to understanding the development of his metaphysics of nature from his earliest writings into the *Opus postumum*.

The Third Analogy has been one of the most neglected aspects of the
Critique of Pure Reason, and it has received far less attention than

the other two Analogies of Experience. This is unquestionably due to the difficulties inherent in trying to make the Third Analogy's contents consistent with what Kant elsewhere says about the conditions of possible experience and the nature of a priori knowledge. These difficulties have led some influential commentators to be quite dismissive about the philosophic value of the text itself. They have either stated forthrightly or implied that the Third Analogy simply does not merit serious attention because of the anomalous and, moreover, disreputable character of its proof.[21]

If this proof were indeed philosophically disreputable, and if the Third Analogy therefore *deserved* to be neglected, then our concern with the argument against empty space could hardly be of much significance except to shed light on a flaw in Kant's theory of knowledge. But it will be an altogether different story if we can show how the argument against empty space opens up a dimension of Kant's transcendental theory of experience that cannot even be addressed unless the argument is understood in all its ramifications. In fact, the Third Analogy's proof contains something of extraordinary value for our understanding of modern philosophy's history. Establishing that this is so, however, requires answering conclusively two main objections that may be raised against this interpretation.

The first objection would likely be raised by most of the commentators who have considered the Third Analogy's argument against empty space. It is that Kant uses this argument merely to illustrate the rule under which we can have—in other words, "make"—the experience of coexistent substances in space. Thus, Kant merely *exemplifies* a category's application to appearances by referring to empirically determinable features of our experience of objects in space; he does not intend to establish a material transcendental condition by means of an *a priori* existence proof.[22] The second objection cannot be gleaned so readily from the existing secondary literature.[23] It is that even if Kant does offer an a priori existence proof for a material transcendental condition, this must be judged a mere aberration with regard to the fundamental tenets of his transcendental theory and the argumentative procedures of transcendental critique. The mode of proof in question thus represents a derailment within the Transcendental Analytic. It should not be taken seriously, since it presupposes a concept of transcendental conditions of experience that does not belong to Kant's theory of a priori knowledge.

Does Kant's argument against empty space, then, *necessarily* involve an a priori existence proof that establishes a material transcendental condition of possible experience? If it does, should we take this at all seriously? My argument in this book is that we must respond affirmatively to both of these lead questions.

A Prospectus of the Argument

Part one of this study examines the basic problems that the Third Analogy poses for Kant's transcendental theory. Chapter 1 analyzes, reconstructs, and translates Kant's proof of the principle of community (that is, of reciprocal causal action) developed in the Third Analogy. Chapter 2 explores in detail the central phases of Kant's argument. The Third Analogy occupies a pivotal position within Kant's transcendental theory of experience, and this position is required by the argument against empty space. At the same time, Kant does not provide enough information for us to understand the full import of his argument. In particular, Kant does not make explicit the link he requires between the concepts of cosmologically ubiquitous "world-matter" and transeunt causal influences. This result motivates examining the broader context of Kant's views about matter, force, causal influence, and cosmic aether in order to interpret properly that crucial link. Accordingly, chapter 3 examines passages from the Amphiboly chapter of the Transcendental Analytic and from the *Metaphysical Foundations of Natural Science* that bear on this issue. This examination prepares the way for the discussion, in parts two and three, of the historical context and the development of Kant's views about dynamical community (i.e., reciprocal causal action) and aether theories.

Part two examines the historical background of the idea of dynamical community and the main stages of its development in Kant's precritical writings. Chapter 4 reviews some central features of Leibniz's and Wolff's metaphysics, focusing on two basic issues: (1) the conception of the commerce of substances, analyzed in terms of universal harmony between individual substances (monads); and (2) the metaphysical grounding of a science of dynamics on the basis of an Aristotelian concept of substantial force. Chapter 5 then traces the development of Kant's thought on these issues through his precritical writings between 1746 and 1770. The concept of transeunt substantial force is central to Kant's early attempts to give an account of dynamical community that could present an alternative to the Leibnizian monadological theory of the universal harmony of substances.

Part three examines the development of Kant's views about cosmic aether as a solution to the problem of transeunt causal influences and matter. Chapter 6 treats corpuscular and dynamical theories of matter in modern natural philosophy prior to Kant. This provides the background in contemporaneous physical theory necessary for understanding Kant's views about physical aether and its role in the development of his dynamical theory of matter. Chapter 7 recounts the history of Kant's views on these issues up to the publication of the *Metaphysical Foundations* and shows we must regard the history of Kant's theory of matter as the attempt to achieve a coherent dynamical aether theory—a theory based on the conception that physical aether is a universal continuum, or plenum, of material forces.

Part four draws these interpretive materials together to resolve conclusively the questions presented at the outset. Chapter 8 presents the argument that there is indeed a transcendental existence proof in the Third Analogy and that we must take this proof very seriously in view of what ultimately is involved in Kant's transcendental theory of experience. The proof of the existence of a physical aether undergirds Kant's proof of dynamical community (i.e., reciprocal action) in the Third Analogy. Moreover, the aims and issues involved in such a proof are central to Kant's continued reflections on these matters in the *Opus postumum*. Chapter 9 argues that the type of investigation of the material conditions of possible experience in the Third Analogy and the *Opus postumum*, i.e., Kant's "transcendental dynamics," is rooted in the reappraisal of speculative considerations on space and dynamical community in the *Inaugural Dissertation* and in Kant's metaphysical reflections from the decade preceding the publication of the first *Critique*. The Third Analogy's argument against empty space thus provides a key to understanding the development of the critical philosophy. A bridge to Kant's late work on the transcendental theory of experience puts us in a position to evaluate the fundamental revision of the idea of transcendental idealism that he undertakes in the final fascicles of the *Opus postumum*. Far from being alien to the critical project, this revision is a logical outgrowth of the Kantian theory of our knowledge of material nature. The common judgment about the anomalous character of this theory in the *Opus postumum* reflects the inadequacy of the standard interpretation of Kant.

In sum, examining carefully Kant's argument against empty space in the Third Analogy provides an important opportunity to reassess both the intentions behind and the achievements of Kant's account of the conditions of objective experience by showing how his central concern with the dynamical plenum links his transcendental theory of experience to his metaphysics and epistemology of natural science, and how these are linked to contemporaneous metaphysics, epistemology, and history and philosophy of science. At the same time, establishing the crucial connection between the Third Analogy and the *Opus postumum* lets us understand why Kant was willing to make the dynamistic view of material nature the cornerstone of his final system of transcendental idealism.

PART I

Dynamical Community, Influences, and Matter Everywhere

The Third Analogy of Experience has not been given its proper due in the history of expository commentary on the *Critique of Pure Reason*. Textual exegesis of the Third Analogy has certainly not been of predominant concern to twentieth-century commentary on the Transcendental Analytic.[1] As for the Analogies of Experience as a whole, interpretation has concentrated on the various problems inherent in Kant's endeavor to establish that a priori concepts of substance and causal sequence are necessary for our experience of nature. Although the transcendental principle of community has not been completely ignored, much of its proof has often enough been found to be of purely antiquarian interest.[2] Several more recent expositions of the Transcendental Analytic seem to view the Third Analogy as a mere supplement to the First and Second Analogies. The principle of community has thus apparently been regarded as a kind of appendage to the principles of the permanence of substance and time-sequence according to the law of causality.[3] I do not maintain here that twentieth-century commentary on the Analogies of Experience amounts to nothing more than the progressive downgrading of the Third Analogy's systematic role. But there has in fact been a tendency to place this role in the background of interpretive concern. What follows contests this trend.

CHAPTER I

The Transcendental Principle of Community and Its Proof

§ 1: Community and the Unity of the World-Whole

       In the context of Kant's system of principles, the principle of community embodies a judgment achieved a priori by the understanding. More particularly, it presents a synthetic judgment achieved by the transcendental power of judgment through its employment of a pure concept of the understanding. This employment takes place under the condition furnished by that concept's transcendental schema.[1]

       Let us consider first the category which underlies the principle of community. The category of community is the concept of reciprocal action between agent and patient (*Wechselwirkung zwischen dem Handelnden und Leidenden* [A80/B106]). Kant explicates the sense of this relation in an addition to the 1787 edition of the first *Critique*. At B111–113 he accounts for the agreement between the category of community and the form of judgment from which it derives. He proposes that the sphere (*Sphäre*) of disjunctive judgment is represented as a whole divided into parts and that these parts must be conceived as coordinated, and thus as reciprocally determinative. He then maintains that the same procedure of the understanding is involved when the understanding represents to itself that sphere as when it thinks of things combined to form a whole:

> Now a similar connection is thought in a *whole of things*, since one thing as effect is not *subordinated* to another as cause of its existence, but

is simultaneously and reciprocally *coordinated* with it as cause in respect of the determinations of the other (as, for example, in a body whose parts reciprocally attract and resist one another); which is an entirely different kind of connection from that which is encountered in the mere relation of cause to effect (of ground to consequence), in which the consequence [*Folge*] does not in its turn reciprocally determine the ground, and thus does not constitute with this a whole (as is the case with the creator and the world). (3:97.3–12)

Four aspects of this description require emphasis at this point. First, the relation which is thought through the category of community is the connection *in* a whole of things (*Verknüpfung in einem Ganzen der Dinge*). Second, these things are identified as substances. Third, in a whole of such things, each substance, as a cause, is simultaneously and reciprocally coordinated with the other substances with respect to some (as yet unspecified) determination of those substances. Fourth, the connection in any given whole of things (or substances) must be distinguished from the connection at issue in the mere relation (*im bloßen Verhältnis*) of cause and effect, i.e., in that causal relation which does not constitute a whole.

The special relevance of the distinction that Kant draws between the mere relation of cause and effect and the reciprocal causal determination of substances will occupy us below (chapter 2, § 2). We must now obtain a more detailed understanding of the first three aspects mentioned. Specifically, we need to determine more precisely the concept of thing or substance that underlies the relation of community. I refer to Kant's treatment of the schema of community at A144/B183–184:[2]

> The schema of community (reciprocal action) or of the reciprocal causality of substances in respect of their accidents is the coexistence of the determinations of the *one* with those of the *other* in accordance with a universal rule.

Apart from its definition of the relevant transcendental time-determination, this passage contains two further specifications regarding the relation of community: (1) Community is defined as the reciprocal causality of substances in respect of their accidents. (2) The constituents of this relation are individual substances.[3] On these terms, we can say (bearing in mind the definitional account of community at B111–113) that the category of community, when subjected to the condition furnished by its transcendental schema, has its application to the relation of a whole constituted by substantial particulars that interact reciprocally in respect of their accidental determinations.[4]

So much for Kant's most basic account of community. What, then, is included in the whole of reciprocally interacting substances to which the schematized category[5] is referred? To answer this, we may turn to the two versions of the principle of community or coexistence. According to the different formulations of 1781 and 1787, this transcendental law of nature[6] asserts that the following are necessary features of our experience of objects:

(A) All substances, insofar as they are coexistent, stand in thoroughgoing community (i.e., reciprocal action among each other). (A211)

(B) All substances, insofar as they can be perceived in space as coexistent, are in thoroughgoing reciprocal action. (B256)

Notice the reference to totality contained in both formulations of the principle of community or coexistence.[7] The principle is concerned not with just any coexistent substances or with some multiplicity of substances that happen to be perceivable in space as coexistent. Rather, it asserts that *all* (perceivably) coexistent substances stand in thoroughgoing community or reciprocal action. Thus, the principle of community presents a synthetic a priori judgment that specifies the condition under which our cognitive relation to the empirically relevant totality of substances in space can take effect.

What exactly does Kant have in mind with this statement about the empirically relevant totality of substances? I refer here to the note contained in Kant's general remarks on the Analogies at A218/B265:

> The unity of the world-whole, in which all appearances are to be connected, is manifestly a mere consequence of the secretly assumed principle of the community of all substances that are coexistent: for if they were isolated, then they would not as parts constitute a whole; and if their connection (reciprocal action of the manifold) were not already necessary for the sake of their coexistence, then one could not make the inference from the latter, as a merely ideal relation, to the former, which is a real relation. But as we have shown in the appropriate place: community is actually the ground of the possibility of an empirical cognition of coexistence, and one thus only makes the inference from this cognition back to that community as its condition.

We can conclude from this that the principle of community is an a priori judgment about a knowable totality both grounded in and constituted by the thoroughgoing reciprocal action between coexistent substances. It is thus a proposition concerning the unity of a world-whole. But that means that the transcendental principle of community is implicitly a principle of the unity of the world-whole in which, as Kant states, *all* appearances are to be connected.[8] How exactly does this connection of appearances come to be established?

§ 2: The Proof Structure of the Third Analogy

I will divide Kant's proof for his principle of the community of all substances in space into four main parts.[9] There are two principal arguments by which the requisiteness of the category of community for our possible experience is demonstrated. I label these *core argument 1* (B256–258)[10] and *core argument 2* (A211–215/B258–260).[11] Each of these demonstrates that the category of community is a necessary condition for our experience of coexistent substances, but they are very differently accentuated. It is the second argument—i.e., the original core argument of 1781—that introduces the central theme of our expository enterprise, namely, Kant's a priori argument against empty space. There are also two sets of supplementary considerations on the core arguments. Each set is taken unaltered from the first edition of the *Critique*. *Elucidation 1*[12] (A213–214/B260–261)[13] consists of a detailed definitional explication of the relation of community. It is linked analytically to the argument against empty space in core argument 2. In elucidation 1, Kant seeks to establish two essential positions: (1) The relation of substances at issue in the principle of community includes the totality of empirically knowable world-bodies (*Weltkörper*) and physical objects. (2) Our perceptual cognition of these entities depends on the existence of *influences*, which operate continuously throughout space; *light*, which operates between the world-bodies and the perceiving subject; and *matter*, which is distributed in space. *Elucidation 2* (A214–215/B261–262)[14] does two separate things: It integrates the preceding argumentation with Kant's theory of apperception. It also provides a transition to the general remarks on the Analogies at B262–265.

CORE ARGUMENT 1

This segment of Kant's proof consists in three steps, as follows:

1. B257=3:180.24–181.6: Besides pointing out, parenthetically, the contrast between the themes of the Second and Third Analogies, Kant

lays out the basic meaning of the concept of coexistence (*Zugleichsein*). He also clarifies a fundamental premise of his proof, which is that the known coexistence of perceived things depends on the reversibility of sequences of perceptions in empirical intuition.[15] It is with reference to this reversibility that he determines how we are able to recognize that things are coexistent.

> Things are *coexistent* when in empirical intuition the perception of the one can follow upon the perception of the other reciprocally (which, as was demonstrated for the second principle, cannot occur in the time-sequence [*Zeitfolge*] of appearances). Thus, I can direct my perception first to the moon and afterwards to the earth or, conversely, first to the earth and then to the moon; and because the perceptions of these objects can follow one another reciprocally, I say they exist at the same time [*existieren zugleich*].[16]

2. B257=3:181.16–19: Kant now furnishes a formal definition of coexistence (= *die Existenz des Mannigfaltigen in derselben Zeit*)[17] and proceeds to specify the ground by which it can hold true with respect to the things of perceptual experience. The epistemological requirement for this ground is given by two negative factors: (a) time itself cannot be perceived;[18] (b) the synthesis of imagination in apprehension[19] would reveal nothing more than our single perceptions of things, each in its turn. According to (a), we cannot gather simply from the fact of things being posited in the same time that the perceptions of them can follow one another reciprocally. According to (b), the synthesis of imagination in apprehension would not reveal objects that are coexistent. Nor would that synthesis reveal that the coexistence of these objects is necessary for the perceptions of objects to follow upon one another reciprocally. Given these factors, both the necessity and the logical attributes of the category at issue are evident:

> Now coexistence is the existence of the manifold in the same time. But one cannot perceive time itself in order to gather from things being set in the same time that the perceptions of them can follow one another reciprocally. Thus, the synthesis of the imagination in apprehension would furnish [*angeben*] only each one of these perceptions as a perception that is present in the subject when the other is not, and vice versa, but not that the objects are coexistent—i.e., the synthesis would not reveal that if the one is there, the other is also there in the same time—and that this [coexistence] is necessary, so that the perceptions can follow upon one another reciprocally. Consequently, for these things that exist externally to one another, an intellectual concept of the reciprocal sequence [*Folge*] of their determinations is required in order for us to say

that the reciprocal sequence of perceptions is grounded in the object, and thereby for us to represent the coexistence as objective.

3. B257/3:181.19–27: This final step of core argument 1 does three things: (a) It defines more precisely the relation of substances linked to the concept of the reciprocal sequence of determinations. (It determines this relation as one of influence and, more particularly, as one of community or reciprocal action.) (b) It makes it explicit that the coexistence of substances is a relation of substances in space. (c) It demonstrates that the cognition of this coexistence of substances is possible *only* on the supposition of their reciprocal action, which is to say, *only* under that condition of possible experience supplied by the category of community.

> But the relation of substances in which the one contains determinations the ground of which is contained in the other is the relation of influence; and when reciprocally this contains the ground of the determinations in the other, the relation is that of community or reciprocal action. Thus, the coexistence of substances in space cannot otherwise be known in experience than on the presupposition of a reciprocal action between them; this is therefore the condition of the possibility of things as objects of experience.

CORE ARGUMENT 2

As is true of core argument 1, Kant's second core argument consists in three steps:

1. A211/B258=3:181.23–36: This step coincides fully with step one of core argument 1, although it contains a more developed account of why the problem of our perceptual cognition of coexistent things must be resolved with reference to the reversibility of sequences of perceptions. In core argument 2, Kant (a) defines the coexistence of things; (b) regresses to the problem of how we know that things are in one and the same time; (c) determines the necessary condition of our knowledge of coexistence (namely, that the order in the synthesis of apprehension of the manifold of things is indifferent); and (d) justifies this determination by showing the consequences of assuming that the order in the synthesis of apprehension is not indifferent with respect to coexistent things.[20]

> Things are coexistent so far as they exist in one and the same time. But how does one know [*woran erkennt man*] this: that they are in one

and the same time? When the order in the synthesis of the apprehension of this manifold is a matter of indifference; i.e., when it can run from A through B, C, D, to E or reversewise from E to A. For if it were in time sequentially (in the order that starts from A and ends in E), then it would be impossible to begin the apprehension in the perception of E and advance backwards to A, because A belongs to past time and therefore can no longer be an object of apprehension.

2. A212/B258−259=3:181.37−182.14:[21] As is true of its counterpart in core argument 1, this step expounds upon the requirement that there must be a specific ground for the objective, empirical representation of coexistence. In putting forward this requirement, Kant utilizes (as he also does in core argument 1) the notion of what I will call the "singularity in sequence" of perceptions. He does not, however, directly employ the notion of the non-perceivability of time. Instead, he introduces his argument against empty space: (a) If substances, as appearances, were not connected by reciprocal influences, then their coexistence would not be an object of any possible perception; nor would the perceived existence of any one substance lead to the perceived existence of any other substance. (b) That is, if substances were separated from one another by empty space, it would not be possible to distinguish between an objective causal sequence of appearances and the coexistence of substances as appearances. (c) Thus, given the existence of any two substances (A and B), there must be something by which they reciprocally determine their respective positions in time; for that is the condition on which they can be empirically represented as coexistent substances.

> Now assume this: that in a manifold of substances as appearances, each of these were completely isolated, i.e., that no one of them acted on the other and received influences reciprocally from it. I then maintain that their *coexistence* would be no object of a possible perception, and that the existence of the one could lead by no path of empirical synthesis to the existence of the other. For if one proposes that they were separated by a completely empty space, then the perception that advances from the one to the other in time would indeed determine the existence of the latter by means of a succeeding perception, but it would not be able to distinguish whether the appearance follows objectively upon the first, or is rather coexistent with it.
>
> Besides mere existence, therefore, there must be something through which A determines for B its position in time, and also reversewise B for A, because only on this condition can the substances in question be empirically represented as *coexistent*.

3. A212–213/B259–260=3:182.14–26: Having established that there must be something besides existence for substances (*A* and *B*) to be empirically represented as coexistent, Kant proceeds to exhibit this condition as a relation of dynamical community. He then establishes that such a relation is a transcendental condition that must apply to *all* appearing substances insofar as they are coexistent:

> Now only that which is the cause of the other or of its determinations determines for the other its position in time. Every substance (for only in respect of its determinations can it be an effect [*Folge*]) must therefore contain within itself the causality of certain determinations in the other and, at the same time, the effects of the causality of the other; i.e., they must stand (immediately or mediately) in dynamical community if coexistence is to be known in any possible experience. Now in respect of the objects of experience, everything is necessary without which the experience of these objects would not itself be possible. Thus, it is necessary for all substances in the [field of] appearance, so far as they are coexistent, to stand in thoroughgoing community of reciprocal action in relation to one another [*in durchgängiger Gemeinschaft der Wechselwirkung unter einander*].

ELUCIDATION I

Elucidation 1 (A213–214/B260–261=3:182.27–183.12) first provides a terminological specification of the concept of community. Kant stipulates that community (*Gemeinschaft*) does not, according to his usage, refer to a merely external juxtaposition or communion (*communio*) of parts. Rather, we must understand it as dynamical community, which corresponds to the Latin *commercium* and its grammatical denotation of an intercourse of parts. Dynamical community—*commercium* —is then declared a condition of the empirical cognizability of spatial community (*communio spatii*). The sense of this declaration is explained by means of a restatement of the argument against empty space. But rather than repudiating the possibility of void space by means of an indirect proof, Kant now forthrightly asserts that the following features can be attributed (*anmerken*)[22] to our experiences: (1) Only continuous influences at all positions in space can lead our senses from one object to another. (2) The light acting between our eyes and world-bodies[23] effects a mediate community[24] between ourselves and these bodies, thereby demonstrating the coexistence (*Zugleichsein*) of the latter. (3) We cannot change our location (i.e., we cannot perceive the change of our spatial location relative to objects) except under the fourfold provision that (a) the presence of matter everywhere makes possible the perception of our position; (b) this matter[25] establishes (although only mediately) the co-existence (*Koexistenz*) of even the most remote objects; (c) this matter establishes the coexistence of these objects by establishing its own coexistence (*Zugleichsein*) correlative to them; and (d) this matter establishes its coexistence solely by means of its reciprocal influence.[26] Kant generalizes on these assertions by stating that except for dynamical community (which, as is now clear, is rooted in the action of influences, light, and matter), all continuity in the synthesis of perceptions of objects would be lacking. Consequently, experience itself would not be possible as a synthesis of empirical representations having any temporal coherence. Kant emphasizes that the possibility of empty space *per se* is not refuted by this conclusion. There may well be empty regions of space that escape the reach of our perceptions. But in this sense, empty space is obviously not an object of possible experience.

> In our [German] language the word *community* [*Gemeinschaft*] is ambiguous, and can mean either *communio* or *commercium*. We use it here in the latter sense, as that of a dynamical community without which even local community (*communio spatii*) could never be empirically known. It can easily be attributed to our experiences that only continual influences in all positions of space can guide our sense from one object to another; that the light that plays between our eye and the world-bodies effects a mediate community between us and them, and thereby shows the coexistence of the latter; that we can empirically change no location (perceive this change) without matter everywhere making possible the perception of our position and this [matter] being able, only by means of its reciprocal influence, to establish its coexistence, and thereby (though only mediately) the coexistence of even the most remote objects. Without community, every perception (of an appearance in space) is broken off from the other, and the chain of empirical representations, i.e., experience, would begin entirely anew with a new object, without the preceding one being able to have the least connection with it or to stand in temporal relation [*im Zeitverhältnis stehen*] to it. By this, I do not by any means want to refute empty space, for it may always be there where perceptions do not at all reach, and thus where no empirical cognition of coexistence takes place; but it is then for all our possible experience no object whatever.

ELUCIDATION 2

As was previously pointed out, this segment of the Third Analogy (A214–215/B261–262=3:182.27–183.12) has two distinct aims. It connects the preceding arguments with the critical theory of apperception.[27] It also provides a transition between the Third Analogy and the retrospective comments on all three of the Analogies of Experience at B262–265. The actual proof of the principle of community is concluded with the achievement of the first aim. Thus, rather than taking the passage as a unit, I will consider it under the two separate headings mentioned in the text.

Communio apperceptionis. A214/B261=3:183.13–26: In this passage Kant determines exactly how the subjective unity of consciousness with respect to coexistent objects depends on a perceptual synthesis ruled by the category of community. His purpose is thus to show how this aspect of the subjective or empirical unity of apperception is grounded in the transcendental unity of self-consciousness. The justification for this interpretation is given below in chapter 2, where I discuss the passage in view of the relationship between empirical and transcendental apperception. Here, I give only the translation:

> The following can serve for elucidation. In our mind, all appearances, as contained in a possible experience, must stand in community (*communio*) of apperception; and so far as the objects are to be represented as connected in coexistence, they must reciprocally determine their position in one time, thereby constituting a whole. If this subjective community is to rest upon an objective ground, or be related to appearances as substances, then the perception of any one substance, as ground, must make possible the perception of the other, and vice versa, so that the succession, which is always encountered in perceptions as apprehensions, is not attributed to objects, but rather that these can be represented as coexistent. This, however, is a reciprocal influence, i.e., a real community (*commercium*) of substances, without which the empirical relation of coexistence could not take place in experience.

Compositum reale. A214–215/B261–262=3:183.26–31: The connection of appearances intrinsic to the real community of substances— i.e., the connection of appearances achieved through a synthesis of perceptions conforming to the categorial function of community— is the relation of a *compositum reale*.[28] This term designates the third of the three foundational dynamical relations, namely, the relation of composition, as distinguished from the relations of inherence and consequence.[29]

> So far as they stand outside one another and yet in connection, the appearances constitute through this *commercium* a composite (*compositum reale*), and such composites are possible in a variety of ways. The three dynamical relations, from which all remaining ones spring, are therefore those of inherence, consequence, and composition.

CHAPTER 2

Problems in the Third Analogy

The main target of the next series of analyses will be the a priori argument against empty space and the notions of influence and matter affiliated with it. I therefore do not claim to provide a completely exhaustive explication of Kant's proof of the principle of community. My primary aim is to bring to light the central questions that the void-space argument raises for Kant's transcendental theory, namely, (1) what is the status of the Third Analogy in Kant's theory of objective experience? (2) what is encompassed by the relation of community? (3) how does a material transcendental condition fit into Kant's account of the a priori possibility conditions for outer experience? and (4) how does this account relate to the theory of apperception at issue in the Third Analogy? Before turning to the investigation of these issues, however, I will comment on Kant's use of the concept of influence and on his views about the most basic structure of the relation of community.

§ 1: Relation of Influence and Relation of Community in Core Argument 1

The first core argument presents no fundamental difficulties: Kant's terminology by and large conforms to his basic account of community. But several items are in need of further clarification. These are found in the argument's third step, which demonstrates that our perceptual cognition of the coexistence of substances depends on the presupposition that they interact reciprocally. The relevant lines are as follows:

> But the relation of substances in which the one contains determinations the ground of which is contained in the other is the relation of influence; and when this [relation] reciprocally contains the ground of the determinations in the other [relation], it is the relation of community or reciprocal action.

In proceeding from the characterization of the relation of influence to its description as a relation of community, Kant identifies the former as a relation of substances in which the one *substance* contains determinations the ground of which is contained in the other *substance*.[1] He also identifies the relation of community with the relation of influence, insofar as the *relation* of influence[2] reciprocally contains the ground of the determinations in the other *relation* of substances. Two sets of comments are in order in view of these points.

(1) According to the terms stated, the relation of community might be understood as a kind of expansion of a more basic "one-way" relation of causal influence between substances. That would mean that we could take the relation of community to be essentially a combination of one-sided relations of causes and effects established between things in space. On this interpretation, the concept of causality underlying Kant's use of "influence" in the Third Analogy would be intelligible as a merely derivative product obtained by conjoining the a priori concept of substance from the First Analogy with the concept of causality treated in the Second Analogy.[3] But at B111[4] Kant takes considerable care to demonstrate the inadequacy of any interpretation like this. There, Kant does stipulate that community—defined as the *causality* of a *substance* in the determination another (or others) reciprocally (*die Kausalität einer Substanz in der Bestimmung der anderen wechselseitig*)[5]—originates in the combination of the first two categories of relation. However, in the same context he goes on to express the following caution:

> let it not be thought that the third category is for this reason a merely derivative concept, and not a primitive concept of the understanding. For the combination of the first and second concepts in order to bring forth the third requires a special act of the understanding, which is not identical with that performed in the case of the first and second. Influence, i.e., how a substance can become the cause of something in another substance, is not at once to be understood from the circumstance that I combine the concept of a *cause* and that of a *substance*.[6]

Kant here explicitly maintains that influence is not intelligible apart from the act of the understanding that gives rise to the category of community. He also maintains that, although the concept of community is obtained by combining the concepts of substance and cause, the act of combining is nonetheless a *special* act of the understanding that generates a *primitive* concept (*Stammbegriff*). Thus, to grasp what influence is—that is, to grasp *how* one substance can become the cause of anything in another—a special act of the understanding is required; and this act exhibits precisely the function of the understanding that makes possible the representation of the community of substances or, in other words, the causality of a substance in the determination of another *reciprocally*. Strictly speaking, then, influence must be a feature unique to the category of community as a primitive concept of pure understanding. But if this is true, then there seems to be a certain redundancy inherent in Kant's terminological specifications regarding the relation of influence in step three of the core argument 1.[7] According to what he says at B111, the relation of influence in question is in some sense *eo ipso* a relation of community;[8] for the very notion of influence is presented as being unintelligible apart from the special act of pure understanding through which the concept of reciprocal causal determination is originally acquired.[9]

(2) The relation of community described in the passage taken from core argument 1 is considerably more complex than the relation described in Kant's definition of the schema of community (A144/B183–184). In presenting this definition, Kant portrays community simply, in terms of the reciprocal causal relation between particular substances. He does not give any further description of the structure of this relation in his treatment of the schematization of the categories. But that does not appear to be true of our passage from the Third Analogy. Provided that we take the text at its syntactical face-value, we seem to be dealing not only with a multipolar relation of reciprocal action but with a multilayered relation as well.[10] When referring to a *relation* of substances that contain reciprocally the ground of the determinations in another *relation*, Kant seems to have in mind individual clusters of mutually interactive substantial particulars that interact reciprocally with other individual clusters of substantial particulars.

The text of the Third Analogy does not by itself allow us to determine the significance of this conception of the relation of community in core argument 1. We will, however, eventually be able to return to this problem after treating, in chapter 7, Kant's theory of matter.[11]

Consideration of the difficulties that Kant had in determining the fundamental form of reciprocal action between material substantial particulars in space will shed light on the structure of the relation at issue in the addition to the 1787 version of the Third Analogy.[12]

§ 2: The First Argument against Empty Space

Let us direct our attention to the second step of core argument 2, which introduces Kant's argument against empty space into the Third Analogy. I have already summarized the main stages of this argument. It is now appropriate to translate the passage expansively to make fully explicit the inference moves contained in it:

1. Assume that in a manifold of substances (as appearances)[13] each substance is completely isolated. That is, assume that no one substance acts in another substance and receives reciprocally influences from the latter.[14]

2. Two things follow from this assumption: (α) the coexistence of those substances would be no object of a possible perception; (β) the existence of the one substance would not lead by any path of empirical synthesis to the existence of the other or others.[15]

3. These consequences are necessary; for if we assume that substances are separated from each other by completely empty space, then (α) the perception that advances from one substance to another in time would indeed be able to determine the existence of the latter substance by means of a succeeding perception;[16] but (β) it could not distinguish whether the appearance follows objectively upon the former or else is coexistent with it.[17]

4. Therefore, besides mere existence, there must be something by which any one substance ("A") determines for another ("B") the latter's position in time, and vice versa.[18]

5. That is so, because it is only on this condition that these substances can be empirically represented as coexistent.[19]

Two features of this formulation of the argument against empty space require separate commentary: first, the concept of influence and its connection with the notion of empty space; and second, the opposition that Kant recognizes between the concept of the objective sequence of appearances and the concept of the coexistence of substances as appearances. I will take these in reverse order.

Objective Sequence and Coexistence. Let us consider jointly points 3 and 4 of the void-space argument's expansive translation in view of the problem of objective sequence and coexistence. The necessity of a transcendental condition for the empirical representation of coexistence is established with reference to three items: a synthesis of perceptions that determines the existence of substances; an objective sequence of appearances; and the coexistence of appearances. In view of these items, we must comprehend Kant's deductive procedure as being far more elaborate than it is in core argument 1. In step two of core argument 1 Kant moves from what I have previously called the "singularity in sequence" of perceptions in the synthesis of imagination to the necessity of the category of community for our experience of coexistent substances. In core argument 2, however, he proceeds indirectly (by means of the hypothesis of empty space). In step three of core argument 2 he acknowledges the advancement of perception from one substance to another in time. He thereby recognizes the demand for a condition by which the coexistence of appearances is distinguishable from an objective sequence of appearances and by which substances can thus be empirically represented as coexistent.

In core argument 1, then, the necessity of the category of community is demonstrated in view of the merely subjective sequence of apprehension. But in core argument 2 the transcendental condition at issue (i.e., dynamical community) is put forward in view of the possibility of differentiating between the objective forms of the sequence of appearances. Kant's task in core argument 2 is therefore to establish the possibility of distinguishing between the irreversible sequence of appearances required for the determination of a non-reciprocal causal relation and the reversible sequences of appearances required by the reciprocal causal relation between substances. More particularly, he must show how the distinction between these two relations can be made within a sequence of perceptions in time that determines the existence of substances as appearances.

It is evident that the solution to the problem of objective sequence and coexistence bears directly on the question of the relationship between the Second and Third Analogies.[20] According to point 3 of the void-space argument, the possibility of determining in empirical intuition an irreversible objective sequence of appearances has as its negative provision the a priori determinability of the coexistence of the appearances of substances. That is, the determination of what *is* an objective, irreversible sequence is predicated on the determination of what is *not* coexistence (and vice versa). The possibility of determining what constitutes an objective sequence of appearances thus does not depend *solely* on the categorial rule of synthesis that distinguishes it from a merely subjective sequence of apprehension; for the application of this rule depends on the possible determination of the coexistence of substances (as appearances), and consequently on the categorially ruled synthesis of perceptions necessary for the empirical representation of the coexistence of substances. Accordingly, it is evident that the Third Analogy cannot be a *mere* supplement to the Second Analogy. It is, rather, both supplement and presupposition.[21] The two transcendental principles—the principle of community and the principle of temporal sequence according to the law of causality—are mutually supporting.[22]

In light of the foregoing, it is appropriate to ask whether the solution to the problem of objective sequence and coexistence does not also contain implicitly an assertion about the relationship between the First and Third Analogies.[23] Let us approach this question by juxtaposing points 2.β and 3.α of the void-space argument in core argument 2. If we assume that substances are isolated from one another by empty space (i.e. if we assume that there is no dynamical community between substances), then (2.β) the existence of one substance would not lead by any path of empirical synthesis to the existence of another (or others); and (3.α) the perception that advances from one substance to another in time would be able to determine the existence of the latter. There is evidently an inconsistency in Kant's argumentation. For granted the isolation of substances by virtue of empty space, consequence 2.β denies and consequence 3.α affirms the determinability of the existence of particular substances in an empirical synthesis or synthesis of perceptions. If we accept 3.α, then the First Analogy could have its application independent of the Third Analogy with respect to temporally consecutive perceptual experiences of objects. Given a sequence of perceptions in time, the principle of permanence would thus necessarily hold true of any individually identifiable substance existing in space without reference to the condition under which a relation of coexistence between substances can be ascertained. On the other hand, if we accept 2.β, then the independent status of the First Analogy is clearly excluded. Under this interpretation, the principle of the permanence of substance can have no concrete application independent of the principle of community. For it presupposes the encompassing causal context of experiential unity that the principle of community defines and rules. As far as the founding of the actual unity of experience is concerned (as distinguished from the order of presentation of the Analogies of Experience), the principle of community must be a presupposition of, as well as a supplement to, the principle of permanence—at least to the extent that the latter principle concerns the existence of a multiplicity of particular substances as appearances.[24]

Which of the alternatives just presented represents Kant's basic position? In entertaining this question, let us inquire into the ramifications of the second interpretation for the Third Analogy's relation to the Second Analogy of Experience. Consider again proposition 2.β—the existence of one substance would not lead by any path of empirical synthesis to the existence of another. If we take this as expressing Kant's basic position, then we must also hold that the Third Analogy plays a crucial role in establishing that the principle of temporal sequence according to the law of causality serves as an a priori necessary principle of experiential unity. This means that the argument against empty space establishes not merely the condition by which we can distinguish between the objective sequence of appearances and the coexistence of substances. It also establishes that even the irreversible sequence of appearances involved in our cognition of a one-way or non-reciprocal relation between a cause and its effect presupposes the relation of reciprocal action between substances as appearances. Because perception cannot advance from one substance to another except on the condition of reciprocal action (or non-empty space) between substances, then *any* experience of an objective causal sequence of appearances presupposes that every possible synthesis of our perceptions of substances as appearances must conform to what is required by the principle of community.[25] It follows that each experience of a causal sequence of appearances is possible only as integrated fully with a more encompassing experiential unity, i.e., the unity of experience in which all substances, insofar as they can be perceived in space as coexistent, are in thoroughgoing reciprocal action.

As far as core argument 2 alone is concerned, these considerations of the relationship between the Third Analogy and the First and Second Analogies remain purely conjectural. This is because the information that Kant provides in core argument 2 does not allow us to decide between the alternatives presented by propositions 2.β and 3.α. But when elucidation 1 is taken into account, the balance clearly shifts in favor of 2.β, which denies the possibility of empirical synthesis in the event that substances do not interact reciprocally. In summarizing the import of the void-space argument, Kant states:

> Without community every perception (of an appearance in space) is broken off from the other, and the chain of empirical representations, i.e., experience, would begin anew with each new object without the preceding one being able to have the least connection with it or to stand in a temporal relation [*im Zeitverhältnis stehen*] to it. (A213–214/B260–261)

That is to say that *no synthesis* in the sequence of our perceptions of objects could possibly take place except on the condition that objects or substances in space stand in the relation of dynamical community, a condition that is satisfied only if *all* our experience of objects is underpinned by the transcendental principle of community.[26] In other words, our experience of objects *in general* could not exhibit coherence through time unless the cognitive relation to the omnicomprehensive dynamical community of appearing things in space were already in principle established. Taken together, core argument 2 and elucidation 1 show that Kant's thinking on this issue is not without its internal tensions. Nevertheless, the 1781 text of the Third Analogy shows Kant's propensity to regard the possible synthesis of perceptions ruled by the principle of community as the basis of all possible experience of spatial objects through time, and hence to recognize that the condition of such synthesis is the condition of any particular objective experience.

This means, first of all, that we must interpret the Analogies of Experience as containing an integrated set of mutually supporting principles. But it also means that there is a sense in which Kant is prepared to recognize the systematic preeminence of the Third Analogy within the theory of objective experience established collectively by the Analogies.[27] This sense of preeminence or systematic priority does not, of course, make it necessary for us to revise the notion that the three transcendental principles of the Analogies are, logically speaking, mutually supportive.[28] It involves rather the position that Kant's theory of objective experience is best regarded as a theory of dynamical community, given that all our experiences of substances and causal sequences of appearances are understandable as partial or delimited aspects of the encompassing experiential unity governed by the principle of community.[29]

Influence and Empty Space. Apart from the Third Analogy, the concept of empty space figures prominently in the *Critique of Pure Reason* in two separate contexts, namely, in the Anticipations of Perception and in the First Antinomy. I will begin by very briefly discussing its role in the Antinomy in order to clarify two concepts of empty space relevant to Kant's theory of a priori knowledge.

Kant's presentation of the first conflict of transcendental ideas sets up two principles of reason in opposition to each other. Whereas the thesis asserts that "[t]he world has a beginning in time and is also contained [*eingeschloßen*] within limits in terms of space"(A426/B454), the antithesis asserts that "[t]he world has no beginning and no limits in space, but is infinite in respect of both time and space"(A427/B455). The supporting argument for the antithesis purports to refute the thesis indirectly by clarifying what is entailed by the assumption of empty space and time.[30] As regards space, the argument is directed against the claim that the world, conceived as an absolute whole, is related to empty space beyond its limit. It is supposed to demonstrate that the thesis requires the world's relation to "*no object*" (A429/B457), and hence the limitation of the world by nothing. The dogmatist argument in favor of the antithesis thus attempts to show the self-refuting quality of the thesis, thereby establishing the truth of the proposition that the world must be "infinite in respect of extension" (A429/B457).

Kant's critical solution to the antinomy also eschews the notion that the world is related to empty space.[31] But in contrast to the dogmatic position represented by the antithesis, which assumes the absolute or transcendental reality of space,[32] Kant's rejection of empty space is based on his doctrine of space's transcendental ideality:

> Space is merely the form of outer intuition; it is no real object that can be outwardly intuited; and it is no correlate of appearances, but is rather the form of appearances itself. Space, therefore, can absolutely (by itself alone) not obtain [*vorkommen*] as something determinant in the existence of things, for it is no object at all; it is only the form of possible objects. Things as appearances, therefore, do determine space, i.e., among all its possible predicates (magnitude and relation) they make this or that one belong to what is real; but space, as something self-subsistent, cannot conversely determine the reality of things in respect of magnitude or shape, because it is nothing real in itself. Hence, a space (whether it be full or empty) can well be limited by appearances, but appearances cannot be limited *by an empty space* beyond them. (A432–433/B460–461)[33]

Consider in particular the final sentence of this passage. Although the Kantian theory of space excludes the notion that appearances are limited by empty space beyond the realm of appearances, it does not rule out the idea that space may be delimited by appearances. Consequently, Kant's rejection of the transcendental reality of space does not by itself repudiate the supposition that there can be empty space *within* the world of appearances (*mundus phaenomenon*).[34] The possibility of empty space, of course, is not positively established by this consideration. Still, that possibility cannot simply be dismissed, for any given space can be limited by appearances, whether it is full *or empty*. In the note that he appends directly to this assertion, Kant states that empty space limited by appearances—i.e., empty space within the world— "at least does not contradict the transcendental principles and may therefore be granted in view of these" (A432–433/B460–461).

Given the Third Analogy's argument against empty space, this last statement obviously raises questions about the logical coherence of Kant's account of empty space in the *Critique of Pure Reason* as a whole. The charitable interpretation therefore has to be as follows: In the context of the critique of dogmatist metaphysics, the possibility of empty space within the world of appearances must be granted *in view* of the transcendental principles of our knowledge of objects. That is because the assumption of this empty space is not *formally* inconsistent with any one of these principles simply as stated. Clearly, this is what Kant has in mind in the First Antinomy. For in the context of his theory of objective experience he is quite explicit that none of his transcendental principles can lend support to the assumption of empty space within the world, and he insists that some of the proofs of these principles positively refute this assumption.

We have already established this last point for the Third Analogy. We may now turn to the Anticipations of Perception and thus to the principle of the intensive magnitude of appearances ("In all appearances the real, which is an object of sensation, has intensive magnitude, i.e., a degree" [B207]).[35] In the proof of the Anticipations, Kant shows generally that the principle of intensive magnitude does not allow for an explanation of sense perception that could be used to establish empty space within the realm of appearances. He also demonstrates how this restriction gives rise to a criticism of a common form of scientific explanation. While our main interest at this stage lies in understanding the nature of this criticism, the general frame of Kant's argument against empty space in the Anticipations warrants review.

(1) In addition to (pure) intuition, appearances contain the matters (*Materien*) of some object in general as an object of perception. That is, they contain the real (*das Reale*) of sensation.[36] By itself, sensation provides only for the consciousness that the subject is affected.[37] It is thus

a merely subjective representation in which neither the intuition of space nor that of time is encountered.[38] The real of sensation must therefore be assigned an intensive instead of an extensive magnitude.[39] Inasmuch as they contain sensation, then, all appearances, or objects of perception, must have an intensive magnitude, i.e., a degree of *influence* on the senses.[40]

(2) All reality in perception has such a degree which, though infinitely diminishable, is nevertheless always of some determinate magnitude.[41] Any determinate or extensive magnitude presented in empirical intuition thus allows of infinite variation in the degree of intensity of the real that fills it.[42] But no possible perception, and consequently no possible experience, could prove the complete privation of all that is real in the appearance.[43] That is to say, "never can a proof of empty space or of an empty time be derived from experience" (A172/B214). This conclusion is unavoidable; for the complete privation of the real in sensible intuition cannot be perceived, nor can it be inferred from any appearance and the variation in that appearance's degree of reality. Moreover, such privation may not even be supposed as a means of explaining this variation.[44]

Kant holds that these last assertions provide the basis for his criticism of one of the fundamental assumptions of mechanistic natural philosophy, namely, the supposition that perceived variations in the quantity of matter in different objects of equal volume (or extensive magnitude) can be explained in terms of interstitial empty space. The repudiation of this supposition involves two main steps: first, the establishment of the non-empirical and *merely* metaphysical status of the assumption of empty space; and second, the formulation of a transcendental proof based on the concept of intensive magnitude.[45] This procedure is intended to enable us to conceive of variations in the quantity of matter without being forced to have recourse to the notion of empty space within material objects. But Kant also places severe restrictions on what can be accomplished regarding the concept of matter by means of strictly transcendental argumentation. He emphasizes that his proof does not furnish the actual point of departure for the empirical account of perceived or measurable variations in the quantity of matter for corporeal entities of a given volume. And it cannot even be employed to interdict categorically the mechanistic mode of explanation and its metaphysical supposition of interstitial empty space; for that would involve a *transition* from the systematic level of the principles of pure understanding to the level of empirical principles.[46] The aim of transcendental proof can only be to demonstrate two things: (1) According to the transcendental principle at issue, the nature of our perceptions makes *possible* a non-mechanistic mode of explanation, i.e., a system of explanatory principles that do not require the supposition of invariable or absolute *realia* and empty space. (2) One therefore assumes on non-empirical grounds —and falsely—that whatever is real in the field of appearance must be invariable (or absolute) in the degree of the reality that it exhibits (i.e., in the intensity of its causal influence on the senses), and that perceived variations in the quantity of matter can thus only be accounted for in terms of changes in the aggregation of discrete and qualitatively invariable *realia*.[47]

One might be tempted to think that Kant simply has no business discussing principles of natural philosophy in the Anticipations of Perception. After all, the transcendental principle of the intensive magnitude of appearances is concerned with the quality of the real of sensation, and Kant maintains that sensation is a merely subjective representation that must be understood in abstraction from the intuition of space and time. It may thus seem that when discussing variations in the quantity of matter, he fails to distinguish properly between the matter of objects as the real of sensation and matter as it exists in space. Consequently, he appears to be open to the charge of conflating his doctrine of the material quality of sensation with a metaphysical account of matter as that which fills space.[48]

But Kant does precisely the opposite. In emphasizing the restricted scope of his transcendental proof, he makes it fully clear that his account of the real of sensation does nothing more than open up the possibility of a non-mechanistic explanation of matter in space.[49] His account therefore does not encroach upon the domain of this type of explanation and the principles of the non-mechanistic theory of matter to which it gives rise.

Before returning to the concept of empty space in the Third Analogy, three facets of the preceding reconstruction of Kant's thinking in the Anticipations of Perception need to be brought into sharper focus. First, the argument against empty space in the Anticipations takes the form of a transcendental proof that cannot infringe upon the systematic region of empirical natural science.[50] Kant's proof thus establishes the possibility of a non-mechanistic mode of explanation. But it can do no more than that. Non-mechanistic principles based on the rejection of interstitial empty space have merely the status of explanatory hypotheses; they are not themselves derivable from, or required by, the principle of pure understanding at issue in the Anticipations of Perception. Second, the Anticipations' argument against empty space remains firmly anchored in the problem of the a priori determinability (*Antizipierbarkeit*)[51] of the real of sensation, and its general conclusion is applied mainly to objects of determinate extensive magnitude or volume that exhibit such sensuous content. The focus of Kant's concern with the problem of empty space in the Anticipations is therefore physical bodies taken as the particular objects of outer perceptual experience.[52] Even when Kant refers to heat,[53] he has in mind a material entity, or at least a material quality, that fills a determinate space.[54] Finally, owing to its particular focus, the argument is concerned with the internal composition, i.e., the fine structure, of physical bodies. According to Kant, the mechanistic mode of explanation necessarily involves the assumption that this internal structure cannot be perceived, and that there is therefore an experiential gap or hiatus between the perceivable qualities of physical bodies and the domain of objects treated by any possible empirical science of corporeal entities. Moreover, even where Kant does argue a priori (i.e., from the nature of our perception)[55] against the postulation of interstitial empty space and in favor of a non-mechanistic mode of scientific explanation, he does not assert that his argument is sufficient to bridge such a gap. He does not contend that his transcendental proof makes possible any direct transition between a principle of pure understanding and the part of the general doctrine of corporeal nature that is defined by empirical principles *per se*.[56]

The broader significance of these points will become clear below in our discussion of the development of Kant's dynamical theory of matter (chapter 7). What is interesting at this juncture is the fact that we can better understand Kant's treatment of empty space in core argument 2 of the Third Analogy by comparing and contrasting it with the corresponding treatment in the Anticipations of Perception. On the one hand, both arguments against empty space proceed strictly a priori and without assuming any empirical principles; both are directed against the notion of empty space within the phenomenal world; and both arguments are, for obvious reasons, concerned with the objects of outer perception. But on the other hand, the argument of the Third Analogy is not immediately anchored in the problem of the a priori determinability of the real of sensation, this being in itself a merely subjective representation taken in abstraction from all spatial and temporal properties. Rather, the argument of the Third Analogy against empty space is constructed in view of the epistemological demand to constitute a relation of appearances as the spatial relation of coexistent substances. Granted this point of departure, its explicit concern is not with the notion of space *within* physical bodies; it is rather with the space *separating* substances existing within the horizon of outer perceptual experience. Hence, its objective is not (or at least is not primarily) to furnish the basis for an alternative mode of scientific explanation. It does not establish the metaphysical grounds of an explanatory hypothesis by which the internal composition of material objects can be accounted for empirically in non-mechanistic terms. Rather, it aims to specify and establish the condition of the connection of perceptions by which objects constituted in the sequence (*qua* synthesis) of perceptions can at all be empirically represented as coexistent substances. This condition is, quite simply, that the space *between* all substances, as appearances, must prove to be a non-empty space if the relation of substantial coexistence is to be empirically representable to us.[57]

The role and implications of the hypothesis of empty space in the Third Analogy's first argument against empty space are by now reasonably clear. But notice that our entire problematic has reversed itself with the preceding determination of the condition for our empirical representation of coexistence: What is *non*-empty space between substances? A seemingly naive approach offers itself here: what is this non-empty space filled (or determined) by? To reply to this, we must analyze properly the concept of influence at hand in Kant's argument.

In point 1 of the Third Analogy's first argument against empty space (see p. 26 above), Kant asks us to assume that there can be substances completely isolated from one another. These are substances that do not exchange influences reciprocally. In point 3 of the argument Kant characterizes these as entities separated by empty space. It is thus obvious that he identifies causally isolated substances as substances separated by empty space. Since the argument as a whole cannot be logically coherent apart from this identification, we must infer that empty space is minimally definable as space *not* determined by a relation of influence. It is, in other words, dynamically undetermined space. But this raises the issue of non-empty space as something dynamically determined, i.e., something determined by a relation of influence. What exactly does it mean to say that space is determined by a relation of influence? How does space come to be dynamically determined?

Consider closely the concept of influence at hand in point 1 of Kant's argument (p. 26 above). Since we are concerned with reciprocal action, it is clear that whenever one substance acts on or in (*wirkt in*) a substance from which it receives reciprocally influences,[58] then it must also somehow exert influences on, or at least transmit influences to, that substance. Two features of this description of interaction need to be stressed: (a) at the respective poles of the relation of reciprocal action, influences are both received and transmitted; (b) at least grammatically, "influence(s)" has a substantive denotation. Thus, we are presented with a relation of influence or reciprocal action that is definable in terms of the reciprocal *trans*-action or mutual *trans*-mission and reception of influences. If we are to take the passage under consideration in its grammatical integrity (as obviously we must), then it is at least plausible to comprehend the space between substances that is determined by a relation of influence as the very space that is determined—filled—by causal agencies called influences.[59] Provided this supposition is correct, these are elements that establish the relation of causal reciprocity between substances and that, in doing so, make possible the connection of perceptions by which the coexistence of these substances is known in empirical intuition. But this means that influences provide objective conditions (or preconditions) by which a sequence of perceptions, determined by the category of community, can occur at all. In short, the word "influence" denotes an a priori specifiable condition of possible experience. If we provisionally accept this interpretation, then we must surely ask how the role of such a condition fits into Kant's critical theory of a priori knowledge.

At this point, several explanatory comments are in order. It goes without saying that Kant comprehends the void-space argument as the means of establishing the epistemic necessity of the category of community, a category that offers the rule for the empirical representation of the relation of coexistent substances. But what is remarkable about the argument is that Kant seems to locate the condition of the category's application to appearances not *only* in its transcendental time-determination qua formal and pure condition of the sensibility,[60] but also in the determination of space as a dynamical field.[61] Bearing this peculiar field concept in mind, let us turn to the second formulation of the argument against empty space in the Third Analogy.

§ 3: The Second Argument against Empty Space

Consider in succinct formulation the quintessential tenets of the void-space argument of elucidation 1:

(1) Continuous influences at all points of space make possible (for us) the perception of a manifold of spatially separate objects.

(2) Inasmuch as it effects a mediate community between the subject and world-bodies, the action of light makes possible our cognition of the coexistence of these bodies.

(3) Matter makes possible the perception of local change (motion) relative to our given standpoint.[62] It does so inasmuch as it (a) makes possible the perception of our location in space and (b) demonstrates by means of its reciprocal influence both its presence throughout space *and* the coexistence of all empirically knowable objects in that space.

The passage under consideration certainly does not make our interpretive task any easier. It compounds the entire set of difficulties connected with the question of how we are to understand the role of influence in Kant's theory of a priori knowledge. The postulation of continuous influences at all spatial positions does at least substantiate our previous contention that non-empty space is space determined—indeed, uninterruptedly determined—by causal agencies operating between substances. But light and matter are two entirely novel factors injected into the void-space argument, and Kant makes no effort to determine precisely how they are linked to the concept of influence. That the three elements are conceptually linked is contextually evident, but the foundations of their linkage are by no means revealed. Yet, whatever the basis of the relation between the elements may be, one thing seems clear from the outset: Kant's focus remains the conception of dynamically determined (i.e., non-empty) space as something that contains certain a priori conditions of objective experience. In the second formulation of the void-space argument, this conception is refined in a significant way: as components of dynamically determined *cosmic* space, the three elements figure as conditions of our experience of the empirically relevant *totality* of coexistent objects. And although these elements serve as conditions of our possible experience of this totality, Kant is able to posit their existence by appealing to the empirical actuality—that is, to the *given* perceptual contents—of the totality itself.[63] We must not be led astray by this appeal to the empirically given. At issue here are indeed non-subjective causal conditions of objective experience. But they are nonetheless a priori specifiable epistemic conditions; for they are conditions without which that synthesis of perceptions that forms our experience of coexistent objects could not occur. Moreover, they are conditions that are coupled with the representation of space as a single, omnicomprehensive field of continual causal influences.

Obviously, we need to ask how all this fits in with the formalism of understanding and intuition that is intrinsic to Kant's conception of a transcendental doctrine of elements and, more generally, to his idea of transcendental philosophy as such.[64] To exhibit fully the meaning this formalism, it would be necessary to lay bare the programmatic structure of the entire *Critique of Pure Reason*.[65] Since that is not possible here, it must suffice to sketch out several of its central features. By formalism of understanding and intuition I mean the approach to the question of knowledge that starts with a fundamental methodological requirement of transcendental critique. The requirement is that the conditions of our possible experience of objects must be determined by means of the exposition of the formal conditions of sensibility (space and time as forms of intuition and as pure intuitions), and by means of the analysis of the functions of pure understanding in its necessary relation to productive imagination and pure sensible forms.[66] This methodological requirement goes hand in hand with the position that all synthetic a priori knowledge is possible *only* insofar as it expresses the formal conditions of a possible experience.[67] This position involves the cognitive limitation expressed in one of the main results of the Transcendental Analytic, namely, Kant's determination that "the understanding can never accomplish a priori anything more than to anticipate the form of a possible experience in general" (A246/B303).[68]

Taken together, the requirement, the position, and the limitation just described necessarily lead to the following claims regarding the material aspect of our experience: (1) The matter of perception and of appearances can only be represented *in* perception, and so only a posteriori (A166/B208, A720/B748).[69] (2) Inasmuch as this matter can be given empirically only in a determinate manner, nothing can be "had" regarding it a priori except "indeterminate concepts of a synthesis of possible sensations, insofar as they belong (in a possible experience) to the unity of apperception" (A723/B751).[70] (3) Owing to this indeterminacy, it is not the *existence* of appearances that can be known a priori, but only their *relation* of existence (A177–179/B220–222).[71]

It is difficult to see how the implicit characterization of influence, light, and matter as conditions of possible experience could be made to harmonize with the transcendental formalism at the heart of Kant's theory of our a priori knowledge of objects. In some sense, the conditions of possible experience at issue in elucidation 1 are inseparable from the objective contents of our experience of coexistents, and so they cannot be purely formal conditions (in the sense just delineated). They are conditions of experience that must therefore have some determinate material character.[72] But they are also conditions that, despite their material character, cannot be *merely* given, and therefore representable *solely* a posteriori; for it is precisely because they are necessary conditions of possible experience that they must—if they are to conform to the idea of transcendental critique—be subject to a priori determination and deduction.[73] And indeed, they are conditions that must be thus determinable in respect of their existence as given components of the spatial field of outer appearances. Thus, with influence, light, and matter it seems that we are being confronted with general a priori conditions of possible experience and, moreover, with necessary and transcendental conditions of the synthetic unity of the manifold of appearances in a possible experience.[74] But even as general a priori conditions of possible experience, they are still actual components of the field of outer perception in which objects are known as coexistent substances. As such, they must be *material* conditions of our *possible* experience of coexistent objects in space.[75] What is the significance of this curious facet of material apriority intrinsic to the conditions of our experience and knowledge of coexistents? Why does it surface in the midst of the Transcendental Analytic? And what are its implications for Kant's idea of transcendental philosophy?

Before attempting to come to grips with these questions any further, let us see if we can shed some light on the relationship between influence and matter.[76] Elucidation 1 contains two good sources of information from which we can at least begin to fathom what might be involved in this relationship. The first source lies in the phrase "unless matter everywhere makes possible for us the perception of our position" (*ohne daß uns allerwärts Materie die Wahrnehmung unserer Stelle möglich macht*) (A213).[77] How is the adverb "everywhere" to be understood? More particularly, how is it to be understood in relation to the matter by which the perception of our position is possible?

We might maintain that *allerwärts* has no direct link to the notion of matter as something existing in space, but modifies solely the action by which we make the observation of our position possible. In other words, we could understand Kant as saying that we make the observation of our position *everywhere possible* by determining our position relative to given matter, this being the variety of material bodies (e.g., the celestial bodies) observable in space. Accordingly, the phrase pertains only indirectly to the question of the existence of matter in space. And in any event, it does not suggest that matter must be distributed in all parts of space in order for the perception of our spatial position to be possible.

This interpretation cannot be refuted out of hand, but it is not the only plausible one. An alternative understanding is offered when we take the second source of information into account. Consider Kant's characterization of matter as that which "only by means of *its* reciprocal influence can establish *its* simultaneous existence and thereby the coexistence of even the most remote objects" (*nur vermittelst ihres wechselseitigen Einflusses ihr Zugleichsein und dadurch, bis zu den entlegensten Gegenständen, die Koexistenz derselben . . . dartun kann*) (A213/ B260).[78] In keeping with the interpretive scheme presented in the preceding paragraph, we might assert that matter, thus characterized, should simply be regarded as the sum-total of observable objects.[79] But another way of explicating these lines is to comprehend Kant as referring to the activity of a single material entity diffused throughout space. Under this reading, "matter" is not a merely generic term denoting the manifold of empirically knowable individual objects, or even the aggregate of qualitatively diverse materials that may exist in the space separating these directly perceivable objects. Rather, it designates some kind of ontologically homogeneous cosmic material distributed continuously throughout space. Now if matter is definable along these lines, then it also makes sense to think that the use of *allerwärts* in the present case does pertain directly to the existence of a matter distributed in all parts of space.[80]

The second way of explaining the relationship between "matter" and "everywhere" is obviously open to debate. But its plausibility is greatly enhanced when we consider the continuum, or plenum, of influences mentioned earlier in elucidation 1 (and implicit in the second step of core argument 2).[81] Even if we are not prepared to admit that "matter" designates anything more than the manifold of directly observable material objects, we are still left with Kant's assertion that these are objects connected by reciprocal influences, and indeed by influences that are *continually* operative at *all* positions in space. So precisely what is the link between this notion of a dynamical continuum and the conception of matter as something that only by means of *its* reciprocal influences establishes *its* simultaneous existence throughout space (and thereby establishes the coexistence of all observable objects)? If we are to grasp adequately the fundamental significance of the argument against empty space, must we not suppose that in both instances Kant is thinking of a *material* continuum of activity in space, and that he is in effect declaring that this is an a priori necessary condition of possible experience?

We ought to make this supposition. Even if the relationship between influence and matter (not to mention light) remains unclarified, it still follows from Kant's line of argument that our experience of coexistent objects depends on the a priori determinable function of a continuum, or plenum, of influences. Specifically, it depends on the epistemic function of a dynamical continuum that encompasses all possible content of the field of our perceptual experience of those objects, and that is therefore inseparable from this objective field of appearances. But this is to say that there is a universal material condition (see p. 40 above) that is also an a priori necessary condition of our experience of objects. Hence, the primary significance of Kant's argument against empty space must lie in this: it demonstrates that the possibility of our experience of objects in space is predicated on the *transcendental* function of the entire field of dynamical interactions that lies within the horizon of outer perception, and it thus establishes the existence of this dynamical plenum as a material transcendental condition of our knowledge of sensible nature.

The preceding considerations of the two versions of the argument against empty space have established two things: First, Kant's tendency is to maintain that the possibility of our experience of any and all objects in space depends on the category of the community of substances as a rule of experiential unity. This is compatible with the fact that the three principles of the Analogies of Experience constitute a set of mutually supporting principles. But despite—indeed, because of—the integrated quality of this set, the recognition of Kant's tendency leads us to conclude that theory of objective experience contained in the Analogies as a whole is best regarded as a theory of the dynamical community of substances. In this sense, the Third Analogy has a certain pride of place in relation to the other two Analogies. Second, in his endeavor to critically ground the principle of community as a transcendental law, Kant tacitly makes it evident that the existence of an encompassing dynamical field of material causal activity is a necessary condition for our experience of the empirically relevant totality of objects (or substances) in space. Taken together, these factors lead up to the following claim: by means of his argument against empty space, Kant is in effect proposing that the unity of all objective experience is rooted not *only* in the formal constitution of human sensibility, and that it issues not *only* from the constitutive cognitive accomplishments of pure understanding. Thus, Kant's argument against empty space shows, implicitly, that a theory of our a priori knowledge of objects cannot be constructed entirely on the foundation of a transcendental formalism of intuition and understanding alone.[82]

§ 4: *Communio Apperceptionis* and Original Synthetic Unity of Self-Consciousness

A fully adequate treatment of the problem of the unity of apperception at issue in elucidation 2 would require a lengthy discussion of the general theory of apperception that underlies the entire Transcendental Analytic. It would also demand a detailed investigation of the theory's historical forerunners, as well as the examination of its origins in Kant's theoretical philosophy prior to 1781.[83] These comprehensive tasks cannot be undertaken here, but it is nonetheless necessary to determine precisely the sense of Kant's considerations on the unity of apperception in the Third Analogy. I will begin by dividing up and paraphrasing the passage already translated in chapter 1 under the heading of *communio apperceptionis* (see p. 22 above):

1. (a) Inasmuch as they are contained in a possible experience, all appearances[84] must stand in the community (*communio*) of apperception. (b) If the objects[85] are to be represented as connected in a relation of coexistence (*als zugleich existierend verknüpft*), they must reciprocally determine their respective position(s) in one time, and thereby constitute a whole.

2. (a) If this subjective community is to have an objective ground, i.e., if it is to be referred to appearances as substances,[86] then the perception of any one substance, as ground, must make possible the perception of the other substance (or other substances), and vice versa. (b) This reciprocal determinability of our perceptions of substances (which is made possible by means of their reciprocal ground and consequence relation) is necessary; for otherwise the sequence encountered in perceptions, as apprehensions,[87] would be ascribed to objects, and these objects would therefore not be representable as coexistent.

3. (a) This[88] is a reciprocal influence, i.e., a *real* community or *commercium* of substances. (b) Without such real community, the empirical relation of coexistence would not be possible.

In summarizing the import of this argument in chapter 1 (see p. 22 above), I stated that Kant determines how the subjective unity of consciousness with respect to coexistent substances depends on a perceptual synthesis ruled by the category of community. I inferred from this that his purpose is to show how an aspect of the empirical unity of apperception is grounded in the transcendental unity of self-consciousness. I thus take the community (*communio*) of apperception at issue in step 1(a) of the argument to be the same as what Kant elsewhere terms "empirical unity of apperception," "subjective unity of consciousness," and "empirical unity of consciousness through the association of representations."[89] Accordingly, I understand Kant's reference to *this* subjective community (*diese subjektive Gemeinschaft*) in 2(a) to pertain to a specific form of the community (i.e., the empirical unity) of apperception, namely, consciousness conceived with reference to the reciprocal determination of perceptions by which objects come to be representable as coexistent.[90]

My understanding of Kant's concept of the community of apperception needs some explanation. It opposes the interpretation offered by H. J. Paton, who is the only previous commentator to have paid close attention to the passage. Paton understands the *communio apperceptionis* of step 1(a) to be the "necessary unity which is implied in the unity of apperception and articulated in the whole scheme of the categories."[91] According to this interpretation, Kant's references to the community of apperception cannot be references to empirical unity. They pertain rather to the transcendental unity of apperception, i.e., the original synthetic unity of self-consciousness. Paton further identifies the subjective community at issue in step 2(a) as a particular configuration of such a priori necessary synthetic unity of self-consciousness, i.e., "the togetherness of appearance in one time as a whole for thought."[92] He then argues that an objective ground of this unity is required so that the particular appearances thought of as being together in one time can be regarded as coexistent objects in space, and thus "not merely as combined in one time by an arbitrary act of the mind."[93]

There are two basic types of difficulty with this line of interpretation. First, there is the terminological difficulty inherent in characterizing the transcendental unity of apperception as *subjective*. This certainly runs counter to Kant's insistence in the *Critique of Pure Reason* that all transcendental unity of apperception or original synthetic unity of self-consciousness is objective and, moreover, objectively necessary.[94] Second, there are the logical peculiarities involved in the assumption that the subjective community of apperception, understood as a configuration of transcendental or original synthetic unity, *requires* an objective ground in order for the combination of appearances not to be merely arbitrary. If that subjective community is indeed an original synthetic unity, then it must already contain this kind of ground as an intrinsic condition of its possibility; and there is in consequence no reason to think that the appearances in question could be combined arbitrarily. On the other hand, if the subjective community of apperception does not contain such a ground, then it simply cannot be the transcendental unity of apperception or any possible configuration of this kind of objective and a priori necessary unity.

Clearly, Kant's concept of the subjective community of apperception can only be that of an empirical unity. But how exactly is this empirical unity of apperception with respect to coexistent objects connected with Kant's account of the transcendental unity of apperception, as we should expect it must be in the context of the Transcendental Analytic? The answer to this question lies in a proper understanding of the objective ground brought into play in the second step of Kant's argument.

This is the ground by which the subjective community of apperception is referred to appearances as substances through a synthesis of perceptions. More particularly, it is the ground provided by the category of community as the formal condition of possible experience that allows the relation of reciprocal influence—the real community (*commercium*) of substances—to be determined from a sequence of perceptual apprehensions. In other words, the ground in question is the formal transcendental condition through which a relation of appearances can be determined as an objective relation of coexistent substances from a sequence of perceptions. It is therefore a condition of the synthetic unity of perceptions according to pure concepts of the understanding. As such, it is a ground intrinsic to the kind of unity of apperception that furnishes the principle of all employment of the understanding: the transcendental or original synthetic unity of self-consciousness.[95]

Things are therefore exactly as we should expect to find them in the context of the Transcendental Analytic. Two distinct concepts of the unity of apperception are at work in the passage under consideration: First, an empirical unity of apperception explicitly characterized by Kant as *communio apperceptionis;* this is empirical apperception understood in terms of the consciousness of a whole of objects that are representable as coexistent. Second, the transcendental unity of apperception that grounds all such empirical unity. This is pure, transcendental apperception understood in terms of the a priori and necessary relation of self-consciousness to the objects constituting the perceivable whole of dynamically interacting substances.[96]

Now let us recall here what this whole of substances includes. Consider once more the principle of community itself, which asserts that *all* substances, insofar as they can be perceived in space as coexistent, are in thoroughgoing community or reciprocal action (B256). Consider also the corollary of this proposition, namely, the principle of the unity of the *world*-whole in which all appearances are to be connected (see pp. 15–16 above). Given these specifications of the domain of Kant's principle, we can see that the objective and necessary unity of self-consciousness at issue in elucidation 2 is a configuration of transcendental unity established with respect to the connection or synthesis of appearances through which we know a world-whole of dynamically interacting substances.[97]

§ 5: Results

It is now possible to bring into proper focus both the positive results achieved and the questions left unanswered by this chapter. We have been able to draw four main conclusions: First, the tendency of Kant's thinking in the Third Analogy (at least in those parts of the text taken unaltered from the first edition of the *Critique*) is to underscore the preeminent significance of the Third Analogy within the systematic framework of the Analogies of Experience.[98] This tendency is discernible in Kant's inference that in the absence of dynamical community, *no* synthesis of perceptions or empirical representations would be possible. Second, through the synthesis of perceptions conforming to the categorial rule of community, a dynamical relation of reciprocally interacting substances is constituted for (and by) the subject. This relation encompasses the world-whole in which all appearances are to be connected. Third, the non-emptiness of space, which depends on the presence of influences, light, and matter, is a prerequisite of that connection of perceptions by which objects known in the sequence of perceptions are empirically representable as coexistent, reciprocally interacting objects. Finally, we have adduced that the unity of self-consciousness, which grounds (and is grounded in)[99] the synthesis of perceptions governed by the category of community, involves the establishment of a necessary relation between the apperceptive subject and the world-whole of reciprocally acting substances.

The main difficulties that we have encountered all stem from Kant's argument against empty space. Recognizable above all in elucidation 2, they revolve around (1) the relationship between influence(s), light, and matter; and (2) the aspect of non-formalistic apriorism inherent in Kant's tacit claim that these elements furnish a priori specifiable conditions of possible experience.

CHAPTER 3

Influence, Matter, and Force in the Transcendental Analytic and the Metaphysical Foundations of Mechanics

This chapter explores the relationship between the material conditions treated by Kant in the Third Analogy. It also formulates the problems for Kant's transcendental theory that are raised by the consideration that any material condition of experience can serve as a transcendental condition. I am concerned, first, to reveal a link between the matter mentioned in elucidation 1 and the influences that Kant in core argument 2 and elucidation 1 asserts to be operative at all spatial positions. This link is in fact furnished by the concepts of attractive and repulsive force which, in the *Critique of Pure Reason,* are thematized in the Amphiboly of the Concepts of Reflection. Accordingly, the notion of matter and the idea of a universal continuum, or plenum, of influences adumbrated in the Third Analogy can plausibly be understood in connection with Kant's dynamical theory of matter. Second, I lend support to this position by discussing the relationship between the Third Analogy and the *Metaphysical Foundations of Natural Science* of 1786. The systematic correlation that Kant acknowledges between the transcendental principle of community and his Third Law of Mechanics presupposes the explanation of matter in terms of original forces of attraction and repulsion. A number of consequences for Kant's philosophic system follow from this presupposition, if we accept that the dynamical theory of matter plays any role in establishing the principle of community as a transcendental law of nature. Finally, after addressing the two objections to my reading of Kant's argument against empty space that were mentioned in the introduction, I provisionally characterize the conception of a priori knowledge that emerges when material conditions are regarded as epistemic conditions; I then formulate the problems that this conception generates for Kant's idea of transcendental philosophy.

§ 1: Material Substance and Force in the Amphiboly of the Concepts of Reflection

To reveal a connection between Kant's notions of a continuum of influences and matter, let us here consider some passages from the Appendix to the Transcendental Analytic containing some explicit criticisms of Leibniz.[1] Besides touching on the problem of matter in transcendental idealism, these passages exhibit features of Kant's transcendental idealist response to the Leibnizian idea of the preestablished harmony of individual finite substances, or monads, a response on Kant's part that presupposes the fundamental assumptions of a dynamical theory of matter. The background to this response and its impact on the development of Kant's metaphysics of nature will be a major theme of parts two and three below. Of immediate interest to us are several sets of definitional considerations that are relevant to the concept of influence employed in the void-space argument of the Third Analogy.

(1) Whatever the role of influence in Kant's critical ontology of substance, it is clear from these considerations that the individual terminal of the mutual transmission and reception of influences can only be substance as appearance or *substantia phaenomenon*.[2] More particularly, it is substance as perduring (*beharrliche*) appearance in space, an appearance that is identical with matter.[3]

(2) As *substantiae phaenomena*, the spatially interrelated substances in question can be said to have internal determinations. But these entities are nonetheless clearly distinguishable from Leibnizian monads— i.e., from *substantiae noumena*, which act solely through purely internal powers of representation (*Vorstellungskräfte*) and which are thus completely free of any possible external reciprocal causal relations established by way of physical influence.[4] The determinations of phenomenal substances are therefore only comparatively internal. Consequently, substance, as appearance in space, must be conceived as a complex of relations; and it must be understood as something that

contains external relations, since what is only comparatively internal consists in external relations.[5] Yet some of these relations are independent and perduring. It is through them that we are given a determinate object, and the perduring appearance in space which contains them furnishes the first substratum (*das erste Substratum*) of all outer perception.[6]

(3) Substance is known *only* by the action of attractive and repulsive forces, inasmuch as the former ground the attractive capacity of matter and the latter its fundamental property of impenetrability.[7] These forces are thus constitutive features of the empirically employable concept of matter; and by direct implication, they are constitutive for the concept of substance as appearance.[8] As perduring appearance in space, substance is definable as impenetrable extension (*undurchdringliche Ausdehnung*), which is what furnishes the first substrate of all outer perception.[9]

According to these stipulations from the Amphiboly chapter, to "receive reciprocally influences from" a substance in space (see p. 36 above) ought to occur with respect to an entity that, conceived as a complex of relations, is equivalently definable as matter, perduring appearance in space, impenetrable extension, and the first substrate of all outer perception; is knowable only on grounds of the action of attractive and repulsive forces; and is attributed impenetrability and the capacity to attract as its fundamental empirically relevant properties. Now on these assumptions Kant would seem logically constrained, in the general context of the Transcendental Analytic, to identify influence with attractive and repulsive force. That is, given (a) that both the influences of the Third Analogy and the attractive and repulsive forces of the Amphiboly chapter have, grammatically, a substantive denotation and are described as having an active causal role; (b) that substance, as appearance in space or matter, is known *only* by the action of attractive and repulsive forces; (c) that this substance is constituted as a complex of relations and, moreover, as that which contains merely external relations; and (d) that the alternative Leibnizian assumption of purely internal relations of substance necessarily leads to an understanding of force as a noumenal (or monadic) force of representation, and hence to the metaphysical postulate that finite substances are completely isolated from all external causal action or any relation of influence—given all this, it seems that in Kant's account of substance as appearance, "influence" could refer to nothing else than the materially constitutive efficacy of attractive and repulsive force.

Nowhere in the first *Critique* does Kant expressly identify influence with material force. But if the identity of influence and such force could be firmly established, then the link between the continuum of influences and the "matter everywhere" in the void-space argument would also be ascertained. If *all* matter is known *only* as something constituted by the action of attractive and repulsive forces, and if influence can be understood in terms of these forces, then our entire problem concerning material conditions of possible experience could be formulated in terms of a cosmic matter conceived as a universal continuum of attractive and repulsive forces. In other words, it could be understood with reference to the object of a dynamical theory of matter.

But whatever the logical constraints under which Kant is in fact operating, he certainly has ample reason not to connect forthrightly the concepts of matter and influence by means of the dynamical concept of material force. Making this connection explicit would constrain him to admit that a dynamical theory of matter is required for the deduction of a *transcendental* principle. And that admission would thoroughly problematize the relationship between transcendental principles and metaphysical principles of corporeal nature that is central to Kant's plan for a comprehensive system of transcendental philosophy.[10] In particular, it would seem to involve the effacement of the line of demarcation between the transcendental part of the metaphysics of nature and the special metaphysical science of corporeal nature that Kant draws in the *Metaphysical Foundations of Natural Science* of 1786.[11] Thus, if the fundamental tenets of a dynamical theory of matter are in fact prerequisites for the deduction of a transcendental law of nature, then it is unclear how the distinction between the transcendental and special metaphysical disciplines could be upheld rigorously. There will be more to say about this implication in the next section.

§ 2: Influence, Force, and Kant's Third Law of Mechanics

A separate problem also pertains to the architectonic plan of Kant's metaphysics of material nature, but it concerns most directly the connection between two types of special metaphysical principle rather than the relationship between these principles and transcendental laws. I shall comment on the connection between the principles of the Mechanics and the Dynamics of material nature as it was viewed by

Kant in the *Metaphysical Foundations* of 1786. My intention is to shed further light on the broader architectonic ramifications of the relation of influence, matter, and force in the Transcendental Analytic by considering Kant's treatment of the systematic correlate to the principle of community. This correlate is the Third Mechanical Law or the Mechanical Law of the Equality of Action and Reaction,[12] which states that "In all communication of motion, action and reaction are always equal to each other" (4:544.32–33).

In his proof of this metaphysical law of nature, Kant explains that the concept of reaction involves a specification of the pure concept of reciprocal action employed in the transcendental principle of community.[13] It is this special metaphysical concept of causal reciprocity, obtained through the application of the category of community to motion as the fundamental determination of objects of the outer sense, that furnishes the mechanical concept of community; and the employment of this concept of community presupposes the theory of matter formulated in the Metaphysical Foundations of Dynamics.[14] Kant holds that the necessity of presupposing the dynamical theory of matter for the deduction of the Third Mechanical Law derives from the fact that the fundamental laws of mechanics pertain to matter defined as the movable insofar as, *qua* movable, it has moving force (*das Bewegliche, so fern es als ein solches bewegende Kraft hat*).[15] According to this definition, the force of a matter set in motion is regarded as something present in that matter in order to communicate (*mitteilen*) its motion to another.[16] But the capacity of any matter to exert this force, and thus to communicate its motion, rests upon its ability to impart (*erteilen*) motion by means of original (i.e., materially constitutive) forces of attraction and repulsion.[17] In his theory of rational mechanics, Kant repeatedly attempts to clarify the sense in which the laws involving the mechanical concept of force presuppose the dynamical laws of the interplay of attractive and repulsive forces.[18] The following passage from the First Remark to the Third Mechanical Law and its proof is the one most directly relevant to our concerns:

> One cannot at all think how the motion of a body *A* must necessarily be linked to the motion of a body *B* except by thinking forces that appertain to them both (dynamically) before all motion, e.g., repulsion; and one can now prove that the motion of body *A* is by the approach toward body *B* necessarily linked to the approach of *B* toward *A* and, if *B* is regarded as at rest, is necessarily linked to the motion of *B* . . . toward *A*, so far as the bodies with their (original) moving forces are considered to be in motion merely relatively to one another. This latter can be fathomed [*eingesehen*] fully a priori through the fact that whether body *B* is

at rest or moved in respect of empirically cognizable space, it must necessarily be regarded as moved in respect of body A and, moreover, as
moved in the opposite direction: otherwise, no influence of the body
upon the repulsive force of both would occur, without which influence
no mechanical action whatever of matters upon one another, i.e., no
communication of motion by impact, is possible. (4:550.10–25)[19]

I shall disregard the details of the "construction of the communication of motion" (4:549.6) at issue in these lines.[20] It is sufficient to note
what follows from Kant's mechanical account of reciprocal action: that
the specification of the concept of influence required by this special
metaphysical account of the community of material objects in space is
unintelligible—indeed, is *unthinkable*—except with reference to the
dynamical concept of force.[21] In other words, the mechanical concept of
reciprocal causal influence cannot be understood, or even entertained,
apart from the fundamental determinations of the dynamical concept of
matter. To say this, of course, is not to claim that the mechanical concepts of community and influence and the associated concept of force
can be explicated reductively *in terms of* the dynamical concept of
material force.[22] But it is to assert that there is a *necessary* connection between these mechanical concepts and the dynamical account of
matter— and thus between Kant's special metaphysical principle of
community (i.e., the Third Mechanical Law) and the foundations of his
metaphysical dynamics.

This connection certainly cannot be used at this juncture in any
straightforward way to support the thesis that the concept of attractive
and repulsive force supplies the link needed to establish the relationship
between matter and the continuum or plenum of influences in the Third
Analogy's argument against empty space. As I have already pointed out,
such a thesis implies that tenets of a dynamical theory of matter are
required for the deduction of the transcendental principle of community, and that these tenets must in consequence be regarded as crucial
components of the transcendental part of the metaphysics of nature.
The contents of this transcendental part, however, are not directly at
issue in Kant's treatment of the relationship between the Dynamics
and the Mechanics of 1786. Still, the connection that Kant explicitly
acknowledges between the dynamical concept of matter and the mechanical concepts of community and influence is clearly relevant to
our thesis. It is so because understanding the relationship between
Kant's dynamical account of matter and his special metaphysical principle of community enables us to determine with greater precision the

architectonic ramifications of the argument against empty space for Kant's critical metaphysics of corporeal nature.

If the concept of attractive and repulsive (i.e., material) force is the key to understanding the connection between matter and the continuum of influences in the Third Analogy, we can see that Kant has recourse to a dynamical account of matter for the deduction of the general (i.e., the transcendental) principle of community. It follows, then, that he presupposes the basis of a dynamical theory in order to ground *transcendentally* his special metaphysical principle as a law of Mechanics. This means that the special metaphysical principle is grounded not only "horizontally" with reference to a dynamical theory that, according to Kant's architectonic conception of the 1780s, must be treated as a special metaphysical discipline placed on the same level as his Mechanics. Indirectly, the special metaphysical principle is also grounded "vertically" by means of the fundamental concept of a dynamical theory of matter. For the application of the category of community to matter as something that has moving force presupposes that the general principle holds good as an a priori principle of the unity of experience and thus as a transcendental law of the causal uniformity of nature.[23] But the Third Analogy's argument against empty space shows that Kant establishes the universal validity of his general principle of community by introducing a material transcendental condition. And our thesis implies that this condition cannot be understood properly separate from the concept of material force that forms the basis of Kant's dynamical theory of matter.

Thus, to establish his special metaphysical principle as an a priori law of his Mechanics, Kant must ground it with reference to the general principle of community that furnishes a transcendental law of nature. Yet if our thesis concerning influence, matter, and force is correct, he establishes this general principle as a transcendental law by bringing in a universal material transcendental condition that must be understood in terms of material force. This means that Kant's transcendental theory of experience must employ a concept taken from a metaphysical discipline which is supposed to be subsidiary to the system of the principles of pure understanding. Kant in effect must borrow the basic concept from the theory of matter treated in his special metaphysical Dynamics and import it into his transcendental theory. Otherwise, he cannot intelligibly establish the general principle of community as a transcendental law of nature capable of supporting an a priori law of Mechanics.

In sum: if our thesis is correct, the dynamical account of matter plays a crucial role at *both* of the architectonic levels relevant to Kant's metaphysics of corporeal nature. That is because neither the general (or transcendental) principle of community nor the corresponding special metaphysical principle is established as an a priori law of nature without recourse to the fundamental concept of a dynamical theory of matter.

There is, of course, no crucial systematic problem involved in making the dynamical account of matter or material force the presupposition for understanding the mechanical concept of reciprocal causal influence. On the other hand, an extremely significant difficulty arises if Kant does indeed require the dynamical account of matter in order to establish the general principle of community as a transcendental law of nature. For it is entirely unclear how he could uphold rigorously the distinction that he draws between his transcendental theory of experience and his dynamical theory of matter if the concept of material force plays an essential role in the proof of his transcendental principle of the dynamical community of substances. We cannot avoid facing this issue if we want to understand fully Kant's theory of objective experience.

§ 3: Cosmic Matter, Substance as Appearance, and the Transcendental Unity of Apperception

The line of inquiry pursued thus far began by asking whether Kant's argument against empty space necessarily involves an a priori existence proof for a cosmic matter. Our investigations have furnished reasons for holding that it does, even if this raises significant problems for Kant's transcendental theory and its relation to the metaphysics of corporeal nature. Three main factors support our position: (1) Kant's argumentation in the Third Analogy makes the unity of objective experience depend on the transcendental function of the entire field of dynamical interactions. (2) There is reason to think that Kant is constrained to view this field as a continuum, or plenum, of attractive and repulsive forces. (3) There are indications that the mention of "matter everywhere" in elucidation 1 must be understood as a reference to this material continuum.

The first of these factors suffices by itself to deflect much of the force of the first objection against our reading of the void-space argument (see p. 7 above). According to this objection, an *a priori* proof of existence is not to be found in the Third Analogy since all that Kant is doing in elucidation 1 is exemplifying the application of the sche-matized category of community to appearances by addressing signifi-cant empirically ascertainable features of our perceptual relation to ob-jects in space. This objection is not entirely off target, for it is indeed the case that in elucidation 1 Kant is describing how we "make" expe-rience by establishing a cognitive relation to the empirically accessible totality of coexistent objects.[24] But it is precisely this description that shows how untenable it is to suppose that Kant's appeal to the actual contents of that experience involves nothing *more* than reference to what is empirically given. Our analysis has shown that the cognitive relation in question is possible only on the condition that the entire field of em-pirically accessible objects is constituted as a whole of uninterrupted dy-namical interactions. The analysis has also shown that the account of this condition requires the a priori deduction of a material condition of possible experience. Specifically, I have argued that this account un-avoidably involves the ascription of a transcendental function to the universal field of dynamical interactions that exists within the horizon of our possible perceptual experience of material objects. But if this omnicomprehensive dynamical field has such a function, then we must admit that Kant's deductive procedure itself amounts to an a priori ex-istence proof for *some* kind of non-subjective entity that supplies a tran-scendental condition of our knowledge of objects in space. From the standpoint of Kantian epistemological formalism, of course, the fact that this condition is required at all must appear exceedingly odd; for in any given perceptual experience of objects, that condition must be un-derstood as belonging objectively to the encompassing field of percep-tion in which all objects are known. That is to say, it must present itself as a basic feature of precisely that *empirically* determinate aspect of the world that is subject to the a priori rule furnished by the category of community. This is true even if the material condition in question is not anything like a particular object of empirical intuition.

An illustration of the conformity of appearances to a principle of the purely formal unity of experience? Certainly, Kant's deductive proce-dure in elucidation 1 is just *that*—but not *just* that. Whatever else fol-lows from this procedure, it surely demonstrates that human under-standing must be considered capable of accomplishing far more with respect to our a priori knowledge than merely anticipating the *form* of a possible experience (again, contrast A246/B303).[25] This must be the case as long as Kant is prepared to insist that the theory of the a priori determinable form of perceptual experience precludes any material and non-subjective condition from serving as a transcendental condition of our perception of objects in space.

Does, then, the argument against empty space represent nothing more than a conceptual derailment within the framework of Kant's transcendental formalism? This query raises the second objection to acknowledging the presence of an a priori existence proof in the Third Analogy, which is that we must regard such a proof as a mere aberration in the theory of the possibility conditions of objective experience presented in the *Critique of Pure Reason* (see p. 7 above).

If anything, the second objection appears to have been strengthened by our investigations, since we have seen that the 1787 addition to the Third Analogy does not introduce the kind of transcendental condition at issue in the argument against empty space. It therefore seems that the development of the critical theory of a priori knowledge between 1781 and 1787 shows Kant's propensity to delete any reference to the material quality of the universal causal setting within which our perceptual experience of objects can take place. The proof added to the second edition places explicit and exclusive reliance on the non-perceivability of time, which takes up all the logical space that would otherwise be available for the determination of that quality. This points to the conclusion that the forward movement of Kant's thought is toward a properly expurgated account of the strictly formal conditions of our experience of coexistents. Accepting that conclusion would evidently require us to admit the incoherence of Kant's argumentative strategy in the Third Analogy as a whole; and it may mean the reduction of the Analogy's valid content to that of the 1787 addition. But on the other hand, it would presumably be a bearable price to pay for redeeming the rest of Kant's transcendental theory—or at least for preventing this formalistic theory's contamination by some sort of "precritical" material residue.

The second objection therefore clearly places the burden of proof on anyone who does maintain that we must take seriously Kant's void-space argument. Is there, then, any reason to think that Kant did *not* regard—and would not have regarded—the results of the argument against empty space as a conceptual derailment within the Transcendental Analytic, but rather as something crucial to his critical theory of a priori knowledge? One obvious reason, of course, shows itself in the fact that he did not delete the void-space argument from the second edition text of the Third Analogy. But in view of the second objection, the response to this statement of fact is equally obvious: It is that Kant ought to have deleted that argument and altered the entire text accordingly; and he ought to have done this for one simple reason: he should have recognized the basic inconsistency between the two phases of his deductive procedure in the 1787 text. It thus seems that if we are to have any warrant for taking the argument against empty space seriously, we need to go well beyond the obvious differences between his proofs for the transcendental principle of community. What exactly does that demand of us?

Consider once more the summary that Kant gives of the import of his argument against empty space in elucidation 1:

> Without community, every perception (of an appearance in space) is broken off from the other, and the chain of empirical representations, i.e., experience, would begin anew with each new object without the preceding one being able to have the least connection with it or to stand in a temporal relation [*im Zeitverhältnis stehen*] to it. (A213–214/B260–261)

The position taken here is that no synthesis in the sequence of our perceptions, and hence no synthetic unity of our objective perceptual experience, is possible apart from the relation of dynamical community or thoroughgoing reciprocal action between all substances as appearances in space. As we have shown (see pp. 28–30 above), Kant is not unambiguous in his support for this position in the original core argument of the 1781 edition. Moreover, the position is simply not addressed in the new core argument of the 1787 edition, where Kant relies on the nonperceivability of time in order to clarify the problem of determining the relation of coexistence from the sequence of single perceptions of objects (see pp. 17 and 19 above). Accordingly, there seems to be reason to think that the position that Kant takes in his summary statement from elucidation 1 does not represent the central epistemological problematic of the Third Analogy.

On the other hand, we must bear in mind as well that the *appended* 1787 core argument cannot, due to its exclusive reliance on the nonperceivability of time, address the position that Kant obviously does support unambiguously— *at least in elucidation 1*. The appended argument cannot, in other words, address the epistemological problematic which Kant in fact responds to when he maintains that the existence of an all-inclusive dynamical plenum is an a priori necessary condition for all possible unity of our experience of objects in space. Thus, if we are to take seriously the Third Analogy's argument against empty space, we must understand how the position articulated by Kant's summary statement in elucidation 1 comes to be a central issue for his theory of objective experience. We must also determine the extent to which that position remains central to his theory after 1781.

The Third Analogy's argument against empty space establishes that our knowledge of the relation of dynamical community is made possible by a material transcendental condition. Thus, before taking up the tasks just mentioned, we will have to give a conclusive response to our interpretation of that void-space argument. Clarifying the preconditions for this response will occupy us for the next four chapters. Yet before setting out on this course, it is worth putting up some signposts to mark our way through the mass of theoretical material that we need to investigate. Let us therefore focus here on two specific problems generated by the theoretical position that impels Kant to maintain that our experience of objects depends on the existence of a dynamical plenum. These can be brought out best with reference to the notion of a single cosmic matter (or, as the case may be, a universal continuum of attractive and repulsive forces).

We must first ask how this matter is actually related to the particular objects that *appear* to us as coexistent substances. How exactly does it fit into Kant's doctrine of appearance if the individually identifiable material objects of empirical intuition are the only substances that we can know directly as appearances in space? Even if the cosmic matter in question is not directly observable or ascertainable by any ordinary empirical means, it is still located *between* all perceivable substances in space. Consequently, it is in *some* sense part of the objective content (or contents) of the spatial field of appearances, an objective content known through the synthesis of perceptions by which objects come to be empirically represented as coexistent substances. But how can it possibly belong to this field if it is, at the same time, an a priori necessary condition of our experience of these substances as appearances? Kant certainly does not answer this question anywhere in the *Critique of Pure Reason*.[26] If it is to be answered, we will have to take into account other textual resources.

The second problem concerns Kant's conception of the unity of apperception. I have argued that the objective and necessary unity of apperception treated in elucidation 2 of the Third Analogy is the configuration or mode of transcendental unity required for our cognition of a world-whole of dynamically interacting substances. In treating this conception, I showed that the kind of unity of self-consciousness in question concerns the connection in the synthesis of perceptions by which the empirical representation of coexistent objects is made possible (see pp. 45–46 above). This means that the a priori necessary conditions for the unity of such synthesis are conditions of one's consciousness of oneself as a subject related cognitively to a causally unified whole of spatial objects. Now Kant insists in elucidation 1 that no unity in the synthesis of perceptions through time is possible apart from a dynamical plenum as a condition of synthetic unity. Thus, if cosmic matter, understood as a continuum of forces, is what furnishes this a priori necessary *material* condition, it follows that it also supplies a condition for the unity of consciousness with respect to the knowable world-whole of interacting substances. For without the transcendental function of such matter as the medium of all reciprocal action between substances as appearances, no connection of our perceptions of objects would be possible; and consequently, there could be no unity of consciousness with respect to objects in space. The *concept* of this kind of unity of apperception would indeed furnish a subjective and formal condition of our possible experience of these objects, or indicate the unified complex of such conditions. But it could have no application to any objective experience if cosmic matter did not exist as a condition of the possibility of *all* our experience of objects.

We would expect Kant to explicate these implications with reference to his account of the subjective and formal conditions of the unity of experience. Above all, we would expect him to explain the epistemological position that he takes in the Third Analogy in view of his argument that the synthetic unity of apperception is the "highest point" (B135) upon which hinges all employment of the understanding, the whole of logic, and transcendental philosophy as such. Since Kant does not do this in the *Critique of Pure Reason,* we must inquire into whether he ever adequately addresses the issues that the argument against empty space raises for his account of the unity of apperception.

In focusing on these last two sets of questions pertaining to Kant's doctrine of appearance and theory of apperception, my purpose has been to clarify what is at stake when we investigate the developmental background of the Third Analogy's argument against empty space. To the extent that the issues just discussed underlie what some have regarded as Kant's "disreputable play" with the notions of causal reciprocity and mutual determination,[27] the line of inquiry that we will now follow is something of far more than merely antiquarian interest. It weighs heavily upon the very meaning and tenability of Kant's concept of transcendental knowledge, and hence upon his idea of transcendental philosophy.[28]

PART II

The Historical Background to Kant's Critical Theory of Dynamical Community

The main problem that must be addressed in parts two and three is the relationship between force and influence in Kant's account of the dynamical community of substances. This second main division thus treats the historical background of the idea of dynamical community and the roles that this idea plays in Kant's philosophy prior to the *Critique of Pure Reason*. Chapter 4 considers certain features of Leibniz's and Wolff's metaphysics. The discussion is structured in view of two general aspects of Leibniz's philosophy: (1) the conception of the commerce of substances, as seen in relation to the Leibnizian postulate of the universal harmony of individual substances; (2) the metaphysical grounding of a science of dynamics with recourse to an Aristotelian concept of substantial force. Chapter 5 examines Kant's employment of the idea of the commerce of substances between 1746 and 1770 by examining Part 1 of the *Essay on Living Forces*, Proposition 13 of the *Nova dilucidatio*, and Sections 1 and 4 of the *Inaugural Dissertation*. Determining Kant's views about influence and force in these texts enables us to discern the crucial links between Kant's early metaphysics and Leibniz's and Wolff's metaphysics of substance. More generally, it enables us to understand how Kant's conception of the basis of dynamical community allows him to distance himself from the major rationalist responses to the problem of the communication of substances found in seventeenth- and eighteenth-century philosophy. The need to clarify the presuppositions of Kant's alternative response to this problem will lead us to examine his theory of matter in part four below.

CHAPTER 4

Substance and Substantial Force in Leibniz and Wolff

§ 1: Universal Harmony and the Commerce of Substances in Leibniz's Metaphysics of Substance

Seen in relation to the seventeenth-century rationalist problematic of the communication of substances, the primary task of Leibniz's general ontology is to establish the genuine individuality of substances with reference to a system of the universal harmony of created beings. Opposing the Cartesian and Malebranchean as well as the Spinozistic metaphysics of substance, Leibniz grounds the interrelatedness of the postulated infinite multitude of qualitatively distinct simple substances in the principles of the perfection and plentitude of creation.[1] His basic metaphysical conception is therefore that of a harmonious world of substantial activity in which each of the *prima constituentia,* i.e., each monad,[2] contains within itself its essential representational link to all other monads. According to this conception, the individuality of any given substance is determined by the relation through which it expresses, reflects, or represents from its unique point of view the reality of all substances that were brought (and are continually being brought) into existence along with it.[3]

In keeping with the monadological interpretation of substance, Leibniz denies what I shall henceforth term "transeunt action" or "transeunt causation."[4] He characterizes this crucial feature of his thought in *De ipsa natura* in the following terms: "As to what can be established about the *transeunt actions of created entities*, . . . : The *community* [*commercium*] of substances or monads, namely, arises not from an influence, but through an agreement proceeding from divine preformation, so that each and every substance is accommodated to the outside while it follows the intrinsic force and the laws of its own nature."[5] Leibniz's denial of transeunt causation—in other words, his rejection of *influence réelle* coupled with his affirmation of an *influence idéelle* that denotes the purely internal spontaneity of all substantial change—does not, however, imply that the monad is an ontologically isolated entity.[6] Leibniz does indeed employ the metaphor of the monads' windowlessness. Accordingly, he maintains that each monad must be comprehended with reference to its representational activity as a world concentrated into itself (*concentratio universi*).[7] But precisely *as* thus determined, each monad must express the infinite totality of qualitatively distinct created substances. The self-contained character of substance is the ground of its all-encompassing representational function, so "the nature of every substance carries a general expression of the whole universe."[8] The Leibnizian monad provides, therefore, "the concept of an individual substance that contains [*enveloppe*] all its phenomena, such that nothing can happen to substance that is not generated from its own ground [*qui ne lui naisse de son propre fond*], but in conformity to what happens to another . . . ."[9] Given this self-contained but nonetheless all-enveloping nature of substance, the notion of external transeunt action or real influence is not only unintelligible in the strict metaphysical sense; it is also philosophically superfluous.[10]

Leibniz's concept of the monad thus satisfies the requirements of the traditional definition of substance as *ens per se subsistens* even while it counters the tendency inherent in Cartesian and Spinozistic rationalism toward an "isolationist" interpretation of the ontological independence of substance.[11] In his letter to Arnauld of June 1686, Leibniz argues that the independence of finite substances does not preclude that they exist in community with each other.[12] This community or commerce (i.e., *commerce*), however, consists in the reciprocal correspondence (*l'entraccord*) of the expressive activities of the individual substances constituting the universe. Leibniz holds that such harmony of expression or representation is a function of the purposive activity evidenced by continual divine production, and that it is the phenomenally manifest reciprocal accommodation of substances stemming from this divine activity that permits us to speak of the action of any one finite substance upon any other. Action must therefore be comprehended as the distinct expression by (or in) one substance of the cause (or ground) of change in another. Consequently, the commerce of substances, which consists in the reciprocal correspondence of finite substances' activities, must be understood in terms of this account of action, and not in terms of any *real* physical influence or real physical dependency.

§ 2: Leibniz's Aristotelian Dynamism and the Idea of a Transition from Metaphysics to Corporeal Nature

We have just seen that Leibniz's account of the universal harmony of individual substances involves a metaphysical principle of action based on a conception of representational activity.[13] Let us now turn to the application of this principle in Leibniz's philosophy of nature. We will consider the role played by substantial force in his attempt to define the rational principles of finite knowledge that express the lawfulness of corporeal nature in view of its infinite manifoldness and diversity.[14]

Presupposing the monadological interpretation of *ens qua substantia,* Leibniz's account of substantial force aims to furnish the complete metaphysical groundwork for a science of dynamics.[15] For a concise formulation of the fundamental architectonic assumptions upon which this science is built, I refer to the criticism of § 64 of Descartes's *Principia philosophiae* (Part 2) contained in Leibniz's *Animadversiones in partem generalem Principiorum Cartesianorum* (1692).[16] Leibniz argues there the following points: General metaphysical principles and the explanatory principles of particular natural phenomena are to be cleanly separated from each other. Mechanical principles and the corresponding general laws of corporeal nature are necessarily true within their own sharply delimited domain. But they are derivative of higher-order metaphysical principles inaccessible to sensuous cognition.[17] These metaphysical principles pertain to unextended substance or, respectively, to force defined as the power to act (*potentia agendi*). It is this force that effects the transition from metaphysics to corporeal nature (*transitus a metaphysica ad naturam*) or, conversely, the transition from the material to the immaterial. Since they derive from principles of perfect reason, the laws of this force have a cognitive status superior to that of mathematical principles per se.[18]

The broader implications of these assertions will be discussed below in the treatment of Leibniz's criticism of the metaphysical foundations of seventeenth-century corpuscularianism (see pp. 100–101). Here, we direct our attention to the characterization of force as *potentia agendi* and as something that effects the transition (*transitus*) from metaphysics to nature.

In the opening paragraph of *Specimen dynamicum* (1692), Leibniz begins by clarifying his intention to supersede the Cartesian account of corporeal substance by asserting the priority of force over extension (In rebus corporeis [est] aliquid praeter extensionem, imo extensione prius . . . nempe ipsam vim naturae ubique ab Autore inditam).[19] This allows him to affirm that the Aristotelian principle of form is needed for the philosophical account of nature. He does this in view of four main facets of his doctrine of force: (1) the characterization of force (*vis naturae*) as that which is constitutive of substance itself; (2) the concern to sharply distinguish this concept of force from the Scholastic notion of *potentia;*[20] (3) the correlative interpretation of force in terms of *conatus* or *nisus*, i.e., as something between mere potency and completed act;[21] and (4) the affirmation of the fundamental correctness of Aristotle's own concept of form as *entelechy*, and Leibniz's corresponding attempt to make this concept fully intelligible.[22]

By superseding the Cartesian concept of corporeal substance and by advocating the Aristotelian principle of form, Leibniz sets the stage for an interpretation of material being in terms different from those of inert matter and externally communicated motion. Leibniz thus retains what he takes to be the rational core of the Aristotelian conception of substance. In effect, Leibniz's theory of force involves the rehabilitation and reconstruction of the matter-form composite as the pivotal concept of the metaphysics of corporeal nature.[23]

Leibniz's concern to revive the Aristotelian explanatory scheme by means of the concept of substantial force underlies his description of the structural and material features of the aggregation of monads and corporeal interaction.[24] He holds that the following four ontological expressions of substantial force constitute the nature of a complete corporeal substance and supply the grounds of all corporeal interaction: primitive active force, primitive passive force, derivative active force, and derivative passive force.[25]

The analysis of primitive active force (*vis activa primitiva*)[26] yields the fundamental metaphysical principle that substance perdures through all processes of phenomenally manifested corporeal interaction. Primitive active force thus furnishes the basis of the identity of any particular

body through the alterations that it undergoes as the result of its interactions with other bodies. It also provides for the continuity and conservation of action within corporeal nature as a whole. Primitive passive
force (*vis passiva primitiva*)[27] is the ground of corporeal extension, by
which a body appears as material mass. The passive capacity demonstrated by any body to resist changes in its state of motion and to hin-
der penetration by other bodies is also explained in terms of primitive
passive force. Derivative active force (*vis activa derivativa*)[28] results
from the modification or limitation of primitive force, a limitation that
takes the form of the phenomenally manifested conflict of physical bodies. Derivative active force is subject to distribution by virtue of this
conflict. It therefore does not perdure in any single body during the
course of its interaction with other corporeal substances. Since it is comprehensible as the internal action generated within a body when this is,
phenomenally speaking, acted upon by some other body or bodies, derivative active force allows us to explain how bodies have the capacity to
resist actively penetration and changes in their states of motion. Derivative passive force (*vis passiva derivativa*)[29] is the purely quantitative
modification of primitive passive force. We know it in terms of the mea-
sures of any material mass's resistance to penetration and change in its
state of motion.[30]

Leibniz insists that primitive force pertains solely to completely general causes. As a strictly metaphysical principle, it is the object of purely
rational apprehension. It is thus not linked immediately to the actual
laws of corporeal interaction in the phenomenal realm. On the other
hand, derivative force does pertain directly to such observable interaction. Its analysis leads to the systematic formulation of the fundamental laws of corporeal dynamics. These are laws of action that are known
not only by reason, but are also proved by the evidence of the senses:

> But having distinguished and presupposed these basic general points,
> from which we learn that every body always acts on account of its form
> and that every body is always acted upon and resists on account of its mat-
> ter, we must now proceed further and, in this doctrine of derivative forces
> [*virtus*] and resistances, treat the extent to which bodies are efficacious
> with different strivings [*nisus*] or, on the other hand, the extent to which
> they counterstrive in various ways; for to these derivative forces and resis-
> tances apply the laws of action that are understood not only through rea-
> son, but are also confirmed by sense itself through the phenomena.[31]

It is in view of this mixed epistemic quality of derivative force's laws
that Leibniz holds force to be something that effects the transition

from metaphysics to nature (see p. 65 above).[32] Accordingly, Leibniz's science of the fundamental laws of corporeal dynamics mediates between the purely rational principles of the metaphysics of substance and the level of explanation at which the particular laws of empirical physics are formulated.[33] There is thus no gap in Leibniz's system of natural philosophy between principles of pure reason and the concepts and rules governing empirical inquiry. The Leibnizian *transitus a metaphysica ad naturam* does not involve any break between the metaphysics of corporeal nature and physics as an empirical science.

§ 3: Dynamism and Rationalism in Wolff's Transcendental Cosmology

Wolff's metaphysics of nature demonstrates a number of structural parallels with Leibniz's doctrine of the universal commerce of substances and theory of substantial force. Like Leibniz, Wolff accounts for the composition of physical bodies with recourse to the aggregation of simple substances. He formulates a concept of "world" in terms borrowed directly from Leibniz's theory of the universal connection of substances and principle of universal harmony.[34] Wolff clearly distinguishes between dynamical and mechanical principles of explanation in natural philosophy. Regarding the former, he differentiates between *vis activa* and *vis passiva* in order to explain the active causal and the inertial properties of composite bodies. In keeping with this distinction, Wolff purports to adhere to the Leibnizian critique of the Cartesian notion of corporeal substance. He also complies with Leibniz in advocating the Aristotelian conception of substantial force and in criticizing the Scholastic doctrine of *potentia* or *facultas*.[35] Finally, in stating the general laws of corporeal interaction, Wolff distinguishes between primitive and derivative force. He maintains that active force is directly relevant to the actual formulation of physical laws.[36]

On closer examination, though, these parallels prove to be superficial. They tend to conceal the fundamental differences between Wolff's transcendental cosmology and Leibniz's metaphysics of corporeal nature.[37] Above all, Wolff's use of the concept of *substantia simplex* does not preclude his rejection of the essential features of the Leibnizian concept of the monad.[38] This is evident at various junctures in the *Cosmologia generalis* (1737).[39] But it receives its most succinct formulation in chapter 1 of the *Vernünftige Gedanken* (1720), or *Deutsche Metaphysik*,[40] where

Wolff is expressly concerned to give a dynamical account of substance. I refer here to his definition of substance as a simple thing that contains within itself the source of its alterations, and hence provides its own principle of individuation.[41] In view of this definition, Wolff appeals to the Leibnizian idea of substantial activity.[42] Yet in spite of this appeal, Wolff is unwilling to go along with the metaphysical consequences of accepting the Leibnizian idea.[43] In § 215 of the companion volume to the *Vernünftige Gedanken*,[44] Wolff makes it clear that he keeps his distance from the Leibnizian version of the dynamical concept of substance.[45] Although he grants that the constitutive elements of things must be simple substances, he is unwilling to decide whether to give his stamp of approval to Leibniz's doctrine of monads. By constraining us to accept that "all simple things should have one and the same kind of force," the Leibnizian doctrine leads us to ascribe a representational function to all types of substance, and Wolff is quite cautious about taking this step.

Wolff's caution has important consequences for his interpretation of Leibnizian universal harmony.[46] In §§ 598–600 of the *Vernünftige Gedanken*,[47] he expresses his misgivings about Leibniz's "opinion" (§ 598) that the whole world is represented in each simple thing. Wolff contends that, since "the internal state of each simple substance relates to everything else in the world" (§ 600), all things are harmoniously attuned to each other. But at the same time, Wolff claims that Leibniz "neither sufficiently explains nor proves" (§ 600) the basic idea of substantial activity that he uses to make this universal harmony intelligible. Thus, while recognizing that Leibniz explains in terms of representational activity how the internal states of substances are related, Wolff insists that the nature of substantial activity must remain an open question.

In the *Cosmologia generalis*, Wolff remains true to his agnosticism regarding the question of substantial activity. He does not choose to portray definitively the internal workings of the elements constituting composite bodies.[48] Although he does provide a structural description of the observable universal connection of substances, he does not, at least within the systematic confines of his transcendental cosmology, attempt to determine the specific grounds of this relation. Within the framework of his science of "world" he postulates the facticity of such connection as something generally grounded in sufficient reason. But unlike Leibniz, he does not, and cannot, establish that it is the very nature of each finite substance to exist as something connected with all other substances.[49]

Before turning to Wolff's analysis of force, one further dimension of the account of substance given in the *Cosmologia generalis* merits special mention in anticipation of our further treatment of Kant. Despite

Wolff's refusal to engage in speculation about the intrinsic determinations of the simple substances or elements, he does not hesitate to maintain that these are *physical* unities. In the remark to § 182 of the *Cosmologia generalis,* Wolff establishes the link between his own concept of the element and the Leibnizian description of the monad as a metaphysical unity. In § 186 the element is termed *atomus naturae* in order to distinguish it from the Democritean *atomus materialis.* And after stating in § 187 that the elements of material things are atoms of nature, though not material atoms, he claims that "[i]t is evident for this reason why atoms of nature are called in such a wise, doubtless because the nature of things does not admit atoms other than such as are considered in themselves indivisible—so much so, indeed, that they cannot even be divided by means of divine omnipotence. They are also called physical atoms. On account of their indivisibility *atoms* are also called *monads* or *unities,* and indeed *physical* as opposed to *arithmetic* ones."[50]

Wolff's justification for this terminological and conceptual scheme in view of his professed agnosticism about the intrinsic nature of substance need not occupy us here. What is interesting is his concern to establish that the elemental constituents of composite entities are physical unities, as distinguished from metaphysical unities in the Leibnizian sense.[51] There will be more to say about this when we discuss Kant's dynamical theory of substance.

The basic definition of force in Wolff's natural philosophy is in keeping with the conception of force that underlies his general account of substance. Since force is attributed to the elemental constituents of composite bodies, it may be termed substantial; but its nature cannot be subject to any more specific determination.[52] This limitation applies in particular to the active and passive forces to which Wolff refers when distinguishing between dynamical and mechanical explanation. These forces are phenomenal and thus pertain to the domain of confused representation to which merely sensuous knowledge is confined. Hence, their ontological status can only be that of the likeness or image of substance (*instar substantiae*).[53] It follows, then, that we may not rank the corresponding dynamical principles higher than mechanical principles, all of which are based on the concept of extension. Wolff does attribute *vis activa* (or *vis motrix*) and *vis passiva* (or *vis inertiae*) to physical bodies. But his aim in doing so is not to *ground* mechanical principles in higher metaphysical principles. It is merely to complement the mechanical principles.[54]

We now come to the distinction between primitive and derivative force. Contrary to Leibniz, Wolff's analysis of force into its primitive and derivative dimensions is carried out solely in view of *vis activa*.[55] Moreover, Wolff places a limitation upon the intelligibility of derivative force that is quite foreign to anything acceptable to Leibniz. We can recognize this limitation in § 365 of the *Cosmologia generalis:*

> *Derivative forces are explained in an intelligible manner by rules of motion.* For since derivative forces result from the modification of primitive force . . . , derivative forces can be explained intelligibly when you have specified the ground of the modification of the same forces. . . . Wherefore, since moving force has been modified according to the rules of motion in the conflict of bodies from which derivative force results . . . , one can understand through those rules why, in a given case, primitive force is modified in one way rather than another, and consequently why the ground of the modification is yielded by them . . . , and so to that extent why the derivative forces are explained intelligibly by the rules of motion.

The key to understanding the significance of this passage is found in Wolff's notion of the rules of motion (*regulas motus*). In § 302 he defines these as the rules according to which moving force is modified or limited through the interaction (*conflictus*) of bodies. In the corresponding Remark, he states that he has *already* demonstrated these in his work on the foundations of mechanics and that they would be subject to empirical confirmation in his experimental philosophy.[56] By rules of motion, Wolff thus has in mind physical laws of corporeal interaction formulated and established at a systematic level inferior to that of transcendental cosmology.[57] Consequently, in § 365 he means that the analysis of derivative force must be couched in terms of particular physical laws. These empirically confirmable laws of nature, however, are formulated *independently* of the distinction between primitive and derivative force.

Wolff's intentions concerning his criterion of intelligibility for derivative force are hardly clear. Indeed, his reasoning on this point seems positively disingenuous. (Among other things, we are left wondering what the epistemological relevance of the distinction between primitive and derivative force might be, seeing that Wolff does not give derivative force a properly foundational role to play in relation to the aforementioned special laws.) At any rate, though, the indications are that there is an unbridgeable gap in Wolff's general theory of physical law. On the one hand, there is force regarded as *instar substantiae* and as *vis derivativa;* this is force understood according to the particular laws that are actually apposite to our knowledge of corporeal nature. On the other hand, there is force conceived as an intrinsic determination of elemental constituents, the nature of which is simply not subject to any further specification. The surreptitious empiricism evident in Wolff's understanding of the relationship between substantial force and physical law marks a basic departure from Leibniz. The latter undertakes the analysis of force in order to establish a priori the possibility of the conceptual transition from the purely rational principles of the metaphysics of substance to the physical laws that describe the phenomenal manifestations of substantial activity. In allowing a gap between purely rational principles and such laws, Wolff thus denies himself the opportunity to follow the underlying logic of Leibniz's metaphysics of substance in its application to the doctrine of corporeal nature. Wolff is in no position to complete the deductive progression from (1) a principle of action or substantial activity apprehended in terms of the monads' perception and appetition; to (2) primitive force, which is in principle intelligible in terms of monadic activity; to (3) the modification of primitive force, i.e., derivative force, and the fundamental laws of motion corresponding to it; and finally to (4) the level of particular mechanical principles.

Before going on to Kant, one further aspect of Wolff's treatment of substance and force needs to be brought into sharper focus, even if it may be obvious from what we have just discussed: the lack of commitment that Wolff demonstrates toward the theory of transeunt causation. This is quite evident in the *Cosmologia generalis*. After stipulating that there is an active and a passive principle in the substantial elements, Wolff makes the following claims in a remark added to § 294: We cannot establish whether the reciprocal causal action between the elements is merely apparent as long as the nature of the principles in question remains undecided. Although we must ascribe force to the individual elements or simple substances that constitute material things, this does not mean that we can determine the essential character of this force. We can indeed demonstrate generally the way in which the force of bodies results from the forces of aggregated simple substances. But we cannot explain this more clearly as long as the specific differentiae of force are unknown. That is no problem, however, since such explanation is neither necessary nor philosophically fruitful. It suffices for us to know that each of the elements or substances in question has an active principle by which it continually acts and a passive principle by which it is acted upon—or at least *appears* to be acted upon.

CHAPTER 5

Dynamical Community, Physical Influence, and Universal Harmony in the Development of Kant's Metaphysics

This chapter treats the early developmental stages of Kant's conception of dynamical community as a relation of universal physical influence. Prior to the *Critique of Pure Reason,* Kant intended his metaphysical theory of substance to resolve conclusively the modern problem of the communication of substances. Kant's resolution of this problem required him to offer a fully intelligible explanation of transeunt substantial force in connection with the idea of physical influence. In this frame of reference, we will examine Kant's precritical views of the relationship between finite substance, force, and space. We will able to see why Kant's early accounts of the community of substances as a spatial relation of universal physical influence led to the investigation of the dynamical theory of matter, which is the subject matter of part three.

§ 1: Force, Substance, and Space in the *Essay on Living Forces*

The scientific content of the *Essay on Living Forces* (1746) has been amply examined in the secondary literature. I therefore will not be concerned with the details of Kant's proposals for settling the *vis viva* controversy.[1] I will consider only part 1 of the *Essay,* where Kant lays out the theoretical groundwork for his attempted solution. The general task of part 1 is to furnish "several metaphysical concepts of the force of bodies in general" (1:17.17). In pursuing this goal, Kant seeks to establish the proper relationship between the notion of the connection (*Verbindung*) of particular substances and the concept of active or substantial force. This relationship presents a crucial philosophic problem for Kant, since he assumes that individual substances are completely independent:

> A substance is either connected with and related to other substances external to it, or it is not. Because every self-subsistent [*selbständige*] entity contains within itself the complete source of all its determinations, it is not necessary for its existence that it stands in any connection with other things. That is why substances can exist and nonetheless have no external relation to other substances, or stand in any real connection with them. (1:21.35–22.5)[2]

Kant's account of substance in the *Essay* thus involves an extreme version of what I will henceforth call the principle of ontological isolationism.[3] While Kant assumes with Leibniz that the world is composed of a multiplicity of substantial individuals, his isolationist viewpoint is diametrically opposed to the conception of substantial activity and reciprocal accommodation entailed by Leibniz's principle of universal harmony.[4] For Leibniz, the idea that substance is the complete source of its determinations is put forward in order to exclude precisely the kind of theory of substance and its external relations that Kant offers in the *Essay on Living Forces.*

Granted the isolation of particular substances, Kant can stipulate that all connectedness and relations between substances must originate in the reciprocal actions and effects of their forces (1:21.30–33). His special purpose in part 1 of the *Essay* is thus to describe the preeminent role played by force in the interaction of substances, particularly in the interaction of composite corporeal substances. This means that he must demonstrate that essential or active (*wirkende*) force is the source of motion within the corporeal realm, and that it is therefore the causal ground of all interaction between physical bodies.

In view of the issues raised by Leibniz and Wolff, as discussed in chapter 4 above, one aspect of Kant's view of active or essential force needs specially to be considered here. Kant maintains, with explicit reference to the opening paragraph of Leibniz's *Specimen dynamicum* (see p. 66 above), that the origins of his concept of active force can be traced to Aristotelian *entelechy* and, moreover, that his use of this concept derives directly from Leibniz:

> It is said that a body in motion has a force. For everyone designates as acting the overcoming of obstacles, the stretching of springs, and the shifting of masses. If one looks no further than what the senses teach, one will consider this force to be something communicated entirely and solely from the outside, something that the body does not have when at rest. With the sole exception of *Aristotle*, the whole throng of philosophers prior to *Leibniz* was of this opinion. It was believed that the obscure *entelechy* of the former is the secret of the actions of bodies. None of the Scholastics, all of whom followed Aristotle, comprehended this enigma, and perhaps it was not made to be comprehended. Leibniz, to whom human reason owes so much, was the first to teach that an essential force is present in a body and which belongs to this even prior to extension. *Est extensionem imo extensine prius;* these are his words. (1:17.9–24)

Thus, the appropriation of Leibniz's concept of *vis activa* underlies Kant's description of the role of essential force in corporeal nature.[5] Kant points out that the Leibnizian concept preserves an essential feature of the Aristotelian account of substance. And significantly, he defends what he takes to be the genuine (i.e., the Aristotelian/Leibnizian) version of this concept not only against the Scholastic notion of *potentia;* he also argues against the reductivism that he sees as inherent in Wolff's identification of active force with *vis motrix*.[6] In attributing this moving force to a body "in order to have a ready answer to the question about the cause of motion" (1:18.11–12), Wolff is open to the same charge of explanatory vacuousness as can be leveled against the Scholastics; for whoever employs the notion of *vis motrix* in this way "is to a certain extent making use of an artifice that the Scholastics exploited when, in investigating the grounds of heat or cold, they resorted to a *vis calorifica* or *fragificiente*" (18.13–16).[7]

Yet despite his criticism of the Wolffian account of substantial force, Kant in fact follows Wolff in assuming that only active force is pertinent to the metaphysical grounding of the laws of motion and corporeal interaction. In the *Essay,* the concept of passive force is not in evidence as one of Kant's metaphysical concepts of the force of bodies. Moreover, although Kant favors the vintage Leibnizian version of active force, there is in the *Essay* nothing like the treatment of substantial force that is essential to Leibniz's grounding of his science of dynamics, namely, the deductive movement from the concepts and principles of primitive force to those of derivative force, and finally to the level of special mechanical concepts and laws. What we do discern in Kant's utilization of Leibnizian active force is this: Kant furnishes the elements of a theory of space and then goes on to determine the fundamental lawfulness of nature in terms of *Newtonian* principles of natural philosophy. He achieves these objectives in §§ 9–10 of the *Essay*. His line of argument there runs as follows:

(1) Space is the product of the real interaction of corporeal substances. This means that space, and consequently extension, depend on the capacity of those substances to establish their mutual external connection by means of essential, active force. According to this relationist conception of space, the attributes of extension all derive from essential force, which operates between all substances.[8] The tri-dimensional character (*die dreifache Abmessung*) of space thus derives from the properties of substantial force.[9]

(2) The essential force by which any substance acts in union with its external counterparts is conceivable only as something exerted in conformity with a certain law, a law that is exhibited in the nature of its efficacy (*sich in der Art seiner Wirkung hervortut*).[10] Thus, the general law by which the dynamic spatial relations are determined must derive from the particular laws according to which substances strive (*suchen*) to unify themselves by virtue of their essential forces.[11]

(3) When applied to the mathematical foundations of natural philosophy, the preceding considerations on the relationship between essential force and space furnish these four principles:[12] The substances comprising our world possess substantial forces that operate in unison according to Newton's inverse-square law of universal attraction or gravitation. The connection of substances that originates in conformity with this law of force interaction has the property of being tri-dimensional. The Newtonian law of force interaction (or more precisely, the Newtonian law of the interaction of substances by virtue of Aristotelian / Leibnizian essential force) is metaphysically arbitrary in the sense God could have chosen another law of force if it had so pleased Him. Another law of force would have given rise to spatial extension with properties and dimensions different from those of our own world.

Before leaving the *Essay on Living Forces*, there is one further issue in Kant's early theory of substance and force to consider. Should we understand the action of essential force to fall under the heading of transeunt causation and physical influence in the sense discussed above in chapter 4 (see pp. 63–65)? In part 1 of the *Essay*, Kant's treatment of physical influence (§§ 5–6) revolves around the mind/body prob-lem.[13] He introduces this by asking how matter is capable of producing representations in the human soul by means of physical influence. He maintains that the difficulties traditionally encountered in responding both to this problem[14] and its counterpart (i.e., the question whether the soul is capable of setting matter in motion) disappear when we con-ceive of the force of matter not in terms of motion, but rather in terms of its effects in other substances. Thus, the question whether the soul can cause motion, i.e., whether the soul has moving force (*bewegende Kraft*), is transformed into the question whether the soul's essential force is capable of acting externally *upon* other entities, thereby bring-ing about changes within them. When posed in this fashion, the ques-tion can be answered affirmatively; for the soul must be capable of act-ing externally merely because it has a specific place in the universal network of external relations established by the reciprocally acting sub-stances: "One can answer this question in an entirely decisive manner by saying that the soul must be able to act outwardly by reason of the fact that it is in a location. For when we analyze the concept of what we call location, we find that it suggests the actions of substances on [*in*] each other" (20.35–21.3).[15] According to Kant, the same considerations apply to influence taking place in the opposite direction, i.e., to what happens when external matter changes the internal state of the soul:

> For matter that has been set in motion acts on [*in*] everything spatially connected with it, and hence it acts also on [*in*] the soul; that is, it changes the internal state of the soul insofar as this state relates to what is external. Now the entire internal state of the soul is nothing other than the summation [*Zusammenfassung*] of all its representations and con-cepts. And insofar as this internal state is related to the exterior, it goes by the name of *status repraesentativus universi*. Thus, by means of the force that it has while in motion, matter changes the state of the soul through which it represents to itself the world. (1:21.13–24)

Kant seems here to be responding to his mind/matter problem on the basis of a monistic conception of substantial force. He assumes that the same concept of essential force can be employed to explain both the universal dynamic relation of substances constituting the physical world and the relation *through* which that world comes to be represented *in* the mind of the knower.[16] He thus seems to maintain that the material causal condition through which the represented object (i.e., the spatial universe) is constituted is also a fundamental epistemic condition for representing the object itself. If that is so, then the concept of physical

influence cannot be limited to the relation of transeunt causation established between external matter and the soul. Rather, the concept
must be applicable to the entire domain of substances relevant to human cognition. Specifically, the universal spatial relation of substances
and its Newtonian lawfulness would have to be intelligible in terms of
the same agency of transeunt causation or physical influence that establishes the relation between the physical world and the cognitive faculty
that represents this world.

This interpretation of Kant's view of the relation between the faculty
of representation and the corporeal universe receives some corrobora-
tion in § 10 of the *Essay*. After describing the Newtonian lawfulness and
tri-dimensional character of the universal relation of substances,[17] he
goes on to state: "The impossibility that we notice in ourselves of representing to ourselves a space of more than three dimensions seems to
stem from the circumstance that our soul *as well* [*ebenfalls* (emphasis
mine)] receives the impressions from without according to the inverse-
square relation of distances, and because its nature itself is so constituted as not only to be thus affected, but also to act outside itself in this
way" (1:24.31–25.2). Whatever Kant's reasons for attributing transeunt
efficacy to the substantial forces of corporeal substances, though, an explicit treatment of physical influence within the corporeal universe is not
central to the metaphysical problematic of the *Essay on Living Forces*.
For that, we must turn to the *Nova dilucidatio*.

§ 2: Physical Influence, Space, and the Universal Commerce of Substances in the Nova Dilucidatio

The metaphysical groundwork laid out in part 1 of the *Essay* of 1746 has one very basic unstated presupposition: the connection
(*Verbindung*) of substances most directly pertinent to a science of nature is the universal spatial relation of coexistent entities. We can hardly
overlook the structural similarities between this connection and the relation of dynamical community treated in the first *Critique*. But further
analysis of Kant's early thought is necessary in order for us to reveal the
actual terminological foundations of the Third Analogy. I refer at this
juncture to Proposition 13 of the *Nova dilucidatio* (1755).[18] Kant's *principium coexistentiae* states:

Through their existence alone, finite substances stand in no relation to each other, and have no community at all, except insofar as they are sustained by the common principle of their existence—namely, by the divine understanding—as arranged in reciprocal relations. (1:412.36–413.2)

To understand what is entailed by this proposition, let us first direct our attention to the main part of its proof, where Kant offers the following argument:[19] Despite the ontological isolation of particular substances, there is, manifestly, a reciprocal connection of all such entities in the universe. Since substances are isolated from one another, this encompassing interconnectedness can only be due to a common cause, namely, to God understood as the general ground of all existents. Hence, the factually ascertainable existence of the universal commerce (i.e., the dynamical community) of things is intelligible only with reference to the constantly creative and representational activity of the divine intellect.[20]

We must pay especially close attention to two facets of this argument. The first has to do with the linkage between Proposition 13 and part 1 of the *Essay on Living Forces*. Both of the central tenets asserted in Proposition 13—the ontological exclusiveness of all finite particular substances; the role played by the divine intellect in the establishment and conservation of the reciprocal connection between them—are found in the *Essay* as well. The isolationist conception of finite substantial individuals and the corresponding requirement for a transcendent ground of the community of substances thus represent important elements of continuity in the development of Kant's metaphysics between 1746 and 1755.

As for the second facet: Taken by itself, Proposition 13 may lead us to conclude that Kant's theory of dynamical community is based merely on the two tenets just mentioned. Yet the proof of the principle of coexistence shows that the theory requires a third basic tenet as well. Kant supposes that the knower is faced with the cognizable facticity or actuality of the reciprocal connection of *all* substances. Because of this third factor, he argues not merely from the bare fact of the coexistence of particular substances to the position that their reciprocal connection requires an objective ground (in this case, the activity of the divine intellect). Rather, he presupposes their *empirically manifest* universal commerce and then establishes the necessity of the objective ground for this all-encompassing dynamical community.[21]

Kant's overriding concern in his treatment of the principle of coexistence is with the role of divine causation in establishing and preserving the reciprocal connection of substances. He does not explicitly mention the concept of essential or active substantial force in the proof of his metaphysical principle of coexistence or in its further elucidation.[22] But when he discusses the specific applications of the principle, it becomes clear that he has carried over from the *Essay* of 1746 the basic principles of natural philosophy originally linked to the concept of substantial force. Two sets of these are relevant for our purposes:

(1) All spatial determinations (*locus, situs, spatium*) are products of the external connection and mutual determinations of substances.[23] As such, they arise not from the mere positing of the existence of substances. They must be established by the creative, representational activity of the divine intellect. Since representation in the divine intellect is, in the final analysis, metaphysically arbitrary, it follows that substances could exist without being in any place (*locus*) and consequently without having any relation to our particular universe.[24]

(2) The concept of space derives from the concept of the commerce or dynamical community of substances, and this kind of community must be understood in terms of the action and reaction that occurs between corporeal substances.[25] Given that space is constituted through this physical interaction, the lawfulness of corporeal nature—indeed, the fundamental law of nature itself (*lex primitiva naturae*)—can be expressed in terms of Newtonian attraction:

> If the external appearance of this universal action and reaction throughout the entire expanse [*ambitus*] of space in which bodies stand in relation to one another consists in their mutual approach, it is called *attraction*, which, since it is brought about by co-presence alone, extends to all distances whatever, and is *Newtonian attraction* or universal gravity. Accordingly, it is probable that this attraction is brought about by the same connection of substances by which they determine space and that it is therefore the most primitive law of nature that matter is bound to obey. (1:415.8–14)

In sum: The account of the origin of spatial relations, the derivation of the concept of space, and the description of the fundamental lawfulness of corporeal nature already presented in the *Essay* of 1746 have their place in the *Nova dilucidatio* as well. It is true that the Leibnizian concept of essential force is no longer in evidence in the metaphysical treatise of 1755. But by supplying the elements of a relationist theory of space, and by combining these elements with the Newtonian law of universal attraction, Kant retains the peculiar amalgamation of principles of natural philosophy that already informs his thinking in the earlier treatise.

It is in view of these principles that we must ask whether Kant accepts real interaction between substances. Does he maintain that the community of substances in the corporeal realm takes effect by means of transeunt causation? Does he therefore understand this dynamical community as a relation of physical influence?

Consider here the final application of the principle of coexistence (*Usus 6*):

> Since all substances, insofar as they are contained in the same space, stand in reciprocal community, and thus in reciprocal dependency in respect of their determinations, the universal action of spirits on bodies and of bodies on spirits can, hence, be understood. But no substance of any kind has the power of determining others distinct from it by that which belongs to it internally (as was proven).[26] (This happens, rather, only in virtue of the connection by which they are linked together in the idea of the infinite being.) Consequently, whatever determinations and changes are found in any of them, they indeed always refer to what is external. But physical influence in the proper sense is excluded, and there is a universal *harmony* of things. (1:415.17–24)

Although Kant once again initiates the discussion of physical influence in view of the mind/body problem, he now clearly demonstrates that what he says applies generally to the community of all substances regarded as a spatial community. And although he at first appears to reject physical influence, he declares further on that

> there is real reciprocal action between substances or community through truly efficient causes. For the same principle that establishes the existence of things also makes them subject to this law, and hence community is established by means of the determinations that attach to the origins of their existence. For this reason, one is as justified in saying that the external changes can be produced in this way through external causes as one is in saying that the changes that occur within a substance are ascribed to an internal force of the substance, although the natural efficacy of this force, no less than the foundation of the external relations just mentioned, depends upon divine sustentation. However, the system of the universal community of substances formed in this way is certainly somewhat superior [*emendatius*] to the popular system of *physical influence*, for it reveals, of course, the origin itself of the reciprocal connection of things—an origin that is to be sought outside the principle of substances considered as existing in isolation, regarding which that worn-out system of efficient causes chiefly deviates from the truth. (1:415.32–416.4)

Thus, the traditional account of physical influence must be rejected in favor of Leibnizian universal harmony. But Leibniz's peculiar interpretation of the idea of universal harmony as involving a doctrine of preestablished harmony is equally unacceptable.[27] By universal harmony, Kant has in mind a relation of real influence established through transeunt causation (*per causas vere efficientes*). He insists, however, that the objective ground and origin of this universal relation must be considered an essential part of the doctrine of physical influence.

§ 3: Universal Dynamical Community, Transeunt Forces, and Physical Influence in the *Inaugural Dissertation*

Two main features of the *Inaugural Dissertation* will prove crucial to our understanding of Kant's theory of dynamical community and its ultimate impact on his transcendental theory: (1) the role that he assigns to the concept of dynamical community in his doctrine of the form of the intelligible world; (2) the way in which he relates his exposition of the concept of space to the theory of dynamical community. At present, I will comment only on the first of these. Discussion of the second point is reserved for the concluding chapter (see pp. 176–180), where I examine the implications of Kant's dynamical account of matter for the overall development of his critical theory of space into the *Opus postumum*.

In Section IV of the Dissertation, the concept of the commerce or dynamical community of substances assumes a preeminent position in Kant's metaphysics. Stated simply, the principle of the form of the intelligible world *is* the idea of the objective and transcendent source of the reciprocal connection of substances, a connection that is established by means of transeunt forces and that is thus constituted as a relation of physical influence. To understand the relationship between force and influence that underlies the theory of dynamical community in Section IV, let us first turn to § 2 of Section I. This contains Kant's foundational analysis of the concept of world (*mundus*).

The definition of "world" requires drawing the distinction between its material and formal "moments" (2:389.22). In discussing the former,[28] Kant's strategy is no longer to begin with a philosophically stringent conception of finite substance. He does not take as his point of departure the isolationist concept of substance, as is the case in both the *Essay on Living Forces* and the *Nova dilucidatio*. Rather, he first establishes the common ground between ordinary usage and his metaphysical definition of matter and substance. He then formulates the task of reason (*problema rationis*) that emerges in view of this commonality, which is to account for how the unity of a world comes to be realized out of the multiplicity of its substantial components. Given the agreement between his conception of "world" and ordinary usage, he then emphasizes the distinction that must be drawn between his approach to the problem of world unity and the corresponding Spinozistic approach.[29] He also makes it clear that the description of substance required by the definition of "world" must be kept separate from the general cosmological problematic of the temporal succession of the states of the world.[30]

As is implicit in the historical contextualization of his task of reason with reference to the Spinozistic theory of substance, Kant formulates the problem of world unity in conformity with the assumption that there is a multiplicity of coexistent substances. By doing this, he completes the transition from the material to the formal "moment" of the definition of world.[31] It is important that we arrive at a very precise understanding of this latter dimension of Kant's conceptual analysis, for the determination of "form" lays the foundation for the preeminent position that the concept of dynamical community assumes in Kant's metaphysical theory of 1770.

Kant is concerned first of all with form consisting in the "co-ordination" as distinguished from the "subordination" of substances (2 : 390.5 – 6). He is therefore concerned with the reciprocal and homonymous relation of the parts constituting a whole. In causal terms, this means that the relation denoted by "form" is one in which any given substantial component is related to its counterparts as something simultaneously determinant and determined. The relation cannot be that of one-sided causal dependency.

Second, Kant shows that the reciprocal and homonymous relation which determines the form of a world is a *real* and *objective* one. It is not a relation dependent on any merely arbitrary representational activity:

> This coordination is conceived as *real* and objective, not as ideal and based on the subject's bare power of choice, by which one may fashion any multiplicity whatever into a whole by adding together at will. For by taking several things together, you bring about without toil a *whole of representations,* but not therefore the *representation of a whole.* (2 : 390.11–15)

In keeping with this distinction between representational totality (*totum repraesentationis*) and the representation of a whole (*repraesentatio totius*), Kant argues[32] that if there were unconnected wholes of substances, then the sum-total of these would amount to nothing more than a multiplicity of worlds encompassed by a single thought (*pluralitas mundorum una cogitatione comprehensorum*). This representational totality or merely ideal unity does not do justice to the true import of the interrelation of substances indicated by the relation of co-ordination. By this, Kant has in mind a unified world-whole constituted by individual substances bound together in reciprocal interaction.

The third step in Kant's explication of the formal aspect of the world is the description of the *essential* form (i.e. the principle of the possibility) of a world composed by reciprocally interacting substances. This is where the concepts of transeunt force and influence explicitly come into play:

> But the connection constituting the *essential* form of the world is seen as the principle of *possible influences* of the substances constituting the world. For actual influences do not pertain to the essence, but to the state; and transeunt forces themselves—the causes of influences—presuppose some principle by which it may be possible that the states of several things, the subsistence of each of which is for the rest independent of the others, relate mutually to each other as states determined by a ground. If you abandon this principle, transeunt force in the world cannot be assumed as possible. (2:390.18–26)

Kant's thinking about transeunt force in this passage is not easily understandable, but let us specify the major points either stated or assumed. Apart from the interposed claim that substances are independent of each other with regard to their subsistence (one gathers from this just how peripheral the isolationist account of substance has become), Kant's basic claims are as follows: The connection that constitutes the essential form of a world must be a principle of *possible* influences between substances; for *actual* influences do not pertain to the essence of a world, but merely to its given state.[33] Transeunt forces, being the *causes* of such actual influences, pertain to the given state of a world. They thus presuppose some principle that makes it possible for the substances to exist in a relation of reciprocal causal dependency with respect to their states. Apart from this principle, the possibility of transeunt force operating *in* a world is not grounded.

In establishing the necessity of a principle of the possibility of transeunt force, Kant's foundational conceptual analysis has involved the characterization of the material aspect of "world" in terms of a multiplicity of coexistent substances. It has also led to three specifications of "form." He has defined form as a logical relation of co-ordination,[34] as an objective and real relation of the sum-total of substances composing a world, and as the principle of the possibility of the reciprocal causal determination of substances through transeunt forces. The analysis has progressed to the idea of the principle of a world whose actuality must be comprehended in terms of the reciprocal causal action between coexistent substances. This reciprocal action takes place by means of transeunt *force*, and this force is the ground of all *real* connection between coexistent substances. It is precisely the principle of the possibility of this real connection that furnishes the theme of Section IV of the Dissertation (*De principio formae mundi intelligibilis*).[35]

The procedure by which Kant exhibits the principle of the form of the intelligible world is, basically, an expanded version of the proof and elucidation of Proposition 13 in the *Nova dilucidatio*. I summarize here the main stages of the argument presented in §§ 17–22 of the *Inaugural Dissertation*.[36]

(1) Given a multiplicity of substances, the principle of their possible dynamical community (*principium commercii inter illas possibilis*) is not established by their existence alone. Besides this, there must be something by which their mutual relations can be comprehended. Thus, if dynamical community is to be established, there must be a specific ground (*ratio peculiaris*) that determines it.

(2) Assume that the whole of substances is a contingent whole. Assume also that the world consists of contingent entities. It follows from this that the cause of the world must be a transcendent entity (*ens extra mundanum*).[37]

(3) Assume, moreover, that the substances of the world are all equally dependent upon a single ground for their existence (*substantiae mundanae sunt entia a alio, sed non a se diversis, sed omnia ab uno*). It follows that the unity in the conjunction of these substances must derive from that ground, namely, from the one creator God.

(4) If the previous inference from the given world to a single cause of all its parts is valid, so too will be the reverse line of reasoning, i.e., the deductive movement from a common cause to the connection of all parts or component entities. In this way, the fundamental connection of all substances (*nexus substantiarum primitivus*) will be a necessary one by reason of the conservation of all things through a common principle (*per sustentationem omnium a principio communi*); and the harmony of substances founded in this way will take place in accordance with common rules.

(5) This relation of substances is a generally established harmony

(*harmonia generaliter stabilita*). It contrasts with the individually established harmony (*harmonia singulariter stabilita*) at issue in Leibnizian preestablished harmony and in Malebranchean occasionalism. According to both of these main types of metaphysical explanation, the
dynamical community of substances is externally determined by the
common cause of existence. But only generally established harmony allows us to postulate the universal dynamical community of substances
by means of transeunt causation or physical influence. And only this
idea of dynamical community allows us to comprehend the world as a
real whole:

> If, therefore, the *conjunction* by which all substances form a unity were
> *necessary* through the conservation of all substances by one being, then
> the universal dynamical community [*commercium substantiarum uni-
> versale*] of substances will be through *physical influence,* and the world
> will be a real whole; if not, the community will be sympathetic (i.e., har-
> mony without true dynamical community), and the world will be but an
> ideal whole. (2:409.20–25)[38]

To use two terms that Kant later employs in the *Critique of Pure Reason* (see p. 15 above), the "unity of the world-whole" is conceivable as a
"real relation" only if the universal connection of substances is understood as a relation of physical influence.

§ 4: Summary and Conjectures

We can now bring together the various strains of Kant's
treatment of dynamical community prior to the 1780s. At each stage in
the development of his theory of dynamical community, Kant postulates the existence of a multiplicity of substances. In all three of the writings considered, he holds that the existence of substantial particulars
supplies a necessary, but not a sufficient, condition for the universal interrelation of substances. Besides the creative activity of God, such a
relation involves the real connection or real reciprocal action of finite
substances.

In the *Essay* of 1746 and in the *Nova dilucidatio,* Kant's metaphysical
point of departure is an extreme form of ontological isolationism that
is in at least one respect diametrically opposed to the fundamental assumptions of Leibniz's account of substance and universal harmony.[39]
Kant's position is put into sharpest focus in Proposition 13 of the *Nova*

dilucidatio. There, the independence of each finite substance with respect to its counterparts is absolute. For that reason, the intelligibility of the observable universal reciprocal connection of substances requires not only the creative representational activity of God. It also requires that finite substances should be linked to each other in a relation of physical influence. Whereas Leibniz considers physical influence to be unintelligible and philosophically superfluous, Kant takes it to be indispensable for his metaphysical theory of substance; and he maintains that it must be made intelligible in terms of a principle of universal harmony. In the *Inaugural Dissertation*, Kant's isolationism comes to be of peripheral concern to him. But he is still occupied with giving an account of a system of universal harmony on the basis of the concept of physical influence.

In the *Essay on Living Forces,* accounting for the universal connection of substances requires a concept of essential or active force. The origins of this concept are found in Kant's interpretation of Leibnizian *vis activa.* This interpretation involves the rejection of Wolff's reductivist understanding of active force and the affirmation of the original Leibnizian (and hence "Aristotelian") account of substantial force. But at the same time, Kant's interpretation incorporates Newtonian attraction or universal gravitation as the expression of the fundamental lawfulness of nature. In the *Nova dilucidatio,* the role of force is not discussed. Nevertheless, dynamical community involves the *real* reciprocal action of substances, i.e., the *commercium per causas vere efficientes;* and the universal relation of finite substances is understood as a relation of physical influence. The basic structure of this relation is portrayed with reference to the idea of Newtonian attraction. In the *Inaugural Dissertation,* the role of force is once again explicitly revealed: transeunt forces, as causes of influences, furnish the world-immanent material grounds of a system of physical influence that conforms to the requirements of the principle of universal harmony.

The basic problem guiding our investigations in this chapter and, more generally, in the second part of our overall investigation is the relation between influence and force. In view of this, a problem of the utmost importance arises at this juncture: what is a *transeunt* force as the *cause* of an *influence?* Should we understand it in terms of Leibnizian/ Aristotelian active force? Or should we explicate it with reference to Newtonian attraction? Kant, however, does not supply a clarification of the concept of transeunt force here in question in either the published text of the Dissertation or in any of the metaphysical fragments and lecture transcriptions that are even remotely relevant to the Dissertation's metaphysical project.[40]

The obvious rejoinder to this line of inquiry, of course, is to ask why he should do so. And indeed, if we disregard for a moment our guiding question, it seems that Kant would be, in 1770, in a position to put forward two good arguments for not furnishing that definition in the Dissertation itself. First, although transeunt force pertains to the formal aspect of "world," it is still true that transeunt forces serve as causes of *actual* influences, and so pertain to the *given* state of the world (see p. 84 above). The implication is that the concept of transeunt force can play no direct role in the treatment of the principle of the form of the intelligible world; for this treatment is not concerned with actual influences but rather with the principle of *possible* influences between all finite substances constituting our world. The use of the concept of transeunt force, therefore, has no direct bearing on the role assigned to the concept of dynamical community in the Dissertation. Consequently, the concept of transeunt force does not require further clarification.

Second, even if this concept is linked to the concept of dynamical community, the latter is, essentially, *conceptus intellectualis*.[41] Thus, to the extent that the problem of the principle of the form of the intelligible world revolves around this function of the intellect's real use, the employment of the concept of dynamical community in the exposition of that principle must take place at a theoretical level where any definitional considerations on transeunt force would conflict with Kant's underlying systematic intentions in the Dissertation.[42] It would lead to the encroachment of empirical principles upon the use of pure understanding. And that would be inconsistent with fundamental methodological assumptions of a work that we are supposed to regard as providing a propedeutic science for metaphysics.[43]

The second argument against the appropriateness of our question about transeunt force and influence may well be on target as regards both the distinction between empirical and metaphysical knowledge and Kant's broader architectonic concerns in the Dissertation. Nevertheless, we should not let it obscure a counterargument that can be directed against the first. In fact, it is precisely in view of the first argument presented that we can establish our question's appropriateness. We may do this by putting forward a two-pronged claim: Kant *must* be able to provide a coherent account of transeunt force as cause of an influence; and he must be able to do so not only with respect to the achievement of the concept of dynamical community, but also with respect to its employment (as *conceptus intellectualis*) in the exposition of the aforementioned principle of form.[44] For despite the fact that transeunt force plays no part in this exposition, it is still true that the concept of dynamical community at issue in Section IV is the concept of the universal community of substances through *physical influence* (*commercium substantiarum universale per influxum physicum*).[45] Hence, if transeunt force as cause of influence is not subject to further clarification, then the distinctive feature of Kant's a priori concept of community must remain vague and unclarified. This would expose Kant to a variety of objections. For one thing, he would be in no position to counter the classical Leibnizian objections concerning the lack of intelligibility and superfluousness of physical influence. And more ignominiously, he would be open to a charge of terminological redundancy and explanatory vacuousness similar to the charge that he himself brings against Wolff's *vis motrix* in the *Essay on Living Forces* nearly a quarter of a century prior to the *Inaugural Dissertation*.[46] In sum, we can justly contend that a properly explicated account of the causality of transeunt force is necessary even if it does throw into question the distinction between empirical and metaphysical knowledge, and even if it does therefore wreak havoc with the architectonic plan for theoretical metaphysics that Kant advocates in 1770.

But even apart from these considerations, we need to keep in mind the broader historical context of Kant's early theory of dynamical community. The development of this theory represents not merely Kant's endeavor to offer an alternative to Leibniz's version of the theory of universal harmony, a version that requires us to assume a mutual accommodation as opposed to the real reciprocal dependency of substances. Beyond this, it embodies Kant's explicit response to one of the questions that determined the course of seventeenth- and eighteenth-century metaphysics beginning with Descartes, namely, the problem of the communication of substances.

Kant's response requires him to subject a concept of "world" to an analysis that results in the derivation of a concept of dynamical community. In carrying out this task of reason, Kant lays claim to an independent position not only with respect to Leibniz's doctrine of preestablished harmony, but also with respect to the occasionalist account of causation and the Spinozistic theory of substance. Thus, granted the centrality of the idea of physical influence for the completion of that task, the admission of any ultimate obscurity regarding the relationship between force and influence would amount not merely to the acknowledgment on Kant's part that a pivotal concept of his metaphysics prior to the *Critique of Pure Reason* is unintelligible; it would also be tantamount to renouncing his claim to a separate pedestal in the gallery of rationalist resolutions of a fundamental problem in modern thought, namely, the metaphysical problem of the communication of substances.

If we now recall our discussion of the relationship between force and influence in § 1 of chapter 3, it becomes apparent that Kant's claim to have assumed such an independent position concerns something more than merely the prehistory of the critical theory of a priori knowledge of the 1780s. What, then, are the areas of tangible contact between the two treatments of the relationship between force and influence? And what bearing do they have on the capacity of the critical theory of a priori knowledge to respond to a basic problem of post-Scholastic metaphysics?

In approaching these issues, we must take into account an important difference between the two treatments. In chapter 3 (see p. 50), we were confronted by the demand to identify influence with force. We articulated this demand in view of the fact that Kant discusses substance in space (i.e., matter) as something containing external relations and as something knowable only as constituted through the action of attractive and repulsive force. In the present context, however, given the characterization of transeunt forces as *causes* of influences between substances, that identification seems unfeasible. If "influence" has a definite meaning in the context of the *Inaugural Dissertation,* then it must pertain to the purely *internal* changes in individual substances, and not to the external or relational determinations of substances. In other words, the concept of influence must be tied to the causal ground of alteration in the intrinsic determinations of the self-subsistent, finite entities mentioned in passing in Section I of the Dissertation (see p. 84 above). Hence, according to the information actually provided by Kant in 1770, a transeunt force ought to be a kind of external triggering mechanism for the changes that occur within substantial entities. More precisely, it should be the extrinsic efficient cause of change in substances, each of which is the complete source of all change in its alterable determinations, and is therefore capable of existing apart from any causal connection with its finite counterparts. Thus, while the relationship between force and influence in the *Inaugural Dissertation* points back toward a rigorously isolationist understanding of the ontological independence of particular substances, the corresponding relationship in the Transcendental Analytic of the *Critique of Pure Reason* does not do so—or at least it does not obviously or necessarily do so. In view of this contrast, then, it is reasonable to suppose that Kant's movement away from the isolationist description of substance, the result of which we encounter in the Transcendental Analytic, has something to do with the comprehension of forces of attraction and repulsion as the forces actually *constitutive* of substance in space or matter. We have already seen, in chapter 3, that the fully intelligible employment of the intellectual concept of dynamical community within the critical theory of a priori knowledge depends on the clarification of the relationship between force and influence. We have also seen that this clarification depends in turn on a proper understanding of the materially constitutive efficacy of attractive and repulsive force. There is now reason to suspect that this requires not so much the systematic marginalization of the isolationist portrayal of substance as its dissolution.

In what follows, we will be occupied mainly with a concept of force whose referent is the constitutive forces of matter or substance in space. We will examine the role played by this concept in Kant's achievement of a non-isolationist understanding of *material* substance in the context of his dynamical theory of matter. In undertaking this task, however, we must not lose sight of the major issue raised at the end of this chapter: what does Kant mean when he writes about a causal *relation* between forces and influences? We will be able to return to this question in part four, after our investigation of the dynamical account of matter has prepared the ground for responding to it adequately.

PART III

Dynamical Aether in Kant's Philosophy of Nature

Kant's dynamical conception of physical aether as a continuum of moving forces is an essential component of his theory of matter. He formulated this conception systematically in a number of his early works, and it represents a central part of his concern in his philosophy of nature to furnish metaphysical foundations for physics. Given this centrality, what follows will explore the relationship between the concept of physical aether and the ontological and epistemological ramifications of Kant's theory of matter.

Chapter 6 clarifies a number of historical presuppositions of Kant's dynamical theory by bringing out basic metaphysical and epistemological implications of corpuscular and dynamical theories of matter in seventeenth- and eighteenth-century natural philosophy. Chapter 7 investigates the development of Kant's theory up to 1786 to show that Kant's attempts at constructing a philosophically viable theory of matter are best understood with regard to three interrelated factors: (1) Kant's concern to overcome the isolationist conception of substance; (2) his theoretical need to achieve a coherent dynamical account of matter as material substance; (3) the reasons that ultimately lead him to base this account of matter or material substance on the idea of a universal continuum of attractive and repulsive forces. Examining the development of Kant's theory of matter in view of these issues will show, in part four, that an a priori existence proof for a dynamical cosmic matter is present in the Third Analogy and, moreover, that it is a crucial feature of Kant's transcendental theory of experience.

CHAPTER 6

Corpuscular and Dynamical Theories of Matter in Seventeenth- and Eighteenth-Century Natural Philosophy

This chapter selectively probes the context of seventeenth- and eighteenth-century natural philosophy. Its theme is the two types of theory of matter that were of overriding importance during this period. The investigation revolves around the concepts of matter at the core of these theories. I will therefore be treating (1) the corpuscular concept of matter, according to which physical entities are composed of minute and discrete substantial parts; and (2) the dynamical concept of matter, according to which physical entities are constituted by the interplay of moving forces. Historically, both concepts were coupled with wide-ranging theological speculations. These will be excluded from the following discussion. I am concerned here solely with the roles played by the two concepts in the explanation of physical phenomena. My aim is to provide a definition of the dynamical concept of material substance and to make clear the most general implications that this concept holds for physical ontology, for epistemology, and for explanatory strategy in physics. Understanding these implications will allow us to grasp the full spectrum of issues that underlie Kant's attempts to provide a philosophically well founded theory of matter.

§ 1: Fundamentals of the
Corpuscular Philosophy

Corpuscularianism—the corpuscular or mechanical philosophy—became a dominant form of natural philosophy during the seventeenth century. It was closely connected with the emergence of modern physical science and with the science of mechanics in particular.[1] Corpuscular theories of matter were utilized by the major figures of the seventeenth-century scientific movement and were integral to what can be called the mechanical scheme of nature.[2] They thus belong to the way of thinking about nature that had its origins in the speculative atomism of the Greeks and that achieved experimentally grounded definitiveness during the nineteenth century in conjunction with various chemical theories.[3]

The type of thought associated with seventeenth-century corpuscular theories has been seen to represent a "half empirical, half speculative stage between Democritus and Dalton."[4] A corpuscular theory is the kind of theory of matter that assumes local motion and a particulate matter as the basis for explaining the physical world. Accordingly, we can say that seventeenth-century natural philosophers employed the corpuscular concept of matter if their accounts of natural phenomena were framed in terms of the local motion of discrete particles and their properties, i.e., if they accepted that mobile particles—corpuscles—do in fact exist and that the essential properties of the corpuscles serve as starting points for any theoretically adequate portrayal of appearing physical reality.[5] The use of the corpuscular concept of matter required, therefore, that mobile particles should be understood as the most basic elements relevant to the scientific explanation of the physical world.

I assume that whatever else a philosophical account of nature may be concerned with, it must be capable of fulfilling at least four interrelated requirements. First, it must determine the ontological status of the physical world's material aspect. Second, it must explain the various qualities which empirically cognizable things take on successively or simultaneously. Third, it must describe the nature of the constituent components of experienced things. And fourth, it must render intelligible how those things interact.[6] Corresponding to these requirements, four general principles of the corpuscular philosophy emerge from the characterization of corpuscles as fundamental entities:

(A) The matter of which external objects or bodies are composed is itself substance.

(B) All qualities of bodies are the effects of the primary affections (or primary properties) of this matter, i.e., of the invariant, objective determinations of the constituent corpuscles.

(C) The corpuscles must be conceived as very small versions of particular perceived things.

(D) The interaction between the corpuscles and between the things composed by them is definable in strictly mechanistic terms.

The import of each of these principles, which are common to all versions of the corpuscular philosophy, needs to be elucidated in some detail.[7]

(1) The significance of the corpuscular characterization of matter as substance is best brought out by considering the role played by the principle of matter in the Aristotelian scheme of nature.[8] According to Aristotelian thinking, natural change takes place by the actualization of forms in matter, matter being the substratum of qualitative change. The concretely experienced physical existent or substance is a matter/form composite that is subject to generation and destruction, to coming into being and passing away. Matter does not denote any one specific and definite thing that can be identified as an ultimate constituent of the natural realm. It is, essentially, the correlate of form.[9] In comparison with the Aristotelian view of matter, the corpuscular identification of matter and substance represents a decisive elevation of the ontological status of matter. Matter is the ever-perduring and self-subsistent physical existent as such.[10] The corpuscular account of nature is thus based on a concept of *material* substance, something for which there is, strictly speaking, no place in the Aristotelian scheme of things.[11]

(2) The corpuscular doctrine of properties is integrated with a theory of the objective grounds of sense perception. Central to this theory is the distinction between primary and secondary properties, according to which the properties of corpuscles provide the essential attributes of any object offering itself to scientific scrutiny. Although the corpuscles themselves are not directly perceivable, they are supposed to exhibit primary properties (e.g., size, figure, bulk, solidity)[12] by virtue of which they act on the sensory organs of the knowing subject. They are also supposed to determine the natures and the mode of interaction of material substances. The basic claim is that these properties are perceived as they really are *in* the object. In other words, they are perceived properties; but

they are also essential properties of the imperceptible elementary components of material substance. On the other hand, secondary properties (colors, tastes, etc.) are not absolute properties of the object. They are experienced owing to the relation between the perceptual constitution of the subject and the external objects affecting it. Although they are in fact perceived as particular positive properties, they do not correspond to any properties in the given object. Secondary properties are produced in the knowing subject by means of the corpuscles. Secondary properties are purely relational and reflect the particular dispositions and powers that things have by virtue of their primary (i.e., their corpuscular) constitutions and that can be correlated with the subject's sensory operations and affections.[13] According to the doctrine of primary and secondary properties, all properties or qualities encountered in the physical world can therefore be explained in terms of the varying configurations of the corpuscular components of perceived material substances; but not all properties are equally real.[14]

(3) The third principle follows directly from the corpuscular doctrine of properties. The belief that fundamental entities are very small versions of perceived things is based on the supposition that they share the same essential properties with these things. In other words, the characteristics of perceived things that are both universal and invariant must be ascribed to fundamental entities too. This entails that our assumptions about the internal constitutions of observable bodies depend on the presupposition that the primary properties of bodily parts are the same as the primary properties of the wholes.[15] At issue here is a principle of microstructural explanation that posits the reality of material entities characterized solely by primary properties. The underlying supposition is that, although the corpuscles are imperceptible (or are at least not distinctly perceivable) in the context of ordinary sensory experience, there can be no "representational gap" between the corpuscles and observable bodies with their particular primary properties. Thus, the corpuscular philosopher accepts the notion of an *analogy of nature* that directly links the concept of the invisible corpuscle to the empirical representation of precisely those observable macroscopic structures and essential corporeal properties that the concept is employed to explain.[16]

(4) On the corpuscular view of physical action, matter is determined by its purely mechanical behavior. The corpuscular account of matter thus requires a mechanical view of causality, according to which all causes are external and efficient. On the macrocosmic level, causal action consists in the impression of forces upon observable bodies, these being

entities that are set in motion and pass on their received motion by way of impact.[17] The same processes take place at the microstructural level, where rigid and impenetrable corpuscles rearrange themselves by collision, thus altering the perceived properties of bodies. On the mechanistic view, physical bodies and the corpuscles of which they are composed exhibit no aspect of internally generated activity. Ideally, any powers attributable to matter are reducible to its passive, inertial quality of resisting changes of motion.[18] Matter is therefore counterposed to force (or power) to the extent that the latter is understood as an active material principle. Taken in relation to matter, force is a superadded causal principle. It is the purely external condition of the causal efficacy of matter.[19] It follows from this that the particular substances composed by corpuscles cannot, strictly speaking, be regarded as causally efficacious. One may, indeed, speak of material substances as things that have a disposition or power to act and to produce effects in other substances. This ascription of causal efficacy, however, must in principle be analyzable in terms of the microstructural constitutions of those substances and the extrinsic conditions under which they exist. Causal powers are not part of the nature of material substances.

§ 2: Rationalist and Empiricist Interpretations of the Dynamist Project

The centerpiece of dynamism (or the dynamical philosophy) is the concept of ontologically primitive moving force. In the eighteenth century, this concept supplied the foundation for theories of matter that utilized the notion of an interplay of attractive and repulsive forces. These dynamical theories were often worked out in conjunction with accounts of a gravitational aether and also with theories of imponderable fluids put forward for the explanation of light, heat, electricity, and magnetism.[20] It is a sensible procedure to discuss eighteenth-century dynamism in view of its continental (primarily German) and its British lines of development.[21] In doing this, however, we must bear in mind that the philosophical traditions in question influenced each other to a very considerable degree precisely in the domain of dynamical theories. Thus, the attempt to clearly distinguish between the two streams is based on heuristic principles of presentation rather than concrete historical analysis. Nevertheless, by adhering to these principles we arrive at the following crude, but useful, portrayal of eighteenth-century dynamism's origins and its main directions of development.

The dynamical philosophy had its continental roots in Leibniz's mon-adological concept of substance, and consequently in the postulate of the ontological primacy of force with respect to corporeal substance. The Leibnizian factor was of overriding importance for Wolff and the Wolffian School.[22] It also presented the fundamental point of reference for R. J. Boscovich and Kant in their respective attempts at working out a synthesis of Leibnizian and Newtonian philosophies of nature. It was with Newton and, more particularly, with Newtonian forces of attraction and repulsion that British dynamism had its inception. British dynamists' concern with these forces must also be seen against the backdrop of empiricist criticism leveled against the epistemological justification for the corpuscular concept of matter and, more generally, against the concep-tual foundations of seventeenth- and eighteenth-century science. The work of J. B. Priestley exemplifies this connection between dynamism and empiricism.

To bring to light the principles underlying dynamical theories, I will first very briefly sketch out the relevant facets of Leibniz's and Newton's philosophies of nature. I will then summarize some of the basic posi-tions taken by two contemporaries of Kant—Boscovich and Priestley—who represent the two directions taken by dynamist thinking during the eighteenth century.

Leibniz. Here, I will discuss only the aspects of Leibniz's analysis of substance and substantial force that are directly pertinent to his criticism of the corpuscular philosophy.[23] The first relevant as-pect concerns the concept of corporeal substance as such. In his mature work on natural philosophy from the 1690s, Leibniz's criticism of cor-puscular assumptions is directed against what he considers to be "that crude notion of corporeal substance that depends on the imagination alone and that some years past was introduced through an abuse of the (by itself admirable and most true) corpuscular philosophy."[24] In bas-ing their account of nature on this concept of corporeal substance, the fault of the corpuscular theorists is twofold: they assume that the essence of body is either extension alone or else extension and impenetrability; and they conceive of bodies as exhibiting no feature of internally gen-erated activity.[25]

According to Leibniz, the genuinely philosophic account of corpo-real entities must begin with the assumption that the substantial thing is essentially determined to act.[26] Thus, understanding the nature of corporeal substance requires the supposition that there is an intrinsic force or power of acting in things that can be grasped adequately by the intellect alone.[27] According to this intellectual principle of force or power, all properties of bodies and all corporeal interactions are intelligible only as phenomenal manifestations of ontologically primitive forces.[28] Under this view, therefore, it is force that constitutes the inner nature of bodies (*intima corporum natura*).[29]

Leibniz's concept of force is essential to his monadological interpretation of substance.[30] Although the fundamental entities that constitute the world can be *represented* by means of analogy with the geometrical point, they can be conceptually *apprehended* only in terms of original activity and primitive force.[31] Thus apprehended, they form substantial unities (*unités substantielles*) or "*atoms of substance,* that is, real unities absolutely destitute of parts, which are the sources of actions, the first absolute principles of the composition of things, and, as it were, the last elements in the analysis of substantial things. One could also call them metaphysical points. . . ."[32]

We must be very precise in our understanding of the descriptions of matter and corporeal substance that follow from Leibniz's metaphysical theory of substance. "Matter" refers to the corporeal properties of extension and inertia and to the capacity of physical bodies to resist penetration, but it does not denote any self-subsistent physical existent. As is true for classical Aristotelianism, whose matter/form composite Leibniz seeks to rehabilitate,[33] there is, strictly speaking, no place for a concept of material substance in the Leibnizian scheme of things.[34] The natural philosopher is entitled, of course, to call the perceived material thing a corporeal substance. But usage like this is legitimate only as long as it is clear that the material thing remains an entity constituted by the aggregation of monads, and hence that it does not share the ontological status of these non-extended and essentially non-material metaphysical unities.[35]

Newton. In keeping with the corpuscular viewpoint, Newton assumes the existence of a particulate matter characterized by the primary properties of extension, hardness, impenetrability, mobility, and inertia.[36] But contrary to the orthodox corpuscular tenets, he also affirms the reality and, moreover, the ubiquity of active force in nature. Specifically, he maintains that attractive and repulsive forces (or powers) cannot be ignored in a truly comprehensive theory of the physical world. Central to our comprehension of Newton's view of force is Query 31 of the *Opticks*.[37] Appealing to the principle of the self-conformability (or analogy) of nature, Newton declares there that, just as long-range forces such as gravity operate between observable physical bodies, so too must short-range forces of attraction and repulsion operate between the fundamental particles of which such bodies are composed.[38] Although Newton does not purport to be able to treat the action of these forces quantitatively, he thinks it is crucial to fit them into mathematical physics. He intends to show that an experimentally based theory of matter can, at least in principle, obtain results comparable to those of the dynamics of the macrocosmic world presented in his *Principia*.[39]

In following this plan, Newton is concerned to explain the interactions and visible properties of various materials by determining the ways in which elementary particles are rearranged by the forces operating between them.[40] He conceives all particles of matter to be surrounded by attractive and repulsive forces that, by entering into varying combinations, change the internal corpuscular constitutions of bodies in ways that alter their observable properties.[41] Newton's conception of the primitive form of force interaction is not entirely clear, but in Query 31 he writes:

> There are therefore agents in Nature able to make the particles of bodies stick together by very strong attractions. And it is the business of Experimental philosophy to find them out. . . .
>
> Since metals dissolved in acids attract but a small quantity of the acid, their Attractive force can reach but to a small distance from them. And as in Algebra, where Affirmitive quantities vanish and cease, there Negative ones begin; so in Mechanicks, where Attraction ceases, there a Repulsive virtue ought to succeed.[42]

Newton thus apparently holds that attractive force is transformed into repulsive force at a minute distance from any given particle.

Newton's concern with interparticulate forces has important consequences for the aether hypothesis discussed in Queries 18–24 of the *Opticks*. In employing this hypothesis, he postulates the existence of a universal medium that, being particulate in its fine structure, is rare, subtle, and elastic. The aether is something that dilates and contracts. It condenses, has graduate density and vibrates. By virtue of its rarity, this medium penetrates all bodies and poses no resistance to their motions. By virtue of the elastic force associated with its microscopic particles, it is "expanded throughout all the heavens," and thus can serve as the cause of gravitation.[43]

Query 21 contains a key passage pertaining to Newton's conception of the aether:

> As attraction is stronger in small magnets than in great ones, in proportion to their bulk; and gravity is greater in the surfaces of small planets than in those of great ones, in proportion to their bulk; and small bodies are agitated much more by Electric Attraction than great ones; so the smallness of the rays of light may contribute very much to the power of the agent, by which they are refracted. And so if any one should suppose that *aether*, like our air, may contain particles which endeavour to recede from one another (for I do not know what this *aether* is) and that its particles are exceedingly smaller than those of air, or even than those of light: the exceeding smallness of its particles may contribute to the greatness of the force, by which those particles may recede from one another; and thereby make that medium exceedingly more rare and Elastick than air, and by consequence exceedingly less able to resist the motions of projectiles, and exceedingly more able to press upon gross bodies, by endeavouring to expand itself.[44]

Recent scholarship has shown that in entertaining the notion of the elastic force of physical aether, Newton here attempts, conjecturally, to reduce forces that appear to act at a distance to a single and all-pervasive interstitial force of repulsion.[45] With regard to the microstructure of the aether itself, he comes very close to introducing the concept of a universal force aether. He does retain vestiges of the corpuscular conception of matter. But—at least in this particular context—his tendency is to view aether as being, basically, a dynamical continuum, since its causal efficacy derives from the operations of repulsive force between infinitesimally minute material particles.

Boscovich. In his *Theoria philosophiae naturalis redacta ad unicam legem virium in natura existentium* (1763), Boscovich formulates a theory of matter that accounts for the properties of bodies and the forms of corporeal interaction purely in terms of moving forces (*vires*). He considers that his theory of interacting forces represents a system "midway between that of Leibniz and that of Newton, a system that, to be sure, takes very much from both and also differs very much from both" (§ 1). Boscovich conceives of matter as something spatially permanent but without extension, given that its fundamental constituents are unextended focal points, or centers of exertion, of attractive and repulsive forces. Observable material bodies emerge from the relations established between these centers of force in accordance with a single law of the oscillatory transformation of repulsion into attraction and vice versa. The various configurations of the force-centers formed according to this law are subsystems within the universal system of corporeal nature constituted through the action of the two elemental forces.

For our purposes, two aspects of Boscovich's dynamical theory need to be given special emphasis. First, Boscovich rejects what Leibniz calls the "crude concept" of corporeal substance as something that could furnish a model for explicating the internal constitution of matter. Insofar as matter is defined by force, questions about the particulate structure of matter must yield to questions about the form—i.e., the law—of force interaction. Thus, the adequate understanding and representation of this form cannot be grounded solely with reference to the individual thing encountered in ordinary sensory experience. This factor is well illustrated in § 132 of the *Theoria* by Boscovich's appeal to the intellect as the proper cognitive source for comprehending his force-center model: "[W]e could never acquire through the senses any idea pertaining to matter that did not involve at the same time extension, parts, and divisibility. And for that reason, as often as we presented to the mind a point, we would, unless we made use of reflection, obtain the idea of a sort of ball—an extremely small one, to be sure, but still a ball having two distinct and opposed surfaces." Boscovich does not deny that all of our ideas concerning matter originate in sensory experience. Nonetheless, he argues that without the intellectual apprehension of the point-center of force, we should never be able to get beyond the fixation on the perceived structure and the geometrically determinable extension of material things that is characteristic of corpuscular thought.

The second factor to underscore is the idea that furnishes the governing principle of Boscovich's theory of natural philosophy. We can recognize this in the description of the grounds of material nature's systematic coherence given in § 2 of the *Theoria:*

> [The theory of mutual forces] derives its simple and perfectly nonextended first elements from the theory of Leibniz. From the Newtonian system it has the mutual forces that vary as the distances of the points vary from one another; and likewise from Newton it has not only the kind of forces that determine the approach of the points and that are commonly called attractions, but also forces of a kind that determine their recession and are called repulsions. Moreover, this conception of the forces is such that, where attraction ends, there, with a change of distance, repulsion begins, and vice versa. That, of course, is what Newton proposed in the final Query to the *Opticks,* and he illustrated it by the example of the transition from positive to negative, as obtains in algebraic formulae. This feature, however, is common to both systems as well

as to my own, namely, the point that any particle of matter is connected with every other particle, no matter how remote, in such a way that in accordance with a change in the position, however small, of any one of them, the determinations to motion in all the rest are altered; and unless perchance these all destroy one another, which is infinitely improbable, some motion . . . will thereupon be brought about in all of them.

The main point in question here is a conception of physical reality that borrows from both the Leibnizian monadology and Newton's idea of a world system but that also explicitly acknowledges Newtonian forces of attraction and repulsion to be the basis of appearing physical reality. These forces act lawfully and continuously with varying degrees of intensity between all aggregates of force nuclei. They thereby provide for the causal connection between all the materials of the physical universe. Boscovich proposes that the material world as a whole is constituted as a dynamical continuum in conformity with an a priori demonstrable Newtonian law of force interaction.[46]

Priestley. The epistemological difficulties inherent in postulating the existence of a realm of imperceptible objects led many British philosophers, including Priestley, to reject the corpuscular account of nature.[47] They found untenable the notion that our experience of physical things and processes should be explained in terms of invisible corpuscles characterized by primary properties.[48] Before going into Priestley's view of matter, I will very briefly consider some basic elements of eighteenth-century empiricist criticism of the doctrine of primary and secondary properties and the conception of material substance that this doctrine involves. I will limit my remarks to some criticisms put forward by Berkeley and Hume.

By appealing to the immediate contents of sense experience, Berkeley and Hume undertake to relegate primary properties to the domain of the secondary, thereby collapsing the distinction between the two kinds of property. They maintain that the existence of all knowable properties of matter depends on the sensory activity and mental processes of the perceiver.[49] They employ a similar strategy in their epistemological destruction of the concepts of force and power associated with the corpuscular doctrine of material properties.[50] Berkeley denies that this concept can be vindicated with reference to ideas of sense or to ideas of reflection.[51] In the context of his general analysis of causation, Hume rejects the idea that the ascription of causal powers to bodies and matter can be philosophically justified by investigating the origin of our idea of cause and effect.[52] It follows from Berkeley's and Hume's arguments that our knowledge claims about the external world cannot be rationally justified if the analysis of sense perception requires the portrayal of an affective relation between the percipient and material substances having absolute existence. According to Berkeley, the very concept of material substance is epistemically insupportable.[53] Similarly, Hume maintains that when we reason from cause and effect, we must conclude that none of the purportedly secondary qualities of material objects can have a mind-independent existence; and that "[w]hen we exclude these sensible qualities there remains nothing in the universe, which has such an existence."[54] There is thus for Hume a "direct and total opposition" between the results of our causal inferences and the evidence of the senses that persuades us of "the continu'd and independent existence of body."[55]

Writing in the final decades of the eighteenth century, Priestley combines the dynamical conception of matter with a theory of knowledge designed in part to counter the phenomenalistic dimensions of Berkeleyan and Humean empiricism, which he considers to be inimical to the pursuit of natural philosophy. This leads Priestley to emphasize the role of the concept of force (or power) in the account of our knowledge of the external world. We can discern the centrality of this concept for Priestley's theory of knowledge in a passage from the *Disquisitions Relating to Matter and Spirit* of 1782:[56]

> From the manner of expressing our ideas, we cannot speak of powers or properties, but as powers and properties of some kind of thing or substance, though we know nothing at all of that *thing* or *substance* besides the powers that we ascribe to it; and, therefore, when the powers are supposed to be withdrawn, all idea of substance necessarily vanishes with them. I have, therefore, the same right to say that matter is a substance possessed of the properties of attraction and repulsion only, as another has to say, that it is a substance possessed of the property of impenetrability together with them, unless it can be proven that the property of attraction or repulsion necessarily implies, and cannot exist without, that of impenetrability. Whether it be possessed of any of these properties must be determined by experiment only.[57]

We may summarize Priestley's views on matter and empirical knowledge by commenting on three facets of this passage: (1) the relation between the force (power) and substance; (2) the identification of powers with the properties of material substance; and (3) the confirmation of the strictly empirical nature of our knowledge of matter.

Substance and Force. Like Leibniz (and Boscovich), Priestley makes his concept of substance dependent on the concept of force or power. What distinguishes him from Leibniz can best be traced to his particular philosophic context. The special care that Priestley takes to establish the reality of substantial force with reference to the immediate contents of sensory experience is motivated not by the requirements arising from rationalist conceptions of "substance" and "world," but rather by the empiricist demand that our knowledge of external things must conform to the character of such experience. By satisfying this demand, Priestley provides himself with epistemological leverage for affirming the objective reality of material substance in the face of the objections put forward by thinkers such as Berkeley and Hume. These are objections that, as we have seen, revolve around the corpuscular definition of matter. Ultimately, Priestley's argument in favor of material substance is based on his view that the concept of force or power emerges from ordinary perceptual experience and must therefore be employed to structure the scientific portrayal of physical reality.[58] Given this view, the appeal to sensory experience does not demand the rejection of the scientific account of nature as an account of a system of real things causally responsible for perceptual appearances.[59]

Forces and Material Properties. Priestley's claim about the legitimacy of asserting that matter is "a substance possessed of the properties of attraction and repulsion only" amounts to a denial of the corpuscular doctrine of material properties. Specifically, this claim cuts away the foundations of the distinction between primary properties and the relational properties (i.e., the secondary qualities and the forces or powers) that material things have by virtue of their corpuscular constitutions. If all properties of matter can be understood in terms of attraction and repulsion—if even those properties (e.g., impenetrability) commonly thought to be basic to the scientific definition of matter may therefore be functions of these forces—then clearly there is no conclusive theoretical basis for drawing the kind ontological distinction between primary and secondary properties which the corpuscular theorists held to be crucial to the account of both physical reality itself and the foundations of our perceptual knowledge of objects.

Force and Empirical Criteria of Perceptual Cognition. Since it relates to Priestley's actual derivation of the dynamical concept of material substance, the third facet needs to be treated in greater detail than the preceding two. In his *Disquisitions,* Priestley discusses the way in which we are able to obtain a dynamical concept of matter. His point of departure is the common opinion about matter. According to this opinion, "matter is necessarily a *solid* or *impenetrable* substance, and naturally or of itself, destitute of all *powers* whatever, as those of *attraction* or *repulsion* etc." [60] The notion that matter is solid or impenetrable substance is supposed to be derived directly from tactile sensation. [61] But the analysis of sensation and the account of practical experimentation show that the common opinion concerning solidity is actually founded on resistance, i.e., on something that "is never occasioned by *solid matter,* but by something of a very different nature, *viz.,* a *power of repulsion* always acting at a real, and in general, assignable distance from what we call body itself." [62] Rigorous sensory analysis and the proper understanding of the import of experimentation for empirical cognition also lead us to conclude that attraction is not a property foreign to matter. Granted that any body, which is experienced as something apparently impenetrable, must have a definite shape, Priestley proposes that "no such *figured thing* can exist, unless the parts of which it consists have a *mutual* attraction, so as either to keep contiguous to, or preserve at a certain distance from each other. This power of attraction, therefore, must be essential to the *actual existence* of all matter, since no substance can retain any *form* without it." [63] When contrasted with repulsion—a power directly sensed as resistance—attraction is thus indeed an inferred constituent of the physical world. Yet it is still something "absolutely essential" to the "very nature and being" of matter. [64]

In sum: Priestley shows how we obtain the dynamical concept by examining our sensory experience and experimental activity. He thereby establishes that repulsion is the primary criterion for our recognition of the existence of matter. He establishes further that attraction, as an inferred though nonetheless constitutive force of matter, is the basis of all corporeal formation.

We need to note one further aspect of Priestley's empirical derivation of the dynamical concept, since this will be directly relevant to the discussion of Kant in the next chapter. As is shown by his treatment of attraction, Priestley conceives of matter as something particulate. Although he does not go into detail about this point, he very probably has in mind a force-center model of the structure of matter. This interpretation is supported by the fact that he considers Boscovich's point-center theory to offer a plausible explanation for the different kinds of body which we experience. [65] Nevertheless, he is not concerned to formulate a comprehensive theory of the interaction of forces:

In this *metaphysical work,* I have confined myself to the exclusion of the property of *impenetrability,* which is generally considered as essential to all matter, and to the claim of the property of *attraction and repulsion,* as appearing to me not to be properly what is *imparted* to matter, but what *really makes it to be what it is,* in so much that, without it, it would be nothing at all; which is giving it the same rank and importance that has usually been assigned to the property of *solidity and impenetrability.*[66]

A coherent theory of force interaction would require "consideration of the *internal structure of matter,*" as well as clear answers to "queries concerning physical indivisible points."[67] But given the lack of experimental data, Priestley deems any conclusions drawn about this structure to be unavoidably speculative and therefore inappropriate for the type of doctrine in which his dynamical concept has its place.

§ 3: Metaphysical and Epistemological Ramifications of the Dynamist View of Nature

What are the implications of the dynamical conception of matter for a comprehensive philosophic account of nature that satisfies the four requirements stated at the beginning of this chapter? By generalizing on the assumptions involved in Boscovich's systematic dynamical theory and in Priestley's epistemological reflections regarding the dynamical concept, we arrive at the following principles:

- The matter of which bodies are composed is itself substance, and substance is definable in terms of moving force (attraction and repulsion).

- All properties of bodies or material substances are the effects of the interplay of the substantial moving forces.

- The apprehension of the form — or law(s) — of force cannot rely on any direct representational link to the things of ordinary perceptual experience.

- Force interaction cannot be comprehended in strictly mechanistic terms (in the sense defined above in § 1).

Thus, the dynamical definition of matter preserves the status of matter as the self-subsistent physical entity or material substance. It does not therefore require the demotion of matter as substance to its standing in the Aristotelian scheme of nature. Rather, the dynamical definition secures the ontological status of matter as substance, which is only partially achieved by the corpuscular conception of material substance. In making the philosophical account of nature independent of the "crude concept" of corporeal substance, the conception of matter as moving force furnishes a more stable basis for the rational justification of assertions about the reality of material substance than the corpuscular view of things could provide.

The acceptance of forces as the causal grounds of all experienced properties of things necessarily involves the rejection of the foundational role played by the corpuscular primary properties. It can be established that some material properties are more fundamental than others, as is necessary for the practices of natural science.[68] But contrary to the explanatory procedure of the corpuscular theorists, there is in the dynamical view neither the need for, nor the possibility of, driving an "ontological wedge" between fundamental and secondary properties of matter. In superseding the corpuscular doctrine of primary and secondary properties, dynamist thinking makes all properties relational (in the sense discussed above); and it makes them all equally empirical manifestations of the activity of those forces that present material reality to the knowing subject.

The dynamical concepts of substance and material properties can be grounded with reference to the actual contents of our perceptual experience of an outer world. Nevertheless, the repudiation of the crude concept of corporeal substance entails that the link between the concept of matter (or material substance) and the empirical representation of the structures and properties of observable bodies is broken. One might argue that in postulating indivisible, non-extended points for the purpose of representing the interplay of forces, the eighteenth-century dynamist continues to work with a principle of microstructural explanation. But even granting this, it is plain that the corpuscular analogy of nature is effectively dissolved: the elemental constituents of the physical world can no longer be regarded as minute versions of perceived things.

Intrinsic to dynamical theories is a conception of causal action that is in essential respects opposed to the notion of causation underlying corpuscular theories. Efficient causality is retained, but its character is transformed: the mechanistic paradigm of rigid or absolutely non-elastic particles communicating action by impact yields in dynamical theories to the conception of forces operating with varying degrees of intensity.[69] These forces, which are constitutive of matter as it is known, are at the same time the self-activating principles of the causal efficacy of matter in the physical world as a whole.

Let us bring to a close the main line of argument followed in this chapter. Both corpuscular and dynamical concepts give matter the status of substance, but they lead to radically divergent doctrines of material properties and causal action within nature. The dynamical concept of material substance is achieved through criticism of the ontological underpinnings of, and the epistemological warrant for, its corpuscular predecessor. It is a concept of remarkable versatility. It conforms to the conceptual requirements of the intellect but complies with the evidence of the senses. It lends itself equally well to the formulation of an a priori demonstrable law expressing the elemental form of force interaction and to an empirical derivation of basic material properties that sets out from an analysis of sensory experience. It can be employed to justify the construction of a world system that is anchored in a metaphysical insight into the possibility of matter and that remains true to the legacy of the Leibnizian monadology. But it can also be fitted into a theory of knowledge intended to satisfy the relatively modest demand to counter the phenomenalistic destruction of material substance without engaging in speculation about the fine structure of matter. We will see all of these factors at work in the development of Kant's theory of matter.

CHAPTER 7

The Theory of Physical Aether in Kant's Philosophy of Nature

Kant's writings on the philosophy of nature have been the subject of intense scrutiny over the past two centuries, and it is not my intention to add to the voluminous literature on any given special aspect of Kant's relation to the natural sciences. Rather, my aim is to chart a developmental undercurrent present in Kant's natural philosophy for a period of more than forty years. This undercurrent affects significantly the different courses that Kant takes in working out his views on matter. Understanding its function in his thought provides the proper context for interpreting not only Kant's theory of matter but also those aspects of that theory that are indispensable for understanding the Third Analogy.

The history of Kant's views on matter is ordinarily divided into five separate phases: (1) Two of Kant's works from 1755 involve a theory of matter based on the corpuscular concept of matter and Newtonian forces of attraction and repulsion. These categories underlie the account of cosmogenesis in the *Universal Natural History* and the general aether theory of *De igne*. In the former treatise, Kant supposes that originally there was an elementary matter diffused throughout cosmic space. In the latter, he posits the existence of an imponderable elastic matter that fills the spaces between the corpuscles making up composite bodies. (2) The *Monadologia physica* of 1756 embodies Kant's first attempt to formulate a theory of matter based on strictly dynamistic principles. A monadological concept of matter, according to which bodies are composed of the spheres of activity of attractive and repulsive forces, provides the foundation for this theory. (3) During the early to mid-1770s, Kant repudiates the notion that the monadological concept of matter can furnish the foundation for a dynamical theory of matter. Physical aether, conceived as an imponderable elastic matter continuously diffused throughout cosmic space, supplies the condition of corporeal formations and serves as a ground of the community of physical bodies. Kant thus regards this aether as the generative source of all corporeal entities in that space and as a material substrate that allows for their causal interaction. (4) In Part 2 of the *Metaphysical Foundations of Natural Science* (1786) Kant constructs what in effect is a "double-faced" dynamical theory. Seeking to respect the restrictions on the scope of our rational cognition of nature imposed by the critical theory of a priori knowledge, he works out a theory of matter that conforms to his previous repudiation of his monadological concept of matter. But at the same time, he finds himself constrained to make use of this monadological concept when attempting to represent the relation of forces through which matter as we know it is constituted. (5) In the earlier fascicles of the *Opus postumum* (i.e., the manuscripts composed during the period of 1786 through 1799) Kant revises the dynamical theory of the *Metaphysical Foundations*. He puts in its place the rudiments of a systematic theory of matter, using the concept of a force aether as his point of departure. The concept of a universal continuum, or plenum, of material forces is thus expressly made the centerpiece of the dynamical theory.

According to this standard interpretation,[1] the history of Kant's systematic considerations on matter consists in the formulation of two different types of theory—the corpuscular and the dynamical—with the latter having four quite distinct and discontinuous phases. The implication is that we should not view this history as a process of reformulation and refinement of a single theory. The standard interpretation is not in need of essential revision. Yet in this chapter, and in the corresponding section in chapter 8 (see pp. 158–163 below), I will show the history of Kant's considerations on matter to have greater coherence than is suggested by the schematic summary just presented. In particular, I will show that an important element of continuity in Kant's natural philosophy originates in his characterization of physical aether as an imponderable elastic matter. I will establish that the concept of physical aether, which obviously is central to Kant's thinking in the first, third, and fifth of the phases described, is a highly significant feature of the other two phases as well. And I will make it clear that Kant's concern to specify the nature of physical aether and to determine its proper role in

metaphysical and scientific explanation is what enables us to understand best the undeniable aspects of discontinuity exhibited by the historical development of the Kantian dynamical conception of matter. The
achievement of these objectives will be completed in chapter 8, which is
devoted mainly to the discussion of the *Opus postumum*. In the present
chapter, I will concentrate on the first four stages in the unfolding of
Kant's views.

§ 1: Corpuscular Matter, Force, and Aether in 1755

In the *Universal Natural History,* we witness the union of
the concept of matter and Newtonian forces that provides the key to understanding all subsequent developments in Kant's theory of matter. In
1755, these forces are conceived as grafted onto a corpuscular matter and
are fitted into a conjectural description of cosmogenesis:

> After setting the world in simple chaos, I applied no other forces for
> developing the greatest order of nature than attractive and repulsive
> forces—two forces that are both equally certain, equally simple and,
> at the same time, equally original and universal. Both are borrowed from
> the Newtonian worldly wisdom. The first is by this time a force of na-
> ture placed beyond any doubt. The second, to which the natural science
> of Newton can perhaps not grant as much clarity as the first, I accept
> here only in the sense in which no one denies it, namely, in the case of
> the finest dissolution of matter, as, for example, in vapors. On these very
> simple grounds I derived without artifice the following system, . . .
> $(1:234.26-235.5)^2$

In accounting for the cosmogenetic process, Kant thus postulates
the existence of minute material particles that are differentiated according to their specific densities and that are endowed with attractive and
repulsive forces.[3] These forces are the grounds of the mechanical action
of corpuscular matter from which there results the formation of, and
impartation of motion to, the major bodies of the solar system. This
formative process occurs in conformity with the laws of divine understanding. But it also takes place in accordance with its own purely immanent Newtonian lawfulness. It is by hypothetically reconstructing
this process of systematic ordering that Kant intends to put in place the
physical part of a cosmic science, the mathematical part of which is furnished by Newton's *Principia.*[4]

In Kant's view of cosmogenesis, the observable lawfulness of the solar system derives from a natural inclination (*natürlicher Hang*)[5] of matter. Kant proposes to explain the formation of the solar system and the stellar systems of the universe in terms of the mechanical laws of a matter whose self-ordering motion tends toward increasingly perfect harmony in the workings of all its parts. To this end, he assumes the existence of an elementary matter out of which all bodies are generated. This corpuscular elementary matter, which obeys the laws imposed upon it by the creator, was originally dispersed throughout space.[6] The formative process undergone by the elementary matter involves the emergence of composite bodies of incrementally increasing mass as the result of the action of attractive and repulsive force. The entire process tends toward a state of universal equilibrium in the interactions of all bodies, i.e., a condition of least action (*ein Zustand der kleinsten Wechselwirkung*),[7] in which the conflict of the forces is reduced to a minimum. Granted the validity of the analogy of nature, the philosophic account of this process explains the lawfully ordered mechanical workings of the solar system and the totality of stellar formations.[8]

Two facets of the Kantian conception of cosmogenesis are especially relevant to our concerns. First, we should note that the theoretical reconstruction of the cosmic process contains a proof of empty space. The first step in this proof opposes the Cartesian assumption that there is a mechanical aether present in interplanetary space to the Newtonian assumption that there is no such matter capable of establishing a community of influence (*Gemeinschaft des Einflüßes*), i.e., dynamical community, between the planetary bodies.[9] The second step is to establish the fundamental correctness of the Newtonian position by integrating it with Kant's own account of cosmic history:

> In the present condition of space in which the orbs of the whole planetary world revolve, there is to be found no material cause that could impress or direct their motions. This space is completely empty, or at least is as good as empty. Thus, it must once have been differently constituted and filled with matter that was sufficiently capable of transmitting motion to all the celestial bodies to be encountered therein and of making this motion agree with its own motion, thus bringing them all into agreement with one another. And after attraction cleansed the aforementioned spaces and collected all the diffused matter into particular clumps, the planets had henceforth, with the once impressed motion, to continue freely and unaltered in their orbits in a non-resisting space. The reasons for the first adduced probability definitely require this concept; and since between the two cases no third case is possible, this concept

can be regarded with a high degree of approval, which raises it above the probability [*Scheinbarkeit*] of an hypothesis. (1:262.21–263.5)

Kant thus formulates an a posteriori proof for empty space that contrasts markedly with the arguments against empty space that we have encountered thus far. It is important, however, to recognize that his rejection of an interplanetary material plenum applies solely to a community of influence sufficiently powerful to generate the reciprocal impartation of motion between the major planetary bodies. Kant explicitly confirms this restriction in a note preceding the passage just quoted: "I do not investigate here whether this space can be called empty in the most genuine sense. For it is in any case enough to observe that all matter that may happen to be present in this space is not powerful enough by far to give rise to any effect with respect to the moving masses in question" (1:262.32–36). The argument against empty space therefore does not establish that the space in question is entirely devoid of matter.

The second thing to note is that, in the context of the theory of cosmogenesis, Kant's argument in favor of *mechanically* empty space leads to the idea that attraction is the source of the immanent lawfulness and causal uniformity of all matter in motion.[10] But attraction is not *merely* the source of such lawfulness and uniformity. It is "that certain natural law, which brings it about that all matter, in its self-restriction through reciprocal action, ultimately puts itself in a state in which one matter incurs from another as little change as possible. . . ." (1:340.12–15). As Newtonian universal attraction, attractive force is itself the embodiment of the primitive law governing the orderly formation and conservation of corporeal nature as a whole—past, present, and future.[11]

Kant assumes in the above quoted passages the reality of both short-range and long-range forces of attraction. In the *Universal Natural History*, the short-range efficacy of attraction is responsible for the original excitation (*Regung*) of nature that initiates the formation of the elementary matter. As is true of all corporeal systems, our solar system began to evolve at locations where particles of the elementary matter possess relatively stronger short-range forces of attraction.[12] It was at these locations that the formation of composite bodies originally occurred. On the other hand, long-range attraction acts on the whole of material reality. All systems of celestial bodies are reciprocally connected by this form of attractive force. Kant calls it the universal relation that unites the parts of nature in one space (*die allgemeine Beziehung, welche die Teile der Natur in einem Raum vereinigt*).[13] It furnishes the principle of all the formations of matter encountered in space, and it also provides for their conservation through time.[14]

As he does in the *Universal Natural History,* Kant uses in *De igne* a corpuscular concept of matter in conjunction with Newtonian forces of attraction and repulsion. He also underscores the key role played by attractive force in scientific explanation. As far as the theory of matter is concerned, the most obvious difference between the two writings is that in *De igne* Kant attempts to combine these factors into a general theory of physical aether. The theme of *De igne* is the different functions in nature to be attributed to an imponderable elastic matter that operates in conjunction with short-range Newtonian forces. Kant intends to explain different states of matter and various thermal and optical phenomena in terms of the efficacy of this elastic matter.

In Section 1 of *De igne,* Kant maintains that in order to explain liquidity and solidity, as well as the deformations undergone by solid bodies, we must assume the existence of an elastic matter capable of penetrating into the intercorpuscular spaces of ponderable matter. The observable fluid states of various materials are therefore not explicable straight away on purely corpuscular (in this case Cartesian)[15] grounds. Similar considerations apply to the explanation of the mechanical action of ponderable fluids and the solidity or hardness of bodies.[16]

In Section 2, Kant seeks to establish the connection between his *materia elastica,* as treated in Section 1, and the imponderable fluids employed in the explanation of thermal phenomena.[17] The connection is yielded by the supposition that the range of such phenomena must be understood in terms of the action of interstitial elastic matter — namely, the wavelike action of the *materia ignis* or *materia lucis.* Kant's central concern in *De igne* is therefore to establish that his intercorpuscular elastic aether is the same as caloric and light aether. He proposes that the "matter of fire is nothing other than the elastic matter (described in the preceding section [i.e., in Section 1 of *De igne*]) that holds together the elements of bodies with which it is intermixed" (1:376.18–20). And since we assign the name of heat to the "undulatory or vibratory motion" (376.20) of this aether, it follows that "the matter of heat is nothing other than the aether itself (the matter of light) compressed by means of the strong force of attraction (or adhesion) of bodies into their interstices" (377.16–18).

The unified aether theory of *De igne* is incomplete in a number of very basic ways.[18] Kant does not give any precise description of the material composition of the aether itself. Is it, then, corpuscular in nature? Is it endowed with its own attractive or repulsive forces? Kant shows some inclination to make repulsion the primary means by which the aether acts.[19] But he characterizes the aether's causal efficacy merely in terms of the pressure that it exerts and by the undulatory motion that is supposed to occur in concert with the short-range attractive forces affiliated with the corpuscular components of ponderable matter. He does not stipulate whether that action must in turn be explained through corpuscular motion and forces of attraction and repulsion. He also leaves it undecided whether the aether is present in all of physical space. Since he maintains that the aether serves as a light aether, he would seem to be obliged to admit this.[20] But the cosmological orientation characteristic of the *Universal Natural History* is simply not a central feature of Kant's scientific thinking in *De igne*. Even where he is occupied with describing the role of the aether as *materia lucis*, his interest is limited to the explanation of certain commonly occurring terrestrial phenomena.[21]

§ 2: The Physical Monadology of 1756

The *Monadologia physica* represents Kant's first concerted endeavor to work out a truly comprehensive theory of matter based on dynamical principles. His avowed purpose in constructing his physical monadology is to establish the proper relationship between geometry, as applied in the science of mechanics, and metaphysics.[22] The latter, characterized as a science of the nature itself of bodies (*scientia ipsius corporum naturae*),[23] treats the causal sources of the phenomena of material nature. It counters the phenomenalistic bent of the geometrical science, seeing that geometers (i.e., the mechanical theorists) are "those who only chase after the phenomena of nature" and are consequently "always just that far removed from the recondite understanding of first causes" (1:475.13–14).

There thus appears to be an inherently conflictual relationship between the two theoretical disciplines in question. Since bodies consist of parts, it is a crucial task of metaphysics to determine the nature of these parts and their combination. In particular, metaphysics must establish whether bodies fill space by virtue of their corpuscular constitution or else through the mutual conflict of their forces. But it seems nearly impossible to unite metaphysics with geometry in the attempt to complete this task, since metaphysics seems inevitably to oppose geometry in its responses concerning the infinite divisibility of space, the reality of empty space, and the determination of the grounds of universal attraction gravitation.[24] Kant, however, intends to put an end to apparent disagreement between geometry and metaphysics by instituting a clear division of labor between them. His division is based on the assumption that the elemental constituents of bodies are intrinsically active. This involves a reinterpretation of the Leibnizian monad in terms of *physical* unity. That, Kant holds, is possible if monadic activity is comprehended in terms of the operations of Newtonian forces. Accordingly, Kant aims to explain the elemental internal constitution of matter by employing the notion of a sphere of activity of attractive and repulsive forces. His goal in the *Monadologia physica* is thus to derive these forces from the very nature and primitive properties of the elements of bodies (*ex ipsa elementorum natura et primitivis affectionibus*).[25]

In view of the discussion of Leibniz's, Wolff's, and Kant's general theories of substance in chapters 4 and 5 above, the significance of Kant's concept of the monad can be summarized as follows: In agreement with Leibniz, but contrary to Wolff, Kant does not hesitate to employ the vocabulary of a monadological account of substance. In agreement with Wolff, but contrary to Leibniz, Kant makes it clear that the monadological concept relevant to the metaphysical foundations of natural science applies solely to corporeal entities.[26] In agreement with both Leibniz and Wolff, the Kantian monad is defined in terms of its simplicity, indivisibility, and unity.[27]

In accordance with his own metaphysical postulate of the ontological independence of finite substances, Kant contends that all connection between the physical monads must be conceived as a purely external relation. This last point is established by the proof for Proposition 2 of the *Monadologia physica:*

> Bodies consist of parts, each of which has an enduring existence separate from the others. Since, however, composition by such parts is nothing but a relation, and hence a determination that is in itself contingent and that can be denied without violation of the existence of the parts related, it is plain that all composition of bodies can be annulled, leaving standing all the parts that were formerly bound together. Moreover, when all composition is abolished, the parts that are left are plainly not composite, and they are thus completely free of a plurality of substances, and hence are simple. Any body whatever, therefore, consists of absolutely simple parts, i.e., of monads. (1:477.9–17)

We encounter in these lines the naturo-philosophic correlate to the general metaphysical concept of substance found in the *Essay on Living Forces* and the *Nova dilucidatio:* It is the "isolationist" concept of substance applied to the notion of the composite body. This application requires that the elementary constituent of bodies, i.e., the monad, should be thought of as capable of permanent existence apart from any connection with other monads. Composition, understood as the mutual connection of monads, is therefore a metaphysically contingent relation.

Now to the basic features of Kant's account of attractive and repulsive force:

> since the principle of all internal actions, or the force inherent in the elements, must be a moving force, and one, indeed, that is applied from without because it is present to what is external;[28] and since we are unable to conceive of any force for moving what is co-present other than a force that endeavors to repel or attract; and since, furthermore, if one posits repulsive force alone, one will not be able to understand the combination [*colligatio*] of elements so that they form compound bodies, but only their diffusion, whereas if one posits attractive force alone, one will indeed be able to understand their combination, but not their determinate extension in space—[since all this is so, then] one can already in a way understand in advance that whoever is able to deduce these two principles from the very nature and fundamental properties of the elements will have made no mean contribution toward explaining the inner nature of bodies. (1:476.6–15)

Kant endeavors here to establish the status of attraction and repulsion as principles of the existence of composite bodies. He claims that the ground of intrinsic substantial (or monadic) activity must lie in moving force (*vis motrix*).[29] And he claims that the only *conceivable* force for moving what is co-present is one that strives to drive back and draw towards—to repel and attract. His principle of substantial activity in corporeal nature thus involves the employment of an *a priori* concept of moving force. Employing this concept seems to impel Kant well beyond Wolff's agnosticism regarding the intrinsic determinations of substance. Yet the concept cannot be made intelligible in terms that Leibniz would find acceptable either, for Kant seems to derive it by means of an implicit appeal to our primitive kinesthetic experiences as embodied subjects situated in a world of coexistent material objects. The upshot is that Kant's a priori concept of substantial force is not based on principles that are purely rational in any Leibnizian sense.

Three particular features of Kant's physical monadology will prove to be decisive for our understanding of the overall development of the dynamical aether theory.

(1) Despite its simplicity and indivisibility, the Kantian monad fills the entire space of its presence.[30] Each monad determines its particular space in the form of a sphere of activity (*sphaera activitatis*) within which force is continuously exerted. To the extent that each monad is conceived to manifest its presence in space, it must be represented as such a sphere with force being exerted from its center. Force, therefore, gives rise to the extensive quantity of the presence (*quantitas extensiva praesentiae*) of each substance. It is also what establishes the external relation of substances by means of which space is filled and through which space is constituted. Consequently, space, which is infinitely divisible and does not consist of primitive and simple parts,[31] must be defined as the phenomenon of the relations of united monads (*phaenomenon relationis unitarum monadum*) or as the phenomenon of the external relations of substances (*externae substantiarum relationis phaenomenon*).[32] Yet the monad itself, as the subject of external determinations, can be assigned no spatial attribute. Thus, for the individual monad "space" denotes the ambit (*ambitus*) of its external presence. Spatial determinations are therefore external or relational determinations, and each monad also has internal determinations that are not subject to division in the way that external relations are. To argue against this, Kant insists, is to commit a crude fallacy in metaphysical reasoning:

> It is as if you said: God is internally present to all created things by the act of conservation; accordingly, he who divides the mass of created things divides God, because he divides the ambit of His presence. There is nothing more absurd that can be said than this. The monad, therefore, which is the primitive element of the body, insofar as it fills space, has in any case a certain extensive magnitude [*quantitas extensiva*], namely, an ambit of activity. In this, however, you will not encounter a plurality of things, of which each one by itself alone, separated and isolated from another, would have its own permanence . . . ; accidents do not exist without their substances. (1:481.32−482.3)

The analogical reference to the phenomenal omnipresence of God is intended to clarify how it is possible for the ambit of substantial activity to be divided without substance being subject to division in terms of its internal (i.e., its non-phenomenal) determinations. Kant thus seeks to indicate a way of understanding the divisibility of the external (i.e., the accidental) determinations of substance without having to assume the divisibility of substance itself.[33] Consequently, according to the isolationist account of substance, which obviously is at issue in the passage just quoted, the elemental constituent of physical bodies can be a *physical* unity without being a *material* entity, if by the latter we mean something that can appear in space.[34] Granted this distinction, and bearing in mind the definitional considerations of material substance presented above in chapter 6 (see pp. 97 and 109–110), we can say that Kant's dynamical theory of matter in the *Monadologia physica* is not, strictly speaking, grounded in a concept of material substance. And we may gather that a concept of material substance capable of satisfying the requirements of a dynamical theory of matter will presuppose the rejection of purely internal determinations of substance and the corresponding interpretation of force as a merely external determination of ontologically isolated entities.[35]

(2) Repulsion, which is an expansive force exerted from the center of the monad's sphere of activity, makes its appearance as material impenetrability and, more particularly, as the impenetrability of the aggregations of monads composing bodies. We experience it directly through sensation in the form of contact.[36] There is no correspondingly direct sensory experience of attraction, the consequence being that the existence of this force must be something that is inferred: we conclude that by repulsion alone there could be no bodies having definite volume. The explanation of corporeal volume, or extensive magnitude, requires that the monads of which bodies are composed possess attractive forces that counteract the expansive efficacy of repulsion. It is by means of attraction that the limits of the monads' spheres of activity are set and bodily volume is determined. Thus, only through the unified operations of the two forces are corporeal entities of determinate volume possible.[37] Kant claims that this last consideration completes the essential task of his physical monadology. He is satisfied to have demonstrated the reality of attraction and repulsion and their standing as points of departure for scientific explanation.[38] He does attempt to estimate the rates of decrease in the strength of the two forces with respect to distance from the centers of the monadic spheres of activity.[39] Yet he maintains that determining the specific laws of the two forces' reciprocal action—the laws of action through which bodies are actually constituted—goes beyond what can plausibly be accomplished by a metaphysical treatise.

(3) Having shown that impenetrability and corporeal volume are fundamental properties of matter, Kant goes on, in Propositions 11–13, to treat three further properties of bodies, viz., mass, specific density, and

elasticity. In Proposition 13, the final step of his deductive procedure in the *Monadologia physica,* he explicitly makes the connection between elasticity and repulsive force.[40] He considers elasticity to be a material property directly derivative of repulsive force, inasmuch as this force is exerted from the ultimately impenetrable focal point of the monad's sphere of activity. Through repulsion, the monads constituting physical bodies act reciprocally upon one another to constitute a primitively elastic medium containing no empty space (*medium in se et absque vacuo admisto primitive elasticum*).[41] It is this conception of a material plenum that gives Kant the opportunity to address the question of physical aether:

> *Corollary.* Elements are completely impenetrable, i.e., they cannot be fully excluded from the space they occupy by any external force, however great. However, they are compressible, and they also constitute compressible bodies, since, obviously, they yield somewhat to an external force pressing them together. Whence the origin of the primitively elastic bodies or media, among which we may in advance legitimately count the aether or matter of fire. (1:487.14–18)

The characterization of physical aether as a primitively elastic matter in the final sentence of the *Monadologia physica* represents the incorporation of the aether concept of *De igne* in the dynamical theory of matter. Although Kant considers the elementary constituents of this imponderable matter to be perfectly impenetrable, he conceives of the aether as a dynamical continuum, the material quality of which derives from repulsive force.

§ 3: The Fragments on Physics of the 1770s

During the thirty years separating the *Monadologia physica* from the *Metaphysical Foundations of Natural Science* (1786), Kant offers no further published systematization of his thinking on the dynamical account of matter.[42] We do, however, possess a number of handwritten fragments that illuminate what happens to the dynamical theory after the physical monadology. The Reflections on Physics are exceptionally valuable for our understanding of the conceptual tensions in the published theory of 1786, as well as Kant's reasons for revising this theory in the earlier fascicles of the *Opus postumum*. The relevant Reflections are dated between 1773 and 1776.[43] We can easily recognize in these sketches certain suppositions that are radically opposed to the corresponding tenets of the *Monadologia physica* but that are also consistent with those of the *Metaphysical Foundations*. On the other hand, the most striking feature of the 1770s Reflections—namely, Kant's willingness to entertain the idea that a general theory of matter must be constructed on the basis of a concept of dynamical cosmic aether—has no obvious connection with the deductive procedure of the earlier physical monadology. Moreover, it appears to be incompatible with some fundamental assumptions of the 1786 treatise. These factors will be taken up in due course. But let us first consider several points that the 1770s Reflections clearly share with the *Monadologia physica*.

One point in common is that attraction and repulsion continue to be the moving forces relevant to the dynamical account of matter. In addition, the most general explanation of the relations between the two forces and the derivation of the fundamental properties of matter are at least superficially similar to what was presented in 1756. Repulsion is what fills space and is responsible for corporeal extension and impenetrability. Attractive force limits the expansive effect of repulsion, thereby making bodies of determinate volume and shape possible. By means of their mutual conflict, the two forces thus give rise to all empirically identifiable physical particulars in space, including bodies of measurable dimensions and mass. These forces are also the fundamental conditions of community (*Fundamentalbedingungen der Gemeinschaft*) between all material particulars.[44]

In keeping with these basic assumptions, Kant criticizes corpuscular or mechanical explanation and rejects the notion that its basic categories of *atomos* and *inane*,[45] i.e., physically indivisible particulars and empty space, can serve as the proper basis for a philosophic account of material nature. (This criticism, incidentally, is already implicit in the *Monadologia physica*. See especially Proposition 13.) He does maintain that this kind of explanation is legitimate within its properly restricted domain. It is useful when our immediate concern is to determine the mechanical laws of motion. Nevertheless, such laws cannot be understood except with reference to artificially produced machines. Consequently, they are not in themselves sufficient for explaining the phenomena of nature. As Kant puts it, they do not serve to explain nature, but merely art (*Sie gehören also dazu, nicht die Natur, sondern die Kunst zu erklären*).[46] The principles of dynamical explanation, on the other hand, are not taken from art; and dynamical explanations therefore derive from nature itself, i.e., from moving forces operating according to universal laws (*aus bewegenden Kräften nach allgemeinen Gesetzen*).[47]

We may now approach the major lines of divergence between Kant's early physical monadology and the elements of the dynamical theory contained in the 1770s Reflections. First of all, let us consider the basic description of physical aether in the Reflections, a description that has its origin in *De igne* and is simply carried over from the *Monadologia physica*. The aether is an elastic matter and a pervasively expansive medium whose causal efficacy is a function of repulsion.[48] The explanation that Kant provides for cohesion is of special interest with respect to this basic portrayal. As imponderable matter, the aether has the capacity to penetrate all material things and, by co-operating with the force of attraction, to cause material parts to be pressed together by its undulatory motion or vibrating action.[49] It must therefore be the cause of the cohesiveness of matter. Accordingly, cohesion cannot sensibly be regarded as the effect of an independent force of matter. And as long as we accept the principle of dynamical explanation, cohesion cannot be considered a fundamental material property derived from a special metaphysical principle.[50]

It may at first seem that Kant could quite handily put forward this explanation of cohesion within the framework of his earlier physical monadology. But by closely examining the role of the aether concept in this type of account, we can recognize a decisive difference between the thematic orientations of the two versions of the dynamical theory in question. The crucial distinguishing factor is that by the 1770s physical aether is explicitly deemed to be the *universal* source of all physical bodies and all corporeal formations involving the property of cohesion: "The aether is pressed together by the attraction of all matter of the *universe* and is the generative source [*Gebährmutter*] of all bodies and the ground of all cohesion" (14:295.5–7). Now if we grant that the cohesiveness of matter can result only from the mediating action of the aether, then we can infer further that all of space must be continuously filled by the aether: "No space can be empty of the aether if the cohesion of bodies derives from this aether; for cohesion would then cease where there would be space devoid of the aether [*wo das Leere des aethers wäre*]. The outer aether has community with the internal aether of bodies. . . . All oscillations of the outer aether must correspond to those of the inner aether" (14:443.4–10). Moreover, since it continuously fills space, the aether must be regarded as "the universal repulsive [*treibende*] force diffused throughout the whole of nature, a ground of community throughout the entire *universe*" (14:343.1–2).

Thus, contrary to the *Monadologia physica*, Kant's dynamical theory is now expressly concerned with the role of physical aether as the material ground of all corporeal formations and as a basis of the causal uniformity and lawfulness exhibited by the universal system of corporeal interactions. In effect, the explicitly cosmological orientation of the *Universal Natural History* has been made central to the dynamical theory of matter as a result of Kant's employment of the aether concept in his explanation of material properties.

Given this orientation, we would expect Kant to be concerned with questions about the physical aether's material constitution and about the ontological status of the corporeal particulars included in the aether's field of activity. Kant addresses these issues in a passage from Reflection 44:[51]

> If the world is comparatively infinite, then the aether that is condensed by gravitation has everywhere [*allenthalben*] the same density. . . . Matters [*Materien*] can be regarded as so many different attractive points, according to whose measures there is a densified aether [*nach deren Maaße ihre Masse ein verdichteter aether ist*], and hence aether is not a special kind of matter, as concerns impenetrability, but rather all matters consist of aether, which is drawn together [*angezogen*] in different degrees. This attraction is not that of gravitation, but rather that which checks the tremors [*Zitterungen*] of the aether. (14:334.1–336.6)[52]

Two facets of the monistic conception of material reality articulated in these lines are of direct interest to us. First, although Kant makes no attempt here (or elsewhere in the 1770s Reflections) to determine mathematically the laws governing the interaction of the forces constituting the aether, he nonetheless does go well beyond his most general conceptual determination of the relationship between attraction and repulsion. He puts forward the idea that there must be a *universal* conflict of attractive and repulsive forces, which is not included in the general notion of force interaction. In doing this, he postulates the existence of a single force of repulsion that he regards as the ground of all material reality.[53] He also holds what I shall henceforth call collective and distributive views of attraction.[54] According to the collective view, attraction is Newtonian universal attraction acting formatively upon the whole of the cosmic aether. Considered distributively, attraction is a short-range force that acts to check the wave action of the aether, thereby limiting the dispersive effects of repulsion upon material particulars in space.[55] These material particulars are conceived in conformity with the model of individual centers of force. Kant maintains that because these matters exert attractive forces of varying strengths, they are able to constrict the aether, the result being the formation of heterogeneous material masses or composite bodies.[56]

The second point of interest is that the idea of universal force interaction contrasts markedly with the idea underlying the basic model of the relation between the fundamental forces presented in the *Monadologia physica*. In 1756, Kant's starting point for determining the form of the reciprocal dependency of attraction and repulsion was the concept of the individual monad and its particular sphere of activity,[57] and he made no attempt to get beyond the theoretical limitations imposed by this point of departure. Specifically, in 1756 he did not aim to conceptualize how the reciprocal action of the forces associated with the physical monad actually gives rise to the formation of composite bodies. Nor was he concerned to demonstrate how his provisional determination of the laws of force might figure in a physical theory that treats the various interactive systems of such bodies. Much less did he lay the groundwork for the construction of a universal system of dynamical interactions beginning with the relations between individual monads, as Boscovich, for instance, endeavors to do in his *Theoria philosophiae naturalis* (see pp. 103–105 above). But it is precisely the idea of a universal system of dynamical interactions that furnishes the conceptual foundation for the model of force interaction at issue in Reflection 44. By the 1770s, Kant is thus willing to set out from the assumption that the whole of physical space is determined by (or as) a continuum of forces. Material particulars, conceived as heterogeneous features, or modes, of the universal material continuum, are now intuitively *representable* with the aid of the notion of individual centers of force or focal points from which forces are exerted. The reality of these features, however, is *intelligible* only with reference to the inclusive field of the aether's activity, a field that is internally configured through the limitations imposed on repulsion by the twofold force of attraction. The aether itself is therefore not an ontologically derivative product. Its reality is not reducible to the relations of monadic individuals or any corporeal particulars located within the all-encompassing field of its causal activity.

We must bear in mind that this idea of aether as the substantial ground of material reality is not the only conception of the universal continuum of matter found in the 1770s Reflections. There are Reflections from this period that show Kant's propensity to assume that physical aether (also aethers) and the bodies and corporeal systems formed by its action are ontologically distinct.[58] It is also not clear how the monistic conception of the universal force continuum relates to the concept of cosmic aether that Kant employs in his explanation of cohesion. Nevertheless, we encounter all the essential elements of a dynamical theory that takes the concept of a universal force continuum as its cornerstone. According to this concept, the basis of material reality consists in repulsive force. This force, operating together with the twofold formative principle of attraction, fills continuously the entirety of physical space and establishes the community of all corporeal systems.[59]

Thus, the tendency toward a radical change in the thematic orientation of the dynamical theory has become evident by the mid-1770s. Kant continues to make use of the notion of the centerpoint of force. But this is now employed heuristically as a way of representing how corporeal entities and systems can emerge from the ground of material existence. The physical monad with its sphere of activity no longer serves as a fundamental entity in this physical ontology. And the concept of the physical monad can therefore no longer provide the basis of the dynamical theory of matter.[60] The monadological concept of substance no longer undergirds the theory of matter, which can now be understood as a dynamical aether theory.

The elimination of the monadological interpretation of substance from the philosophy of material nature is acknowledged at various junctures in the 1770s Reflections. The most explicit statements concerning this point are found in Reflection 41, where monadology in general is repudiated as the basis for our knowledge of appearances:

> The monadology cannot serve for the explanation of appearances, but for distinguishing the intellectual from appearances in general. The principles of the explanation of appearances must all be sensible. (14:153.12–14)
> Every mode of explanation is physico-dynamical, not metaphysico-dynamical. (161.1–2)[61]

In short, dynamical principles for the explanation of material nature —in other words, physico-dynamical principles—must be kept strictly separate from the principles that presuppose any monadological concept of substance. The latter, i.e., metaphysico-dynamical principles, cannot be applied to explain physical phenomena. Taken in the context of Kant's concern to provide metaphysical foundations for natural science, they serve merely to establish the distinction between purely intellectual cognition and sensible cognition understood as the knowledge of appearances.[62]

The Reflections on Physics of the 1770s provide ample evidence of Kant's efforts to explore the epistemological ramifications of his demand for physico-dynamical explanation in connection with the concept of *substantia phaenomenon*.[63] Reflections 40 and 42 are especially noteworthy in this respect, since Kant articulates there his view of the relationship between force, matter, and substance as appearance. I recapitulate analytically his main positions:[64] (1) The ground of the material aspect of appearances is force, which, as moving force, is the external cause of sensation. (2) The subject of force is the object of outer appearance, which in turn is matter in the narrowest sense. (3) This matter is the phenomenal substrate (*substratum phaenomenon*) or the permanent appearance that fills space and that therefore does not consist of the absolutely simple or absolutely indivisible. (4) The particular object of outer appearance (i.e., the permanent appearance; the object of force; matter in the narrowest sense) is the subject of the original principles (or conditions) of motion; it is a corporeal unity (i.e., a physical body) constituted through the interplay of attractive and repulsive force.

In view of the underlying metaphysical assumptions of the 1770s dynamical aether theory, what is remarkable about these considerations on matter, or substance as appearance, is their apparently exclusive focus on the individual physical body and its internal constitution. The fact that Kant has expunged the monadological concept of substance from physico-dynamical explanation does not motivate him to develop a doctrine of substance as appearance that focuses on the idea of a universal system of dynamical interactions. In view of this, we must raise a very basic question about the status of physical aether in Kant's account of substance: how can any aether—especially one conceived as a universal continuum of the constitutive forces of matter, as the generative source of physical objects, and as a ground of the causal community of all objects in space—be fitted into the theory of the phenomenal determinations of substance at issue in the lines just summarized from Reflections 40 and 42? More particularly, how can a dynamical cosmic aether be introduced into an account of *substantia phaenomenon* that is essentially the same as the one given in the Transcendental Analytic of the first *Critique*—and that therefore gives rise to the same line of questioning about cosmic matter and matter as appearance that we pursued in chapter 3 (see pp. 49–51 and 59 above)? If we accept that during the 1770s Kant entertains the option of regarding physical aether in general as both the total complex of the moving forces of matter and as the generative ground of particular perduring appearances (i.e., observable physical bodies), then we need to ask another question: how can this ground, if it indeed is matter, appear *as* matter? If Kant is not prepared to espouse the notion of matter as *substantia noumenon,* which obviously cannot be reconciled with the concept of matter as appearance, then it seems imperative for him to construe either his aether (as generative ground) or the empirically given physical body (as product of that ground) as an "appearance of the appearance." In other words, if he is willing to make a universal force continuum the material ground of *all* that appears as substance in space, then presumably he ought to prepare the epistemological terrain for making a fundamental distinction between first-order and second-order appearances. Yet there is no direct evidence that Kant was prepared to recognize any such requirement during the 1770s.

Before going on to the *Metaphysical Foundations,* I want to discuss one further set of consequences of Kant's rejecting all forms of the monadological interpretation of substance as the basis for a dynamical account of material nature. We have already seen that the concept of substance presupposed by Kant's physical monadology is the "isolationist" concept as applied to physical bodies. We have also seen, in chapter 5 (pp. 73–74 and 78–79), that the isolationist concept rests upon the idea that the finite substantial particular is independent with respect to its finite counterparts. Finally, we have seen in the present chapter that the dynamical theory of the *Monadologia physica* is not, strictly speaking, founded on a concept of *material* substance in the sense specified in chapter 6 (pp. 97 and 109–110). In the Reflections of the 1770s, we seem to find not so much the marginalization of the isolationist interpretation of substance (see p. 91 above) as we do the demand for its dissolution. This demand is implicit in the considerations on the ontological status of corporeal particulars that we have encountered in Reflection 44. The emphasis that Kant places there on the inclusive substantial reality of a single material entity in space ought to lead him to deny expressly the causal self-sufficiency of individually identifiable particulars. Moreover, from his blanket repudiation of the monadological interpretation of substance and his advocacy of physico-dynamical explanation it follows that no essential determinations of substance can consist in the non-spatial or purely internal determinations of monads if these determinations are to be relevant to the explanation of physical phenomena. Rather, all substantial determinations appropriate to physico-dynamical explanation must be analyzable in terms of the universal and materially constitutive efficacy of attractive and repulsive force. Thus, whatever the difficulties that the dynamical aether concept presents for Kant's critical doctrine of substance as appearance, it seems that phenomenal substantiality ought to be attributable solely to the total complex of the original forces that constitute matter as permanent appearance in space.

At the same time, however, it is plain from the Reflections that Kant in no way abandons the terminology previously used in his physical monadology to characterize the dynamical community of self-subsistent substances:

> *Principle.* A substance in the world is only the cause of a change in another substance insofar as it changes itself; hence, it acts only by means of a principle of community. The ground of all community is the composition (*Zusammensetzung*) or connection through one force or the other, by which substances determine each other reciprocally. (14:173.1–6)
>
> The fundamental conditions of the community between matters, . . . since there is no action without reciprocal action (*Wechselwirkung*), [are] attraction and repulsion. (14:192.1–193.3)[65]

Despite Kant's general elimination of the monadological conception of substance from his theory of matter, he still holds that attractive and repulsive forces establish the possibility of the dynamical community of particular substances in space. And it seems that a material particular can be the cause of change in another only if the source of change lies in its own internal determinations. Thus, while Kant insists that the dynamical community of material particulars must be understood with reference to the operations of attractive and repulsive forces, he does not clearly indicate that these transeunt forces are the essential determinations of matter as phenomenal substance. We can see, then, that by the mid-1770s Kant's theory of matter shares more of the basic tenets of Priestley's or Boscovich's natural philosophies than it does the metaphysical principles that underlie his earlier monadological and isolationist conception of substance. But it is not obvious that he is willing to acknowledge explicitly that his non-monadological theory of matter requires a dynamical concept of *material* substance. Nor is it apparent that he is prepared to attribute substantial reality to the total complex of the materially constitutive forces, as opposed to the empirically identifiable material particulars constituted through the interplay of these forces.

§ 4: Aether and the Dynamical Theory of 1786

The *Metaphysical Foundations of Natural Science* contain Kant's major published attempt at systematizing his thinking on the dynamical theory. The Dynamics is the second part of this work. It is thus the second main part of the special metaphysical science that results when the principles of pure understanding are applied to the object of the outer sense,[66] i.e., to matter whose fundamental determination is "motion, . . . by which alone the outer sense can be affected" (4:476.11).[67] As in all phases of the dynamical theory, the Dynamics builds on the supposition that attraction and repulsion are the original forces of matter. Echoing the position first established in the *Monadologia physica,* Kant gives these forces the status of a priori starting points of physical explanation by virtue of the fact that they are the only forces that can be *conceived* as being constitutive of matter.[68] He proposes to determine the fundamental properties of matter by conceptualizing the relationship between the two original forces. In doing this, he emphasizes the role of repulsion as the ground of experienced material reality and as that which supplies the primary criterion of our cognition of matter. According to its dynamical definition, matter is first of all known as that which fills space by means of repulsion, and which thus is presented to the senses as something possessing original elasticity and offering resistance to penetration.[69] The impenetrability of any given material space is therefore a property that derives from repulsion; and insofar as matter is revealed to the outer senses as something real in space (*sich als etwas Reales im Raume unseren äußeren Sinnen offenbart*),[70] impenetrability is its fundamental property.[71] The priority of repulsion in the order of cognition, however, must not be understood in a merely sensualistic manner, for the understanding itself must choose the filling of space by repulsion in order to designate (*bezeichnen*)[72] substance in space. It is repulsion, not attraction, that provides us with the concept of a determinate object (*bestimmter Gegenstand*)[73] in space. But by repulsion alone, matter would not be knowable as something contained within definite boundaries, for the expansive efficacy of repulsion would lead to the infinite dispersion of what is real in space. Thus, if matter is to be the object of outer sense, repulsion must be countered by attraction. By itself, attraction or attractive force cannot be sensed, or, as Kant puts it, by itself attraction cannot present a determinate object of sensation (*ein bestimmter Gegenstand der Empfindung*).[74] It is therefore an inferred force as far as the account of our perception of outer objects is concerned. Yet it is not for that reason a derivative force. It too is a fundamental force in terms of which the constitution of all material things of the outer sense must be understood. Thus, repulsion first provides us with the concept of a determinate object in space; but this concept requires that the basic relation between the two forces be specifiable.[75]

The Dynamics carries over from the Reflections on Physics the general repudiation of the monadological concept of substance. In keeping with the fundamental tenets of his theory of transcendental idealism and his critical doctrine of space, Kant accepts the infinite divisibility of matter as appearance. Accordingly, he works out the details of a general criticism of the monadological conception of substance. He directs this against the concept of the physical monad and also against Leibniz's theory of substance as applied to the problem of matter and space.[76] He also explicitly states that his concept of matter is one of *material* substance, i.e., the concept of "that in space which of itself, i.e., separated from all else existing outside it in space, is movable" (4:502.31–33). Now since "the concept of a substance signifies the ultimate subject of existence," and since "matter is the subject of everything in space that can be attributed to the existence of things," it follows that "matter as the movable in space is the subject therein" (503.5/6–7/11–12). The same reasoning applies to all parts of matter: "all parts of matter will likewise be substances," for they are "themselves subjects if they are themselves movable, and thus apart from their combination with other juxtaposed parts are something existent in space" (503.12–13/15–17). Consequently, we can infer that "the proper [*eigene*] mobility of matter or of any part thereof is at the same time a proof that this movable thing, and each of its moving parts, is substance" (503.17–19).

Evidently, the concept of material substance at issue in the *Metaphysical Foundations* has its primary application to the individually identifiable material particular and its parts. The definitional considerations on material substance do not include any mention of the total complex of attractive and repulsive forces as something that constitutes a universal system of corporeal interactions. We have already encountered a similar situation with regard to the corresponding considerations from the 1770s (see p. 129 above). Given Kant's propensity during the 1770s to make the aether concept the central category of his dynamical theory, we have seen that these considerations give rise to two ways of posing a single problem: how is physical aether to be integrated with the critical doctrine of matter as appearance? and what is the status of this aether in the account of *substantia phaenomenon*? Kant, however, does not seem to be confronted by either of these questions in 1786, for he does not emphasize the role of any concept of physical aether in the main body of the Dynamics. The idea of physical aether as a universal continuum of moving forces is simply not part of his basic exposition of the concept of matter.[77] This exposition does not show the tendency on Kant's part to represent material particulars as ontologically derivative structures within the field of activity of a universal force continuum. Consequently, the general rejection of the monadological conception of substance, which is implicit in the above definition of material substance, simply does not engender the problem of integrating the universal dynamical plenum with the critical doctrine of matter or substance as appearance. Kant, it seems, is not confronted by any implicit demand to make his definition of material substance applicable to anything besides the variety of physical bodies or corporeal particulars encountered in ordinary empirical intuition.

On closer examination, though, things turn out to be not nearly as unproblematic as they first appear. A basic aim of Kant's exposition of the dynamical concept of matter is to construct (*konstruieren*) this as the concept of something in motion that fills space to a determinate degree.[78] Accomplishing this requires that some reference be made to a law of the relation of the original forces. As he did in the *Monadologia physica,* Kant maintains in the *Metaphysical Foundations* that the actual determination of this law is a purely mathematical problem and that it consequently cannot be of primary concern to the metaphysics of nature.[79] Nevertheless, he finds himself unable to suppress his inclination to indulge in what he calls an anticipatory observation in behalf of such a constructive procedure (*eine kleine Vorerrinnerung zum Behuf des Versuchs einer solchen vielleicht möglichen Konstruktion*).[80] We can hardly accuse Kant of theoretical immodesty or lack of caution in making such an observation. In following his inclination, however, he makes an explicit appeal not merely to the heuristic representation of the centerpoint of force exertion but also to the concept of the physical monad and its sphere of activity. In doing so, he in effect tries to make the basic relation of the original forces intelligible with recourse to precisely the monadological concept of substance that he expressly rejects as a viable basis for dynamical explanation. Given his acceptance of the infinite divisibility of matter as material substance, the justification for this appeal to a monadological interpretation of substance has been dealt with severely in the secondary literature,[81] and there is no need here to go into the particulars of the problem at hand. It suffices to say that Kant himself is quite willing to admit the inherent deficiencies of his attempted construction:

> I see well the difficulty of this way of explaining the possibility of a matter in general. The difficulty consists in the fact that if a point cannot immediately drive another by repulsive force without at the same time filling the whole corporeal space up to the given distance by its force, then this space, as would seem to follow, would have to contain several repellent [*treibende*] points. That contradicts the presupposition and was refuted above (Theorem 4) under the name of a sphere of repulsion of the simple in space. (4:521.14–20)

Kant's difficulty, then, is that his attempt to determine the basic relation between the original forces seems unavoidably to lead to physical monads characterized by spheres of activity. In order to avoid having to assume the reality of these entities, Kant finds himself constrained to draw a number of distinctions regarding the concept of material space at issue in the dynamical theory. The passage in which these are articulated is one of the more remarkable pieces of argumentation found in Kant's writings. The argument is as follows:

We must make a distinction between "the concept of an actual space, which can be given, and the mere idea of space that is thought solely for the determination of the relations of given spaces, but which is in fact no space" (4:521.21–24). The physical monadologist assumes that there are actual spaces "to be filled from a point dynamically, namely, through repulsion" (521.25–26); for these are supposed to "exist as points before any possible generation of matter therefrom" as well as to "determine, by the sphere of activity proper to them, the space to be filled that could belong to them" (521.26–28). On this physico-dynamical hypothesis, matter cannot be infinitely divisible, since its "parts, which immediately repel one another, have nonetheless a determinate distance from each other" (521.30–32). On the other hand, when we correctly think of matter as continuous magnitude, there can be no distances between the mutually repellent parts, and consequently "no increasing or decreasing spheres of their immediate activity" (521.35–36). Now since matters (*Materien*) are subject to expansion and compression, we represent the distance between the nearest material parts as growing or diminishing.[82]

But since "the closest parts of a *continuous* matter touch one another, whether this matter is further expanded or compressed" (521.30–522.1), we must think of the distances between these parts as being infinitely small; and we must think of this infinitely small space as "filled in a greater or lesser degree" (522.2–3) by the repulsive force of each material part. Hence, it is "only the idea of space that serves to render intuitable [*anschaulich*] the expansion of matter as continuous magnitude, [but] whether the idea is indeed in this way actual cannot be conceived" (522.4–6).

Kant might be, and in fact has been,[83] taken to task for this line of reasoning. What primarily interests us, though, is not the soundness or unsoundness of the argument in question, but rather the motives for his obvious lack of optimism regarding the actual execution of the dynamical account of matter's possibility. We may accept that determining the basic law of the relation between the original forces goes beyond anything that a metaphysical dynamics can properly be expected to accomplish. But why should that lead us to contend that it is not possible to construct, even provisionally, an intuitively representable model of "real" force interaction as long as we adhere to a radically non-monadological interpretation of substance? And why should it lead us to maintain that clarifying the conceptual prerequisites for constructing such a model compels the natural philosopher to introduce crucial elements of a concept of substance that are inherently inconsistent with the fundamental tenets of a non-monadological theory of material substance?

Kant would presumably respond to this line of questioning by asserting that it reflects an exaggerated concern with an issue of secondary importance to the metaphysics of material nature. This we may gather from his cautionary statement that "from the difficulties of the construction of a concept, or rather from the misinterpretation of that construction, one must not raise any objection to the concept itself" (4:522.12–14). But given that the purpose of the *Metaphysical Foundations* as a whole is to provide principles for the construction of concepts pertaining to the possibility of matter in general,[84] such a response is nonetheless bound to raise the curiosity of the reader, especially the reader who is conversant with the prior history of the dynamical theory. After all, during the 1770s Kant had already employed a dynamical concept as the basis for explaining the physical world without wedding his essential description of matter to a monadological representation of the relation between the fundamental forces. Why, then, does he now, in

1786, insist on making use of such a representation if doing so precludes his dynamical theory from offering an intuitively portrayable model (not to mention a conceptually coherent account) of the most basic relation between these forces? To answer this, I will single out two closely related aspects of the Dynamics, each of which has a bearing on the type of aether theory with which Kant had been occupied during the 1770s.

Let us turn first to the second corollary to Theorem 8 of the Dynamics.[85] Kant argues there that the possibility of all given matter depends on the filling of space to a determinate degree through the conflict of attraction and repulsion. He asserts that this most general metaphysical determination of the possibility of a determinate material thing (*bestimmter materieller Gegenstand*)[86] permits us to have the *a priori* insight that elasticity and weight are universal properties (*allgemeine Charaktere*)[87] of matter. But since attraction can be viewed either distributively (as short-range attraction between material parts) or collectively (as Newtonian universal attraction or gravitation), the property of cohesion cannot be the subject of any corresponding a priori insight.[88] Kant assumes that if cohesion is understood to be a universal (or fundamental) property of matter, then it would have to be explained in terms of short-range attraction operating between immediately juxtaposed material parts. But this explanation of cohesion is not legitimate in the context of the metaphysics of nature:

> The *action* of universal attraction, which all matter exerts immediately on all matter and at all distances, is called *gravitation;* the endeavor to move in the direction of greater gravitation is *weight*. The action of the universal repulsive force of the parts of every given matter is called its original elasticity. This, therefore, and weight make up the only a priori fathomable [*einzusehende*] universal characteristics of matter, the former being internal and the latter involving an external relation; for the possibility of matter itself rests upon these two grounds: *cohesion,* when it is explained as the reciprocal attraction of matter restricted solely to the condition of contact, does not belong to the possibility of matter in general, and hence cannot be known a priori as bound up therewith. This property would thus not be metaphysical but physical, and hence would not belong to our present considerations. (4:518.17–31)

Kant holds that only the most general determinations of repulsion and attraction are relevant to the metaphysics of corporeal nature. He claims that the explanation of a material property by means of short-range attraction would automatically make this a physical property, as distinguished from a metaphysical property, since it calls for a specification of the concept of force beyond that of original or materially constitutive force. Kant thus plainly supposes that every attempt to explain a property like cohesion in the context of his *Metaphysical Foundations*, including the attempt to do this by bringing into play an additional dimension of attractive force, must blur the distinction between the metaphysical principles of natural science and the concepts and principles employed in the empirical part of physics.[89] The implication is that offering an account of the possibility of corporeal formation like the one actually given in Reflection 44 from the 1770s (see p. 126 above) is an illicit undertaking. For it would be tantamount to effecting, to use Leibniz's phrase, "a transition from metaphysics to nature (*transitus a metaphysica ad naturam*)."[90] In other words, it would amount to the completion of a direct transition from the metaphysics of corporeal nature to the level of the empirical part of physics. That, of course, is something we can expect Kant to take all steps necessary to avoid. Such a transition would render problematic the very distinction between a priori and empirical knowledge and so would lead to the destructuring and implosion of the architectonic configuration of the critical metaphysics of nature.

We thus have good reason to conclude that for Kant in 1786 the integrity of the critical system of philosophy hinges on eschewing the type of theory of matter and the basic model of force interaction that he had entertained in the context of his 1770s aether theory. While his reasons for taking this position are not clear at this juncture, we can see why Kant is willing to pay the price inherent in having recourse to physical monadology in his exposition of the dynamical concept of material substance: the theoretical focus on the individual physical body and its parts, which is evident in the monadological model of the relation of the original forces, allows him to bypass the dangers to the critical theory of a priori knowledge that are engendered by the 1770s theory; and the monadological model of the relation between the original forces offers him a basic point of reference for maintaining that focus.

The concern for the architectonic integrity of the critical system is reflected, indirectly, in the General Remark to the Dynamics, where Kant employs the concept of physical aether to show that cohesion need not be explained by appealing to a fundamental material force. To understand the ramifications of this employment, we must first see how Kant undertakes to achieve his main purpose in the Remark, which is to establish the legitimacy of dynamical explanation over and against the presuppositions of the corpuscular philosophy.

One might expect that this general task would have been completed in the main body of the Dynamics. But fully in keeping with the tentative tone of his dynamical account of the possibility of matter, Kant insists on the purely methodological character—and indeed, the merely problematic status—of scientific explanation based on the general metaphysical principle of the dynamics of material nature.[91] This insistence occurs in the context of a criticism of corpuscular assumptions that builds on the rudiments of criticism contained in the Reflections of the 1770s. Kant rejects the corpuscular notion of solid and absolutely impenetrable material parts, and he defends the dynamistic supposition of repulsive force and "true" attraction or immediate action at a distance.[92] Accordingly, he argues against the notion that interstitial empty space must be assumed for the explanation of differences in the density of matter.[93] But despite these considerations, he holds that the advantage accruing to dynamical explanation is merely relative. The Dynamics of 1786 represents nothing more than a methodologically employed metaphysics (*methodisch-gebrauchte Metaphysik*).[94] It offers a set of principles that can plausibly *compete* with the assumptions of the corpuscular philosophy. By means of dynamical principles, the field of the natural sciences is indeed indirectly broadened to the extent that corpuscular principles, which entail the elimination of the original forces of matter from nature, lose their undisputed validity.[95] Nevertheless, the merely methodological character of metaphysical dynamics becomes evident as soon as we venture beyond the most general definitional considerations pertaining to the dynamical concept of matter.

Kant emphasizes that the restrictions on dynamical explanation at the metaphysical level preclude the natural philosopher from giving an a priori account of particular material properties. As he says, one "must . . . guard against going beyond what makes the universal concept of matter in general possible and against wanting to explain a priori the particular or even specific determination and variety of matter" (4:524.23–26). The explanation of particular physical properties involves insight into the possibility of the fundamental forces (i.e., attraction and repulsion). Consequently, one would have to be able to determine the possible forms of interaction between these forces, thereby making a priori judgments about the entire range of their connection and effects (*Verknüpfung und Folgen*).[96] But given the reservations expressed in the main body of the Dynamics about even an "anticipated" provisional model of force interaction in behalf of a "perhaps possible construction," that undertaking is excluded from the outset. To be sure, it is legitimate to put forward hypotheses pertaining to the relation of the two fundamental forces—but only as long as one bears in mind that the truth of one's constructive suppositions can never be ascertained.[97]

Now according to Kant, it is precisely with regard to constructive hypotheses about material nature that mathematico-mechanical (i.e., corpuscular) explanation demonstrates its superiority over its metaphysico-dynamical competitor.[98] Assuming interstitial empty space and the existence of a completely homogeneous matter, the corpuscular theorist explains the immense variety of physical properties and effects "by means of the manifold shape of parts, with empty spaces interspersed" (4:525.2–3). Thus, as long as it permits "foreign forces" (525.5) to be superadded to matter, this mathematico-mechanical mode of explanation possesses a significant advantage over the dynamical mode; for "the possibility of the shapes as well as of the empty intermediate spaces can be demonstrated with mathematical evidence" (525.5–7). Dynamical explanation shows its greatest deficiency in precisely these areas, since it conceptually transforms homogeneous matter into fundamental forces "whose laws we are not in a position to determine a priori," and concerning which "we are not in a position reliably to indicate the manifold of such forces sufficient for explaining the specific variety of matter" (524.8–10). As proponents of the dynamical concept, we thus "lack all means for *constructing* this concept of matter and for presenting as possible in intuition what we had thought universally" (524.10–12).

Still, despite the clear advantage that corpuscular explanation brings to the project of a mathematical physics,[99] it must ultimately relinquish its favored position to its dynamistic competitor.[100] Not only does it presuppose an epistemologically unwarranted concept and deny intrinsic causal efficacy to matter. It must also give to the imagination a license that is neither subject to empirical constraints nor proper to natural philosophy as a rational enterprise.[101]

Kant holds that the crucial premise in favor of mechanical or corpuscular explanation derives from our supposed need to assume empty space between the absolutely impenetrable particles of a homogeneous primitive matter in order to account for the specific differences (i.e., the special properties) exhibited by physical entities.[102] Hence, the viability of dynamical explanation depends on its adroitness in effectively countering the force of this putative theoretical requirement. The key move that the dynamist has to make is therefore to emphasize the capacity of repulsion to fill space with varying degrees of intensity. And granting this capacity, "one would not find it impossible to think of a matter (as, for instance, one imagines [*sich vorstellt*] the aether) that entirely filled its space without any void and yet with incomparably less quantity of matter, at an equal volume, than all bodies which we can subject to our experiments. The repulsive force in [*an*] the aether must in relation to its own attractive force be thought as incomparably greater than in all other matters known to us" (4:534.5–11). The argument against empty space, i.e., the argument by which dynamical explanation establishes its ultimate superiority over corpuscular thinking, leads naturally to the hypothesis that there is a cosmic aether that fills space by virtue of the expansive force of repulsion operating in concert with the aether's force of attraction. Yet however much credibility the aether hypothesis lends to dynamical explanation, the reality of the entity in question must remain undecided as long as a priori insight regarding the possibility of the original (or fundamental) forces of matter lies beyond the scope of our reason. The existence of the aether is therefore to be entertained merely as a counterplay (*Widerspiel*)[103] to the corresponding corpuscular assumption of empty space.[104]

The considerations on cohesion in the General Remark to the Dynamics exemplify the role of the aether hypothesis in dynamical explanation. In keeping with the restrictions that he imposes on dynamical explanation in the Corollary to Theorem 8, Kant declares himself unable to furnish an adequate account of the possibility of matter and its specific variety (*Spezifische Verschiedenheit*)[105] from the fundamental forces. Nonetheless, he does undertake to construct a framework for the a priori classification of the special properties of matter. Cohesion figures as the second cornerstone of this framework:[106]

> (2) Attraction, insofar as it is thought as efficacious merely in contact, is called "cohesion." . . . Cohesion is commonly assumed to be an altogether universal property of matter, not as if one would be led to it already through the concept of a matter, but because experience demonstrates it everywhere. But this universality must not be understood *collectively*, as though every matter through this kind of attraction acted *simultaneously* upon every other matter in cosmic space—in the same way as gravitation—but merely disjunctively, namely, as acting upon one matter or the other, of whatever kind these might be, that come into

contact with it. For these reasons, and since this attraction, as is demonstrable on various grounds, is not a penetrating force but only a surface force, . . . I thus hold this attraction in contact to be no fundamental force of matter but only a derivative one; but more on this later. (4:526.12–35)

Just as he does in the corollary to Theorem 8 of the Dynamics, Kant distinguishes here between the collective view of attraction (i.e., Newtonian gravitation) and the distributive view according to which attraction is thought of as a short-range force acting between juxtaposed materials. We can legitimately classify the property of cohesion with reference to the latter, since short-range attraction is commonly held to be an original force of matter. But further consideration shows that the ground of cohesion is more likely a merely derivative force. We are referred elsewhere for a more detailed treatment of this last point— specifically, to the considerations on the dynamical definition of empty space in the General Remark to the Phenomenology.[107]

In dynamical terms, empty space is "space that is not filled, i.e., space in which nothing else resists the penetration of the movable" (4:563.19– 21). It is, in other words, space devoid of the materially constitutive action of repulsive force. This can be either empty space *in* the world (*vacuum mundanum*) or else, provided the world is represented as limited, empty space *outside* the world (*vacuum extramundanum*). Since the necessity of postulating empty space within the world is already supposed to be laid to rest by the criticism of corpuscular assumptions in the General Remark to the Dynamics, Kant's task in the Phenomenology is to refute its very possibility.[108] Although there is, of course, no purely logical basis for this refutation, there *might* be, Kant argues, a general *physical* ground for eliminating the assumption of *vacuum mundanum* from natural philosophy. Such a ground would be the basis for explaining the possibility of the composition of a matter in general (*Zusammensetzung einer Materie überhaupt*).[109] Even if we are restricted in our ability to achieve insight into this possibility, the following dynamist claims can still reasonably be upheld:

if the *attraction* that one assumes for the explanation of the cohesion of matter should be only apparent and not true attraction; if, rather, it should be merely the effect [*Wirkung*] of a *compression* by external matter diffused everywhere in cosmic space (the aether), which matter is itself brought to exert this pressure only through a universal and original attraction—for which opinion there are a good many reasons—then empty space within matters would be impossible. Even if not logically impossible, it would still be dynamically and thus physically impossible, because every matter would expand of itself into the empty spaces assumed to be within it (since nothing resists its expansive force) and would keep these spaces always filled. (4:563.39–564.9)[110]

These lines contain a justification for postulating the existence of a cosmic aether. If we grant that this cosmic matter serves as the ground or generative source of *all* material formations, its existence will make empty space physically (i.e., dynamically) impossible. Kant's endeavor to refute the *possibility* of empty space within the world in order to lend credibility to dynamical explanation thus culminates in an argument for the existence of a dynamical physical aether. But in keeping with the restrictions imposed by the merely methodological character of his metaphysical dynamics, Kant underscores the problematic status of his argument's conclusion and, by implication, the tentative validity of the general principle of the dynamics of material nature: "no one should be taken aback that this elimination of empty space happens in a wholly hypothetical manner; the claim that there is empty space fares no better. Those who dare to decide this controversial question dogmatically, whether they do so affirmatively or negatively, rely ultimately on nothing but metaphysical presuppositions, as may be gathered from the Dynamics; and it was at least necessary to show here that they cannot at all decide the problem in question" (4:564.16–22).

From the considerations on empty space at hand in the Phenomenology of the *Metaphysical Foundations*, it is clear that Kant must provide good reasons for postulating the existence of a dynamical cosmic aether. Otherwise, he cannot establish the tenability of his dynamist project in opposition to the corpuscular account of matter and the corresponding mechanistic view of nature. It is also evident that placing dynamical explanation on epistemologically firmer footing than we can find in the *Metaphysical Foundations* of 1786 requires something more than just the demonstration of that cosmic matter's mere metaphysical possibility. Yet Kant is quite unwilling, in 1786, to go beyond what his restricted metaphysical argument against empty space establishes. The attempt to do so would require him to establish a priori the reality of a cosmic matter whose action could explain the special properties of matter, i.e., the properties not derivable from the most general determination of repulsion and Newtonian universal attraction as fundamental forces. Such an existence proof, however, would apply to an entity that is in some sense a feature of the objective material content of the field of outer appearances to which all our empirical intuitions of objects are referred, and that thus belongs to the territory of empirical cognition.

How, then, could the distinction between the principles of the meta-physics of corporeal nature and the concepts and principles of the empirical part of physics be upheld under these conditions? Clearly, providing an a priori proof of the aether's actual existence would confront Kant with exactly the kind of transition issue that we have already encountered in discussing Theorem 8 of the Dynamics, namely, the problem of a *direct* transition from the metaphysics of corporeal nature to the empirical part of physics.

We have seen why Kant refuses to make this transition in the context of his Dynamics of 1786. But let us be aware, too, of the collateral costs of his avoidance of the transition problematic—costs that must fall upon the entire project of the critical metaphysics of nature, including its transcendental part. Kant must make use of a concept of substance that is *intrinsically* inconsistent with the non-monadological interpretation of material substance explicitly advocated in the Dynamics of the *Metaphysical Foundations*. At the same time, he must also concede that the general principle of the dynamics of material nature is nothing *more* than the principle of a "methodologically employed" metaphysics. The question, therefore, is whether concepts and principles like these can ultimately satisfy *all* the epistemic requirements established in the transcendental part of the critical theory of a priori knowledge. Kant is in a position, of course, to maintain that his metaphysical dynamics conforms fully to the restrictions imposed upon transcendental argumentation by the principle of pure understanding to which his general dynamical principle is supposed to be immediately subject, i.e., the transcendental principle at issue in the Anticipations of Perception. And since these restrictions are laid down expressly in view of the dynamical mode of explanation (see pp. 33–34 above), we can hardly fault the subsidiary metaphysical discipline for respecting them.[111] Yet it remains to be seen whether any of these restrictions can finally be upheld once the implications of a radically non-monadological theory of substance are properly understood with reference to the material conditions of possible experience that Kant injects into his transcendental theory of dynamical community. Can the classical critical restrictions on the scope of transcendental knowledge be sustained, once those conditions are integrated with a fully coherent non-monadological interpretation of *substantia phaenomenon*? It is with this question in mind that we turn once again to the Third Analogy of Experience.

PART IV

The Theory of Dynamical Community and the Idea of a Transcendental Dynamics

The background is now in place to understand properly Kant's thought in the Third Analogy. Chapter 8 begins by weaving together the threads of argument followed thus far. The main conclusion established in the first section of this chapter is that an a priori existence proof for a dynamical cosmic matter—indeed, for physical aether conceived as a universal continuum of forces—is part of the Third Analogy. I show that the investigations in chapter 4–7 support fully the thesis, put forward in chapter 3, that Kant's references to influences and matter in the Third Analogy must be understood as references to a dynamical theory of matter. In particular, I show that the problem of material transcendental conditions in Kant's theory of knowledge revolves around the idea of physical aether as an all-inclusive plenum or continuum of material forces.

I go on to discuss the epistemological problematic that requires an a priori existence proof for this dynamical matter to show that Kant regards this problematic as an essential feature of his transcendental theory. The second section of chapter 8 explores the connections between the Third Analogy's argument against empty space and the corresponding type of argument found in Kant's late work on the philosophy of material nature: the transcendental aether deduction of the *Opus postumum*. The third and fourth sections of chapter 8 examine the impact of Kant's conception of "transcendental dynamics," which undergirds the *Opus postumum*'s aether deduction, on some fundamental aspects of his theory of a priori knowledge. I determine the character and extent of that impact on the Kantian accounts of substance and the unity of nature, as well as the theory of apperception.

Chapter 9 puts in place the major planks of a general interpretive framework needed for comprehending the developments in Kant's transcendental theory that underlie the Third Analogy and that are openly exhibited by the *Opus postumum*. I argue that, in order to understand the import of these developments, we must bear in mind the intertwining histories of Kant's theory of dynamical community and his dynamical accounts of material nature. In the first section of chapter 9, I examine the doctrine of space that emerges from the transcendental dynamics of the *Opus postumum*. I relate this doctrine to the characterization of space as phenomenal omnipresence that we find in the *Inaugural Dissertation*'s treatment of the ground of dynamical community. In the second section I begin by linking this speculative characterization of space to the dynamical aether theory of the 1770s. I then explore the connections between these dimensions of Kant's writings in the 1770s and the problem of material transcendental conditions contained in Kant's later critical theory of a priori knowledge. Finally, in the third section of chapter 9, I discuss how these issues relate to the culminating phase of Kant's concern with transcendental philosophy, namely, the doctrine of self-positing adumbrated in the final fascicles of the *Opus postumum*. This allows us to make historical sense of the basic changes that Kant's conception of transcendental idealism undergoes in the context of that doctrine.

CHAPTER 8

The Third Analogy and the
Opus Postumum

§ 1: Interim Balance

The investigations up to this point have taken place in view of two lead questions: (1) does the Third Analogy's argument against empty space necessarily involve an a priori existence proof that establishes a material transcendental condition for our experience of objects? (2) If it does, should we take this proof seriously? By the end of part one (see pp. 55–60 above), we found that there is reason to formulate the Third Analogy's problem of material transcendental conditions by concentrating on the function of a universal continuum of attractive and repulsive forces. We were also able to frame the second question in view of Kant's position that no synthetic unity of perceptual experience is possible apart from the relation of dynamical community. Specifically, we asked whether this position represents the Third Analogy's central epistemological problematic.

The second lead question is inseparably linked to the first. This is because the Third Analogy's argument against empty space is supposed to establish that our knowledge of the relation of dynamical community is made possible by a material transcendental condition. Thus, in order to answer the second question, we have had to clarify the preconditions for responding conclusively to the first. In chapter 3, we ascertained our point of departure for undertaking this task by connecting the concepts of influence, force, and matter, and by provisionally ascribing a transcendental function to matter regarded as a universal medium of reciprocal action. The strategy has been to see whether we can justify these conjectural procedures by investigating the developmental background of the theory of dynamical community and the theory of matter at the core of the Kantian metaphysics of corporeal nature.

The task of part two was to shed light on Kant's precritical conception of dynamical community by showing how it relates to the Leibnizian and Wolffian metaphysics of substance and, more generally, to the early modern problem of the communication of substances. We traced the evolution of that conception up to 1770, emphasizing the fundamental importance of physical influence for Kant's "isolationist" conception of substance. Moreover, we found that the concept of transeunt force provides a key to understanding his view of physical influence even where his account of the universal dynamical community of substances no longer requires this isolationist conception.

The goal of part three was to understand Kant's dynamical concepts of substance and the roles played by the aether concept in the history of Kant's theory of matter up to 1786. Against the backdrop of seventeenth- and eighteenth-century natural philosophy, we emphasized especially Kant's view of physical aether as a cosmic matter and universal continuum of attractive and repulsive forces, as the generative source of bodies and corporeal formations in physical space, and as a ground of the community of these bodies and formations. We found this view of physical aether to be articulated most clearly in the Reflections on Physics from the 1770s in conjunction with Kant's repudiation of his early isolationist and monadological conception of substance. But it also turned out to be a significant factor in the dynamical theory of 1786. Indeed, the different uses made of the aether concept underlie the most important dissimilarities between the two stages of the dynamical theory of material substance: the thematic focus on the total complex of materially constitutive attractive and repulsive forces (Reflections) versus the focus on the individually identifiable corporeal entity and its substantial parts (Dynamics); the centrality of the account of corporeal formation by means of the universal aether's action (Reflections) versus the marginalization of this account (Dynamics).[1]

Are the pieces now in place for securing the connection between influence and matter that was suggested in part one? Our investigations plainly support the thesis that the relation of influence at issue in the Third Analogy should be understood as a relation established by transeunt forces of attraction and repulsion operating between observable physical bodies. Moreover, since these moving forces are constitutive for all knowable matter, there is by implication the confirmation of our claim that the universal continuum of influences at issue in Kant's void-space argument must be understood as a continuum of material forces. There is, then, good reason to comprehend the Third Analogy's problem of material conditions of possible experience with reference to the reality of a dynamical matter, the further implication being that an a priori deduction of the existence of a cosmic force aether is in fact a feature of the transcendental part of the Kantian metaphysics of nature.[2]

The confirmation of our original conjectures, of course, is subject to one qualification. We have not discovered any explicit statement by Kant that actually identifies attractive and repulsive force with influence, and so the linkage between influence and matter has not been, and evidently cannot be, directly confirmed. Nevertheless, the investigations thus far provide decisive grounds for concluding that force and influence must be one and the same in Kant's theory of dynamical community. We can now say this not only in view the logical constraints that our analysis of Kant's criticism of Leibniz in the Amphibolies of Reflection brought to light at the beginning of chapter 3 (see p. 50). Even apart from the results of this analysis, our historical studies allow us to see that the Third Analogy contains the basis of Kant's critical response to the post-Scholastic problem of the communication of substances, a response already attempted in Kant's precritical work on metaphysics. The Third Analogy's origins are found in Kant's early concern to present his accounts of the universal dynamical community of substances through physical influence as a specific alternative to Leibniz's theory of universal community through preestablished harmony. Kant's conception of dynamical community ultimately derives from his appropriation of Leibnizian substantial force. But it makes "force" the world-immanent, transeuntly operative causal ground of the real connection, or relation of influence, between ontologically independent substances. As we have seen, the isolationist conception of substance, which underlies Kant's earliest accounts of dynamical community, is by the time of the *Inaugural Dissertation* of 1770 a purely marginal aspect of his metaphysical theory. And by the mid-1770s, he repudiates the monadological theory of matter required by that isolationist conception. This, however, does not lead him to discard the terminology that he had previously used in his monadological theory to explain physical action and the possibility of material bodies. We have seen that he characterizes reciprocal action with reference to materially constitutive forces of attraction and repulsion that operate between particular substances. Indeed, he does this during the same period in which he entertains the option of formulating his dynamical theory of matter as the theory of a single cosmic force aether.

All this might be considered irrelevant to the interpretation of Kant's transcendental theory if the Third Analogy rested in a developmental void. But it does not. It contains the completion of the "task of reason" (see p. 83 above) intrinsic to all versions of Kant's response to the Leibnizian theory of universal harmony. This is the task of explaining, in influxionist terms, the knowable unity of the world-whole in view of the manifold of substantial particulars in space. By 1770, in the *Inaugural Dissertation,* Kant explains the universal relation of physical influence or dynamical community in terms of the action of transeunt forces; and from the mid-1770s his non-monadological accounts of matter and his descriptions of reciprocal action between all material particulars are couched exclusively in terms of transeunt forces of attraction and repulsion. Thus, the historical investigations contained in chapters 4–7 lead to the following conclusion: Kant's references in the Third Analogy to influences operating between substances in space are implicitly references to the material forces treated in his dynamical accounts of matter. There is no plausible alternative to this conclusion, especially when the results of those investigations are combined with the logical issues that emerge when we relate the Third Analogy's argument against empty space to Kant's criticism of Leibniz in the first *Critique*'s Amphiboly chapter.

Nor is it plausible to regard the Third Analogy's references to the existence of matter as anything but the insertion of the idea of a dynamical aether into Kant's transcendental argumentation. In chapter 2 (see pp. 40–41), I discussed the option of interpreting Kant's mention of "matter everywhere" (B260) as merely an allusion to the aggregate of individually identifiable bodies and materials in cosmic space. Yet to insist on this interpretation at this point is hardly credible. Kant's transcendental argument against empty space establishes that the perception of all material particulars depends on their embeddedness within the continuum of influences that determines dynamically the whole space of our outer perception. This continuum of influences—i.e., this dynamical plenum—encompasses the entire field of material objects as objects of possible experience. It therefore includes all possible objective content of this field of appearances. Neither the *Critique of Pure*

Reason itself nor the histories of the theory of dynamical community and Kant's systematic considerations on matter show us any way to understand the nature of such a universal dynamical plenum except in terms of materially constitutive attractive and repulsive forces. But a universal plenum or continuum of these forces is exactly what Kant means by a dynamical cosmic aether.

In sum: In the context of Kant's transcendental theory of experience, "influence" is not intelligible as a term denoting a material a priori condition of possible experience without recourse to the fundamental tenets of a dynamical theory of matter. And in the context of this kind of theory, the connection between the notion of a *universal* continuum of influences and the concept of matter lies in the idea of a cosmic force aether. Hence, if we insist on knowing exactly what Kant means by the terms he injects into his transcendental theory by means of the void-space argument, acknowledging that connection is the only available basis for doing so, once everything that he says about matter and force up to the 1780s is considered. But if we take this step, then we must also admit that an a priori deduction of the existence of dynamical cosmic aether is indeed a part of Kant's transcendental theory.

This conclusion brings us once again to the second objection to our interpretation of the Third Analogy, namely, that an a priori existence proof for any kind of material transcendental condition can only be judged an aberration with respect to the fundamental tenets of Kant's theory and the argumentative procedures of transcendental critique. As noted earlier (see p. 57 above), the 1787 addition to the Third Analogy excludes any mention of, or allusion to, material transcendental conditions. If we combine this point with the supposition that the forward movement of Kant's thinking about the nature of the critical theory of a priori knowledge effectively ceased by the late 1780s, then most everything that we have unearthed in parts two and three might be thought to lend further credence to the claim that the 1781 argument against empty space contains a precritical residue incompatible with Kant's formalistic conception of transcendental knowledge. Accordingly, we would then have strong reasons to regard the entire argument as nothing more than a derailment in Kant's deduction of the transcendental laws of nature, especially when the implications of the transition problematic at issue in the Dynamics of 1786 are properly understood (see pp. 137–144 above). That would mean that there is no good reason to take seriously the argument against empty space. (After all, not even a great thinker is systemically infallible.) And it would follow from this that the argument against empty space does not address the Third Analogy's central epistemological problematic.

There is indeed only one obstacle to taking this interpretive approach—but it is an obstacle presented by Kant himself. The fact is that the definitive elimination of the aether proof from the theory of a priori knowledge does not take place. There are compelling reasons to take seriously the emergence of an a priori existence proof in Kant's transcendental theory and therefore to regard Kant's argument against empty space as the epistemological centerpiece of the Third Analogy. These reasons are given by the fact that Kant expressly fuses the dynamical theory of matter with the transcendental theory of experience in the final phases of his concern with the metaphysics of corporeal nature. It is in the *Opus postumum* that Kant explicates fully the conceptual presuppositions as well as deductive procedure of the aether proof, and then goes on to explore the ramifications of this a priori existence proof for his account of objective experience and his idea of transcendental philosophy.

§ 2: The Aether Deduction of the *Opus Postumum*

It is necessary first to discuss generally the place of the aether proof, or aether deduction, in the *Opus postumum*. For the sake of clarity, I will initially bracket out our previous discussion of Kant's work on physical aether and the dynamical conception of matter. I will also shift the focus of discussion away from the Third Analogy for the time being.

There is one very basic issue that any treatment of Kant's late manuscripts must contend with. It is the notion of a transitional science, which Kant generally refers to as "Transition" (*Übergang*). This science is intended to mediate between, on the one hand, the principles of a special metaphysical science—notably, those principles formulated in the *Metaphysical Foundations of Natural Science* of 1786—and, on the other hand, the particular concepts and methods of empirical physics.[3] In accomplishing its purpose, the transitional science is supposed to fill in a gap in the structure of the Kantian metaphysics of nature (and thus fill out the architectural plan of Kant's transcendental philosophy).[4] The actual passage from metaphysical principles to the empirical part of physics is supposed to take place by means of the systematic formulation of a dynamical theory of matter. This theory of matter is founded on the concept of a cosmic aether. Kant treats physical aether as a continuum of moving forces that furnishes the material ground of interaction between all empirically knowable corporeal entities in space.[5] By setting out from this dynamical conception of a universal material plenum, Kant aims to erect a framework of a priori concepts of moving forces that allows him to specify the elemental material properties encountered in the whole of nature.[6] The particular contents of the transitional science are never definitively fixed.[7] Still, it is clear that in striving to complete the transition to the empirical part of physics, Kant proposes to anticipate experience not just *quoad formale* (with respect to form), but *quoad materiale* (with respect to matter) as well. That is, he claims to be able to determine a priori and according to concepts the genuinely empirical (*das Eigentlich-Empirische*) or that which pertains materially to the actual existence of things as appearances.[8]

The significance, soundness, and even intelligibility of Kant's ambition to present his transitional science have been (and will no doubt continue to be) the subject of fundamental controversy in the secondary literature.[9] Very generally speaking, the conflict of interpretations has hinged on two inseparably intertwined problems: (1) the legitimacy of Kant's proposal to anticipate experience *quoad materiale* in view of his criteria for determining synthetic a priori knowledge; (2) the proper place of the transitional science in the architectonic edifice of the Kantian metaphysics of nature. Apart from the outright rejection of Kant's late philosophic enterprise,[10] the most radical approach to these problems has been to maintain that Kant is not so much filling in a gap in the critical system as he is being driven to expound upon conditions of our experience of objects *in general*. According to this approach, Kant's theoretical labors on the Transition project finally lead him to recognize that he must establish principles of an a priori science of nature that are on an equal footing with the principles of pure understanding. In the *Opus postumum* Kant thus finds himself compelled to construct a *transcendental* dynamics, although the impact of this theoretical discipline on his conception of transcendental philosophy remains substantially unclarified at the end of his career.[11]

I accept the central tenets of this approach.[12] But it will not be my task here to argue systematically in its favor and against competing viewpoints by considering the details of Kant's various sketches of his transitional science. I will instead allow the plausibility of the approach to become plain in view of one crucial aspect of Kant's philosophic reflections in the *Opus postumum,* namely, his endeavor to demonstrate a priori the existence of a continuum of forces in empirically cognizable space.[13]

Kant's stated purpose in providing this a priori proof or deduction is to ground his transitional science. Two problems must be addressed at this point if we are to understand Kant's intentions. The first stems from the limited extent of the aether deduction in the corpus of system sketches and fragments that make up what we call the *Opus postumum.*[14] In the system sketches written prior to the spring of 1799, the deduction is either absent from, or else is not a central ingredient of, Kant's reflections on his transitional science.[15] In the sketches dating from late summer of the same year it appears to be a rather marginal theme wherever it does plainly emerge.[16] It is solely during the period of May through August 1799, and above all in the collection of manuscripts titled Transition 1–14, that Kant's efforts are fully concentrated on formulating an a priori proof of existence for a cosmic aether. All this may, of course, have no real bearing on the ultimate significance of the aether deduction for Kant's thinking in the *Opus postumum* as a whole.[17] (I will, in fact, argue precisely this point below in the concluding chapter.) Still, it is incumbent upon us to ask whether the deduction represents merely an episode in Kant's thought which he increasingly distances himself from once he has clarified its ramifications for his theory of knowledge.

The episodic character of the aether deduction becomes especially pressing when it is taken in conjunction with a second problem. What exactly is the connection between Kant's aether concept and the notion of a system of a priori concepts of moving forces and material properties? Is an a priori proof of physical aether's existence logically indispensable for such a system? At least on the face of things, the answer must be no. We can perfectly well conceive of grounding—and, moreover, transcendentally grounding—a science of a priori concepts of matter without having recourse to an a priori existence proof for a cosmic entity.[18] Furthermore, we might argue that this option is precisely what Kant has in mind in certain phases of the doctrines of self-affection and self-positing adumbrated in the manuscripts composed after November of 1799.[19] In these parts of the *Opus postumum,* Kant links his transitional science to a theory of the integrated functioning of the embodied subject's cognitive faculties. He thereby attempts to provide a subjective deduction of a priori concepts of moving forces and material properties, and it is in the passages where this procedure is thrown into sharpest relief that the aether concept tends to be least in evidence.[20] We could thus plausibly claim that the chronologically discriminating reconstruction of Kant's late thought on the metaphysics of nature shows that he disavows any necessary connection between his transition problematic and the aether deduction.

We will return to both of these problems in due course. At this point, they serve primarily to make it clear that our main question in approaching the aether deduction must be very specific. We must ask why Kant endeavors to demonstrate a priori the existence of a dynamical cosmic aether, in at least *one* phase of the *Opus postumum, despite* the fact that there is no obvious logical link between this existence proof and any elementary system of moving forces and material properties.[21] By beginning with this query, we will be able to understand properly Kant's employment of the aether concept in Transition 1–14. We now turn to the details of this employment.

The aether deduction of the *Opus postumum* is a procedure of transcendental argumentation through which Kant professes to reveal and to submit to a priori determination the causal setting within which the perceptual relation of an embodied knowing subject to an objective world is at all possible. The deduction represents in particular the endeavor to demonstrate, by means of a series of strictly a priori arguments, the reality of the aether as a continuum of material forces present throughout empirically cognizable, cosmophysical space. In Transition 1–14 Kant intends to ground his transitional science by showing that the existence of such an entity is a transcendental condition for our experience of objects in general. This condition, or setting, is defined in terms of the action of attractive and repulsive forces.[22] Kant repeatedly attempts to determine the possible forms of interaction between these forces; for it is their activity that constitutes the universal field-entity, an entity designated as aether (*Äther*), caloric (*Wärmestoff*), and light matter (*Lichtstoff*).[23] The aether[24] is internally self-moved and perpetually in motion, its uniform and uninterrupted wave action being rooted in the efficacy of attractive and repulsive force.[25] By virtue of its spatial ubiquity and the uniformly lawful quality of its activity—a quality that receives its most general expression in the Newtonian law of universal gravitation—the aether furnishes the subject-independent causal basis for the perception of any and all external objects.[26] It is thus *a* condition for our possible experience of the accessible totality of objects; and it is *the* condition necessary for our experience of this totality to demonstrate what

Kant calls a collective unity, as distinguished from a merely distributive unity.[27] The aether is, at the same time, "the *one* object" (*das Eine Objekt*) of this experience, although its existence is not ascertainable by empirical means in the way that the existence of individually identifiable objects of empirical intuition is ascertainable.[28]

These and similar characterizations have been bequeathed to us in generous doses by Transition 1–14.[29] In view of them, the reticence shown by certain commentators toward the aether deduction is understandable.[30] Surely, one may contend, there is nothing like it in the texts of classical criticism! But the previous investigations of the Third Analogy and its background permit us to confute this kind of pronouncement. For whatever its relation to the transition problematic of the *Opus postumum* may be, we can understand the aether deduction as an extension of the transcendental argumentation regarding material conditions of the formal and subjective unity of experience that we encounter in the Third Analogy's argument against empty space. Indeed, the general aim of the late aether deduction is simply to establish, in conformity with a subjective principle of "*one* all-encompassing experience" (*Eine allbefassende Erfahrung*),[31] that our experience of nature is necessarily grounded in an overarching *union* between subjective and formal conditions and material conditions. Kant thus intends to establish that what he calls the *one* object of that experience must itself be understood to have a transcendental function within the cognitive process. This conception of the a priori material basis of the cognitive relation is articulated in passages like the following:

> Now the concept of the whole of outer experience presupposes all possible moving forces of matter conjoined in collective unity and, indeed, in filled space (for empty [space], be it within or outside bodies, is no object of possible experience). But that concept presupposes also a continual *movement* of all matter that acts upon the *subject* as object of the senses; for without this movement, i.e., without the excitation of the sense organs as its effect, no perception of any object of the senses whatever and, hence, also no experience would take place. . . . (21:572.25–573.5)

The reference to continuously filled space is to the *whole* of space in which particular objects of the senses are encountered owing to the continual movement of *all* matter or material forces. This theoretical orientation comes out with particular clarity when Kant treats explicitly the conditions for our experience of the universal dynamical community of material objects.[32] The following passage is especially striking in this respect:

What was said of the existence of such a matter and its inner movement in time is true also of world-space; that is: in the coexistence of all parts of world-space [*im Zugleichsein aller Theile desselben*] this matter sets all corporeal things in community and places the subject in the condition of possible experience of even the most remote corporeal things—e.g., it makes the world-bodies perceptible to the senses and the object of possible experience.

If it is to be an object of possible experience, even the gravitational attraction between bodies influencing each other immediately at all distances implicitly presupposes a matter that lies between them and exists in the continual connection of all parts of space; . . . For the distance that is to be presented to the senses through perception can only by means of an intervening matter be an object of possible experience, regarding which absolutely empty space is simply no object whatever: so that the thought thereof [i.e., the thought of an object in space], because it contains the *existence* of a spatial object in its concept, must unavoidably run up against a matter that fills space.

Caloric [*Wärmestoff*] is therefore not a hypothetical matter conjured up for the explanation of certain appearances given in *experience;* rather, it is a matter that issues by necessity from a priori concepts, but one which is given categorically in behoof of the possibility of *one* all-encompassing Experience as such. (21:562.21–563.15)

Obviously, Kant's exploratory use of language in the last two passages quoted leaves a number of issues unclarified. How exactly should we understand the first passage's apparent reference to *all* matter as single object of the senses? What sense does it make for Kant to say in the second paragraph of the second passage that gravitational attraction can be an *object* of experience? And what exactly does it mean to say there that the *distance* between bodies to be sensuously presented through perception can be an object of possible experience? Still, it is plain that the a priori existence proof that Kant wants to provide pertains to a continuum of moving forces filling the whole of cosmic space. To account for the possibility of unified experience of objects, Kant intends to establish a priori the existence of an encompassing material field of activity as a possibility condition for our experience of individually identifiable corporeal things. He is thus concerned to establish the existence of a universal dynamical entity in accordance with a subjective principle of possible experience.[33] "In behoof of the possibility of *one* all-encompassing experience"—this phrase epitomizes the procedure of a transcendental existence proof that conforms to the *critical* principle at the heart of Kant's theory of our a priori knowledge of objects.[34] No well-founded interpretation of Kant's transcendental theory can afford to ignore the ties between that procedure and the Third Analogy of Experience. The crucial assumptions underlying the Third Analogy's void-space argument are spelled out in Transition 1–14 with explicit reference to the concept of a dynamical aether.

§ 3: Dynamical Community and the Spinozistic Definition of Substance

In whatever way we may view the relationship between the aether deduction and the transition problematic of the *Opus postumum,* we can understand Transition 1–14 as Kant's attempt to clarify a dimension of his critical theory of a priori knowledge already partially revealed by the Third Analogy. It therefore stands to reason that a fuller comprehension of the Third Analogy's significance for the critical theory can be gleaned from the wealth of materials afforded by the *Opus postumum.* The rest of this chapter will clarify some ontological implications of Kant's final version of his dynamical explanation of matter and then take up his account of the aether's role in the theory of objective experience. In this section, I concentrate on the concept of substance presupposed by the dynamical aether theory; in § 4, I will determine with greater precision the nature of physical aether's transcendental function in view of Kant's theory of apperception.

The theory of matter contained in the earlier parts of the *Opus postumum* was developed over a period of more than fifteen years. It is not feasible here to treat it in detail. I will therefore highlight only the crucial import of its development against the background discussed in chapter 7. This lies in the fact that Kant makes the concept of a cosmic aether the thematic centerpiece of the dynamical theory of matter. What, then, happens to the aether concept between the mid-1770s and the earlier fascicles of the *Opus postumum* where Kant's energies are directed mainly toward reformulating his dynamical theory?

The secondary literature has established that the aether theory of the *Opus postumum* represents a refinement of the theory adumbrated during the 1770s.[35] It contains the same description of the aether—as an elastic matter, as an imponderable, all-penetrating expansive medium, and as a universal continuum, or plenum, of forces—as is found in the 1770s Reflections.[36] In the *Opus postumum* Kant also characterizes the aether as a ground of community and, moreover, as the highest ground of all material reality in space, as well as the generative source of all corporeal formation.[37] His basic inclination in the *Opus postumum* thus seems to be to regard the aether as the primordial ground of all observable corporeal particulars.[38] Yet he also shows the propensity to posit an ontological duality of the aether and the materials, bodies, and interactive corporeal systems that are constituted as the result of the aether's all-encompassing action.[39] All this is discernible in the 1770s Reflections as well. The later aether theory, however, is modified in one decisive way. In the *Opus postumum*, Kant offers a blueprint for constructing a symmetrical model of force interaction. While retaining his general dynamistic conception of the formative efficacy of attraction and his notion of repulsion as the ground of experienced material reality,[40] he gives a more differentiated treatment of repulsion. He advocates the collective and distributive views of both attraction and repulsion—not of attraction alone.[41] This symmetrical conception of universal force interaction is at the root of Kant's efforts to determine a priori the specific variety of matter.[42] Kant's project of anticipating experience *quoad materiale*—i.e., his attempt to complete the transition from the metaphysical principles of natural science to the empirical part of physics—thus presupposes what the Dynamics of 1786 defines as an "a priori insight" into the fundamental forces. The Kantian analog to the Leibnizian *transitus a metaphysica ad naturam*—the transition from metaphysics to nature—is therefore predicated on the possibility of formulating an a priori analysis of the four most basic spatial determinations of substantial force.[43]

I have already discussed, in chapter 7 (see pp. 137–138 above), what such a transition means for the architectonic configuration of the Kantian metaphysics of nature as it was conceived during the 1780s: it renders problematic the distinction that Kant draws between a priori and empirical knowledge, and thus it leads to the destructuring of that configuration.[44] I will explore here the main ramifications of the late aether theory for Kant's general account of substance and dynamical community. The issues are framed in an extended passage from the series of system sketches titled Elementary System 1–7 (fall/winter 1798):

> Space is no object of possible experience. Thus, the movable in space, [i.e.,] matter, cannot be represented as a whole that would itself be movable; . . .[45] But its parts must stand against one another in a relation of influence; for otherwise they would not constitute a real whole.—But this influence (and the community of all parts of matter resting upon it) cannot be anything other than attraction and counteracting repulsion,

and not merely as a capacity [*Vermögen*] but as agitating forces whose threefold play (of attraction, repulsion, and oscillation) must have a beginning, namely, that of the moving forces of matter whose system constitutes the principle of the advancement from the Metaphysical Foundations of Natural Science to physics. . . .

One must think of the whole cosmic space as filled [*eingenommen*] in all points by the moving forces (of attraction and repulsion), for otherwise that which is empty of force [*das von aller Kraft Leere*] would be a perceptible object, an object that, hence, would act upon the senses and would be a matter—which [assumption] is self-contradictory . . .

There has to be supposed a primitive (*primitive*) *internal* motion of cosmic matter as the unity of the cause of community, for otherwise motions in view of [*bei*] the unity of space and the relations of matter in respect of its moving forces would not be subject to laws. One and the same matter must also in its internal motion (of attraction and repulsion) be in ceaseless agitation, and it is the *primum movens* thereof. (22:194.17–195.26)

Let us simply disregard here Kant's reference to the aether as the material basis of the conservation of motion through time and focus on the connections between material substance, force, influence, and dynamical community.[46] We can recognize the problem posed by these connections in the now familiar set of issues raised by the aether deduction, namely, the repudiation of empty space, the question of the material ground of dynamical community, and the conception that attraction and repulsion are the constitutive forces of matter.

Consider in particular the first paragraph's explicit identification of the activity or efficacy of attraction and repulsion with reciprocal influence itself. If we take this literally, then these forces, which operate throughout cosmic space and between all coexistent parts of matter, cannot be understood as *causes* of influences, or as that which brings about change *in* other substances (see pp. 89–91 above). Rather, they simply *are* the (relation of) reciprocal influence that constitutes the single real whole—i.e., the real community of all parts of matter—relevant to outer perceptual cognition. This distinction may look like a minor point. But by keeping it firmly in mind, we can finally articulate the fundamental problem that the dynamical concept of matter presents for Kant's conception of dynamical community. We will also be in a position to recognize the deepest source of the difficulties that we have hitherto faced in trying to understand the relationship between influence, matter, and force in Kant's metaphysics.

As we saw in chapter 5 (pp. 87 and 90–91), the view of transeunt force as the cause of an influence in another substance—as something that brings about change *in* another substance—is part of Kant's early isolationist conception of substance. It underlies his precritical accounts of dynamical community. We saw in chapter 7 (pp. 119–120 and 131–132) that Kant's dynamical theory of matter retains this basic view of transeunt force in its treatment of reciprocal action between material particulars. By the mid-1770s, Kant does indeed reject the monadological account of matter that correlates with his general isolationist conception of substance. He also entertains the basic idea of a dynamical theory that denies the causal self-sufficiency and ontological independence of material particulars. But his description of the community of substances in space suggests that a substance supplies the cause of change in another only if the source of this change lies in that other substance's internal determinations.[47] Thus, in the mid-1770s, Kant apparently still tends to regard transeunt forces of attraction and repulsion as merely external triggering factors or stimuli for changes that occur from within particular substances in space. According to this view, those material forces could not be essential determinations of substances as appearances.

This view is entirely consistent with the basic definition of community furnished by the *Critique of Pure Reason* in 1781. The definition stipulates that reciprocal action is the causality of substances in respect of their accidents.[48] It thus presupposes the categorially foundational relation of the particular thing to its variable, and therefore nonessential, properties.[49] Dynamical community is the reciprocal causality of substances *not* in respect of their essential substrative quality, i.e., their permanence in and through time as the substrata of time-determination.[50] According to this scheme of things, a *relation* of influence must be one in which influence pertains to the changing, and therefore accidental, determinations of coexistent substantial particulars.[51]

Now the basic problem with this view of the relation of influence is as follows: Kant's use of the concept of influence in the Third Analogy and, as we have seen, in the *Opus postumum* points toward a radically different understanding of the causality of substance than can be accommodated by his definition of community or reciprocal action. If influence must be conceived in terms of the forces that actually constitute matter as substance in space, and if the relation of influence pertinent to our perceptual cognition of coexistent objects is nothing less than the real whole of substantial activity constituted through the exercise of those forces, then it is unclear how the causality of substance could be characterized except as the action of substance in respect of its essential determinations.[52] According to *this* concept of causality, force is not an accidental determination of any given particular substance. Nor can it be understood in terms of the (causal) relation of any such substance to its accidents.[53] But if that is so, then the viability of the definition of dynamical community at hand in the Transcendental Analytic of the first *Critique* is called into question. The Kantian dynamical concept of matter plainly demands a fundamental rethinking of the entire substance/accident scheme of things that the account of the community of substances presupposes.[54]

That Kant recognized this demand can be discerned at various junctures in the *Opus postumum,* although it is questionable whether his late work contains all the elements necessary for a coherent response to the problem just posed.[55] Yet, however we may judge Kant's success in providing these elements, one thing is quite clear: the attempt to rethink the substance/accident relation in view of the dynamical theory's requirements must bring him face to face with his own criticism of the Spinozistic definition of substance. The *locus classicus* of this criticism appears in Kant's 1790 polemics against Eberhard,[56] in which Kant rejects the proposition "the thing (the substance) *is* a force" as being "contrary to all ontological concepts" (8:224.24–26). According to Kant, a metaphysical theory that assumes the identity of force and substance must forfeit the very concept of substance, namely, "the concept of inherence in a subject" (224.27–28), and put the concept of causal dependency in its place. That, Kant claims, is exactly what Spinoza wanted to do when he made "universal active [*wirkende*] force itself into a substance" (224.31–32). Spinoza thus conflated the two distinct categorial functions at issue:

> A substance does indeed have, besides its relation as *subject* to the accidents (and their inherence), also the relation to these of *cause* to effects. But the former relation is not identical with the latter. Force is not that which contains the ground of the existence of the accidents (for the substance contains this ground). Rather, it is the concept of the mere relation of substance to the accidents, insofar as it contains their ground, and this relation is completely different from that of inherence. (8:224.33–39)[57]

Kant's general assessment of Spinoza is the subject of a line of investigation different from what we have embarked on in this chapter. His concern with the name of Spinoza is of interest at this point only as far as it serves to shed light on the fundamental ontological problem involved in Kant's use of the concept of material force in his account of dynamical community as a relation of influence: if force is what constitutes matter as substance in space, then the concept of force in question cannot be that of the mere relation of substance to accidents.

§ 4: Unity of Matter and Unity of Apperception

How exactly are we to conceive of the transcendental function that Kant attributes to the universal continuum of forces? More particularly, how do we understand this function in relation to the knowing subject's constitutive a priori cognitive accomplishments? Our main problem here is to understand how the active function of the universal force-continuum relates to the specifically subjective transcendental functions. In other words, we need to see how the transcendental function of cosmic matter relates to the particular functions of unity among our representations through which the knowing subject, *qua* individual human subject, establishes synthetic unity in its representations of objects.[58]

The basic aim of the aether deduction is to establish and justify the idea of an overarching union of subjective and formal conditions and material conditions of possible experience by appealing to the subjective principle of *one* all-encompassing experience (*Eine allbefassende Erfahrung*). In view of this principle, the deduction aims to show that the subject's cognitive faculty, as a faculty of representation, must be related to the whole of materially filled space if unified perceptual experience is to be possible. How, then, does Kant understand this relation? To answer this, let me bring to light the main thesis supported by arguments in a number of representative texts from Transition 1–14. (I refer in particular to the following passages from Sheets 11 and 12: 21:578.3–579.4, 601.23–603.2, 603.24–605.4.) Kant contends that the object of the one all-encompassing experience, i.e., the aether regarded as the total complex of the moving forces of matter, is "the basis for the representation of the whole of *one* experience"; it is also "the principle of the unification of all moving forces"(21:578.20–579.2). As the *one* object of outer perception, the aether exerts an all-embracing causal influence that includes the subject's faculty of representation. It thereby constitutes, objectively speaking, the subject-independent basis for the generation of particular perceptions in the subject. But since it is precisely by virtue of this function that the aether constitutes the *one* object represented by the subject, the aether must be conceived in subjective terms, as well as objectively. In other words, there is a single, unified, lawfully operating entity that constitutes the enveloping causal basis for the generation and synthesis of all particular perceptions (or all particular empirical representations). And this objective causal basis is what makes possible the representation of one and the same entity as the *one* object that is known through the subjective synthesis of perceptions. As Kant puts it, the subjective aspect of the dynamical world matter is identical to the objective aspect of the same:

> Now *regarded subjectively*, those perceptions are effects of the moving forces of matter (namely, as empirical representations) and belong as such to the collective unity [*Gesamteinheit*] of *possible* experience. But the collective unity of the moving forces is objectively the effect of the absolute whole of the elementary material [*Elementarstoff*].
> . . . Hence, the subjective moment [*das Subjektive*] of the effects of the . . . agitating forces, i.e., the whole of perceptions, is at the same time the *presentation* of the aforementioned matter, and is thus: identical with the objective moment [*das Objektive*]; that is, this elementary material, as a given whole, is the *Basis* of the unification of all forces of matter into the unity of experience. (21:601.23–602.11)

Obviously, Kant's apparently paradoxical conception that the aether is both the object of outer experience and this experience's a priori necessary causal condition is in need of clarification. We will return to the problem in chapter 9 when we take up Kant's treatment of material space in the *Opus postumum* (see pp. 169–171 below). Let it suffice to say at this point that Kant wants to account for the origin of our cognitive relation to an objective world by showing that the entire unified complex of matter itself provides a condition of formal unity in the connection of empirical representations. The aether thus furnishes an objective *material* condition of formal and subjective unity. That is to say, it furnishes a material condition of cognition without which there could be no combination of any given empirical manifold *into* a synthetic unity, namely, the synthetic unity required by our experience of objects in space.

Kant makes it clear in these passages that the particular formal determinations of the moving forces that affect the senses are, as he puts it, "to be developed out of" the synthetic and non-empirical consciousness of the affected (i.e., the percipient) subject (21:578.5–8). In this way, he

seeks to show that the various operations of the material forces constituting the aether necessarily correlate with certain subjective synthetic
functions that can be specified by means of a priori concepts. Kant's analytic of the subjective side of the subject/object relation thus supports
the central thesis that the aether deduction is intended to establish, i.e.,
the thesis that the unity of our experience of objects depends on the
aether's capacity to *sustain* the affective relation of the percipient subject's faculty of representation to the represented collective whole of
material forces. This thesis implies that our perceptual experience of the
external world depends on the a priori determinable sustentative function of the non-subjective material condition of that unified experience.

The thesis from Kant's late philosophy implies that the unity of perceptual consciousness depends not only on the synthetic functions of
pure understanding with respect to what is given in space and time. For
this unity depends, too, on the a priori determinable function of dynamical matter. Thus, the thesis concerning this dynamical plenum of
cosmic matter undermines the notion that the constitutive principles of
our knowledge of objects could be grounded sufficiently by means of the
exposition of space and time as a priori forms of intuition, and through
the analysis and deduction of pure understanding's synthetic functions
in relation to these formal conditions of sensibility.

We have already encountered this feature of Kant's transcendental
argumentation. It emerges from the Third Analogy's epistemological
standpoint that the existence of a universal dynamical plenum is necessary for there to be any synthetic unity of our perceptions of objects
through time. Kant's treatment of this standpoint in the *Opus postumum*,
then, is nothing fundamentally new. Indeed, the examination of Kant's
late considerations on this standpoint is what allows us to answer conclusively one of the "signpost" questions posed at the end of chapter 3:
whether Kant ever adequately addresses the issues that the Third Analogy's argument against empty space raises for his account of the unity
of apperception (see p. 60). The aether deduction of Transition 1–14
addresses at least the key issue involved, which pertains to the concept
of the original synthetic unity of apperception. Specifically, the *Opus
postumum*'s thesis concerning the function of cosmic matter, or physical aether, leaves fully intact Kant's foundational principle of the synthetic unity of apperception since it does not at all suggest that there
could be anything manifold in intuition that would not be subject to
conditions of the original synthetic unity of apperception. The thesis of

the *Opus postumum* implies merely that this principle of synthetic unity can express, and ground, the necessary unity of experience only insofar as it necessarily *correlates* with a further principle of synthetic unity, namely, the principle that the dynamical aether exists as an a priori necessary condition of all objective experience.[59] To be sure, the aether deduction gives rise to significant problems for interpreting the sense of Kant's philosophic enterprise from the first *Critique* on.[60] But it does not in any sense represent a break with the account of the unity of apperception that already underlies the Third Analogy's central epistemological problematic.

CHAPTER 9

Kant's Transcendental Theory: Heterodox Considerations on Its History

It is now time to put into broadest perspective the type of transcendental theoretic approach that emerges from Kant's position that a universal dynamical plenum is an a priori necessary condition of unified objective experience. To accomplish this, we will first have to determine the aether deduction's place in the theory of experience that Kant seeks to work out in the final stages of the *Opus postumum*. That will allow us to specify what Kant means when he characterizes the aether as the *one* object of outer perception, or as the object of the *one* all-encompassing experience. Understanding the implications of this view of dynamical cosmic matter for the Kantian doctrine of space leads to the further developmental investigations described in the preliminary remarks to part four (see p. 146 above). The goal is to know exactly what Kant intends to say when, in the final fascicle of the *Opus postumum*, he writes of transcendental idealism as a form of Spinozism.

§ 1: Material Space and Phenomenal Omnipresence in 1799/1800

As I pointed out in the last chapter, one way of disposing of the set of questions raised by the aether deduction would be to maintain that it represents merely an episode in Kant's thinking within the corpus of system fragments that make up the *Opus postumum*. At least initially, it seems that this approach might be justified in view of the accounts of self-affection and theoretical self-positing given in the fascicles after Transition 1–14. Between August 1799 and April 1800 (Fascicle 10/11) Kant presents the rudiments of a theory of objective experience by describing how a universal system of dynamical interactions is constituted as the object of perceptual knowledge. This constitution takes place when the knowing subject affects itself by means of given moving forces of matter in accordance with its priori specifiable cognitive functions and its characteristic forms of intuition. In this way, the subject establishes its relation to the unified material system of dynamical interactions that composes the general object of physics.[1] Evidently as a result of his critical encounter with certain arguments from contemporaneous debates about the concept of idealism, Kant comes to regard this cognitive activity of the self-affecting subject as a form of self-positing.[2] Between April and December of 1800, he undertakes to explore the implications that his conception of self-positing holds for his general critical account of theoretical cognition. Primarily in the seventh fascicle of the *Opus postumum*, he seeks to demonstrate how the knowing subject establishes its a priori necessary relation to the unified whole of physical existence in space. He attempts to clarify how the subject is able to conceive of itself as something related cognitively to the all-encompassing objective field of appearances, and is therefore able to regard itself as both observer and author (*Zuschauer und zugleich Urheber* [22:421.9–10]) of the whole of intuition in space and time.[3] He thus shows that the subject is conscious of itself as theoretically self-positing through its relation to the entire field of appearances that is to be investigated by physics as a transcendentally and metaphysically grounded empirical science.[4]

It is not easy to detect in the type of summary presentation just given anything fundamentally inconsistent with Kant's declarations in the *Critique of Pure Reason* that the a priori specifiable possibility conditions of objective experience can only be formal and subjective conditions.[5] Accordingly, one might argue that the foundations of Kant's original transcendental theory are never subjected to serious doubt in the final fascicles, although the doctrine of self-positing may call for some fairly substantial alterations in the architectonic configuration of the critical system.[6] One could thus contend that the purely formalistic approach to the problem of objective cognition, which Kant officially advocates in the first *Critique*, remains basically unchanged in the *Opus postumum*. In particular, one could, it seems, justifiably maintain that the description of theoretical self-positing does nothing more than refine the presentation of the a priori anticipation of the form of possible experience already offered in the first *Critique*. It does not crucially alter Kant's standardly accepted account of the relation between the subjective, a priori determinable formal conditions of theoretical cognition and what is empirically given by bringing into play the idea of a material condition of a priori synthetic unity that the aether deduction is intended to justify.[7] It therefore may seem legitimate to say that the "*Konstitutionstheorie*" of the late manuscripts has abandoned the project of the aether deduction, along with the whole set of problems associated with it. Arguably, then, the supposedly inessential revision of the classical critical (i.e., the strictly formalistic) theory of objective experience represented by the account of self-positing is what leads Kant to refine his concept of transcendental philosophy in the final fascicle of the *Opus postumum*. There, he envisages a comprehensive system of theoretical and practical philosophy based on a concept of transcendental idealism. But this concept remains basically consistent with the view of transcendental idealism espoused in the *Critique of Pure Reason*.

Historically, the approach that I have summarized above has been widely represented in the constructive exegesis of Kant's late manuscripts.[8] But two major objections can be directed against it. First, it is simply not true that the aether deduction is ever conclusively eliminated from the a priori groundwork of physics or the corresponding theory of the objectively constitutive cognitive accomplishments of the knowing subject. Its role in the doctrine of self-affection and self-positing is never definitively fixed. But in all the later manuscripts it is still fully in evidence at important junctures as a significant factor in Kant's reflections on self- positing.[9] Second, and far more importantly: in whatever way we may view the fate of the aether deduction within the *Opus postumum*, we must recognize that the most basic insight supported by this transcendental procedure is never abandoned: that our experience of objects and physical events *in* space is possible only on the condition that the whole of space is completely determined *as* a dynamical continuum or continuum of material forces—and that this space is thus itself determined as the *one* object of outer experience.[10] Throughout the later manuscripts, including Transition 1–14, the condition embraced by Kant's insight is treated in a variety of ways. But the problem of dynamically determined cosmic space does not disappear from the horizon of Kant's continuing reflection on the conditions of possible experience. It makes its appearance at crucial junctures in the theory of self-affection and self-positing. And there is reason to maintain that it is a primary problem, one that determines the forward movement of Kant's thought toward a new conception of transcendental idealism and transcendental philosophy in the final fascicles.[11]

The concept of dynamically determined space is discussed under various terminological headings, the most notable of which are "appearance of the appearance [*Erscheinung der Erscheinung*]" and "*spatium sensibile/perceptibile*" or "*spatium phaenomenon*."[12] In taking up the first designation, Kant clearly attempts to satisfy a theoretical demand already mentioned in connection with the aether theory of the 1770s (see pp. 129–130 above), namely, the demand to work out an account of substance as appearance in space capable of accommodating the concept of a dynamical aether. In his late work Kant draws a qualitative distinction between two orders of appearance. The need to make this distinction derives from the fact that the aether, even though it is that which "establishes [*ausmacht*] the dynamical community of all matter in space," is nonetheless "by itself [*für sich*] no prehensible substance" (21:561.21–23). Although it must be thought of as "an everywhere diffused [*allverbreitete*] and all-penetrating . . . matter that constitutes a self-subsistent whole" (22:325.18–20), it is still "not directly an object of possible experience" (21:562.14–15) in the way that the individually identifiable physical particular is. Hence, it must be conceived as "the appearance of the appearance in the connection of the manifold" (22:325.21–22).

In developing his conception of the two rankings of appearance, Kant explicitly describes "the appearance of the whole of the moving forces of matter" (22:338.7–8) as "appearance of the second order" (22:339.20–21). He holds it to be the "subjective appearance that is prior to the objective, the indirect appearance that is prior to the objective and that makes space into the object of experience" (22:339.26–27).[13] Consequently, the phenomenal presence of material substance refers to "an elementary whole of absolute totality" that is "dynamically omnipresent [*allenthalben gegenwärtig*] and the same as *spatium sensibile*" (22:433.16–19).[14] Although from one point of view space is merely "the form of outer intuitions and the subjective aspect [*das Subjektive*] of the way of being externally affected," it must also be considered a "real relation insofar as it is thought as a principle of the possibility of perceptions" (22:524.1–7). But that is possible only because the "a priori represented substance without particular properties" (22:525.16–17) constituted by the original material forces is something that "makes unlimited space the object of the senses" (525.13–14), thus demonstrating the phenomenal omnipresence of this object: "The presence [*praesentia*] of *one* object in space is, in the concept of space, at the same time [its] omnipresence [*omnipraesentia*], i.e., completely determined, and there is but *one* space and *one* time" (22:526.12–19). What Kant calls the *one* object of outer experience is therefore the phenomenally omnipresent material substance that makes space something dynamically determined.

The considerations of the doctrine of substance as appearance that we find in the later fascicles obviously have a substantial impact on the Kantian theory of space (and time). But what exactly does that impact consist in?

Whether or not he uses the actual vocabulary of his aether theory in the later fascicles, Kant does not cease to treat the universal continuum of moving forces in terms similar to those employed in Transition 1–14. He thus continues to conceive of the dynamical continuum as the condition for "the realization of space as a single object of the senses" (21:564.2–3). He understands it as "hypostatically conceived space" or as "hypostatized space itself, so to speak [*gleichsam*], in which everything is in motion" (21:221.13–14, 224:11–12), and that constitutes "a principle of the possibility of perceptions" (22.524.6). He thereby supplies the elements for the exposition of a concept of space. According to this exposition, "hypostatized" space must, despite its sensible or material quality, pertain to an a priori and necessary representation that undergirds all outer intuition. In effect, Kant works out the rudiments of a metaphysical exposition of a concept of space. In doing this, however, he does not maintain that space, regarded as an a priori condition, is but a mere *form* of intuition or pure intuition.

This challenges the fundamental tenet of the doctrine of space formulated in the Transcendental Aesthetic of the *Critique of Pure Reason*, i.e., the thesis that the quality of space as a condition of the existence of things "lies in our mode of intuition" (B69)—that space is, transcendentally speaking, merely something ideal. Kant tries, and he tries at great length, to mediate between the earlier and later expositions of the concept of space. In the major late manuscripts of the *Opus postumum*, he repeatedly stresses that space in its *primary* signification is but the form of outer intuition and so cannot be an object of perception. In keeping with this position, he maintains that the concept of space denotes merely the formal determinacy of our receptivity for objects of the senses. Accordingly, space is not something objective. It is merely subjective; it is "in me" and is not something "outside of me."[15] Kant thus gives the impression of taking for granted that there is no fundamental inconsistency between the assumptions underlying his account of hypostatically conceived material space, as formulated in the *Opus postumum*, and the conclusions that are drawn from the doctrine of space presented in the Transcendental Aesthetic of the first *Critique*. He is quite often content simply to treat side by side the two different accounts of space in question and to maintain that each of them makes an a priori condition of experience recognizable. Yet precisely these juxtapositions must lead us to question the sense in which the underlying theory of space of the later manuscripts can be deemed internally coherent. A passage in Transition 1–14 exemplifies the theoretical difficulties implicitly confronting Kant:

> Just as every object of the sensibility, we represent to ourselves space in two distinct ways: *first* as something *conceivable* (*spatium cogitabile*), since as a magnitude of the manifold whose parts are outside one another,[16] it lies as a mere form of the object of pure intuition solely in our faculty of representation; but *second*, we represent it also as something perceptible (*spatium perceptibile*), as something existent apart from our representation, which we perceive and can draw to our experience and which as an empirical representation constitutes an object of the senses, i.e., the material that fills space.
>
> An empty space is conceivable, but not perceptible; i.e., is no object of possible experience. . . .
>
> Matter, therefore, merely with the quality [of being] a sensible space, and thus dynamically present in all that is corporeal, must be a self-subsistent, all-penetrating, and uninterruptedly and uniformly diffused whole, and a material that serves as the basis of the moving forces with their motion for the possibility of *one* experience (of all possible coexistents).[17] (21:235.19–27–236.15–20)

On first reading, it looks as though all this might easily fit inside the doctrinal framework of the Transcendental Aesthetic and the theory of objective experience that it supports. There is, of course, the requirement that space must be regarded as something that exists *apart* from our representation. But with that, it seems that Kant is merely referring to the objective perception that springs from the unification of the manifold of a given intuition or, more precisely, to the empirical representation of the object of outer intuition as an object out there *in* space.[18] To use a formulation that Kant employs elsewhere in Transition 1–14, that requirement would constrain us to consider space as "something given outside us in the representation [*ein außer uns in der Vorstellung gegebenes*]" (21:542.5–6), whereby the expression "in the representation" could be interpreted as indicating that space is not something outside us in any transcendental sense.[19]

If this were an adequate explication of the concept of material space at issue, the passage quoted would contain nothing novel vis-à-vis the first *Critique*'s treatment of space in the Transcendental Aesthetic. But the account is not exhaustive. Consider the phrase "something existent apart from our representation" (paragraph 1) in conjunction with Kant's conclusion that the dynamical cosmic matter serves as "the basis for the possibility of *one* experience" (paragraph 3). In other words, consider that phrase in conjunction with the implication that this matter supplies an *a priori* condition for all outer experience as a synthetic unity. Now since it is precisely this objective a priori condition that exhibits the property of being "a sensible (i.e., a material) space" (paragraph 3), it is evident that the concept of material space in question cannot be referred to as a *merely* empirical representation. Furthermore, since material space (as an a priori condition) is constituted as "a self-subsistent whole" of matter (paragraph 3), and since this whole of matter provides the subject-independent causal basis of all outer perception, then the demand for us to consider space as something apart from our representation cannot, it seems, conduce us to consider it as something given outside us *solely* in our *representation* of objects. In short, matter or sensible (i.e., material) space cannot be something that is merely *called* external, or that is represented merely in thought as being outside us, as the classical critical theory of space would have us maintain.[20] And certainly it pertains directly to the a priori knowable features of outer experience. This interpretation is confirmed by a good number of further passages in Transition 1–14, as well as in the manuscripts composed after it.[21]

It is unnecessary for us to take up here the question whether a substantival or else a relationist view of space is implicated by the concept of material space in the *Opus postumum*. The crucial point is merely this: despite the strictures against any objectivistic account of space entailed by the proposition that space is a mere sensible form or form of intuition, space must nonetheless be conceived as something given in reality apart from our representation *independently* of our sensibility.[22] Space must be thought of in this way to the extent that it is known as something completely determined by the *existence* of the universal dynamical continuum as the *one* object of outer experience.[23] Thus, unless Kant is prepared to concede that the sum-total of the matter of outer experience is literally created *ex nihilo* by the individual finite mind in each particular act of perceptual cognition, then the reality attributable to what he calls "hypostatically conceived space" must be, in some sense, an *absolute* reality. But, naturally, it follows from this that the quality of space relevant to transcendental knowledge can no longer consist in the ideality of space (or at least not in its ideality alone). Space is, in some sense, transcendentally real.

It of course remains Kant's prerogative in the *Opus postumum* to argue that our knowledge of the structural properties of materially determined perceptual (i.e., physical) space must conform to the formal constitution of the type of sensibility that underlies all human cognition of an outer world. Specifically, he could (and in fact does) maintain that the space of our actual outer experience is three-dimensional and Euclidean in nature.[24] There thus remains at least this aspect of compatibility between the treatment of dynamically determined space in the *Opus postumum* and the expositions of the concept of space in the Transcendental Aesthetic.[25] Nevertheless, the general doctrine of space at work in the *Opus postumum* seems to conflict unavoidably with the earlier treatment: if we suppose that the aether, understood as the *self-subsistent* material whole or as hypostatically conceived space, provides a principle of the possibility of perceptions, then we must regard such space as something not only empirically real; for it is essential to the meaning of that supposition that space must remain *something*, even when considered in complete abstraction from the strictly subjective condition of all outer appearances.[26] After all, it is the stated purpose of Kant's reflections on the "hypostization" of space to show that we must consider space in exactly this way, given that the existence of the universal continuum of material forces (i.e., physical aether) serves as an a priori specifiable necessary condition of all outer experience. But that means that space is not only something empirically real; it is transcendentally real as well. And that is to say, in Kant's own terms, that its reality is absolute.[27]

§ 2: Space, Aether, and the Idea of Phenomenal Omnipresence in 1770

I have confined my analysis to Kant's treatment of space in the *Opus postumum*. A more thorough discussion of the underlying issues would have to take into account the closely connected treatment of time, which pertains to the aether's role as the material ground for the conservation of motion in the ongoing process of cosmogenesis that shapes our natural history.[28] But at any rate, the considerations on space in the *Opus postumum* confirm the assertion made earlier that Kant's conception of the transcendental function of cosmic matter undermines any pure formalism of intuition and understanding as the adequate basis for a critical theory of our a priori knowledge of objects (see p. 165 above). Moreover, the reflections on the idea of dynamically determined space associated with that conception call into question a pivotal tenet of the particular doctrine of transcendental idealism that Kant had taken to be essential to his critical theory of knowledge and his plan for a system of transcendental philosophy, i.e., the thesis that space is merely transcendentally ideal.[29]

Why is Kant willing to engage in these reflections when his original theory of transcendental idealism, as portrayed in the *Critique of Pure Reason*, stands or falls with the arguments that establish the transcendental ideality of space (and time)? The need to do so is given when Kant in the *Opus postumum* develops, and attempts to address conclusively, the Third Analogy's central epistemological standpoint, i.e., the position that the existence of matter as a universal continuum of forces is necessary if there is to be any synthetic unity of perceptual experience. The conception that space must be something dynamically determined is central to the argument against empty space that establishes this position. And the identification of physical aether with dynamically determined material space is what raises the problem of space's transcendental reality.

In the last section of this chapter we will see how this problem affects Kant's conception of transcendental idealism and, more generally, his idea of transcendental philosophy. Kant's late views on transcendental idealism are articulated in the last written fascicles of the *Opus postumum* in connection with the name of Spinoza. But before going into the contents of these fascicles, some further historical contextualization is required. I will therefore take up the metaphysical account of space that Kant gives in the *Inaugural Dissertation* of 1770 in connection with his treatment of the dynamical community of substances. As I pointed out in chapter 5 (see p. 82), this account is best treated in conjunction with the developmental background of the *Opus postumum*'s theory of space. Accordingly, I will now show how Kant's 1770 considerations on space relate to his dynamical aether theory and his conception of dynamically determined material space. Bringing to light the ramifications of this relationship for the overall history of Kant's transcendental theory of experience will enable us to see why the figure of Spinoza comes to play a central part in the reflections on the nature of transcendental idealism and the tasks of transcendental philosophy that are found in the *Opus postumum*'s final fascicles.

As a way of approaching Kant's metaphysical account of space in the *Inaugural Dissertation*, I call attention here to a fragment on metaphysics that Erich Adickes, the editor of the Academy Edition volumes containing the *Reflexionen zur Metaphysik*, believes was composed during 1769. The reflection bears the number 3986:

> One can suppose that the motion of a body is merely the successive presence of a greater efficacy of impenetrability in space, where it is not substance that changes its place, but rather this effect of impenetrability gradually progresses (*sukzediert*) in different locations, just as air waves do in the case of sound. One can also suppose that there are no substances at all in space, but rather a greater or lesser efficacy of a single highest cause in different locations of space. It would follow from this that matter is infinitely divisible. (17:376.24–377.6)

For preliminary access to the meaning of these lines, we can do no better than to take up Adickes's explanatory comments at 17:377.19–30. Adickes rejects previous editorial conjectures concerning the composition date of the fragment, since these were based on the assumption that Kant still considered space to have absolute reality. According to Adickes, the whole tone of the fragment indicates that this is not the case and that a more plausible reading will set out from one of two views regarding the concept of motion: Motion is either the outer appearance of the internal determinations of substances (a substance being the thing-in-itself); or motion is the phenomenally manifested action of the highest cause (i.e., God). The first of these views is at least ostensibly clear of itself. As to the second, Adickes refers us to Kant's appropriation of the Newtonian idea of *omnipraesentia phaenomenon* as it is discussed in the Scholium in Section IV of the *Inaugural Dissertation*.[30] We will turn to this presently. But beforehand, some brief comments on Section III and on the first article of Section IV are in order.

In Section III of the Dissertation, Kant postulates the ideality of space (and time). He argues that space must be conceived as pure intuition and as the fundamental form of all outer sensations (*omnis sensationis externae forma fundamentalis*).[31] The doctrine of space established by this move is supposed to render untenable all the available treatments of space as something objective and real (*aliquid obiectivi et realis*).[32] This negative implication of Kant's theory applies in particular to both the Newtonian and the Leibnizian accounts of space. According to Kant, each of these different types of account is based on the same fundamental error. Each asserts the absolute reality of space, a reality understood either as a Newtonian absolute receptacle (*absolutum et immensum rerum possibilium receptaculum*)[33] or else, under the Leibnizian interpretation, as something purely relational. (Kant maintains, in other words, that the Leibnizian relationist view of space affirms the absolute reality of space just as much as does the substantival view of the Newtonians.)[34] In the first article of Section IV of the Dissertation (§ 16), however, Kant takes up the question of the reality of space in such a way that he relativizes to some extent his exclusively negative judgment about the objectivistic view of space. The nerve of the argument in § 16 is as follows: Those who regard space as something real find it unnecessary to investigate the fundamental condition of the connectedness of a given multiplicity of entities, and so they do not attempt to determine the principle of the essential *form* of the universe. They consider it superfluous to inquire why entities are related as they in fact are. The connectedness of these things is supposed to be established simply by virtue of the omnicomprehensiveness of space. Yet on *any* account, the concept of space can only refer to the intuitively given possibility of the universal coordination of substances. The more profound question therefore remains, and it is a question answerable by the intellect alone: what is the principle of this relation of all substances that, regarded intuitively, is called space?

Consider closely the pivotal lines of the passage just summarized:

> But beside the fact that, as has already been proved, this concept [of space] pertains rather to the sensitive laws of the subject than to conditions of the objects themselves, *however much reality is ascribed to it* [emphasis mine], it nonetheless denotes merely the intuitively given possibility of universal co-ordination; and thus the question, which cannot be solved except by the intellect, remains yet quite untouched: *on what principle rests this relation of all substances that, regarded intuitively, is called space.* (2:407.1–6)

Despite his adherence to the doctrine of space expounded in Section III of the Dissertation, Kant generalizes here on the problem regarding the principle of the phenomenally manifest dynamical community of substances. And in doing this, he concedes that the problem concerns the objectivistic view of space as well as his own. Moreover, in putting forward the notion of the intuitively regarded relation of all substances (*relatio omnium substantiarum intuitive spectata*), he is in effect formulating for his own use a definition of space that cannot simply be identified with the characterization of space as pure intuition and as the merely *subjective* form of all external sensations. Although he has rejected both the Leibnizian and the Newtonian interpretations of the idea that space is something objective and real, he nonetheless requires a metaphysical principle of spatial determinacy that cannot be completely analyzed in terms of the central features of the concept of space that he adopts in Section III.

Taken together, that concession and this requirement do not justify the charge that Kant's considerations on space in Sections III and IV of the Dissertation are inconsistent. But they do lead us to suppose that Kant acknowledges an *intellectual* principle of the spatial connection of coexistent substances as part of the theoretical instrumentarium that he employs when taking up the problem of the ultimate formal principle of *mundus intelligibilis*. It is with respect to this principle that we need to understand Kant's "Malebranchean" considerations on space and time in the Scholium of Section IV. Our attention here will be directed to the issues implicit in Kant's characterization of space as phenomenal omnipresence:

> If it were fitting to overstep a little the limits of the apodictic certainty befitting metaphysics, it might be worthwhile to investigate certain questions concerning not merely the laws but also the causes of sensible intuition, which can be known only through the *intellect*. For, indeed, the human mind is affected by external things and the world lies infinitely open to its view *only so far as the mind, along with all other things, is sustained by the same infinite power of one being*. For this reason, it senses external things only through the presence of one sustaining common cause; and space, which is the sensuously cognized universal and necessary condition of the compresence of all things, can therefore be called OM-NIPRAESENTIA PHAENOMENON. (For it is not because the cause of the universe is in the same place with each and every thing that it is present to them all; on the contrary, locations, i.e., possible relations of substances, exist because that cause is intimately present to all things.) . . . But it seems more advisable to remain close to the shore of the cognitions granted us by the modest character of our intellect, rather than, like Malebranche, to put out into the open sea of mystical inquiries. His view, namely, *that we intuit all things in God*, is very close indeed to the one expounded here. (2:409.28–410.16)

There are a number of ambiguities in Kant's Latin that we would have to clarify if our goal were the exhaustive explication of this passage.[35] What matters for our present purposes is that we can recognize the following sets of metaphysical claims in the lines translated: (1) The human mind can be affected by external things, and the world is thus accessible to human cognition, only if (a) the human mind is sustained in its relation to those things by the infinite power or force (*vis*) of a single entity, and (b) it is so sustained together with the totality of external things. (2) Space is the sensuously cognized (*sensitive cognita*) general and necessary condition of the compresence (i.e., the coexistence) of these things in their totality. As such, and inasmuch as it can be *thought* as a function of the all-encompassing sustentative activity of the divine creator, space can be speculatively termed *omnipraesentia phaenomenon*.[36] (3) The metaphysical view generated by this speculative determination, i.e., the view that we intuit all things in God, is very close to, although *not* identical with, Malebranche's view.

Let us concentrate first on the second of these sets of claims, seeing that it is the conception of divine omnipresence that refers us back to the requirement clarified in the first article of Section IV (§ 16) of the Dissertation. The proposition that space is thinkable as phenomenal omnipresence provides a metaphysical principle of spatial determinacy that pertains not merely to the subjective, sensuously cognized condition of outer experience, but also to the objective (i.e., the mind-independent) causal ground of such experience. This ground can be known solely by means of the intellect and its non-sensible concepts. Accordingly, the cognitive relation of the human mind to the totality of external objects of the senses can be fully accounted for only with recourse to the intellectual concept of causal connection that allows us to think of space as *omnipraesentia phaenomenon*. Although Kant considers this kind of account to be purely speculative, it nonetheless does bring to completion the task that he sets for himself at the beginning of Section IV in § 16. By referring to the infinite power that sustains our cognitive relation to the totality of external objects, Kant seeks to determine the actual character of the objective ground of that relation of all substances that, regarded intuitively, is *called* space.

In spite of Kant's restrictive appeal to "the shore of cognitions granted us by the modest character of our intellect," the Scholium does not exhibit a fundamental break with dogmatic metaphysics. Nevertheless, we should not underestimate its significance in view of the question that would soon be formulated in the letter to Marcus Herz dated 21 February 1772: "On what ground rests the relation of that in us which is called representation to the object?" (10:130.6–8)

It is well known that Kant's exploitation of this question in all its ramifications is what gives rise to the *Critique of Pure Reason*. Consequently, any claim put forward about the connection between the

Scholium of 1769 and the Herz letter will necessarily pertain directly to the actual origins of Kant's transcendental theory. For obvious reasons, such a claim must be made cautiously and with great precision. I therefore leave it undecided whether the Scholium's reference to the ground of the human mind's relation to the totality of objects represents, as one commentator has contended, "the *first* intimation [*die erste Andeutung*]" of the question posed in 1772.[37] Still, Kant's consideration of that ground in 1769 does at least point *toward* this question. And the very fact that it does so allows us to put into proper focus several queries that are worth stating in view of the history of Kant's theory of knowledge after the *Inaugural Dissertation:* (1) Can we recognize in the development of Kant's transcendental theory *prior* to the *Opus postumum* the transformation of the intellectual principle of causal connection at issue in our passage into the postulate of a dynamical world matter? In other words, can we discern the transformation of the speculative theological principle of divine omnipresence into a critical principle of the unity of perceptual experience? (2) Does that transformation, if it occurs, allow Kant to maintain the elemental structure of the human cognitive relation to the external world that he describes in connection with the principle of divine omnipresence?[38] In other words, does the transformation allow him to establish that the relation of the faculty of representation to the cognizable totality of external objects is made possible by that which completely determines the whole of perceptual space as a dynamical continuum?[39] (3) In bringing about the transformation, is Kant able to follow up on his "Malebranchean" insight regarding the intuition of all things in God? Specifically, is he able to purify that insight of its mystical elements, thus making it receptive to combination with the fundamental tenets of Critical Philosophy?

The first and second of these questions can be answered quite handily in this section in light of what has already been said about the Kantian theory of matter and the dynamical community of substances. The response to the third will require a more extensive treatment pertaining mainly to Kant's engagement with the problem of Spinozism in the final fascicles of the *Opus postumum*.

Let us recall that Adickes has referred us to the Scholium of the *Inaugural Dissertation* in view of the possible connection between Reflection 3986 and Kant's conception of divine omnipresence in the Scholium. As far as Adickes's second reading is concerned, the key phrase in the metaphysical fragment is "efficacy of a single highest cause [*Wirksamkeit einer einzigen obersten Ursache*]." This is to be identified with the power or force of God mentioned in the Scholium, and so the successive presence of the efficacy of impenetrability in space (i.e., the motion of a physical body) should be understood as a localized manifestation of that power. Now besides the two interpretative options suggested by Adickes, there is a third way of reading the fragment in question. It involves interpreting the fragment in light of the aether theory of the 1770s, especially in light of the dynamical concept of the aether articulated in Reflection 44 (see p. 126 above). This reading as well focuses on the idea of the efficacy of a single highest cause in order to explain the successive presence of impenetrability in space. But contrary to Adickes's second reading, it does not identify that efficacy with the power of the *ens creatrix*.[40] Rather, it maintains that the cause in question must be a universal continuum of material forces. From the point of view of Kant's aether theory, then, the efficacy of the single highest cause mentioned in Reflection 3986 is merely the causal efficacy of the aether as an omnipresent material entity. Moreover, the physical body which Kant refers to is comprehensible as a particular spatial field that is determined materially by the relatively greater concentration of repulsion and that is limited by the formative efficacy of attraction. Finally, corporeal motion in general (i.e., the successive presence of a greater efficacy of impenetrability) is not the phenomenally manifested action of God. It should rather be understood in terms of the wave action characteristic of the force aether.

If we bring to mind Adickes's editorial activities and his status as (still) the major authority on the internal development of Kant's philosophy of nature,[41] it is remarkable that he did not entertain this way of reading the Reflection under consideration. Not only is our reading supported by the history of the aether theory up to the mid-1770s. It is also contextually far more plausible than either of the alternatives suggested by Adickes. It can explain why Kant is concerned with concepts of the impenetrability and the infinite divisibility of *matter*, as well as with the existence of a *single* substance *in* space.[42] Nevertheless, this criticism should not be taken as detracting from the value of Adickes's insight about the connection between the problem of space and the idea of phenomenal omnipresence. It is Adickes's insight that allows us to make historical sense of the movement of Kant's thought toward the considerations on material space in the *Opus postumum*. Specifically, Adickes allows us to see that Kant comes to abandon the speculative characterization of space in terms of divine omnipresence in favor of a critically transformed Newtonian idea of phenomenal omnipresence that emerges from the dynamical account of material reality.

The key to understanding this process lies in the most striking feature of the epistemological considerations associated with the dynamical theory of matter and the correlative theory of dynamical community, namely, Kant's concern to work out a theory of objective experience based on the assumption that there is a necessary connection between the faculty of representation of the sensuously embodied self-conscious subject and the material world-whole of dynamical interactions. We have already had occasion to touch upon the precritical origin of that concern, which lies in Kant's view that the *status repraesentativus universi* takes place on the foundation of an ontologically primitive Newtonian law of universal attraction (see pp. 76–82 above).[43] We have just seen the structure of the cognitive relation in question to be articulated explicitly by 1770 in connection with Kant's speculation that the relation between the human mind and the totality of external things is sustained by the common infinite power of a single highest cause operative at all locations in space. And our analysis of the Third Analogy as well as the corresponding parts of the *Opus postumum* has established that the unity of consciousness with respect to the empirically cognizable totality of corporeal entities presupposes the sustentative function of a universal material medium of reciprocal action. In view of this line of development, we can make perfectly good sense of Kant's willingness to engage in the kind of epistemological considerations on space that we find in the *Opus postumum*'s aether deduction and doctrine of self-positing. He is attempting to bring to closure, at the level of his *critical* theory of a priori knowledge, a project that had its inception in his earliest writings on metaphysics and natural philosophy, and which underlies his "intimation" of the question of 1772 that led to the theory of objective cognition contained in the *Critique of Pure Reason*. As we will soon see, pursuing this project must lead Kant to throw into question the meaning of his entire doctrine of transcendental idealism. But that should not keep us from recognizing the nature of the project itself.

§ 3: Spinozism and Realism in Kant's Final System of Transcendental Idealism

There is something odd about the reference to Malebranche mentioned above in connection with the idea of the intuition of all things in God. Apart from the February 1772 letter to Herz,[44] the Scholium of the *Inaugural Dissertation* is the only passage in the entire inventory of Kant's writings in which this is linked to Malebranche. Despite the obvious historical justification for establishing this link,[45] in all other written materials composed after 1772 the idea of the intuition of all things in God is tied to the name of Spinoza. That is invariably the case in the *Opus postumum*, as will be considered presently. But there is also some evidence of a connection to Spinoza by 1775, if not beforehand.[46] In any event, we can establish conclusively that the connection is expressly made by the end of the 1780s at the very latest.

I refer here to Reflections 6050 and 6051. According to the Academy Edition's dating procedures, these were composed perhaps as early as 1776–78, though more likely during the 1780s. In these Reflections, Kant shows his concern to work out a conceptuo-historical scheme for understanding both philosophic fanaticism (*Schärmerei*) and metaphysical dogmatism.[47] Spinozism is seen as the culmination of, and the essential link between, these two streams of noncritical metaphysical thought. Kant purports to locate the origins of fanaticism in Plato's conception of ideas as original divine intuitions or archetypes.[48] He then distinguishes between three distinct developmental stages stemming from the Platonic conception: (1) the mystical view that we now intuit all things in God;[49] (2) the Neoplatonic view that, given our place in the chain of being, we somehow have knowledge of the divine intuitions by our ability to communicate spiritually with creatures of a higher order;[50] and (3) the Spinozistic standpoint of "theosophy through intuition" (18:435.22–23).

Kant discerns the origin of metaphysical dogmatism in the inherently reasonable attempt to put an end to the excesses of philosophic fanaticism by starting out from the Aristotelian principle, "*nihil est in intellectu [quod non fuerit in sensu]*" (18:435.24). But since this type of approach did not investigate how a priori cognitions are possible in accordance with its fundamental principle, it was over the course of time unable to respect the proper limitations of reason's striving to provide the greatest possible unity in knowledge. The result was the Spinozistic account of substance, and consequently the theory of the inherence of all things in a single subject.[51] Hence, just as Spinozism represents the culmination of philosophic fanaticism, so too is "Spinozism the true conclusion of dogmaticizing metaphysics" (18:436.8–9). Moreover, in the absence of the critique of reason, "the sinking back into fanaticism [*der Verfall zur Schwärmerei*]" (18:436.18) cannot be avoided: "If one does not set out on the path of critique, then one must let fanaticism take its course" (18:436.18–20).

According to this kind of historical scheme, metaphysical cognitions not grounded in the critique of pure reason must culminate in Spinozism; and no matter how we view it, Spinozism ultimately can amount to nothing more than a form of philosophic fanaticism:

> The highest grade of fanaticism is that we ourselves are in God and intuit or feel our existence in Him. The second: that we intuit all things according to their true nature only in God as their cause and in his ideas as archetypes. The third: that we do not intuit them at all, but only derive them from the concept of the same, and that from our existence and our rational concepts of things we thus make the inference directly to the existence of God in which alone they can have objective reality. Now from the lowest grade back to the highest: Spinoza. (18:438.17–25)

In short, the two main streams of metaphysical thought that eschew the epistemological discipline of the critique of pure reason merge together in the reservoir of Spinozistic thinking. And the figure of Spinoza thus represents the epitome—indeed, the hypostasis—of any non-critical metaphysical theory that asserts either that the objects of our rational cognitions are purely intelligible or that the origins of our rational cognitions are empirical. Kant's tendency is thus to maintain that the historically dominant Platonic and Aristotelian traditions in metaphysics can in the end lead to nothing more than a form of Spinozism.[52]

In the preceding section, I asked whether Kant ever follows up on his originally "Malebranchean" position regarding the intuition of all things in God by purifying it of its mystical elements (see p. 180 above). According to the historical constructions just described, he clearly does allow for such a position to be stripped of its specifically mystical aspects as long as it is developed to its highest stage. But that obviously does not permit him to put to critical use the corresponding idea of the intuition of all things, for this is now associated with a philosophic standpoint that represents the highest stage of both fanaticism and the dogmatism intrinsic to rationalist metaphysics. In sum, according to what Kant says in the 1780s (provided Adickes's dating is correct), there seems to be no possibility of combining such a *Spinozistic* standpoint with the fundamental tenets of critical philosophy.

None of this ought to be especially surprising, considering the negative judgments passed in the published writings from the 1780s and 1790s wherever Kant mentions the name of Spinoza or considers the

Spinozistic theory of substance.[53] The treatment of Spinozism in the Critical Elucidation of the Analytic of Pure Practical Reason (5:100.15–102.36) is a case in point, and it reveals especially well the deep-seated motives for Kant's standard evaluation of Spinoza. In the Critical Elucidation, the reality of transcendental freedom is seen to require the distinction between the finite acting subject as thing-in-itself and that same subject as appearance. Transcendental freedom thus presupposes the transcendental ideality of time and space, since Kant holds that the attribution of spatial and temporal properties to things-in-themselves must result in the "fatalism [*Fatalität*] of actions" (5:101.19). This consequence holds true as well when the notion of the causality of God as the universal primordial or highest being is entertained. For if we assume the transcendental reality of time, we must accept that the causality of an infinite being is the complete determining ground of the finite subject's actions. Moreover, when existence in time is regarded as an attribute necessary to all finite things-in-themselves, then (so Kant argues) the creative causal activity of the infinite highest being would have to be temporally conditioned.[54] But this implication is inconsistent with the assumption of that being's infinitude and with the postulation of its ontological independence with respect to all finite things. Hence, when the causality of a primordial being is contemplated, and when the distinction between this causality and the finite subject's causality through freedom is demanded by practical reason, only the transcendental idealism of time and space allows us to escape the clutches of Spinozism and its deterministic ramifications:

> if one does not assume that ideality of time and space, *Spinozism* alone remains, in which space and time are essential determinations of the primordial being itself, but in which the things dependent upon it (including ourselves) are not substances, but rather merely inhering accidents: for if these things exist merely as that being's effects *in time,* which would be the condition of their existence in itself, even the actions of these entities would have to be its actions, which it carries out anywhere and at any time. (5:101.37–102.7)

Given considerations like these, it is only reasonable to suppose that any movement on Kant's part toward making his conception of transcendental idealism compatible with *any* type of Spinozistic standpoint would call into question the pivotal concept of the metaphysics of morals, namely, the transcendental concept of freedom. We would expect Kant to avoid doing that at practically all costs. This concept of freedom provides not merely the basis for the critically grounded moral theology whose possibility he is implicitly addressing in the passages just quoted.[55] It is also, as he asserts in the Preface to the *Critique of Practical Reason*, "the *keystone* [*der Schlußstein*] of the entire architectonic edifice of a system of pure reason, even of speculative reason" (5:3.25–4.1). Thus, the attempt to accommodate elements of Spinozism must threaten the systematic integrity of the Kantian critical project in both its theoretical and its practical dimensions. In view of the stakes involved, then, we would expect Kant to continue to draw the sharpest possible line of demarcation between his philosophic project and all modes of Spinozistic thinking.

When seen against this background, it is therefore more than remarkable that Spinoza and Spinozism should ever receive affirmative notice from Kant, as in fact happens in the in the *Opus postumum* in conjunction with his treatment of idea of the intuition of all things in God. Indeed, the favorable light cast upon the figure of Spinoza and Spinozistic doctrine in the final fascicles of the *Opus postumum* simply would not be intelligible if we did not bring to bear the ramifications of Kant's conception of physical aether as a transcendental condition and his corresponding account of dynamically determined material space.

In the last two fascicles of the *Opus postumum*, Kant intends to work out a plan for a comprehensive system of transcendental idealism in view of his theory of self-positing. It is a system that includes the cardinal principles of both our experience of sensible nature and our experience of freedom. One of the most intriguing aspects of Kant's thinking regarding this system is his increasingly affirmative view of Spinoza and Spinozism. Kant repeatedly attributes to Spinoza the idea that we intuit all things in God; and he treats this idea as something that either itself furnishes, or else is necessarily connected with, a formal principle of unity.[56] This Spinozistic principle is what governs the investigation of the formal determinacy of cognition (*das Formale der Erkenntnis*), and Kant clearly weighs the option of making it a, if not the, founding principle of his transcendental theory. Moreover, he explores the possibility of making Spinoza a representative of transcendental idealism and even goes so far as to identify this idealism as a form of Spinozism. A number of passages from Fascicle 7 and Fascicle 1 illustrate well this line of reflection:

> *Spinoza:* that we intuit everything in God and, indeed, according to the formal principle of unity. (22:61.2–3)

> Transcendental idealism is the Spinozism of positing the object in the total complex [*in dem Inbegriff*] of its own representations.

Of Spinoza's idea of intuiting all objects in God. That means as much as comprehending all concepts constituting the formal determinacy of cognition, i.e., the elementary concepts, under *one* principle. (22:64.6–11)

The transcendental idealism of that of which our understanding is itself the author. Spinoza.—To intuit everything in God. (21:15.6–7)

Reason leads the way with the projection of its forms (*forma dat esse rei*), because it alone conveys necessity. *Spinoza*. The elements of cognition and the moments of the determination of the subject through them. (To intuit everything in God.) (21:15.19–22)
    System of trans. idealism through Schelling, Spinoza, Lichtenberg and, as it were, 3 dimensions: the present, past and future. (21:87.29–31)

[Transcendental philosophy] is the *intussusception* of a system of Ideas (inventions [*Dichtungen*] of pure reason) through which the subject makes itself into the object of thought according to a principle and [thus] grounds synthetic unity a priori by means of concepts. It is a principle of the forms (1) of personality in me, (2) of the portrayal of the world, *cosmotheoros*, outside of me, (3) (according to Spinoza) of the system of entities which (in opposition to the principle of experience) [must] be conceived as in me and thereby as outside of me. (21:101.5–12)

Two cautionary notes must be kept firmly in mind when attempting to fathom the significance of conceptual sketchings like these. First, it is important to fully recognize the historically convoluted character of Kant's appropriation of Spinoza and Spinozism in the *Opus postumum*. The assessment of this appropriation will eventually have to take into account not only the entire record of Kant's own criticisms of Spinoza from the 1760s through the 1790s:[57] It will also have to do justice to the fact that Kant's appropriation presupposes his reading of Lichtenberg's epistemological reflections and, at least indirectly, his acquaintance with Schelling's *System des transcendentalen Idealismus* of 1800.[58] A proper understanding of Kant's concern with the name of Spinoza therefore demands a detailed investigation of the role of Spinozism in German philosophy during the second half of the eighteenth century, above all during the 1790s. Perhaps most importantly in this connection, it will be necessary to interpret the treatment of Spinoza given in volume 2 of Lichtenberg's *Vermischte Schriften*, which Kant studied closely during the period in which he composed Fascicle 1. We will also need to determine how Schelling fits into the linkage between Lichtenberg's and Kant's appeals to Spinoza.[59]
    The second factor to emphasize is that Kant's late engagement with

Spinozism does take place fully within the framework of his critical philosophy.[60] His affirmative view of certain features of Spinozism should thus in no sense be regarded as a surrender or retreat to a form of philosophic fanaticism or metaphysical dogmatism. Acknowledging this point is essential for interpreting in a coherent manner the range of judgments on Spinoza delivered in the late fascicles. It puts us in a position to consider what appears to be the outright rejection of all elements of Spinozistic doctrine in a number of passages as part of Kant's effort to divest that doctrine of its enthusiastic and dogmatic elements, thus making it receptive to combination with the fundamental tenets of critical philosophy.[61] Accounting for all of these factors requires intensive research of a sort that is now only at its inception. Yet however that research turns out, the most basic question that guides it will still have to be the following: why is Kant at all willing to entertain the proposition that *Spinoza* qualifies as a representative of transcendental *idealism*—be it the past, the present or, for that matter, the future of that idealism?[62] After all, even a critical appropriation of Spinoza remains an appropriation of —Spinoza. We must therefore ask why Kant is willing to engage in such an exercise when his published writings and the pertinent metaphysical reflections prior to the *Opus postumum* show that he had decisive reason for rejecting any attempt to place his account of transcendental idealism in proximity with any kind of Spinozistic standpoint.

Before proceeding any further, I should mention one very basic way in which Kant's late reflections on Spinoza and Spinozism might be made less intriguing than they have thus far been presented. It is to take those reflections (and, for that matter, most everything else that Kant says in the *Opus postumum*) as evidence of Kant's mental debilitation at the turn of the century, and consequently to regard them as nothing more than expressions of an inherently foolhardy attempt on Kant's part to embellish his thinking with recourse to a figure that loomed large in a then fashionable mode of philosophic discourse.[63] This approach does offer an undeniable practical advantage: Inasmuch as it undercuts the requirement to address seriously the actual philosophic import of Kant's engagement with Spinozism in the late manuscripts, it allows one to avoid any challenges that they contain for the orthodox reading of the critical philosophy as a whole. But if we are interested in bringing to light the reasons that Kant in fact had for confronting the question of Spinozism in the *Opus postumum,* we have no choice but to take up that requirement and to take on the challenges that go along with it.

A more defensible response to Kant's concern with the question of Spinozism can be gathered from our discussion of the dynamics of material nature and the attempt made thus far in this chapter to follow one strand in the development of the critical theory of a priori knowledge from the *Inaugural Dissertation* to the *Opus postumum*. Its point of departure is this: the philosophically serious interpreter must simply face the fact that the late theory of self-positing, which gives rise to the appropriation of Spinoza and the Spinozistic idea of the intuition of all things, cannot be made compatible with the officially stated tenets of the earlier version of the critical theory of a priori knowledge; nor can it be integrated with the particular conception of transcendental idealism that these tenets generate. The reason is that Kant's investigation of the formal determinacy of cognition in the *Opus postumum*'s final fascicles is far broader in scope than the officially stated assumptions of the classical critical theory could possibly allow for.

To see fully the significance this point, we need merely to bring to mind the two main conclusions already drawn in this chapter: (1) Kant's late thinking about the connection between cosmic matter, space, and material conditions of possible experience undercuts the arguments that establish the transcendental ideality of space. (2) Questioning the transcendental ideality of space (and time) is, in Kant's own terms, tantamount to raising the specter of Spinozism. Objectively, then, the systematic problem that emerges from the aether deduction and the treatment of dynamically determined space is to find a way to integrate elements of what Kant himself had previously deemed to be a position of Spinozistic realism with the (or a) theory of transcendental idealism. That Kant in fact recognized and reflected on this problem is evident in the final fascicles of the *Opus postumum*, particularly in the following remarkable passage from Fascicle 1:[64]

> The first act of thought contains a principle of the ideality of the object in me and outside of me as appearance, i.e., of me as a subject affecting itself [*des mich selbst affizierenden Subjekts*] in a system of ideas containing merely the formal determinacy of the advancement towards experience in general (*Aenesidemus*); i.e., transcendental philosophy is an idealism; for experience is not merely an arbitrary aggregate of perceptions. . . .[65]

> We can know objects, either in us or as found outside us, only insofar as we inject into ourselves the *actus* of cognition according to certain laws. The mind of the human being is Spinoza's God (as far as the formal determinacy of all objects of the senses is concerned) and transcendental idealism is realism in the absolute sense. (21:99.5–22)

We witness here the kind of conceptual tension that parallels what we encountered above when discussing dynamically determined space in relation to space as the form of outer intuition (see pp. 172–174). On the one hand, the conception of the ideality of appearances touched upon in the first paragraph lends itself to explication in terms consistent with official critical doctrine—in this case, in terms of the essential connection that, prior to the *Opus postumum*, Kant had established between transcendental idealism and empirical realism on the basis of his supposition that space and time are transcendentally ideal.[66] In view of that connection, the existence of *appearances* is granted only relatively to the conditions of human sensibility. Consequently, outer appearances (and of course space itself) cannot be treated as anything self-subsistent.[67] On the other hand, it is exceedingly difficult to see how the realism in the *absolute* sense mentioned in the second paragraph could be made to incorporate the assumption of such relativity.

One way around the difficulty at hand might be to regard the mention of this sort of realism as nothing more than an oblique reference to the Kantian refutations of material idealism, which are meant to establish that the consciousness of one's own existence (in time) involves the immediate consciousness of the spatial existence of external things.[68] But the argument that the existence of outer objects of the senses does not need to be mediately inferred obviously does not require, or permit, us to renounce the position that the existence of objects, as appearances, is relative to the formal conditions of human sensibility. That is, it does not permit us to reject the tenet that is essential to Kant's original account of empirical realism, and that in effect makes this a realism not in the absolute sense, but rather a realism in a merely relative sense, insofar as it concerns the *existence* of objects as appearances. Now it is unclear what a realism in the absolute sense could mean if it does not involve the renunciation of precisely the kind of relativity regarding the existence of these objects that is demanded by Kant's earlier accounts of empirical realism. The difficulty becomes decisive when we consider that the phrase "realism in the absolute sense" is employed in an interpretation of self-positing which identifies the self-legislative cognitive activity of the *human* subject with Spinoza's God. For we must recall that the Spinozistic standpoint goes together with the rejection of the transcendental ideality of space and time upon which the classical critical conception of empirical realism is based.

In view of the background presented thus far, it makes sense to think that Kant simply means what he appears to be saying; namely, that the account of the ideality of objective appearances must somehow be made compatible with elements of an absolute (or transcendental) realism, if the self-positing human subject is to have knowledge of a unified perceptual world. Now that *may* permit the construction of a system of transcendental philosophy based on a concept of transcendental idealism.[69] But this concept of idealism would have to be radically different from the terminologically corresponding notion from the central critical period.[70] To satisfy its requirements, one would have to see one's way beyond the familiar dualities of the forms of realism and idealism that define the terminological, conceptual, and historical terrain upon which the three *Critiques* were built. And this necessarily would lead one to revise or reinterpret radically the notion that transcendental idealism is but a merely formal idealism, i.e., the notion according to which "everything intuited in space or time, and therefore all objects of any experience possible to us, are nothing but . . . mere representations, which, in the manner in which they are represented, have no independent existence outside our thoughts" (*Critique of Pure Reason,* B518–519).

Recognizing the theoretical need to move beyond the terrain that gives rise to this notion is what motivates Kant to redefine transcendental idealism by means of a doctrine of self-positing that he characterizes with reference to the figure of Spinoza. According to this doctrine, the "Spinozistic" standpoint is engendered by a description of the origins of the subject-object relation that cannot be made compatible with the view of transcendental idealism as a merely formal idealism. For the attempt to integrate that standpoint with a critical theory of transcendental knowledge requires an account of the material basis of the object-relation of self-consciousness that militates against the particular doctrine of space presupposed by Kant's portrayal of transcendental idealism as a merely formal idealism.

If these conclusions are correct, then we can see that Kant was led toward the characterization of his final system of transcendental idealism as a form of Spinozism by way of reflection on the epistemological implications of his dynamistic conception of material reality.[71] Consequently, we can also understand why the elderly Kant had profound reasons expressly to place his final standpoint in close proximity to the positions of his younger contemporaries.[72] Finally, and perhaps most importantly, we can recognize that the seemingly anomalous quality of Kant's late philosophy reflects not the ineptitude of the thinker, but rather the inadequacy of the standard interpretations of Kant's Critical Philosophy.[73]

Kant's late work has now been available in published form for more than sixty years. It is time that we came to grips seriously with what it presents, even if that means giving up some cherished assumptions about the nature of Kant's critical theory of a priori knowledge. I have been concerned to reveal the preconditions for understanding what takes place in the *Opus postumum*. I began by anchoring our investigations in a central text from the *Critique of Pure Reason,* and in this last chapter I have tried to shed light on at least some of the main planks for an interpretive framework that does justice to the developmental complexity of Kant's transcendental theory of experience. I have located these in sources as diverse as the Leibnizian idea of apperceptive subjectivity, the speculative metaphysics of space prevalent in the intellectual milieu of Cambridge Platonism and, finally, Kant's confrontation with the Spinozistic doctrine of substance. Needless to say, my reconstructions have presented a heterodox picture of at least one strand in the unfolding of the critical theory of our a priori knowledge of nature. But if the *complete* history of this theory shows us anything, it is that Kant was finally unwilling to conform to the orthodox view of his critical philosophic enterprise that he himself had so actively promoted during the 1780s and earlier 1790s. Kant was his own severest critic when it came to facing the realist implications of the transcendental theoretic approach already at issue in the Third Analogy of Experience. He remained that to the very end, even if it did bring him up face to face with the positions of some of his more radical contemporaries. We must never lose sight of Kant's capacity to renew and rework the foundations of the Critical Philosophy. And we should not underestimate his will to maintain his place at the leading edge of philosophy's historical progression.

Notes

Introduction

1. "Transeunt" is the proper technical term, used in Kant's era, to designate causal influences that "go out beyond" the causally active substances. It is retained in the *Oxford English Dictionary* in precisely, and exclusively, this sense. I use it here somewhat loosely when referring to both influences and forces. For the justification of this usage, see pp. 49–51 and 148–150 below.

2. For Kant's conception of transcendental critique, see 3:43.27–44.7.

3. See, e.g., 3:50.11–14, 74.9–75.4, 100.25–29, 473.5–18.

4. This supposition is, of course, the key to Kant's Copernican Revolution in metaphysics.

5. See pp. 39–42 below for a detailed discussion of the assertions made in the last two paragraphs. In this context it is important to call attention to a recent investigation by Kenneth Westphal (1997, 139–189) that examines Kant's conceptions of transcendental affinity in the *Critique of Pure Reason*. The aspect of this investigation that most directly concerns my work on the Third Analogy is Westphal's analysis of transcendental affinity in the 1781 version of the Transcendental Deduction. According to Westphal, Kant's treatment of the transcendental affinity of the manifold in intuition (see 4:84.32–85.2, 90.6–91.2) brings to light non-subjective transcendental conditions that are both formal and material. Westphal's discussion of these conditions lends support to my interpretation of the Third Analogy by showing that the Transcendental Analytic of the first *Critique* contains yet another exception to Kant's "formalism." But Westphal does not concentrate on the notion of an a priori existence proof for a dynamical plenum, which is central to my interpretation of the Third Analogy. Also, when investigating the Third Analogy, I will not refer to non-subjective transcendental conditions that are *both* formal and material. Westphal fully justifies this description for the purposes of his analysis of transcendental

affinity by determining precisely how it applies to Kant's conception of sensation (see Westphal 1997, 156 and 164), and there is no inconsistency between the conclusions we draw about the nature of non-subjective transcendental conditions. Yet as we will see presently, understanding the Third Analogy's a priori existence proof requires investigations that go far beyond Kant's accounts of sensation. Moreover, I want to bring out as clearly as possible the differences between the formalistic approach to the question of transcendental conditions that Kant expressly advocates and the type of approach that we actually find in the Third Analogy. Thus, when examining Kant's theory of knowledge prior to the *Opus postumum,* I will generally use "formal" only when describing transcendental conditions that are both subjective and non-material. This is in keeping with Kant's explicitly stated (i.e., his "official") views in the *Critique of Pure Reason* on the a priori necessary conditions of our experience of objects. (As for what happens to the distinction between formal and material transcendental conditions in the *Opus postumum,* see pp. 155–158, 163–174, and 189–191 below.)

6. On Kant's concept of transcendental knowledge, see Pinder 1987, 1–40. For an investigation of the changes wrought upon this concept between the first *Critique* and the *Opus postumum,* see Förster 1989a, 285–304.

7. Cf. George 1981, 240–241, and Aquila 1989, 6–8, 11. Lorne Falkenstein (1995, 104–110) apparently rejects the account of Kant's view of sensation in the Anticipations of Perception that I give here. Falkenstein claims that when Kant correlates sensations with the objects that appear to us, he conceives of sensations themselves as having spatial properties. Falkenstein thus seems to maintain that what Kant calls sensation "in itself" (i.e., sensation regarded in abstraction from further conditions of our possible experience of objects) is necessarily something spatially extended insofar as it correlates with outer objects. But this interpretation is untenable as far as the basic account of sensation in the Anticipations of Perception is concerned. Falkenstein evidently fails to recognize the significance of the distinction that Kant very clearly draws between, on the one hand, the intensive magnitude that must be ascribed to sensation and, on the other hand, the objects of perception to which the intensive magnitude of sensation must be ascribed (see 3:152.16–24). If Kant did not draw this distinction, he would be unable to discuss the intensive magnitude of what is real in all appearances as a specific and delimitable theme for transcendental inquiry in the first *Critique*'s Analytic of Principles. In particular, he could not treat the Anticipations of Perception as being separate from, although inextricably linked to, the Axioms of Intuition and the Analogies of Experience.

8. Regarding the relation between sensation and the matter that *corresponds* to it, see 3:50.6–8, 137.15–18, 474.26–475.5.

9. This brings us to an extremely important point for the argument of this book: *at no point* do I conflate discussion of the "matter of sensation" with considerations on transeunt influences, matter in space, and material forces. My analysis of the Third Analogy thus does not rely on any "sliding" between the two distinct types of consideration (see pp. 35–36 below, where I explain the fundamental differences between Kant's theoretical orientations in the Anticipations and the Third Analogy). This is not, of course, to claim that Kant is

not confronted with very significant difficulties in determining the relationship between the real of sensation and material transcendental conditions. Indeed, the need to deal with such issues is an important factor in his thinking in the *Opus postumum* (see chapters 8 and 9 below). But the conceptual framework for treating them is certainly not developed in the *Critique of Pure Reason*.

10. For a discussion of Kant on the question of the necessary lawfulness of nature, see Thöle 1991, especially 6–38.

11. A more complete sketch of the relationship between transcendental principles and empirical laws would obviously have to include a discussion of the principles of regulatively employed reason as well as the principle of reflective judgment pertaining to the formal purposiveness or systematicity of nature according to its empirical laws (see 3 : 426.21–442.8; 5 : 179.16–186.21, 192.13–194.37; 20 : 201.11–211.5). These principles are indeed transcendental, but Kant does not intend them to be constitutive. I am concerned here solely with the connection between empirical laws and the principles of pure understanding as constitutive principles of our knowledge of objects.

12. Kenneth Westphal (1995a, 43–86; 1995b, 381–409) furnishes two important recent investigations of the *Metaphysical Foundations* and its relation to the concepts and principles of Kant's transcendental theory. Konrad Cramer (1985, 119–161, 307–309) discusses the *Metaphysical Foundations* in view of the problem of non-pure synthetic a priori judgments. Gerd Buchdahl (1988, 672–681; 1992, 288–314) and Michael Friedman (1992a, 136–164) have also provided well-known treatments of the *Metaphysical Foundations*. Westphal (1995b, 409–414; 1998, 335–352) criticizes Buchdahl and Friedman for disregarding or deflating the systematic divisions of labor that Kant establishes between the different parts of his metaphysics of nature. I give concerted criticism of Friedman's work on Kant's natural philosophy in the notes to chapters 7–8 below (see notes 66, 100, and 107 of chapter 7 and notes 9, 12–13, 23, and 40 of chapter 8). For further secondary literature on the *Metaphysical Foundations,* see the notes to § 4 of chapter 7 below.

13. In the *Critique of Pure Reason* (B64), Kant states that "empirical *concepts,* as well as that on which they are based, [i.e.,] empirical intuition, can yield no synthetic proposition other than one that is *also merely empirical,* i.e., is a proposition of experience and that thus can never contain absolute universality and necessity . . ." (3 : 68.13–18). For a thorough discussion of the difficulties that Kant faces in establishing a system of a priori principles on the basis of an empirical concept, see Cramer 1985, 129–161, 307–309.

14. See 4 : 473.35–477.13 (cf. 3 : 92.16–33, 94.15–31, 140.6–16); 5 : 181.15–31.

15. See 4 : 495.27–38, 523.6–17, 551.8–14, 558.22–26. Kant's procedure of specification presupposes that motion is the most basic property of matter since it is "the fundamental determination of anything that is to be an object of the outer senses" (4 : 476.9–16).

16. Kant's account of the relations between transcendental, special metaphysical, and empirical laws becomes considerably more complicated in the *Opus postumum,* where he attempts to construct a "transitional" science that is supposed to mediate between the *Metaphysical Foundations* and the concepts and principles of the empirical part of physics. I discuss this in § 2 of chapter 8 below. At this point, it must suffice to say that Kant does not at first *intend* his

transitional science to call into question the basic architectonic conception of the metaphysics of nature that he had accepted in 1786.

17. See pp. 139–144 below.

18. Kant calls this matter "aether" (see 4:534.6, 564.3).

19. See, e.g., 3:99.30–102.14, 104.6–106.5, 126.27–127.30.

20. See pp. 49–51, 63–68, 87–91, 147–150, and 158–163 below.

21. On this, see notes 1–3 of the preliminary remarks to part one and note 27 of chapter 3 below. At this juncture let me say against those who are inclined to share this attitude merely that Kant's treatment of the principle of community cannot plausibly be ignored in any serious interpretation of Kant's philosophic enterprise in the first *Critique*'s Analytic of Principles. Paul Guyer (1987, 168, 212–214, 224–225, 228, 239, 246, 274–275) has shown conclusively how the three Analogies of Experience form an integrated set of mutually supporting principles. Thus, we cannot disregard any one of the Analogies and expect to understand Kant's theory of objective experience.

22. Cf. Broad 1978, 178–179; Paton 1936, II 318; Strohmeyer 1980, 142; Watkins 1997, 433–434.

23. Pertinent considerations are, however, found in Krausser 1981, 114, 126–128; Lütterfelds 1977, 349–350.

Part I: Dynamical Community, Influences, and Matter Everywhere

1. Emphasis here is on *predominant* concern. The Third Analogy is at least summarily treated in most systematic works on the Transcendental Analytic. The following contain representative commentaries: Aschenbrenner 1983; Bauch 1917; Delekat 1969; Ewing 1938; Findlay 1981; Kaulbach 1981; Körner 1955; and Walsch 1975. (The most detailed exegesis is still to be found in Paton 1936, I 310–331; but see also Guyer 1987, 267–276.) Discussions of special problems from the Third Analogy are found in Broad 1978; Buchdahl 1988; Kemp-Smith 1923; Lütterfelds 1977; Melnick 1973; Paton 1936; Rohs 1976; Strawson 1966; and Strohmeyer 1980. There is, however, no twentieth-century commentary on the Analytic of Principles in which a concerted effort is made to clarify the pivotal position that the Third Analogy holds in Kant's transcendental theory of experience. Generally speaking, contemporary evaluation of the role of the Third Analogy in this theory contrasts markedly with the estimations given by Kant's own contemporaries and immediate successors. On this, see notes 21, 24, and 26 of chapter 2 below.

2. See, e.g., Strawson 1966, 140.

3. What other plausible reason might there be for the lack of attention paid to the Third Analogy in works that purport to contain accounts of Kant's philosophical project in the Transcendental Analytic as a whole? See, e.g., Allison 1983; Bennett 1966; Bird 1962. Bennett goes so far as to claim that the proof of the principle of community is "a failure which is not even incidentally valuable except for a few flickers of light which it throws on the second Analogy" (181).

Chapter 1:   The Transcendental Principle of
             Community and Its Proof

1. See 3:134.28–135.2, 138.35–37, 140.6–16, 161.15–37; 4:160.16–37.

2. This is Kant's sole treatment of community between B111–113 and the Third Analogy.

3. When taken in conjunction with its transcendental time-determination, the category of community thus applies to the relation of coexistence between the accidental determinations of any particular substance (*der Einen*) and the corresponding determinations of another substance or other substances (*der Anderen*) in accordance with a universal rule of synthesis. For the concept of rule at issue here, see 3:133.5–7, 136.28–35, 138.37–139.36, 145.3–7, 184.18–22.

4. Cf. 3:165.10–11; 10:366.7–9; 22:283.23–384.3.

5. That is, the category as both *restricted* in its application and *realized*. On this, see 3:135.21–24, 139.11–37, 161.23–31.

6. See 3:184.26–27.

7. I am supposing here that the principle stated in the second edition represents but a terminological revision of the "ontological" formulation of the first edition. In other words, I assume that the 1787 version of the principle is simply an explication of the original formulation in terms of the possibility of perception, whereby the reference to possible experience that is so central to the critical theory of a priori knowledge (see, e.g., 3:158.15–17, 159.10–11, 199.17–24, 201.36–202.3, 203.6–19) is made fully evident. I thus accept that we can speak unambiguously of a single principle of community or coexistence. For the sake of brevity, I use "principle of community" when referring to the transcendental law of nature in question.

8. That is not to say that the principle of community is concerned with the domain of the cosmological ideas, i.e., with *absolute* totality in the synthesis of appearances (cf. 3:282.25–27, 283.8–15, 286.8–28, 287.15–20, 289.13–20). For the concept of the world-whole as applied to absolute totality, see 3:282.25–29, 299.23–28, 354.17–355.26, 446.33–447.3.

9. My main divisions coincide with those accepted by Paton 1936 (see II 298, 310, and 316).

10. 3:180.29–182.27.

11. 3:181.28–182.26.

12. Regarding my use of "elucidation," cf. 1:413.21–416.4.

13. 3:182.27–183.12.

14. 3:183.13–31.

15. For the concept of empirical intuition, see 3:65.22–26, 74.15–21, 115.11–13, 117.10–30, 125.17–20, 158.25–159.2, 161.2–5, 204.20–205.3. For the concept of perception, see 3:117.20–22, 124.27–30, 152.2–10, 168.8–169.24, 175.10–20; 4:89.5–11.

16. Notice the cosmological orientation of Kant's thinking. In explicating the concept of coexistence, Kant has more in mind than "tables and chairs." Compare his approach with classical empiricist approaches to the corresponding epistemological problem of the continued existence of unperceived objects

(see Berkeley, *Principles,* §§ 4, 6, 9, 18, 20, 24, 27, 33; Hume, *Treatise,* 194–199, and *Enquiries,* 151–153).

17. On the concept of "manifold" employed in this context, see 3:92.19–24, 108.1–4, 108.22–109.1; 111.4–112.12, 115.2–116.13, 168.8–169.7; 4:76.8–14, 77.12–78.19.

18. That time itself cannot be perceived is the pivotal assumption without which Kant's problem of objective experience in the Analogies could not be posed. On this, see 3:159.2–9, 162.8–21, 167.14–168.3.

19. For "synthesis of imagination/apprehension," see 127.21, 168.8–169.16 (cf. 163.1–2), 4:76.8–18, 77.12–30, 79.7–13, 89.2–20.

20. As the history of textual reconstruction and interpretive translation shows, there is considerable room for syntactical maneuvering in these lines:

> Dinge sind zugleich, sofern sie in einer und derselben Zeit existieren. Woran erkennt man aber; daß sie in einer und derselben Zeit sind? Wenn die Ordnung in der Synthesis der Apprehension dieses Mannigfaltigen gleichgültig ist, d.i. von A durch B C, D auf E, oder auch umgekehrt von E zu A gehen kann. Denn, wäre sie in der Zeit nacheinander (in der Ordnung, die von A anhebt, und in E endigt), so ist es unmöglich, die Apprehension in der Wahrnehmung von E anzuheben, und rückwärts zu A fortzugehen, weil A zur vergangenen Zeit gehört, und also kein Gegenstand der Apprehension mehr sein kann.

Consider the assumption of indirect proof by which Kant establishes the necessity of his condition of our knowledge of coexistence. It seems evident that if the subjunctive *wäre* (line 4) is to retain its singular number, then its subject—the pronoun *sie*—must refer to *Ordnung* (*in der Synthesis der Apprehension*) (lines 2–3). The plausibility of this reading is strengthened if we take into account the possible alternatives. One alternative reading (see Erdmann's editorial suggestion at 3:575) would retain the singular number of *wäre,* but would refer *sie* to *Synthesis* (*der Apprehension*). Apart from the grammatical contortions involved, there are two difficulties with this procedure: (1) Kant makes it abundantly clear elsewhere in the Analogies that the synthesis of apprehension *is* always successive in time (see above all 3:163.1–2, 168.8–169.7, 172.36–173.2; 174.28–30). (2) This successiveness is precisely what generates the problem that the passage in question is addressing. Without this successiveness, the problem of our knowledge of coexistence simply would not arise, and there would therefore be no reason to posit indifference in the order of synthesis as a condition of our knowledge. A second alternative reading (see, e.g., Kemp-Smith's English translation of the passage) demands a change in the text itself, substituting *wären* for *wäre* (line 4), thereby linking *sie* (line 4) to *Dinge* (*A, B, . . . E*) (lines 1 and 3–4). But when properly thought out, this interpretation requires the supposition that there is a relation of perceivably coexistent things given independently of the synthesis of apprehension (and, more generally, of the operations of the cognitive faculties). Such a relation would have to be a condition of our experience of coexistence, and it consequently could be known a priori to be given independently of the synthesis of apprehension. That, of course, would also amount to a denial of the problem which Kant is in fact responding to, namely, *how* do we *know* that things are in one and the same time? The passage quoted makes good sense as it stands. I can see no reason not to refer a singular *sie* (line 4) to *Ordnung* (line 2).

21. I follow here the logical sequence of the argument by which Kant establishes the necessity of the ground of coexistence, and not merely the paragraph indention of the printed text. The premise indicator (*Also*) at 3:182.11 makes it clear that we should regard the first sentence of the new paragraph as the conclusion of the argument against empty space. We could, of course, take it as a first premise of the next stage of core argument 1 as well. Presumably, it is the purpose of the indention to make this connection between the two stages evident.

22. Regarding this translation, see Grimm, *Deutsches Wörterbuch*, s.v. "*anmerken.*"

23. This concocted term replaces the usual translation of *Weltkörper* as "celestial bodies." Kant's employment of *Weltkörper* in the present context may fully conform to standard eighteenth-century German usage. If so, he is indeed referring specifically to the variety of celestial bodies as objects of astronomical observation. But he may be using the term to designate any and all bodies regarded as objects of empirical intuition in general (cf., e.g., 18:8.8–15). Support for restricting the term's application to celestial bodies can be found, for instance, in the *Metaphysical Foundations of Natural Science* (see 4:563.19–32). But in the *Universal Natural History* (1755) Kant had drawn a distinction between *Weltkörper* (i.e., the elemental material bodies formed out of the primal matter originally present in space) and *Himmelskörper*, consisting of planets, stars, and stellar formations (see 1:226.29–30, 262.4–8, 338.23–35, 339.8–37, 342.35–37; see also 4:321.2–26).

24. For *mittelbare* (as opposed to *unmittelbare*) *Gemeinschaft*, see 17:573.19–21; 28(1):46.30–33, 435.3–24; 28(2):641.7–20 (cf. 846.36–847.17).

25. The demonstrative pronoun *diese* (3:183.1) is here referred to *Materie* (182.37).

26. Even in the German, the passage at 4:182.36–183.4 almost begs for simplifying reconstruction. But Kemp-Smith's translation has simply too little to do with the Kantian text itself. Guyer and Wood's 1998 translation is far more literal, although I cannot accept their interpretation that *ihr Zugleichsein* (182.2) refers to the simultaneity of particular heavenly bodies instead of the simultaneity of matter everywhere. W. Pluhar's 1996 translation comes closest to mine; and the investigations constituting this book will justify our shared interpretation of the passage.

27. Cf. 3:180.12–20, 184.18–22, 185.2–11.

28. For *compositum reale*, as distinguished from *compositum ideale*, see 3:304.2–22, 306.1–18; Reflections 4314, 4979, 5868–5869. For the formational variability of *compositum reale*, see 3:97.3–7, 185.26–32; Reflections 3788, 4064, 4419; 28(1):431.23–27; 516.20–25. Cf. Baumgarten, *Metaphysica* §§ 224–235, 392–395; Wolff, *Cos. gen.* §§ 60–75.

29. Cf. Reflections 4415, 4493, 4496, 4762, 4979, 5869, 5877, 6404.

Chapter 2:   Problems in the Third Analogy

1. See note 10 below.

2. Following Wille, Kemp-Smith substitutes *jede (Substanz)* for *dieses* at 3:181.22 and translates accordingly. I can see no justification for changing Kant's

text in this instance. Nor do I see any reason to accept Pluhar's translation, which assumes that *dieses* refers to *Substanz*. For further discussion of this issue, see note 10 below.

3. See 3:166.23–28, 167.2–13, 169.17–175.20, 176.30–177.22.

4. 3:96.8–24. This is an addition to the 1787 text.

5. Kemp-Smith imprecisely translates this as "the causality of substances reciprocally determining one another." Guyer and Wood's "causality of a substance in the reciprocal determination of others" is acceptable. But Pluhar's "causality of a substance reciprocally determining [and being determined by] another substance" comes closest to my reading.

6. See also 10:366.16–367.29.

7. This redundancy, however, can be used to counter any attempt to comprehend the principle of community in terms of a dual application of the category of causality. On this point, see Schopenhauer, *Sämtliche Werke*, II 544–549; Paton 1936, II 294–295. See also Guyer 1987, 272–274; Westphal 1995a, 58–65.

8. This does not prevent Kant from having a much broader conception of causal influence in the Transcendental Analytic (see, e.g., 3:121.20–21, 152.23–24; 4:77.3–5, 87.5–8). But in the Analogies of Experience he employs the concept of influence as such strictly in connection with the community of substances or relation of reciprocal action.

9. For Kant's conception of the original acquisition of concepts, see 8:221.226–223.8 (cf. 6:258.9–21, 268.3–30).

10. There are, of course, alternative readings (see the English translations by Kemp-Smith and Pluhar, as well as the editor's note at 3:566–567). These, however, all require either corrections of the available text or else a quite charitable view of what qualifies as acceptable eighteenth-century German grammar (even with respect to Kant's syntactical idiosyncrasies). One plausible textual amendment, which makes the passage at hand agree with the "Schema of Community," is to change the gender of the demonstrative pronoun in the phrase "*wenn wechselseitig diese*" and the definite article in the phrase "*in dem anderen*":

> Nun ist das Verhältnis der Substanzen, in welchem die eine Bestimmungen enthält, wovon der Grund in der anderen enthalten ist, das Verhältnis des Einflusses, und wenn wechselseitig diese [not *dieses*] den Grund der Bestimmungen in der [not *dem*] anderen enthält, das Verhältnis der Gemeinschaft oder Wechselwirkung.

Another interpretation involving a textual change is to construe *dieses* as referring to the ground (*Grund*) that contains, reciprocally, the ground of determinations in the other (*in der anderen*) substance. The relation of influence should thus be conceived as a relation between the causal grounds contained within particular substances. This too is a plausible reading, although it does give rise an interesting question for which there is no obvious answer in the Third Analogy itself: why exactly should Kant entertain the notion of an intrinsic causal *ground* which contains the ground of determinations in another substance when he supposes that the relation of influence is one in which each *substance* contains the ground of determinations in another substance?

Both of the alternative readings can find support in the investigations below (see above all pp. 87–91, 130–132, and 160–162). Yet I am unwilling to undertake a conjectural reconstruction of the printed text unless there is compelling reason to do so, which in the present case I doubt there is.

11. See note 1 of chapter 8 below.

12. A general observation about core argument 1 as a whole is here in order. Notice the great care with which Kant progressively exhibits the concept of thing. He proceeds from (a) the nontechnical (*zugleich sind*) *Dinge* (3:180.29), to (b) *Mannigfaltige* (181.7), to (c) *Gegenstände* (181.13), to (d) *außer einander zugleich existierenden Dinge* (181.17), to (e) (*das Verhältnis der*) *Substanzen* (181.20), and finally to (f) *Substanzen im Raume* (181.24). For similar uses of the concept of thing or object, see, e.g., 3:168.16, 171.14–24, 172.17–33 (cf. 170.11–22). For "substance," see above all 3:166.1/16–17 (for contrasting usage: 163.22–32, 164.25–28).

13. For *Substanzen als Erscheinungen*, see above all 3:164.25–30, 177.18–22, 201.19–21.

14. In his analysis of core argument 1, Eric Watkins (1997, 412–419) shows that Kant's criterion for judging the objective simultaneity of substances is not the reversibility of the order of perceptions, but rather the causality between substances. Unfortunately, his assessment of the Third Analogy's account of this causal relation simply ignores the significance of Kant's use of "influences" in his argument against empty space. Watkins's analysis is textually inadequate, and it therefore fails to come to grips fully with the logical content of Kant's argument.

15. Regarding *Dasein der Substanz*, cf. 3:162.18–21, 163.13–15/18–20, 165.7–9. For *empirische Synthesis*, see 3:127.13–21, 145.21–22, 282.25–30, 343.26–28.

16. Cf. 3:179.33–180.1.

17. Cf. 3:173.27–174.5.

18. For *Dasein* (*der Erscheinung[en]/der Substanz[en]*), see 3:147.4–10, 149.33–37, 159.34–160.8/20–23, 183.32–184.10, 185.2–11, 189.23–28, 189.36–190.4, 190.16–21.

19. In keeping with the editorial decision reflected at 3:182.13–14, my paraphrasing accepts the deletion of the two commas present in all the original versions of the printed text: "weil nur unter dieser Bedingung gedachte Substanzen, als *zugleich existierend,* empirisch vorgestellt werden können." Without the dissolution of the appositive phrase, the clause as a whole might be construed to indicate a relation of substances that must be known to be established independently of the synthesis of imagination in apprehension, and so independent of the categorially ruled cognitive accomplishments of the understanding. For the difficulty involved in such a reading, see note 20 of chapter 1 above.

20. See 3:167.24–168.7, 169.17–170.35, 172.36–173.23, 174.27–175.20.

21. Cf. Hegel, *Gesammelte Werke,* XI 402–409; Schelling, *Werke,* II 468–483 (especially 475).

22. See the references to Guyer 1987 in note 21 of the introduction.

23. Cf. Guyer 1987, 274–275; Westphal 1995a, 58–69.

24. Cf. Hegel, *Gesammelte Werke,* XI 407–409; Schelling, *Werke,* II 476. On Kant's employment of the principle of permanence with reference to the existence of particular substances, see 3:162.28–30, 163.29–32, 165.10–26, 166.16–

17/23–25. For a very different employment, see 3:162.1–6/14–24, 163.9–11/23–36, 164.25–28, 165.9–11.

25. This will be true, of course, only if all appearances encountered in the sequence of time are determinations of substances. But Kant emphatically accepts precisely this condition at the very beginning of the Second Analogy (see 3:167.1–8).

26. Cf. Schelling, *Werke*, II 475–481, 495. Cf. also Anderson 1983, 486–487; Bauch 1917, 255–256; Paton 1936, II 324–325.

27. On the centrality of the Analogies for this theory, see 17:643.1–655.21, 662.29–669.10, 670.13–672.5; 18:84.2–6, 369.21–370.16. Note, incidentally, that core argument 1, which was added to the Third Analogy in 1787, remains neutral with regard to the question of the "preeminence" of the Third Analogy. In core argument 1, Kant establishes the necessity of the category of community for our experience of coexistent objects solely in view of the non-perceivability of time and the successiveness of perceptions in the subject (see 3:181.10–19). The broader systematic issues generated by the argument against empty space simply do not arise in this 1787 addition.

28. If the principles of the Analogies are mutually supporting (cf. the references to Paul Guyer and Kenneth Westphal in note 21 of the introduction and note 23 of this chapter), it makes no sense to say that any one of them has logical priority over the other two.

29. This view is nothing new, of course. Implicit in the passages previously cited from Schelling's *System des transzendentalen Idealismus* (notes 24 and 26) is a reading of the Analogies of Experience that assumes the systematic priority of the Third Analogy. According to Schelling, the categories of substance and causality are but abstract moments or *ideelle Faktoren* (*Werke*, II 478) with respect to the category of community or reciprocal action, and the transcendental principle that employs this concept of reciprocal action has an object domain which encompasses the domains of its two predecessors. Schelling thus grasps the Third Analogy as the culmination of the theory of objective experience articulated by all three of the Analogies. He also understands it to involve the sublation of the idea that nature can ultimately be understood as a system constituted by the interaction of many particular substances:

> We had first determined the object as substance and accidence. But it could not be intuited [*angeschaut*] as such without also being cause and effect. And in turn, it could not be intuited as cause and effect without the substances having been fixed. But where does substance begin, and where does it cease? A coexistence of all substances transforms all into *one*, which is caught up only in eternal reciprocal action with itself [*die nur in ewiger Wechselwirkung mit sich selbst begriffen ist*]. (495)

Cf. Anderson 1983, 486–487; Bauch 1917, 255–256; Paton 1936, II 324–325; Westphal 1995a, 66–69.

30. See 3:294.7–297.5.

31. See 3:348.29–349.36, 353.18–21, 356.8–19.

32. On the absolute reality of space (and time), see 3:61.12–32, 62.24–64.18, 297.8–299.1, 299.19–301.8.

33. Cf. 3:55.2–56.19.

34. See 3:299.19–301.8.

35. See also 3:151.35/152.33–35.

36. See 3:152.5–8.

37. See 3:152.9–10/31.

38. See 3:152.8–9/17–18. For further discussion of this point, see note 7 of the introduction.

39. See 3:152.18, 153.14–15, 153.24–154.1. For the concept of extensive magnitude, see 3:148.22–150.3.

40. See 3:152.3–4/8–9/22–24.

41. See 3:153.16–29, 155.32–35.

42. See 3:156.7–14.

43. See 3:155.32–156.1.

44. See 3:156.3–7.

45. Who would ever have thought that these mainly mathematically and mechanically orientated investigators of nature would base their inference purely and simply on a metaphysical presupposition that they so strongly purport to avoid? They do this inasmuch as they assume that the *real* in space (I may not here call it impenetrability or weight, because these are empirical concepts) is *everywhere uniform* and varies only according to extensive magnitude, i.e., in amount [*Menge*]. To this presupposition, for which they could find no ground in experience, and which is therefore purely metaphysical, I oppose a transcendental proof, a proof that indeed is not supposed to explain the difference in the filling of space, but that does completely cancel the presumed necessity of that presupposition, [which implies that] the difference in question cannot be explained otherwise than on the assumption of empty spaces. It is a proof that has the merit at least of putting the understanding at liberty to think the difference in some other way, should natural explanation concerning this make some other hypothesis necessary. For we then see that although equal [*gleiche*] spaces may be completely filled by different matters [*Materien*], so that there is in none of those spaces any point in which the presence of the matters is not encountered, nevertheless everything real [*jedes Reale*] has, while its quality remains the same, its degree (or resistance or weight), a degree which without diminution of its extensive magnitude or amount can be ever less *in infinitum* before it passes over into the void and vanishes. Thus, a radiation that fills a space, e.g., heat, and similarly every other reality (in the [field of] appearance), can, without in the least leaving the minutest part of this space empty, diminish in its gradations *in infinitum* and nonetheless fill the space with these lesser degrees just as well as another appearance does with greater degrees. My intention here is not at all to claim that things are really like this when it comes to the variety of matters according to their specific density. It is only to establish this from a principle of pure understanding: that the nature of our perceptions makes possible such a mode of explanation, and that one falsely assumes the real of appearance to be uniform [*gleich*] in degree and to differ only according to aggregation and the extensive magnitude thereof—particularly when one even alleges to assert this a priori by appealing to a principle of the understanding. (3:156.21–157.18)

46. See also 3:155.9–27.

47. Kant's presentation of the basic tenets of the corpuscular philosophy without directly mentioning its primary explanatory category—namely, the

"corpuscle"—is a rather remarkable feat in itself. For details on these assumptions, see § 1 of chapter 6.

48. For the dynamical definition of matter as something that fills space, see 4:496.6–9.

49. We should note here that if Kant's account of the real of sensation did not accomplish this, then the principle of the intensive magnitude of appearances could never serve as a basis for his metaphysical theory of matter, as Kant insists it must (see 4:523.5–32).

50. This is made fully explicit at 3:155.22–27.

51. See 3:152.25–153.10, 157.19–158.12.

52. For the identification of physical bodies as the objects of outer intuition, see especially 3:263.9–10, 307.3–9, and 4:233.7–10. But see also 3:24.21–42, 30.8–17, 34.16–35.13, 50.20–27, 66.20–26, 71.3–16, 106.25–28, 191.17–192.2, 192.7–193.6, 358.33–359.10; 4:225.16–22/30–32, 233.23–34, 234.14–20/21–29, 234.30–235.2, 238.35–239.13 (cf. 240.8–11), 242.13–30, 244.11–14/16–20, 245.23–27, 246.5–18/23–25, 248.35–249.1.

53. See 3:157.6.

54. On this, see chapter 7.

55. See 3:157.13.

56. In mentioning this part of the general doctrine of corporeal nature, I am not referring to what Kant at B213 (=3:155.26) calls general natural science (*allgemeine Naturwissenschaft*). Although this general science does presuppose something empirical (namely, the empirical concept of matter in general), its terrain is not determined by empirical principles as such (in this case, by the principles of the empirical part of physics). It is essentially an a priori science, and it thus forms part of the metaphysics of nature (see 4:294.32–295.23, 469.37–470.10).

57. Eric Watkins maintains that since "neither a void nor a causally inert body lying between two substances would contribute to the determination of a substance's place in time, the void/plenum issue is not directly relevant to the Third Analogy. (The Third Analogy could very well obtain for a Swiss cheese universe, one with voids interspaced throughout.) Accordingly, . . . , the Third Analogy could in principle allow for gaps between mutually interacting substances; rather other arguments in the *Critique of Pure Reason* (e.g., Anticipations of Perception) aim to exclude the possibility of a void" (Watkins 1997, 434). I certainly do not deny that other parts of the first *Critique* contain arguments against a void. But no textually well-founded analysis of the Third Analogy can plausibly ignore what Kant in fact has to say about the "void/plenum issue" in his argument against empty space. Moreover, Watkins's appeal to the possibility of a "Swiss cheese universe" is irrelevant to the philosophic point of this argument, and indeed to Kant's entire procedure of transcendental argumentation in the Analogies of Experience. For even if the universe is shot through with voids, we could, according to Kant, have no perceptual experience of them (or of the causally isolated mice that might exist in them). Thus, the principle of the dynamical community of substances could not obtain as a *transcendental* law of nature that specifies an a priori necessary condition for our knowledge of such a universe.

58. See 3:181.1–2.

59. My use of "filled" here is purely nontechnical. I am not pointing specifically to Kant's understanding of the filling of space in his dynamical theory of matter (see. e.g., 1:476.6−15, 480.1−3, 480.36−481.8, 483.31−484.12, 486.36−487.13; 4:496.6−9, 498.27−499.9, 502.11−13, 508.15−18, 511.20−26, 511.28−512.3, 512.17−515.36, 534.5−11, 563.19−24, 563.39−564.9; 14:145.4−12, 296.3−9). I therefore do not claim that Kant has in mind solely the efficacy of repulsive force when referring to influences in space.

60. Compare 3:135.16−14, 138.5−9.

61. Regarding the implications of this claim for Kant's doctrine of the transcendental schematism, see Edwards 1991, 86 n. 32.

62. Cf. 4:481.1−482.13, 556.18−25, 559.28−564.33.

63. This appeal lends itself to contrast with the corresponding procedures followed elsewhere in the Analytic of Principles. On this, see 3:148.22−149.14, 152.25−153.10, 157.19−158.12, 158.25−159.11, 159.34−160.9, 167.14−168.7, 170.4−18, 171.14−175.20 (especially 171.14−24, 173.24−33, 174.24−175.20), 180.12−20, 181.6−27, 186.25−190.21 (especially 186.25−187.4, 187.30−36, 189.35−190.4), 193.25−195.20, 197.25−198.2.

64. See 3:44.24−46.17, 49.6−51.13, 74.1−75.26, 78.22−34, 83.33−84.6, 94.9−14, 109.35−37, 218.27−219.16, 448.19−449.3; 8:404.12−21. Regarding the use of "formalism" in connection with the Kantian idea of transcendental philosophy, cf. 18:40.2−5.

65. In view of this task, see Pippin 1981.

66. For the methodological requirement of transcendental critique, see 3:43.16−44.17. For the concept of the transcendental aesthetic as the exposition of the formal conditions of sensibility, see, e.g., 3:50.1−51.13. For "function of the understanding": 3:86.4−31, 91.14−92.33; 4:82.35−83.8. For the relation of pure understanding to productive imagination and pure sensible forms: 3:111.4−14, 113.2−24, 116.34−117.32, 119.4−120.21, 140.9−16, 144.32−145.37; 4:82.35−83.19, 84.32−89.2 (especially 87.1−89.2).

67. See 3:145.30−37, 186.25−28, 424.4−11; 4:91.37−92.12.

68. See also 3:186.25−35, 190.8−16. For the definitional underpinnings of *Form einer möglichen Erfahrung*, see 3:144.33−144.3, 158.19−25; 4:83.29−32, 93.16−19.

69. 3:152.28−32, 473.10−12. See also 3:50.6−14, 104.6−12, 157.26−158.7, 161.9, 185.24−25, 188.1−2, 189.36−37.

70. 3:475.2−9.

71. 3:159.34−160.8/20−23. See also 3:189.23−190.1 (cf. 193.25−194.20).

72. Cf. 3:185.22−25.

73. For Kant's presentation of the idea of transcendental critique, see 3:43.16−44.2. For the procedure of a priori specification and deduction of conditions of possible experience, see 3:69.10−24, 102.24−32 and 104.21−105.12, 128.5−129.9, 144.32−145.37, 147.7−10, 185.2−11, 186.29−35, 188.6−11, 189.5−6, 474.26−475.35, 482.35−483.17. (See also 4:470.18−19; 18:43.2−5.)

74. Cf. 3:145.26−29; 4:81.14−15.

75. But these are conditions whose concepts would seem to obtain the character of their possibility (*den Charakter ihrer Möglichkeit*) both a priori *and* a posteriori (contrast 3:188.6−11).

76. The "light" that Kant in elucidation 1 supposes to act between world-bodies and the perceiving subject will not be discussed in this chapter. The information furnished by Kant in the first *Critique* and other writings published during his lifetime is simply too sketchy to allow us to determine definitively the significance of his employment of the concept of light in the Third Analogy at this point. In chapters 7 and 8, however, there will be occasion to discuss the notion of a *materia lucis* in connection with Kant's dynamical aether theory. In the meantime, see, e.g., 1:308.34–309.3, 377.16–18, 487.14–18; 14:287.2–291.4; 21:229.10–22, 469.4–10, 515.11–16, 565.3–15, 584.22–585.21.

77. 3:183.37–183.1.

78. 3:183.1–4. Regarding the interpretation and translation of this passage, see note 26 of chapter 1 above.

79. Cf., e.g., Nagel 1983, 202–204. I disagree, incidentally, on all essential points with what Nagel has to say about elucidation 2 in his chapter on the Third Analogy. The source of my disagreement is his treatment of the notion of "mediate community" (3:182.34–35). According to Nagel (200), substances are, in Kant's view, causally *separated* when there is no *direct* interaction between them. But this reading cannot be supported by anything that Kant ever wrote or is reported to have said about the mediate community of substances. (To show the extent of the misunderstanding involved, it would be necessary to discuss what Kant says about the problem of action at a distance in his reflections and lectures on metaphysics, as well as in his writings on the dynamical theory of matter. For a start, see the passages cited in note 76 above.) The correct treatment of the concept of mediate community is furnished in Paton 1936, II 318.

80. Cf. 4:534.5–16, 563.32–564.9; 14:295.5–7, 343,1–2, 334.1–336.6; 29(1) 82.1–30.

81. See 3:182.31–32 and 181.37–182.10.

82. Cf. Edwards 1991, 88. Eric Watkins criticizes me for not recognizing in this article the import of Kant's conditional claim that "*if* one is to have knowledge of coexistence, *then* one must experience mutual interaction" (Watkins 1997, 433 note). Watkins seems to accuse me of identifying this kind of claim, which concerns a transcendental condition, with the categorical (and directly ontological) claim that there is a dynamical field of substances in mutual interaction. But I do nothing of the sort. I argue, just as I do in this book, that Kant effectively makes the presence of a dynamical field (i.e., a universal continuum of influences) an a priori necessary condition for our experience of substances as coexistent objects in space. Since Watkins is not concerned to explicate systematically all dimensions of Third Analogy's proof, he evidently fails to understand the main point of my textual analysis of Kant's argument against empty space.

83. For considerations relevant to this investigation, see Barié 1951, 211–218; Dessoir 1910, 19 ff.; De Vleeschauwer 1934–37, I 299–310; Guyer, 1987, 25–70; Lüdtke 1911, 41–58; Tuschling 1984, 251–278; Westphal 1997, 139–189.

84. Besides the passages cited in note 13 above, see 3:137.34–37, 162.25–28, 164.25–28, 166.16–17, 359.7–12.

85. Regarding the identification of *Gegenstand* with *Erscheinung*, which is implicit in point 1, see 3:162.14–15, 168.8–169.16, 178.1–2, 204.13–14/35.

86. Cf. note 13 above.

87. See the passages cited under "perception" in note 15 of chapter 1 above.

88. There are four possible referents for *Dieses* at 3:183.24: (1) The process of reciprocal grounding by which the perceptions of individual substances make each other possible (183.19–21). (2) The capacity (grounded in the reciprocal determinability of perceptions resulting from that process) to represent objects/substances as coexistent (183.23). (3) The possible representation of objects/substances as coexistent (183.23). (4) Candidates 1–3 taken together, insofar as all three rest upon the function of the category as a pure a priori concept of reciprocal influence or real community (*commercium*) of substances (183.24–25). My own view is that the fourth alternative is the correct one. But the force of Kant's argument will not be affected by a decision in favor of any of the other three.

89. 3:113.6/11–12/19 (see also 3:109.16–19, 113.23; 4:81.23–28, 86.22–27, 87.20–22/32, 90.35). It is thus the type of unity of consciousness that is distinguished from the objective, transcendental unity of apperception (3:113.2–6/26–27) or original synthetic unity of self-consciousness (111.9/27–28). See also 3:109.3–4/35–36, 110.19/33–34, 114.7–9/11–16, 115.6/23, 118.15, 119.16–17/23, 129.27–28; 4:81.34–82.1, 82.4–10/13–16, 83.6/16–17, 84.18, 85.17–18/29–36, 87.14–19, 88.3–5/16/22–25, 90.19/28–30/35–36, 93.11–16, 94.23–28/34.

90. 3:183.14–18. *[D]iese subjective Gemeinschaft* might be construed as referring to a whole of coexistent objects taken independently of any relation to the cognitive faculty (*Gemüt*) and perceptual activity of the subject. But quite apart from the obvious inconsistency with the basic tenets of Kant's transcendental theory implicit in such a reading, it is contextually evident that the whole in question can only be the totality of objects, which *as appearances* must stand in a community of apperception.

91. Paton 1936, II 319.

92. Paton 1936, II 320.

93. Paton 1936, II 320.

94. See the passages cited in note 95 below.

95. See 3:110.11–23, 111.2–3/25–28; 4:87.8–19/32–40.

96. The concept of transcendental unity implicit in elucidation 2—the *commercium apperceptionis*, as it were—can be usefully explicated in connection with the concept of transcendental affinity that Kant treats in his first version of the Transcendental Deduction (see 4:85.8–28, 90.18–91.2). He maintains that all possible appearances belong to the numerically identical whole possible consciousness (*das ganze mögliche Bewußsein*[4:85.14–15]), and that this principle of possible consciousness establishes the transcendental affinity of appearances from which all empirical affinity derives. In other words (see 90.20–34), the transcendental affinity of appearances, which is the objective ground of all association of appearances, derives from a principle of synthetic unity; and this principle requires that all appearances must be apprehended in such a way (*müssen so ins Gemüt kommen*) that they concur (*zusammenstimmen*) in the unity of apperception—a unity that in turn is possible only on grounds of the necessary synthetic unity in the connection of all appearances. Hence, we can comprehend the concept of apperception at issue in the Third Analogy as a form of the whole possible consciousness, i.e., the all-encompassing pure

apperception (*allbefassende reine Apperzeption*—91.18), in which the affinity of appearances is anchored. And we can understand the affinity of appearances that corresponds to the Third Analogy's concept of apperception to be the type of affinity exhibited by the dynamical whole of reciprocally interacting, coexistent substances. What I have called the *commercium apperceptionis* thus refers to a mode of transcendental unity. It is the mode of transcendental unity that pre-supposes that substances, as appearances, must be apprehended in such a way as to concur in *that* unity of apperception that establishes the synthetic connection of appearances as a whole of reciprocally interacting substances. For a highly detailed discussion of Kant's account of transcendental affinity and its background, see Westphal 1997, 139–189. Westphal's analysis of Kant's account of transcendental affinity in the 1781 Transcendental Deduction supports my interpretation of elucidation 2.

97. Cf. Krausser 1981, 126–128.

98. See 3:184.26–27.

99. On this relationship between the unity of apperception and the synthesis functions of understanding and imagination, see 3:108.19–110.35, 111.4–15, 111.25–112.19, 116.18–26, 120.31–34; 4:80.21–81.2, 82.7–25, 82.35–83.19, 84.17–31, 87.8–88.11, 89.21–92.24.

Chapter 3:   Influence, Matter, and Force in the Transcendental Analytic and the Metaphysical Foundations of Mechanics

1. See 3:217.29–218.11, 222.33–223.24, 224.21–27, 228.1–229.13. Kant's criticism of Leibniz in the Amphibolies is based on the claim that Leibniz's intellectual system arises from the failure to distinguish between concepts pertaining to pure understanding and concepts pertaining to the sensibility (see 3:220.22–221.15, 226.20–227.5). The passages considered are concerned with the third pair of the concepts of reflection, the *Inner* and the *Outer*.

2. Cf. 3:117.18–20, 201.19–21; Reflections 5288, 5294.

3. 217.32–34, 218.1–2, 224.21–23, 228.20–21.

4. 3:222.33–223.24, 224.2–20, 228.1–20.

5. 3:217.31–34, 224.21–27, 228.20–23, 229.10–13.

6. 3:228.23, 229.12–13. It may be objected that it makes no sense for Kant to speak of relations as being independent and perduring when the proper subject is substance as perduring appearance, and when the substance in any appearance is the substrate of all change (cf. 3:162.21–24). The objection is entirely legitimate. The source of Kant's difficulty here lies in his insistence that force must be conceived in terms of the relation of substance to its accidental determinations even when his own non-monadological account of material substance shows this to be conceptually impossible. For a discussion of this issue, see above all § 3 of chapter 8.

7. 3:217.34–37.

8. 3:217.37–218.2.

9. 3:228.21–24. See also 4:248.37 and Reflections 5346, 5401, 5402, 6403.

10. See 3:45.13–21, 546.16–547.7.

11. See 4:469.26−470.12.

12. On the relationship between the two a priori laws of nature in question, see 4:548.13−14.

13. See 4:544.35−545.5.

14. See 4:476.7−12, 547.14−19, 548.13−16, 551.18−20.

15. 4:536.5−6.

16. My employment of "*a* matter" in connection with the mechanical definition of matter reflects directly Kant's use of *eine Materie* (4:536.9). This denotes an individuated material in space (i.e., a particular body or part of a body) that interacts mechanically with materials like it. This usage, however, is not limited to the systematic context of the Mechanics. Kant uses *eine Materie* and *Materien* (matters) in a quite general way when referring to material particulars located in space. Accordingly, he usually distinguishes between "a matter" (or "matters") and "matter." The latter term is normally reserved either for matter in general or, as we shall see, for the cosmic matter that furnishes the material plenum, or medium, for all reciprocal causal action between material particulars. Despite the stylistic awkwardness involved, it is essential that translation should distinguish precisely between *a* matter and matter.

17. J. W. Ellington's 1985 translation of the passage (4:536.9−15) ignores the distinction between the (derivative) mechanical communication of motion and the (original) dynamical impartation of motion by means of repulsive and attractive force. Capturing this distinction is crucial, since it is the foundation for Kant's entire theory of mechanics as a special metaphysical discipline separate from the dynamics of material nature.

18. For a treatment of the Dynamics of 1786, see, § 6 of chapter 7.

19. See also 4:536.15−537.4, 547.7−40, 551.18−20.

20. See 545.5−547.6. The classic discussion of the underlying issues is provided by Vuillemin 1955, 300−320. See also Carrier 1993, 404−409.

21. What Kant says here about the communication of motion on the basis of repulsion applies also, *mutatis mutandis,* to attraction. See 4:537.4−10, 546.14−19, 551.18−20.

22. That would be to violate the status of mechanics as a distinct metaphysical discipline; and it is in any event supposed to be excluded by Kant's treatment of the quantity of matter and the mechanical concept of mass (see 4:537.11−26, 539.29−541.26). For discussion of the difficulties Kant faces in this treatment, see the literature cited in note 64 of chapter 7 below.

23. See jointly 4:469.26−470.12 and 551.8−14.

24. Note well, however, that the force of the objection is already substantially weakened by the recognition that elucidation 1 contains merely the explication of what is deduced strictly a priori in core argument 2. Elucidation 1 is *essentially* an elaboration of the first argument against empty space, and its contents are thus analytically linked to the propositions of that argument. Kant is engaged in *dilucidatio,* not *usus* (cf. 1:413.21−416.4). There are thus purely formal grounds for rejecting the supposition that Kant's second formulation of the argument against empty space is *primarily* concerned merely with exemplifying the application of a category to empirically determinate features of the phenomenal world.

25. 3:207.13−14.

26. In the first version of the Paralogisms of Pure Reason, Kant claims that "it is indeed very evident that what I must presuppose in order to know an object at all is not something that I could know as an object" (4:250.34–36). For a criticism of Henry Allison's (1983, 110) handling of the issues here involved, see Edwards 1991, 93 n. 58.

27. See, e.g., Strawson 1966, 140.

28. See 3:43.16–27, 190.24–193.4, 338.21–339.3; 4:232.1–235.22, 238.12–17, 240.25–242.30, 243.24–245.14, 337.29–31.

Chapter 4:   Substance and Substantial Force in Leibniz and Wolff

1. For Leibniz's criticism of Descartes, Malebranche, and Spinoza, see GP I 139–148; II 93–94, 232–234, 239–241, 257–259; IV 364–365; VI 350–351, 581–584. For the idea of the infinite multitude of simple substances, see GP II 49, 51, 74–75, 98, 113, 221, 227, 239, 257, 263–264, 270, 276, 278; IV 364, 432–433, 440–441; VI 598–599, 607, 616. For the infinite variety and manifoldness of substantial attributes: GP II 239 (see also GP II 220–227, 239–241, 249; GM III 521–522). For the principles of perfection and plentitude: GP II 51, 98, 115, 126–127, 239; III 635–636; IV 430–433; VI 598–599, 603–604, 615–616.

2. See GP II 95–96, 267–268, 277–278; III 623, 635–636; VI 598–599, 607–609.

3. For Leibniz's concepts of expression, reflection, and representation, see GP II 51, 57, 74–75, 90, 98, 112–113, 135–136, 263; IV 433–434; 439–440; VI 599, 616. For the idea of continual creation, see GP II 168, 264; IV 439–440.

4. Cf. Broad 1975, 45; Westphal 1995a, 58–61, 65–66, 72–73.

5. GP IV 510.

6. See GP II 93, 135–136, 251, 256–257, 264, 271, 278; IV 439–441, 470, 484–486, 510; VI 598, 607–609, 615.

7. See GP II 252, 278, 553; IV 607.

8. GP II 75.

9. GP II 75. Leibniz is discussing in this instance the mind/body relation, but what he says applies to individual substances generally.

10. See GP II 503.

11. For the classical definition of substance, see Aristotle, *Categoriae* 4b10, 8b15, and *Metaphysica* 1028b33–1029a3, 1038b2–3. (Cf. Wolff, *Ont.* § 771 and *Dt. Met.* § 114; Baumgarten, *Metaphysica* § 191.) Regarding the "isolationist" tendency of Cartesian and Spinozistic rationalism, it is not an exaggeration to say that the seventeenth-century problem of the communication of substances is inherent in the merely negative tenor of Descartes's and Spinoza's definitions of substance:

> By substance we can understand nothing other than a thing that exists in such a way as to require no other thing in order to exist. (*Principia philosophiae* I § 51)
> By substance I understand that which is in itself and is conceived through itself; that is, the concept of which does not require the concept of another thing from which it has to be formed. (*Ethica* I Def. 3)

Leibniz, of course, takes issue with both of these (see GP I 139; IV 364).

12.

> for it follows that every individual substance expresses the entire universe in its own way and in a certain relationship, or, so to speak, according to the point of view from which it regards the universe; and it follows also that its subsequent state is the result . . . of its preceding state, as if there were only God and itself in the world. Thus, each individual substance or complete being is as a world apart, independent of every other thing but God. . . . But this independence does not impede the community [*le commerce*] of substances with each other; for since all created substances are a continual production of the same sovereign being according to the same designs, and since they express the same universe or the same phenomena, they correspond with one another [*s'entraccordent*] exactly. This leads us to say that the one acts upon the other, because the one expresses more distinctly than the other the cause or ground of changes. . . . It is thus, in my opinion, that one must understand the community of created substances with each other, and not in terms of a real physical influence or real physical dependency. (GP II 57)

For Leibniz's further consideration of the positions expressed in this passage, see GP II 74, 136, 168, 264; IV 439–440, 470, 468–487; VI 598, 608–609, 615–616.

13. In particular, it is a principle modeled on the notions of perception and appetition. See e.g., GP II 263, 270–271, 281–282 (not.); IV 509; VI 598, 609, 615.

14. Regarding the relationship between substantial force and Leibniz's principle of action, see GP II 170–171, 184, 248–249, 251, 270, 319, 503; IV 394–397, 469 470, 486–487, 509, 511–512. For the finitude of human knowledge and the limited cognitive perspective of the rational soul, see GP V 46–51, 141–142; VI 178–179, 356–357, 599–600, 603–604, 617–618. See also GP II 324–325; III 623, IV 470.

15. For Leibniz's concept of dynamics, see GP IV 394, 398, 469, 486, 503; GM VI 104, 195, 287. Treatments of this concept in relation to its seventeenth-century context are provided by Dosch et al. 1982, 90–92 and, classically, by Guèroult 1934, 56–109.

16.

> The author concludes the second part, i.e., the general part dealing with the principles of material things, with an observation that seems to me in need of some restriction. He says, namely, that for the explanation of the phenomena of nature no principles are necessary other than those derived from abstract mathematics, or from the doctrine of magnitude, figure, and motion; nor does he acknowledge any matter other than that which is the subject of geometry. I do, indeed, fully agree that all the particular phenomena of nature can, if sufficiently explored by us, be explained mechanically and that the causes of material things cannot be understood on any other basis. But I hold, nevertheless, that this too must be considered: that the mechanical principles, and so the general laws of nature, themselves arise from higher principles and cannot be explained through the consideration of quantity and geometrical matters alone; that there is rather something metaphysical in them, which is independent of the concepts that the imagination supplies and which must be referred to a substance lacking extension. For besides extension and its manifold determinations, there is in matter a force or power to act that brings about the transition from metaphysics to nature, from material to immaterial things. This force has its own laws derived from the principles not merely of absolute and, so to speak, brute necessity, as in mathematics, but from those of perfect reason.

Once these matters have been established in a general treatment, one can after-wards, when accounting for the ground of natural phenomena, develop everything mechanically. (GP IV 390–391)

17. Cf. GP VI 501–505. Cf. also GP IV 422–424, 449–450.

18. For principles of perfect reason as eternal truths present in the divine in-tellect, see, e.g., GP II 48–51; IV 422–424, 427 428, 451–453; VI 600–601, 603, 615. For mathematical principles in the narrower sense, see GP III 58; IV 394–395, 568–569; VI 505, 588–589; VII 355–356, 363.

19. The full paragraph translates as follows:

> We pointed out elsewhere that in corporeal things there is something besides ex-tension, indeed, something prior to extension, namely, that force of nature introduced everywhere by the Creator. This force does not consist in a simple faculty, with which the Schools seem to have been content, but is further provided with an endeavor or striving [*connatus seu nisus*] that would have its full effect unless impeded by a con-trary striving. This striving presents itself everywhere to the senses and, in my judg-ment, is understood by reason to be everywhere in matter, even where it is not re-vealed to sense. But if this may not already be ascribed to God acting through a miracle, then it is certainly necessary that the force should be produced by Him in the bodies themselves; indeed, that it should constitute the innermost nature of bodies, since to act is the mark of substances, and since extension means nothing but the con-tinuity or diffusion of presupposed striving and counterstriving, i.e., resistance of a substance. Extension is thus far removed from being able to constitute the nature of substance itself. Nor does it matter that every corporeal action derives from motion and that motion itself comes from motion already existing beforehand in a body or impressed from without. For if one judges the matter exactly, motion (and likewise time) never exists, since the whole, not having coexistent parts, never exists. And to that extent, there is nothing real in it except for that momentary something [*momen-taneum illud*] which must consist in a force striving towards change. Whatever there is in corporeal nature besides the object of geometry or extension reduces to this. And finally, by this reasoning both the truths and the teachings of the ancients are given proper consideration. Just as our age has already rescued from disdain *Democritus's* corpuscles, *Plato's* Ideas, and the *Stoics'* tranquillity in light of the best possible inter-connection of things, so now the teaching of the *Peripatetics* concerning Forms or En-telechies (which deservedly were regarded as enigmatic, and were scarcely grasped in a proper manner by their own authors) will be summoned back to intelligible con-cepts. Thus, rather than discard this philosophy, which was accepted for so many cen-turies, we think it is necessary to explain it so that it can stand firmly (where this is pos-sible), and, further, to illuminate it and augment it with new truths. (GM VI 235)

See also GP IV 471–472, 478–479 for parallel considerations.

20. Like Leibniz's doctrine of force, the Scholastic doctrine of *potentia,* which includes the metaphysical concepts of *potentia nuda* (or *passiva*), *poten-tia activa,* and *actio,* derives from Aristotle's treatments of *dynamis, energeia,* and *entelecheia.* For a presentation of the Scholastic doctrine, see Thomas Aquinas, *Quaestiones disputatae de potentia,* q.1, a.1, resp. and *Summa theolo-gica,* I, q.xxv, a.1, ad.1.

21. Leibniz's conception of *conatus* should be carefully distinguished not only from the Scholastic interpretation of *potentia* but also from any merely phoronomic interpretation of *conatus,* such as that furnished by Hobbes in chapter 15 of *De corpore.*

22. See Aristotle, *De anima* 412a6–412b2.

23. See GP IV 477–486 (especially 477–479). For classic portrayals of the inertness of matter and the extraneousness of communicated motion, see Descartes, *Principia philosophiae* II §§ 36 (cf. Leibniz, GP IV 442–444), 37, 43. The Leibnizian criticism of inert matter and externally communicated motion applies, incidentally, not only to the Cartesian view of matter as extension, but to all corpuscular accounts of matter (see, e.g., GP II 78, 118; IV 473, 482). There will be more to say regarding this point in § 2 of chapter 6.

24. See, e.g., GP II 268; III 638.

25. See GP II 169–170, 248–252, 324–325; IV 470, 511, 512. Notice in these passages the irreducible factor of matter-form dualism in Leibniz's conception of the force of finite substances. Strictly speaking, the Leibnizian designation of force as *actus purus* applies only to God.

26. Leibniz also characterizes this as *vis substantialis, entelechia seu forma, entelechia primitiva, proton detikon activitatis, vis motrix primitiva, activum primitivum seu substantiale,* and as that which constitutes *lex seriai mutationum.*

27. Also: *materia prima, materia primitiva seu potentia passiva primitiva, principium passiva.*

28. Also: *vis actrix accidentale seu mutabile.*

29. Also: *materia secunda.*

30. The preceding presentation of Leibniz's account of active and passive force is based on the following textual sources: GP II 170–171, 184, 224–225, 241, 248–252, 269–270, 311, 324–325, 375; IV 394–398, 469–470, 511–512. GM VI 236–237.

31. GM VI 237. Dosch et al. 1982, comment extensively on the laws of action addressed in this passage. They maintain that the testing of these laws through perceptual experience shows them to be true "only insofar as they are useful hypotheses for the explanation of phenomena" (107). The laws of action that are, as Leibniz says, "confirmed by sense itself" are thus not a priori truths. This interpretation is acceptable on two conditions: (1) We do not presuppose an account of truth that is inconsistent with Leibniz's theory of judgment. (According to this theory, all true propositions are actually or virtually analytic, and are therefore at least potentially knowable as a priori truths.) (2) We bear in mind that those laws of action, being in principle analyzable in terms of universally harmonious monadic activity, must ultimately be conceivable under the heading of a priori truth. (This is, after all, the whole point of Leibniz's metaphysical analysis of substantial force as it relates to his assertion that the laws of action are understood through *reason.*) For discussions of Leibniz's conception of a priori truth, see Beck 1978, 85–88 and Parkinson 1966, 62–69.

32. Cf. Gurwitch 1974, 352–363, 386–397, 411–424.

33. See GP II 169–170; IV 394–395, 397–398, 444, 469–470. GM VI 236–237.

34. For Wolff's conception of composite physical bodies, see *Cos. gen.* §§ 176–178. (See also *Dt. Met.* §§ 75–80 and *Ont.* §§ 673, 794, 870–873.) For his concept of the physical world, see *Cos. gen.* §§ 48–58 and *Dt. Met.* §§ 540–557. For his terminological exploitation of the principle of universal harmony, see *Cos. gen.* §§ 197–214 (especially §§ 211–214).

35. For the distinction between dynamical and mechanical principles, see *Cos. gen.* §§ 75, 127–128; *Dt. Met.* §§ 607, 614, 616, 623–624, 696–697, 699–700; *Ont.* § 761. For the distinction between *vis activa* and *vis passiva*, see *Cos. gen.* §§ 129–149; *Ont.* § 761. For the critique of Cartesian corporeal substance, the appropriation of Aristotelian substantial force, and the criticism of Scholastic potentia: *Cos. gen.* §§ 142–149; *Dt. Met.* § 117; *Ont.* §§ 716–730, 761.

36. See *Cos. gen.* § 358–365.

37. For Wolff's dogmatic conception of transcendental cosmology, see *Cos. gen.*, pp. 10–14 (*Praefatio*) and §§ 1–9. See also *Dt. Met.* § 541.

38. For Wolff's conception of *substantia simplex,* see *Cos. gen.* § 182 and *Ont.* § 794.

39. See above all *Cos. gen.*, p. 14 (*Praefatio*) and § 142 Remark, § 243 Remark, § 294 Remark. See also *Ont.* § 684 and *Dt. Met.* §§ 595–601.

40. I modernize the spelling of the shortened title of *Vernünfftige Gedancken von Gott, der Welt und der Seele des Menschen, Auch allen Dingen überhaupt.* As is reflected in my endnote citations, this book is commonly referred to as *Deutsche Metaphysik* in order to distinguish it from other works by Wolff that have titles beginning with *Vernünfftige Gedanken*. The 1751 edition of Wolff's text is used by Charles Corr for his 1983 edition, which bears the title *Vernünftige Gedanken* (2), (*Deutsche Metaphysik*).

41. See *Dt. Met.* §§ 75–112, 114.

42. See *Dt. Met.* §§ 115–116. For related considerations on the concept of force at issue, see *Ont.* §§ 722–724, 869–871.

43. The dynamical concept of substance that Wolff employs in *Dt. Met.* (§§ 115–116) contrasts with the non-dynamical concept put forward in his *Ontologia* (see §§ 771, 871). Mariano Campo (1939, 187–188) criticizes the inconsistency involved, which adversely affects Wolff's entire philosophic system.

44. This volume, first published in 1724, was written with reference to the original 1720 edition of the *Dt. Met.*

45.

> Some have assumed I have granted the monads of Mr. Leibniz to be the elements of things, elements having the properties of Leibniz's unities or monads. However, we already see here that this does not at all follow, and I shall presently be able to explain myself in this matter. . . . I have here disclosed my thoughts about Mr. Leibniz's monads and have shown that they have in themselves the universal properties of simple things, and that a force attributable to simple things is ascribed to them. . . . But despite this, I have not been able to decide whether or not to approve of his doctrine of monads. By virtue of what I have demonstrated regarding the universal properties, I do recognize, of course, that the simple things in general—and hence the elements as well—must have a force that continually produces something changeable, and that, moreover, does so in such a manner that the difference of the state of each from all the others is clearly shown. Yet I see no necessity why all simple things should have one and the same kind of force.

46. In one passage (see *Dt. Met.* § 753), Wolff asserts that the representational function of substance can, strictly speaking, be ascribed only to the soul.

47. These sections are from chapter 4 of the *Vernünftige Gedanken*, which corresponds to the entire *Cosmologia generalis* as published in the Latin works.

48. See *Cos. gen.* §§ 183–186, 188, 196, 223.

49. See *Cos. gen.*, pp. 10–14 (*Praefatio*) and §§ 1–4, 7–8, 196–214; *Dt. Met.* §§ 594–598. (The cognitive limitations expressed in these passages are not supposed to apply to the full-fledged natural theological grounding of the universal connection of substances. On this, see *Cos. gen.*, pp. 9–10 (*Praefatio*) and § 204 (with Remark); *Dt. Met.* §§ 928–930, 940, 945, 975, 1037, 1053–1055; *Theol. nat.* I §§ 50–66, II §§ 315–323.)

50. For *unitates arithmeticae* (= *puncta Zenonica*), see *Cos. gen.* §§ 215–218.

51. This point is made by Jean École in his introduction to the 1966 edition of the *Cosmologia generalis* (see p. XXIX).

52. See *Cos. gen.* §§ 167, 176–181, 196–197, 295–301, 365; *Dt. Met.* § 594; *Ont.* § 794.

53. See *Cos. gen.* §§ 167–169, 294 Remark, 295–301.

54. See *Cos. gen.* §§ 75, 127–132, 135–138, 140–149; *Dt. Met.* §§ 614–627.

55. See *Cos. gen.* §§ 358–365.

56. The *Elementa mechanicae* are found in the second book of the *Elementa matheseos universae* (pp. 1–316).

57. See *Cos. gen.* § 303 and Remark.

Chapter 5: Dynamical Community, Physical Influence, and Universal Harmony in the Development of Kant's Metaphysics

1. For analyses of these proposals, see Adickes 1924–25, I 65–144; Polonoff 1973, 5–62; Vuillemin 1955, 198–246. For historical background on the *vis viva* controversy, see Wolff 1978, 290–312.

2. The ontological independence of particular substances has some obvious implications for the metaphysical concept of "world." In the *Essay* of 1746, world is defined as a composite entity consisting of the sum-total of self-subsistent substantial individuals. Given the independence of substance, a thing may well *exist* but not be *present* in the world. The same holds true of collections of substances: if such a collection stands in no relation to our world, but nevertheless encompasses the complex of the relations of the entities composing it, then it must constitute a particular whole, which is to say, a world for itself. Accordingly, it is possible that many worlds have in fact been created, although their existence must remain undecided:

> One cannot say that something is a part of a whole if it stands in no connection [*Verbindung*] with the remaining parts (for otherwise there would be no discernible difference between a real and an imaginary whole), but the world is a really composite entity. Consequently, a substance connected with no thing in the entire world will not at all belong to the world, unless perhaps in one's thoughts. That is to say, it will be no part of the world. If there are many such entities that stand in no connection [*Verknüpfung*] but that have a relation to one another, then there arises from this an entirely particular whole; they constitute an entirely particular world. Hence, one does not speak correctly when in the lecture halls of metaphysics [*Weltwissenschaft*] one always teaches that there could not, in the metaphysical sense, exist more than a single world. It is, in the properly metaphysical sense, really possible that God may have created many millions of worlds; therefore, it remains undecided whether they really exist or not. (1:22.15–32)

Cf. Wolff, *Cos. gen.* §§ 48, 60–61 and *Dt. Met.* §§ 548–550; Baumgarten, *Metaphysica* § 379.

3. I am indebted to Karl Vogel (1975, 125–126) for the characterization of Kant's earlier notion of substance as "isolationist." I use this characterization to bring out the differences between Kant and Leibniz. Note, however, that the characterization conflicts with the assessment of Leibniz's doctrine of substance that Kant himself gives during the 1790s. In his *Preisschrift über die Fortschritte der Metaphysik* (see 20:283.37–284.13), Kant maintains that Leibnizian substance is a completely isolated entity. I do not agree with the assessment, but nothing essential hinges on this point as far as the interpretation of Kant's precritical conception of dynamical community is concerned.

4. For the relationship between the principle of harmony and the problem of "other worlds" in Leibniz, see, e.g., GP VI 107–108, 603.

5. Michael Friedman (1992a, 5) maintains that

> Kant attempts to revise the Leibnizean-Monadology in light of Newtonian physics. . . . Kant breaks away decisively from the Leibnizean-Wolffian conception of active force and interaction. The primary notion of active force is not that of an internal principle by which a substance determines the evolution of its own states, it is rather that of an action exerted by one substance on another substance whereby the first changes the inner state of the second (§ 4: 1,19). Kant has thus imported Newton's second law of motion into the very heart of the monadology.

First of all, as my considerations in this section show, Kant's relation to Leibniz's and Wolff's (quite distinct) conceptions of active force is necessarily a great deal more complex than Friedman seems to be aware of. Second: apart from the fact that Kant does not expressly declare his allegiance to any monadological theory of substance in the *Essay* of 1746, I can find no textual justification for Friedman's claim about the presence of Newton's law. What Kant says in the passage in question is, of course, not inconsistent with Newton's law, even if Newton is not concerned with changes in the internal states of substances. Perhaps Kant did have it in mind when considering the implications of his critical appropriation of Leibnizian active force. (If he did, however, his employment of the Leibnizian concept in the metaphysical foundations of his rational mechanics would have required him to have reservations about the ontological underpinnings of Newton's law. On this, see Kant's rejection of Wolff's *vis motrix* in 1:17.9–24 and the references to Wolff's *Cosmologia generalis* and *Ontologia* in note 6 below, especially the references to Wolff's *Cosmologia generalis*. See also Watkins 1995, 309–315.) In any event, as the first strategic move in his endeavor to set up a (true) "Newtonian" Kant in opposition to a (false) "Leibnizian" Kant, Friedman's Newtonian importation is here of dubious success. I argue below (see in particular note 40 of chapter 8) that Friedman's general endeavor is historically unwarranted and conceptually misguided.

6. See *Cos. gen.* §§ 127–138 (especially 136–137). Cf. *Ont.* §§ 721–744, 761, 771 Remark, 776–777, 794 Remark.

7. Kant's criticism is perhaps not entirely fair. On at least one occasion Leibniz himself identifies *vis activa* with *vis motrix* (see GP IV 511).

8. Cf. Leibniz GP VII 363–364, 372–377, 395–403, 406, 415; Wolff, *Cos. gen.* §§ 46, 52, 134 and *Ont.* §§ 589–590; Baumgarten, *Metaphysica* § 239.

9. See 1:24.12–18.

10. 1:24.11–12.

11. See 1:24.12–18.

12. See 1:24.21–30.

13. See 1:20.12–21.3.

14. Regarding these difficulties, see *Dt. Met.* §§ 763–764 (cf. Baumgarten, *Metaphysica* §§ 761–769), and *Psych. rat.* §§ 573–578.

15. Cf. 2:320.12–321.38, 413.31–414.15. Cf. also Baumgarten, *Metaphysica* §§ 741, 751–752.

16. Cf. Knutzen, *Systema causarum* §§ 20–32, 40–45.

17. 1:24.31–33. On Kant's speculative concern to derive the tri-dimensionality of space from the Newtonian inverse-square law and on his remark about "the highest geometry that a finite understanding could undertake" (1:24.33–34), see Vuillemin 1955, 233–235. See also Friedman 1992a, 5, 25–26.

18. For a discussion of the systematic role played by Proposition 13 in the *Nova dilucidatio,* see Campo 1953, 93–105.

19.

> *Demonstration.* Individual substances, of which none is the cause of the existence of another, have a separate existence, i.e., an existence that can be completely understood without all the others. If, therefore, the existence of any substance whatever is simply posited, there is nothing within it that establishes the existence of others distinct from it. But since a relation is a relative determination, i.e., one that is not intelligible in a substance considered absolutely, it follows that neither it nor its determining ground can be understood through a substance's existence as something posited in itself. If, therefore, nothing further than this were admitted, then there would be no relation between all substances, and hence no community [*commercium*] at all between them. Since, therefore, insofar as individual substances have an existence independent of each other, no reciprocal connection between them takes place; but since it certainly does not fall upon finite things to be the causes of other substances, and since all things in the universe are nonetheless encountered as combined in reciprocal connection— [since all this is true,] it must be confessed that this relation depends on a commonality of cause, namely, on God as the universal principle of existents. But from the fact that God simply established their existence, it does not follow that there is also a reciprocal relation between them, unless the very same scheme that gives existence also established their relations insofar as it conceives of their existences as correlated with each other. From this, it is most clearly apparent that the universal community of all things must be attributed to the concept alone of the divine understanding. (1:413.3–20)

20. Regarding the term *commercium substantiarum,* cf. Baumgarten, *Metaphysica* §§ 448–463. Kant's description of the activity of the divine intellect (in terms of *actus perdurabilis* and *conservatio*) is found at 1:414.1–8.

21. It is with respect to this third factor that we must understand Kant's claim to be the first to have demonstrated that coexistence alone does not suffice to establish the reciprocal connection of substances (see 1:413.22–25). This is not the place to discuss the legitimacy of this claim in relation to the entire "Leibniz-Wolff School," but it is interesting to contrast Kant's considerations on the universal dynamical community of substances with the treatment of universal harmony in Wolff's transcendental cosmology (see *Cos. gen.* §§ 206–214 and *Dt. Met.* §§ 594–600). Assuming the principle of sufficient reason, Wolff

does seem to maintain that reciprocal connection is given with the sheer fact of substances' coexistence.

22. See 1:413.22–414.8.

23. See 1:414.10–13.

24. It is on the basis of his metaphysical voluntarism that Kant deduces the possibility of other worlds (1:414.21–26) along lines virtually identical to those in the *Essay on Living Forces*. See note 2 above.

25. See 1:414.5–8.

26. See the formulation, proof and elucidation of *principium successionis* (Proposition 13).

27. Kant points out that Leibniz's interpretation involves the mere consensus of substances, not their mutual dependency (*proprie consensum, non dependentiam mutuum substantiis indicit* [1:415.25–26]). For related reasons, he also rejects the occasionalist account of community (*commercium substantiarum per causas occasionales Malebranchi* [415.29]).

28.

> I. *Matter* (in the transcendental sense), i.e., the *parts,* which are here taken to be *substances.* We were able to remain wholly unconcerned about the agreement of our definition with the common meaning of the expression, for the only question it raises concerns a problem that arises in accordance with laws of reason, namely, how is it possible for many substances to coalesce into one, and upon what conditions it depends that this one thing is not a part of something else. But indeed, the force of the expression "world," as it is frequently found in common usage, comes to the mind of its own accord. For no one consigns *accidents* to a *world* as its *parts,* but only to its *state* as *determinations.* Hence, the so-called *egoistic* world, which is completely composed of a unique simple substance with its accidents, is not properly called a world, except, perhaps, an imaginary one. For the same reason, one may not attribute to the world as a whole the series of sequents [*series successivorum*] (namely, the series of successive states) as part of it. For modifications are *not parts* of a subject, but are rather something *determined by a ground* [*rationata*]. Finally, I have not put to the test the nature of substances that constitute the world, whether, namely, they are *contingent* or necessary. Nor do I gratuitously stash away such a determination in the definition in order subsequently, as customarily happens, to draw out of it the very same determination by some imposing method of sophistical argumentation. But I shall later show that the contingency of the substances constituting the world can be fully established from the conditions here posited. (2:389.23–390.4)

29. The mention of *mundus egoisticus* (2:389.31) is a direct reference to Spinoza. On this, see Reflections 3803, 5394 and 28(1):206.30–207.1 (cf. Wolff, *Psych. rat.* § 38; Baumgarten, *Metaphysica* §§ 392–393, 395, 438.) A thorough discussion of the underlying issues is provided by De Flaviis 1986, 46–50.

30. For the problem of the succession of states of the world, see Reflections 3905, 4086, 4203–4204, 4326 and 28(1):195.24–30. Cf. Baumgarten, *Metaphysica* §§ 369, 374.

31. See 2:390.5–391.9.

32. See 2:390.15–18.

33. On the distinction between "essence" and "state" of the world, cf. Wolff, *Cos. gen.* § 59 and *Ont.* §§ 143, 168, 705; Baumgarten, *Metaphysica* §§ 40, 226, 369, 467.

34. Cf. Reflections 4047–4048, 4086, 4165, 4169.

35. The question of *essential* form (2:390.26) pertains to *mundus intelligibilis,* not to *mundus sensibilis.* Kant establishes this in Section III, § 13, as follows: The principle of the form of the sensible world is that which contains "the ground of the connection of all things insofar as they are phenomena" (2:398.14–15). Insofar as the world is regarded as phenomenal, which is to say, regarded "in relation to the sensibility of the human mind" (398.17–17), it can have nothing more than a merely subjective principle of form, i.e., "a certain law of the mind by which it is necessary that all the things that can be objects of the senses are seen *necessarily* to pertain to the same whole" (398.19–21). Thus, only the form of the intelligible world can supply the objective ground of connection between finite self-subsistent entities—namely, "the cause by which there is a colligation of things existing in themselves" (398.15–16). (Cf. 2:390.26–391.9; 406.26–407.14.)

36. See 2:407.15–409.25.

37. Cf. Reflection 3907; Wolff, *Cos. gen.* § 90 and *Theol. nat.* § 62; Baumgarten, *Metaphysica* §§ 375, 388, 855.

38. Cf. 1:415.32–416.4 and 2:407.23–30.

39. It is also opposed to at least one of Wolff's different conceptions of substance. See, e.g., *Cos. gen.* §§ 182, 196–214 and *Dt. Met.* §§ 597–602.

40. See above all 28(1):51.18–5315; 28(2):564.6–565.28, 845.12–847.17; 29:822.34–825.19.

41. On this, see 2:394.7–11/25, 395.19–25 (cf. Reflection 4385), 407.5–10.

42. See 2:393.13–19, 394.15–28, 407.5–10.

43. See above all 2:393.29–394.13 and 395.16–26, but also 395.28–31 and 410.20–412.19 (especially 411.21–31).

44. By "achievement" of the concept of dynamical community, I refer to the result of Kant's analysis of "world" in Section I, § 2 (2:289.23–390.26). This should be kept separate from the notion of the "acquisition" of intellectual concepts that underlies Kant's non-empiricist account of concept acquisition in Section II, § 8 (395.19–26).

45. Besides 2:409.22–23, see 407.23–30.

46. Kant was well aware of these difficulties, as can be gathered from the concluding sentence of Section IV (§ 22): "For me, indeed, although the first has not been demonstrated, it has nonetheless been shown to be fully acceptable for other reasons." "First" refers here to "universal dynamical community of substances through physical influence" and to "world" regarded as a "real whole" (2:409.22–23). For the possible "other reasons" alluded to, see § 2 of chapter 9, where the Scholium immediately following the passage just quoted (see 409.26–410.16) is treated in conjunction with Reflection 3986.

Chapter 6: Corpuscular and Dynamical Theories of Matter in Seventeenth- and Eighteenth-Century Natural Philosophy

1. Standard accounts of this connection are given by Boas 1952, 412 ff.; Laßwitz 1963, 3–8; Van Melsen 1957, 127–181.

2. Capek 1962, 79.

3. The relationship between modern atomism (or corpuscularianism) and early nineteenth-century chemical theories is discussed by Toulmin and Goodfield 1982, 229–269.

4. Capek 1962, 33.

5. Some seventeenth-century corpuscular theories that conform to my definition are, strictly speaking, based on non-corpuscular concepts of matter. The classic case in point is Descartes. Rejecting any explicitly atomistic conception of physical reality such as that advocated by Gassendi (see *Animadversiones,* II 374–390), Descartes constructed a theory of nature that, in identifying matter with extension (see *Principia philosophiae,* II §§ 4, 9–11, 20, 22), seems to exclude the employment of the corpuscular concept. But Descartes's basic view of matter did not keep him from assuming that local motion divides matter into particles (mathematically, though not physically, divisible *in infinitum*), and then proceeding to explicate systematically the world in terms of particulate matter and motion (see, e.g., *Principia philosophiae,* II §§ 20, 34–35; III §§ 48–50, 52). I maintain that since Descartes's system of the physical world is constructed in terms of particulate matter and motion, it involves his de facto acceptance of the corpuscular concept. I therefore maintain as well that his general approach to natural philosophy may be classified as corpuscular. These assumptions are in keeping with Robert Boyle's pragmatic criteria for defining what qualifies as a corpuscular approach (see Boyle, *Works,* I 354–356).

6. Cf. Harré 1972, 88. I am especially indebted to Harré for the interpretive framework constructed in this chapter.

7. For an explicit statement of these principles, see Boyle, *Works,* III 37–38.

8. Aristotelianism, which dominated Western natural philosophy from late antiquity to well into the seventeenth century, presented the opponent against which the corpuscular philosophy was defined. Standard treatments of the relationship between Aristotelianism and the establishment of the corpuscular philosophy are provided by Laßwitz 1890/1963, I 263–518 and Van Melsen 1957, 48–126. See also Maier 1949, 1–6.

9. Cf. Lerclerc 1972, 115–121.

10. "Self-subsistent" does not here mean self-sufficient or self-caused. Most all seventeenth-century corpuscular theorists presupposed the dependence of material substance on God as the creator and principle of the conservation of the material world.

11. Cf. Leclerc 1972, 140.

12. Cf. Boyle, *Works,* I 37.

13. Cf. Harré 1964, 63; McGuire 1974, 128; McMullin 1978, 32. (I am indebted to these authors for much of the terminology used in this section.) For the seventeenth-century conception of dispositions, see Boyle, *Works,* III 47–48; Descartes, *Principia philosophiae,* §§ 118, 199. For a discussion of the relevant notion of powers, see Locke, *Essay,* bk. 2 chap. 8 §§ 8 –17, 22–25 and chap. 21 §§ 1–4.

14. This point is made by Heimann and McGuire 1971, 262. Note here that the corpuscular doctrine of qualities contrasts markedly with its Aristotelian predecessor. The Aristotelian philosopher did not follow a reductive approach to the diversity of properties encountered in physical things. The Aristotelian

normally assumed that every quality found in the world exemplifies some particular form and that the forms remain independent of one another even when embodied in a common matter. Although the Aristotelian did not neglect the search for elemental components that combine to determine the complex natures of things—and was therefore prepared to assert that some qualities are more fundamental than others—he did not regard such elemental or primary qualities as the only objective ones, as is the case with the corpuscular theorists. For the Aristotelian, the primary properties of substances furnished the basis for a hierarchy of forms. The higher levels of this hierarchy were thought to presuppose the lower ones. But the new forms appearing at each level were not supposed to be fully analyzable in terms of the forms of any of the preceding levels. For the Aristotelian, all forms, and thus all elements, had some aspect of irreducible specificity. Regarding this account of the Aristotelian conception of properties, see Hesse 1961. For the doctrine of elements that emerges from such an approach, see Aristotle's *De generatione et corruptione* 328b25–338b20. For the historical modifications of Aristotle's doctrine and its role in sixteenth- and seventeenth-century natural philosophy, see Laßwitz 1890/1963, I 151–175, 235–259, 306–518; Van Melsen 1957, 71–126.

15. On this point, see Harré 1970, 265. The explanatory principle in question receives its most influential expression in the third of Newton's *regulae philosophandi* (see Newton, *Opera*, III 2–3).

16. Cf. Harré 1964, 63; McGuire 1974, 128; McMullin 1978, 32. In his Third Rule of philosophic reasoning, Newton stipulates that we are not to "draw back from the analogy of Nature, which is wont to be simple and consonant with itself" (*Opera*, III 4). He uses this principle to establish that the properties universally encountered in our ordinary perceptual experience of bodies (i.e., extension, hardness, impenetrability, mobility, and inertia) must also be the essential properties of the "least particles of all bodies" (4). For a detailed treatment of the significance of Newton's analogy of nature for seventeenth- and eighteenth-century thought, see McGuire 1970, 3 ff. See also Mandelbaum 1964, 81–117.

It is instructive to compare the corpuscular principle of the analogy of nature with the Aristotelian approach to the complex natures of substances. Aristotelian doctrines of the elements (see note 14 above) have these points in common with the corpuscular conception of aggregated corpuscles: they too focus on the notion of the particular object of ordinary sense experience, and they posit no representational gap between perceived physical things and their constitutive components. The dissimilarity between Aristotelian and corpuscular positions shows itself in the respective versions of the components themselves when these are used to explain changes in the natures of those things. It is characteristic of Aristotelian doctrines that (a) the identifiable components of physical entities are in constant change (i.e., are not fully actual), and that (b) this change is necessarily a process of generation, i.e., a changing of elements *into* each other. Through the action of particular forms and by virtue of their common matter, these components are capable of combination conceived as the internal unification of qualitatively diverse materials. Against this view of generation as internal unification, the corpuscular theorist supposed that perceived changes in physical entities can only take place through the rearrangement of minute particles via local motion. Because these particles are fully actual at all times, they are not capable of combination through internal unification. They cannot themselves be literally "trans-formed." For Aristotle's doctrine of chemical combination, see *De generatione et corruptione* 317a12–31, 322b1, 329b22. For treatments of the Scholastic interpretations of this doctrine: Laßwitz 1890/1963, 239–259; Maier 1949, 179–196; Van Melsen 1957, 87–104.

17. For the seventeenth-century paradigm of the communication of motion by impact, see above all Descartes, *Principia philosophiae*, II §§ 49–52.

18. The problem of *vis inertiae* in seventeenth-century natural philosophy is discussed by Koyré 1968, 93–108.

19. On this point, see Heimann and McGuire 1971, 249–250. Locke provides one of the classic formulations of the extraneousness of force in relation to matter by means of his famous billiard-ball analogy:

> A body at rest affords us no *Idea* of any *active Power* to move; and when it is set in motion itself, that Motion is rather a Passion, than an Action in it. For when the Ball obeys the stroke of a Billiard-stick, it is not any action of the Ball, but bare passion: Also when by impulse it sets another Ball in motion, that lay in its way, it only communicates the motion it has received from another, and loses in itself so much, as the other received; which gives us but a very obscure *Idea* of an *active power* of moving in a body, whilst we observe it only to transfer, but not produce any motion. (*Essay*, bk. 2, chap. 21, § 3)

20. This assertion that dynamical theories were often conjoined with theories of imponderable fluids opposes interpretations of eighteenth-century science that rely on a strict dichotomy between "force theories" of matter and "mechanical" (or corpuscular) theories of imponderables (see, e.g., Schofield 1970, 15 ff.; Levere 1971, 5 ff.). The claim that the latter theories were invariably based on corpuscular assumptions does not bear the weight of detailed historical analysis (on this see Heimann and McGuire 1971, 233 ff.). For general information about the history of imponderables, see Adickes 1922, 328 ff.; Hesse 1961, 180–196; Hund, 1978, I 193–212; Rosenberger 1882–90, III 1–70; Toulmin and Goodfield 1982, 194–228.

21. Cf. Hesse 1961, 170–222; McGuire 1974, 121–124, 132–137; Williams 1965, 53–94.

22. For a treatment of dynamist aspects of Wolff's philosophy of nature, see Campo 1939, 209–220. For information on dynamism and the Wolff school, see Polonoff 1973, 77–89; Vogel 1975, 97–113.

23. Leibniz's analysis of substance and substantial force is treated above in §§ 1–2 of chapter 4 above.

24. GM VI 236.

25. See GP IV 470.

26. See GP IV 508.

27. See GP IV 507; GM VI 235, 241–242.

28. See GM VI 235.

29. GP IV 482.

30. See § 1 of chapter 4 above.

31. See GP IV 478.

32. GP IV 482.

33. See § 2 of chapter 4 above.

34. See GP II 135, 257–258, 263, 267, 276. This point is discussed by Leclerc 1972, 244–247.

35. See GP IV 468–470.

36. Besides the references provided in notes 15 and 16 above, see Newton, *Opera,* IV 251–252.

37. Newton, *Opera,* IV 242–264.

38. See Newton, *Opera,* IV 242–243, 258.

39. Cf. Boas-Hall 1972, 94.

40. For examples of this explanatory procedure, see Newton, *Opera,* IV 243–255.

41. Cf. Heimann and McGuire 1971, 238.

42. Newton, *Opera,* IV 255–256.

43. See Newton, *Opera,* IV 223–227.

44. Newton, *Opera,* IV 225.

45. See Heimann and McGuire 1971, 241–246. In other contexts, of course, Newton keeps the door open for mechanical explanations of gravitational force. On Newton's methodological caution regarding the explanation of gravitation, see, for example, De Gandt 1995, 265–272.

46. For the justification of this law of force by means of a metaphysical proof for the (Leibnizian) law of continuity, see *Theoria,* §§ 48–80.

47. For a detailed treatment of this factor, see Heimann and McGuire 1971, 233 ff.

48. Cf. Heimann and McGuire 1971, 261.

49. See Berkeley, *Principles,* I §§ 9, 10, 14; Hume, *Treatise,* 192–193, 225–227.

50. See the references to Locke supplied in note 13 above.

51. See Berkeley, *Principles,* I § 25.

52. See Hume, *Treatise,* 155–172, and *Enquiries,* 60–79.

53. See Berkeley, *Principles,* §§ 15–24, 29, 37.

54. Hume, *Treatise,* 231.

55. See also Hume, *Treatise,* 15–17, 188–194, 211–213, 255–257. Cf. Heimann and McGuire 1971, 263–264.

56. Priestley, *Works,* III 197–337.

57. Priestley, *Works,* III 235–236.

58. See Priestley, *Works,* III 191–192.

59. For Priestley's epistemological realism, see *Works,* III 1–67 and IV 167–196. For his views on Berkeley and Hume, see *Works,* III 45–50 and IV 398.

60. Priestley, *Works,* III 222.

61. The main addressee is Locke. On this, see Priestley, *Works,* III 225; Locke, *Essay,* bk. 2 chap. 4 §§ 1–2.

62. Priestley, *Works,* III 223.

63. Priestley, *Works,* III 223.

64. Priestley, *Works,* III 223.

65. See Priestley, *Works,* III 231–232, 239–240.

66. Priestley, *Works,* III 237.

67. Priestley, *Works,* III 237.

68. Boscovich, for instance, replaces the distinction between primary and secondary properties with the distinction between "general" and "special" properties, all of which he derives from his single law of force-interaction (see *Theoria* § 359).

69. In § 17 of the *Theoria*, Boscovich argues against the notion that the communication of action can take place by means of direct impact between non-elastic materials. He reasons that this would involve a violation of the law of continuity in nature, a law that can be proved true a priori (see §§ 48–62; cf. note 46 above). Priestley, on the other hand, argues against "absolute contact" on strictly empirical grounds (see *Works*, III 227–229).

Chapter 7:   The Theory of Physical Aether in Kant's Philosophy of Nature

1. See Adickes 1924–25, I 145–232, II 1–205; Mathieu 1958, 176–201; Vuillemin 1955, 94–128.

2. See, more generally, 1:222.11–20, 227.16–228.35, 332.20–334.20.

3. See above all 1:261.7–270.21.

4.

These are the grounds of my confidence that the physical part of the science of the world may in future hope to achieve the same perfection as that to which *Newton* raised its mathematical half. Next to the laws by which the cosmic fabric exists in the constitution in which it is found, there are perhaps no laws in the entire investigation of nature capable of receiving mathematical determinations other than those according to which it originated. The hand of a skillful geometer [*Meßkünstler*] would here undoubtedly till fields that are not unfruitful. (1:230.27–35; cf. also 1:24.1–25.33, 415.5–16)

5. 1:223.17.

6. See 1:225.32–228.11.

7. 1:216.16–17.

8. See generally 1:263.16–286.4, 306.13–322.32.

9. See 1:261.1–262.14. For the Cartesian "aether" (or material plenum) and its place in the vortex theory, see *Principia philosophiae*, II §§ 16–23; III §§ 24–33. For Newton's criticism thereof, see *Opera*, II 458–459; IV 234–237. (This criticism is treated in detail by Koyré 1968, 117–129.)

10. See 1:339.21–340.6.

11. For Kant's view of Newtonian attraction as the primitive law of nature, see 1:243.19–21, 244.10–24, 245.6–14, 311.10–15, 314.6–14, 315.28–316.10, 340.3–341.5. (Cf. 1:24.19–25.2, 415.5–16.) For background information regarding this view: Waschkies 1983, 360–409.

12. See 1:263.36–264.29, 312.34–313.14. The role of repulsion (also a short-range force) is in this case to counteract the effects of attraction, so that the incipient process of corporeal formation is not immediately brought to an end due to the establishment of equilibrium in the effects of all the particular forces of attraction. Kant's assumption is that composite bodies of equal mass would instantaneously be formed out of the original elements (i.e., the corpuscles) constituting the elementary matter. On this, see 1:264.29–265.2.

13. 1:308.31–32.

14. See 1:3308.13–309.9. In this passage Kant evidently assumes the existence of a light aether in interplanetary space. He also advocates the relationist view of space that he elsewhere combines with the Newtonian idea of divine omnipresence (on this, see 1:306.33–34, 308.27–30, 312.36).

15. See 1:371.16–18. Cf. Descartes, *Principia philosophiae*, I §§ 54–56. For a discussion of the factual errors involved in Kant's reference to Descartes on this point, see Adickes 1924–25, II 4.

16. Ponderable fluids require an imponderable elastic matter, which keeps the corpuscular constituents of the fluid materials from having any direct contact with each other. The mechanical action of these ponderable fluids can be accounted for only if this condition is met. Also, the mutually attractive particles composing solid bodies do not cohere by the power of attraction alone. Solidity is supposed to be explained in terms of the material property of cohesiveness. But this property of matter is itself intelligible only with reference to an elastic matter located between the corpuscular components of bodies. See 1:372.6–373.30.

17. For general information on Kant's use of various theories of imponderables, see 14:234–457 (editor's commentary); Adickes 1924–25, II 77–159. See also note 20 of chapter 6 above.

18. For a highly detailed treatment of all aspects of obscurity in the aether theory of 1775, see Adickes 1924–25, II 9–15, 41–54, 69–72.

19. See 1:380.8–18, 381.7–8.

20. Cf. 1:308.35–36.

21. See 1:377.9–378.8.

22. Cf. Leibniz, GP VII 355,-356, 363; Newton, *Opera*, II, pp. IX–X. Regarding the problem of this relationship, see Adickes 1924–25, I 148–149; Friedman 1992a, 8–9, 25–27; Polonoff 1973, 77–92; Vogel 1975, 113–120; Vuillemin 1955, 121–122.

23. 1:475.15.

24. See 1:475.19–476.2.

25. 1:476.13–14. Section I of the treatise (Propositions 1–8) explicates the conditions for reconciling geometry and metaphysics that are furnished by the ascription of force to simple substances or monads. Section II (Propositions 9–13) determines the basic form of interaction between attractive and repulsive force. This allows for the specification of the most general properties exhibited by matter and composite bodies.

26. Cf. 2:293.7–18, 323.19–324.14, 414.9–15.

27. See 1:477.9–17.

28. Regarding this reading of *extrinsecus quidem applicatem, quoniam illa praesens est externis,* see the translation supplied by Norbert Hinske in Weischedel's *Immanuel Kant: Werkausgabe* (1968).

29. For Kant's quite different original view of *vis motrix,* see § 1 of chapter 5 above.

30. See 1:480.1–3/11–13, 480.36–481.8.

31. See 1:478.2–3.

32. 1:479.26, 480.27–28. We may note here that Kant is not entirely clear

about whether each monad occupies an extended spatial region on its own, or only when it is related to other monads (see 1:481.1–4).

33. See 1:481.27–32.

34. Which is what Kant means in the Transcendental Analytic of the *Critique of Pure Reason*. See chapter 3 above, p. 50 (cf. also 2:286.25–287.35, 322.21–35, 323.19–324.6). It is worth noting that in his *Träume eines Geistersehers* [*Dreams of a spirit seer*] of 1766, Kant does refer to material unities (2:321.26) and material substances (323,34) when characterizing physical monads. Yet he does so in order to distinguish between spiritual and physical entities. Kant's use of the term "material substance" in this context is based on pragmatic considerations and is technically imprecise. Cf. Vogel 1975, 148–149.

35. There is a tradition of controversy in the secondary literature regarding the relationship between force and the internal and external determinations of substance. The controversy has revolved around three interpretive options: (1) Adickes (1924–25, I 168), for example, identifies the force-center with the sphere of substantial activity. (2) Simmel (1881, 10) identifies the monad as a mathematical point existing at a given location independently of the filling of space through force. (3) Endler (1902, 32) attempts to reconcile these two views by claiming that Kant legitimately gives the term "monad" a dual meaning. A fourth option, the correct one in my view, is presented by Vogel (1975, 178). Vogel argues that Kant does provide two distinct descriptions of the physical monad corresponding to options 1 and 2. But he demonstrates that these descriptions are incompatible and that Kant consequently does not have a coherent concept of substance in the *Monadologia physica*. The price that Kant pays for reconciling geometry and metaphysics is thus an untenable conception of the physical monad.

36. See 1:482.4–6/7–15, 483.11–12.

37. See 1:483.31–484.12.

38. Again, see 1:484.13–16.

39. See 1:484.13–16.

40. See 1:486.36–487.13.

41. 1:486.38.

42. Emphasis is here placed on "systematization." The unsettled character of the theory of matter after the *Monadologia physica* is underscored by the fact that during the 1760s Kant entertains at least three different accounts of matter for the purposes of metaphysical and scientific explanation. On some occasions he simply continues to employ the dynamical concept of the physical monadology of 1756 with no discernible revisions (see 2:279.11–25, 286.25–288.35, 320.12–321.28, 322.14–324.14; cf. 19:69.2–70.33). At other times, he apparently employs the monadological concept in conjunction with a Newtonian (and Boscovichean) law of force interaction (see 2:169.11–22, 179.4–180.4, 198.32–199.5). He also in one instance reverts to the pre-dynamical corpuscular concept of the *Universal Natural History* (see 2:144.9–151.2).

43. It is in view of these dates that we can understand the connections between a number of the 1770s Reflections and passages in the Duisburg *Nachlaß* (see the references to Reflections 4673, 4674, and 4679 in notes 62 and 64 below). A thorough investigation of Kant's theory of knowledge in the 1770s lead-

ing up to the first *Critique* would have to contain a systematic examination of these links.

44. 14:193.1. See also 14:169.1–170.2, 195.6–12, 212.1–213.3, 296.3–9, 457.11–13.

45. 14:151.1–3.

46. 14:153.7–8. See also 14:187.11–12, 211.1–212.2. In claiming that mechanical laws serve to explain only art, Kant wants to show that mechanical explanation relies on the treatment of physical action in terms of apparently direct contact and impact taking place between material parts. Evidently, he assumes that we derive this view of action from the observable workings of human-made machines and that we use this view to account for the interactions of all material things. But no direct reference to teleological explanation is thereby intended.

47. 14:161.4–5. See also 14:151.1–6, 161.3–167.7, 212.3–213.3.

48. See, e.g., 14:316.1–2, 343.1–2, 349.1–350.4.

49. Looking back to the origins of the aether theory, it is especially noteworthy in the 1770s Reflections that Kant's explanation of the various states of matter and material properties is in many ways parallel to the explanation given in *De igne*. See 14:137.1–139.3, 316.1–3, 401.1–12, 418.1–427.4.

50. See 14:138.5–6, 418.1–2.

51. See also 14:287.2–292.4 (cf. 1:376.17–21, 377.15–18, 377.19–378.18; 29:83.18–86.31).

52. On the translation of *Materien* as "matters" see note 16 of chapter 3 above.

53. Compare the treatment of Newton's conception of physical aether in § 2 of chapter 6 above. Adickes discusses the affinity between Kant's and Newton's aether theories in 14:336–342 (editor's commentary).

54. Regarding the expressions "distributive" and "collective," see 4:526.12–35; 14:287.1–288.2; Reflections 4046, 4149, 4169, 4490, 5840.

55. It would seem to follow that distributive attraction performs the role of, or is responsible for, cohesion. But this implication is not made explicit in the passage under consideration.

56. Cf. Adickes 1924–25, I 185. Note the parallels between this portrayal of short-range attraction and Kant's account of the role of attraction in the theory of cosmogenesis of the *Universal Natural History* (see § 1 of this chapter).

57. See especially 1:484.13–485.14.

58. See 14:401.1–12, 409.6–410.7, 419.1–14, 426.1–21, 432.1–34, 439.1–6, 448.2–449.11.

59. The relationship between repulsion as material ground and attraction as the principle of form reminds us of the traditional matter/form composite and its status as the key concept of the metaphysics of corporeal nature. Arguably, this much "Aristotelianism" is endemic to dynamical theories of matter in general. Indeed, it seems to be part of any theory of matter that would undertake to show how particular corporeal unities emerge from the interaction of ontologically primitive forces.

60. On the other hand, we have seen that the aether concept plays a merely marginal role in the *Monadologia physica*. The definition of the aether as primitively elastic "body" and "medium" is achieved in the corollary to the final

proposition of the treatise, where Kant demonstrates determination of the individual monad's elasticity.

61. See also 14:121.4−6, 151.5−6, 187.1−7, 335.5−336.2, 342.1−4.

62. For Kant's conception of the metaphysics of nature during the 1770s, see 14.119.1−6. Regarding the distinction between intellectual and sensible cognition, see 14:162.15−19, 174.4−7 (cf. 2:392.10−398.7, 411.28−31; 10:98.15−36, 130.33−131.10; Reflection 4673 [17:639.29−640.9 and 640.29−641.13]).

63. For the preliminary discussion of this concept, see chapter 3 above (pp. 49−51).

64. The relevant passages translate as follows:

> In every appearance is intuition and sensation. The first contains the form, the latter the matter of the appearance. The form of outer appearance is space; the form of apperception, and thus of all appearance in general, is time. Space and time are conditions (of the principles of all knowledge of nature) a priori. The principle of every appearance according to matter (production of sensation). Force as the ground of relations in space is moving force (or, what amounts to the same thing, the force that resists (the external cause of sensation)). This is the ground of all appearances (space, time, and force). The subject of force, which contains the ground of every outer appearance, and which is thus something as an object of outer appearance in general, is called matter in the narrowest sense. (14:119.7−19 [cf. 350.1−27, 74.9−75.4; 4:476.7−477.13; Reflections 4674 [17:643.1−22], 4679 [17:663.1−2]; 29(1):75.8−25])
>
> Impenetrability and attraction make a body . . .
> 1. The object, which there appears.
> 2. The play of appearances. Motion.
> The object can be known only through forces that are related to motion (as cause or as obstacle), and indeed it is the subject of the original principles of motion . . .
> Of repulsion in a space and materiality. Result [*Folge*] thereof: elasticity.
> Of attraction in space and corporeal unity. Result thereof: cohesion.
> Fundamental forces: *Original elasticity* and *original attraction*.
> Of the *substance* (matter as *substratum phaenomenon*[)]. Imperishability [*Unvergänglichkeit*] of matter, . . .*
> Of the *infinite divisibility* of matter, which completely fills a space. Matter is not regarded as substance in the metaphysical sense ([i.e.,] as the subject in the strict sense); for it is nothing but a *permanent appearance;* consequently, since the appearance does not consist of the *absolutely simple,* matter too does not consist in this. Space determines the possibility of the appearance, and this does not consist in simple parts. (14:181.3−187.7)

*In the lines elided, Kant seeks to clarify the mechanical concept of mass and quantity of matter. He does not directly address there the dynamical concept of *substantia phaenomenon*. But reference to the latter is nonetheless necessarily involved, since he maintains in the 1770s Reflections that the concept of mass must be grounded in the dynamical principle of the original forces of matter (see jointly 14:119.20−23, 122.27−131.2, 187.20−189.3, 211.1−213.3). For treatments of the difficulties inherent in the various attempts that Kant makes during his career to establish the proper relationship between the dynamical concept of matter and the concept of mass, see Adickes 1924−25, I 159−161, 182−184, 214−219, 292−295; Carrier 1991, 215−216; Tuschling 1971, 46−51, 56−61; Westphal 1995b, 395−409.

65. See also 14:169.1−170.2, 195.6−12, 212.1−213.3, 457.11−13.

66. Michael Friedman (1992a) occasionally describes the *Metaphysical Foun-*

dations in terms of an "application of Kant's transcendental philosophy" (see, e.g., 137, 139). This apparently refers to the application of principles of pure understanding as transcendental laws of nature. The application of Kant's transcendental *philosophy* (which includes all concepts and principles of theoretical reason, as well as those of the understanding) to the empirical concept of matter is hardly a step envisaged by Kant in the *Metaphysical Foundations* (see 3:546.16–21; 4;469.7–470.12, 476.7–477.13, 495.27–38, 523.6–17, 551.8–14, 558.22–26). I discuss the relationship between the pure principles of understanding and the principles at issue in the *Metaphysical Foundations* in the introduction to this book (see pp. 4–5 above).

67. See 4:470.10–11, 476.9–12. The determination of the object of external sense as motion contrasts with the corresponding stipulations at 14:119.6–17. The theoretical problems inherent in the new determination are discussed by Tuschling 1971, 90–122. See also Westphal 1995b, 388–395, 405–409.

68. See 4:498.27–499.4.

69. See 4:496.6–9, 498.21–25, 499.6–9, 500.2–6.

70. 4:508.16–17.

71. See 4:502.11–13, 508.15–18, 509.19–20.

72. 4:509.27.

73. 4:510.10.

74. 4:510.24–25.

75. See 4:511.4–26.

76. See also 4:503.20–508.4 (Theorem 4). Regarding the element of self-criticism involved in Kant's general repudiation of monadological accounts of matter, see 14:338–339 (editor's commentary); Adickes 1924–25, I 214–216; Tuschling 1971, 56–61.

77. For the method of exposition followed in the *Metaphysical Foundations,* see 4:478.21–31. For a criticism of the presuppositions of Kant's "imitation of mathematical method" (4:478.21–22), see Tuschling 1971, 111–122. See also Adickes 1924–25, I 252–253; Westphal 1995b, especially 407.

78. See 4:517.18–26.

79. See 4:517.26–518.2.

80. 4:518.33–35. The major upshot of this procedure is that, whereas attraction must be thought to act between attracting points in inverse proportion to the square of the distances at all specifiable distances, repulsion must act in inverse relation to the cubes of the infinitesimally small distances which are thought to separate repelling points. See 4:518.35–521.12 (especially 521.4–12).

81. See Tuschling 1971, 56–61; Vuillemin 1955, 168–169. See also Westphal 1995b, 395–405.

82. See note 16 of chapter 3 above for the translation of *Materien.*

83. See note 81 above.

84. See 4:472.1–12, 475.5–14, 534.31–36. On the conceptual difficulties involved in providing these principles, see Tuschling 1971, 46–51, 111–122.

85. See 4:518.4–31.

86. 4:518.5–6.

87. 4:518.24.

88. Cf. 4:470.18–19.

89. Cf. 4:469.26–470.12, 477.14–20.

90. It is instructive to contrast Kant with Leibniz on this point. For Leibniz, the systematic coherence of the metaphysics of substance, as applied to corporeal nature, depends on the possibility of completing the "transition from metaphysics to nature" (see § 2 of chapter 4 above). For Kant, however, both the architectonic integrity and the empirical open-endedness of the critical system are predicated on the obstruction of any transition from strictly rational principles of the metaphysics of nature to the level of particular physical laws. Here again, Kant's critical apriorism is closer to a theory of knowledge like Priestley's (see § 2 of chapter 6 above) than it is to the Leibnizian explication of corporeal being.

91. The principle states that "all that is real in the objects (*alles Reale der Gegenstände*) of the outer sense that is not a determination of space (location, extension, and figure) must be regarded as moving force" (4:523.21–24).

92. See 4:523.26–27 (cf. 4:511.28–512.3, 512.18–22, 514.12–515.37).

93. See 4:523.29–524.17, 533.6–534.5.

94. 4:524.18–19.

95. See 4:4.8–23.

96. 4:524.34.

97. See 4:524.26–40.

98. Note the shift that takes place between the 1770s and 1786 with respect to the meaning of "metaphysico-dynamical" (see pp. 128–129 above). This change evidently reflects the terminological maturation of the critical theory of a priori knowledge vis-à-vis the 1770s. Since Kant's general metaphysical theory no longer explicitly relies on a monadological concept of substance even for "distinguishing the intellectual from appearances in general" (14:153.13), "metaphysico-dynamical" can now be used to designate the mode of explanation that Kant had earlier termed "physico-dynamical." A less charitable reading, though, might maintain that his employment of "metaphysico-dynamical" reflects the fact that the 1786 version of the dynamical theory does not ultimately avoid reliance upon a monadological concept, and that the attempt to break this implicit dependency must render problematic any possible distinction that Kant could draw between metaphysico-dynamical principles and physico-dynamical principles.

99. Kant has in mind here primarily Cartesian physics, not Newtonian physics (cf. 4:532.40–533.4).

100. In view of the passages under consideration from the General Remark to the Dynamics, Michael Friedman (1992a) distinguishes his approach to the Dynamics (and indeed to the *Metaphysical Foundations* as a whole) from the type of approach advocated here (see also Edwards 1987, especially 148–149). Friedman writes:

> Kant views Newtonian science as in need of a critical analysis or metaphysical foundations: What is lacking in the *Principia* as Newton wrote it? There is a tendency to locate Kant's disagreement with Newton at the level of matter theory: specifically in the contrast Kant sets up between a "mathematical-mechanical" conception of matter and a "metaphysical-dynamical" conception in the General Observation to Dynamics of the *Metaphysical Foundations*. . . . Kant is then seen as opposing . . . Newtonian "atomism" with a "dynamistic" conception of matter growing out of a broadly Leibnizian approach to natural philosophy. (137–138)

Friedman goes on to contend that the attempt to locate Kant's central disagreement with Newton at the level of the theory of matter must be "profoundly misleading" (138), given that "questions of absolute versus relative space and absolute versus relative motion are the central questions to be clarified in any attempt to understand Kant's critical analysis or metaphysical foundations of Newtonian science." (141) Thus, Friedman insists that

> Kant's critical analysis of Newton's *Principia* is an application of transcendental philosophy, an application that is supposed to serve as a realization of that philosophy which illustrates its fundamental concepts and principles *in concreto*. From this point of view we should hardly expect matter theory to be central. (139–140)

Apart from noting that these claims reflect Friedman's propensity to conflate the quite different explanatory tasks that Kant assigns respectively to the Dynamics and the Mechanics (for further details, see notes 23 and 40 of chapter 8 below), there are three sets of responses to direct against Friedman's position:

(1) Historically, all previous commentators on Kant's natural philosophy have regarded the dynamical theory of matter as centrally important to the *Metaphysical Foundations*. To my knowledge, none of these has ever denied that Kant's considerations on absolute versus relative space and absolute versus relative motion are centrally important to Kant's metaphysical project as well. Friedman provides no reference to anyone who has asserted the contrary.

(2) Friedman contends that the theory of matter is not central to Kant's "realization of transcendental philosophy" (regarding the peculiarity of this formulation, see note 66 above). Thus, we would expect Friedman to furnish a systematic treatment of the Dynamics and to discuss critically, and extensively, the substantial body of literature intended to establish the importance of Kant's dynamism for his metaphysics of nature. But Friedman offers no such treatment. Nor does he come to terms with the relevant secondary literature. (The four sources he mentions (138 note) are summarily dismissed without examination.)

(3) As my discussions of the history of eighteenth-century dynamism and the development of Kant's theory of matter and account of dynamical community show, the attempt to set up a "Newtonian" Kant over and against a "Leibnizian" Kant in view of the theory of matter lacks historical justification. It is also conceptually misguided.

101. 4:525.12–19.

102. See 4:532.40–533.21.

103. 4:534.13.

104. See 4:534.12–535.10.

105. 4:525.22.

106. See 4:525.20–24, 526.12–529.25. The other headings in Kant's framework are corporeal volume and density (4:525.26–526.11), elasticity (529.26–530.7), and chemical solvency (530.8–532.9). The most extensive treatment of this classificatory system is provided by Vuillemin 1955, 174–186.

107. According to Michael Friedman's (1992a, 141–149) reconstruction of Kant's argumentative procedure in the *Metaphysical Foundations* as a whole, the Phenomenology turns out to be the pivotal chapter for understanding Kant's systematic intentions. The key component of this reconstruction is the recognition of a step in Kant's argumentation that "proceeds from the observable

(Keplerian) relative motions in the solar system to the law of universal gravitation and the center mass frame of the solar system, as in [Newton's] *Principia*, Book III" (149). Friedman makes it fully explicit (149–150) that his view of Kant's procedure has no direct textual support, and indeed that it seems to be entirely undercut by Kant's failure even to mention Book III of the *Principia* in the Phenomenology. I agree with Friedman's critical self-assessment, especially since Martin Carrier's recent work (1993, 404–416) radically undermines the central assumptions of Friedman's interpretive endeavor. Still, his attempt to remedy Kant's "apparent failure" (Friedman 1992a, 150) is interesting in one important respect. I refer here to Friedman's use of Newton's "moon test" (152) as a basis for establishing an important connection between the General Remark to the Phenomenology and Kant's criticism of Newton in Remark 2 to Proposition 7 of the Dynamics (see 150–159). It is noteworthy that this is the one place in his book where Friedman treats intensively a central issue from the Dynamics, and where he thereby attempts to relate the Dynamics to the other three special metaphysical disciplines contained in the *Metaphysical Foundations*. Most importantly, it seems to be the only place where Friedman acknowledges the sense in which a law of Newtonian dynamics *presupposes* Kant's dynamical account of matter (see 153–154; cf. 4:514.34–515.5).

108. Only empty space within the world is relevant to the metaphysics of corporeal nature. It is either *vacuum dessimatum* (4:563.24–25), i.e., the empty space that is supposed to be part of the volume of matter; or else it is *vacuum coercervatum* (563.26), i.e., the empty space assumed to separate physical bodies of determinate volume. Kant does not consider the difference between these to be essential, since it concerns merely the different places assigned to empty space within the world.

109. 4:563.38.

110. For the distinction between "true" and "apparent" attraction that underpins this passage see 4:514.12–515.37.

111. We can maintain, however, that these restrictions throw into question the sense in which the principle of the Anticipations may be said to ground any theoretical discipline which contains "laws" or "principles of the necessity of that which pertains to the *existence* of a thing" (4:469.27–28; see also 4:467.2–12 [cf. 3:126.9–127.3; 4:93.20–32], 4:469.30–470.1).

Chapter 8. The Third Analogy and the *Opus Postumum*

1. As I pointed out in chapter 2 (p. 25), in the proof added to the 1787 version of the Third Analogy, Kant seems to conceive of the relation of community in terms of individual clusters of mutually interactive substantial particulars that interact reciprocally with an indefinite number of such clusters. The investigations undertaken in parts two and three lead to the conjecture that Kant has in mind a world system of dynamical interactions between variously constituted material particulars and corporeal formations. In other words, he seems to employ the concept of the dynamical community of substances implicitly with reference to the total complex of the constitutive forces of matter

and the heterogeneous material formations arising from the operations of force. Interestingly, the description of the relation of community in core argument 1 of the Third Analogy is roughly contemporaneous with a corresponding shift, which takes place between 1786 (*Metaphysical Foundations*) and 1786/87, in the thematic orientation of the dynamical theory of matter. This shift, which is discernible in the earliest manuscripts of the *Opus postumum*, goes hand in hand with the reemergence of the aether concept as the centerpiece of the dynamical theory's projected final version (on this, see Tuschling 1971, 15–23; cf. also Förster 1987, 547–548 and Westphal 1995b, 407–409).

2. The aether's role as a light matter or *materia lucis* (see, e.g., 14:287.2–290.2 [cf. 1:378.2–18; 4:519.39–520.41; 5:224.22–31] and pp. 117 and 123 of chapter 7 above), incidentally, also puts us in a position to make sense of the final component in the triad of material conditions mentioned in the second phase of the void-space argument. If the transmission of "the light that plays between our eye and the world-bodies" (3:182.33–34) is a function of physical aether as a universal continuum of transeunt forces, then the relationship between influences, matter, and light in the Third Analogy's argument against empty space is fully explainable.

3. See, e.g., 21:162.14–21, 168.15–20, 359.11–17, 368.27–387.14, 402.20–403.9, 407.29–408.5, 477.15–20, 478.23–26, 524.28–525.12, 582.6–16; 22:254.4–7, 263.1–6. (These passages are not cited in keeping with the chronological order of the manuscripts. For the sake of the reader not already well acquainted with the Byzantine textual composition of the Academy Edition *Opus postumum*, I have simplified the standard procedure of citation in the notes pertaining mainly to the earlier fascicles.)

4. See 12:257.8–11, 258.27. For a different, and very interesting, interpretation of the "gap" in Kant's system, see Förster 1987. I should point out here that the passages from the *Opus postumum* cited by Friedman (1992a, 260–264) in support his view of the "gap" in Kant's system are passages that buttress equally well most of the other interpretations offered in the secondary literature (see, e.g., Mathieu 1989, 39–45). I can find nothing in them that could be explained only from Friedman's viewpoint. I therefore conclude with Westphal (see note 9 below) that Friedman does not present evidence that effectively substantiates his interpretation.

5. This conception is already evidenced in the *Oktaventwurf* (see, e.g., 21:378.7–379.6, 383.15–34), but it is most carefully articulated in Transition 1–14 (see 21:219.1–10, 223.10–224.2, 226.25–227.8, 229.23–30, 233.5–8, 235.4–16, 247.2–12, 535.17–537.12, 539.27–540.12, 547.20–548.4, 564.6–12, 565.2–15, 588.17–589.3, 592.7–10). See also the following passages from Fascicle 11: 22:425.23–426.6, 431.4–9, 440.3–15, 457.20–27.

6. See, generally, 21:475.17–477.20, 477.28–478.26, 483.14–484.7, 486.2–27, 490.19–491.4, 504.1–4, 505.5–19, 506.11–19, 508.6–29, 524.5–15, 526.14–20, 527.18–528.5, 530.26–532.15, 615.2–618.6, 621.2–622.6, 628.29–629.17/19–31, 631.1–10, 636.1–637.13, 637.27–639.20, 640.4–17, 642.15–24; 22:149.2–12, 152.15–22, 154.10–14, 155.15–28, 165.13–24, 167.1–18, 169.6–18, 172.22–173.7, 175.2–22, 193.8–194.15, 195.27–196.14, 199.23–200.25, 239.21–241.19, 263.1–6, 265.1–28, 285.1–3, 287.9–29, 354.2–359.13, 384.19–29.

7. Regarding this lack of fixity, see Adickes 1920, 163–166, 199–235, 474–475, 588–591; Edwards 1991, 78–79; Förster 1991, 32–41; Lehmann 1939, 9–11, 30–36, 41–49, 56–65; Mathieu 1958, 203–231, 349–369; Mathieu 1989, 100–110; Tuschling 1971, 164–169; Tuschling 1973, 178–179.

8. See, e.g., (in chronological order) 22:175.2–9, 187.3–15, 263.1–6; 21:627.21–25, 628.17–22, 639.22–25; 22:244.3–9; 21:540.24–541.10, 564.4–12, 574.6–15; 22:334.17–19, 497.20–498.11, 502.3–10, 505.6–13.

9. Michael Friedman's (1992a) recent interpretation of the *Opus postumum* and its relation to the *Metaphysical Foundations* is sharply criticized by Kenneth Westphal (1995b, 409–414) along the following lines:

(1) Friedman ties the Analogies of Experience to Newtonian physics as exemplified by the laws of motion deduced in Kant's Mechanics of 1786. That there is a systematic relationship between the transcendental laws of pure understanding and the special metaphysical laws of the Mechanics is, of course, uncontroversial. But Friedman illicitly welds together the two sets of laws due to his conflation of two quite distinct senses in which Kant uses the term "experience" (i.e., "experience" employed with reference to (a) "the self-conscious experience of spatio-temporal objects"; and (b) "a systematically organized whole of empirical knowledge" [410]).

(2) Correlative to this conflation, Friedman misconstrues Kant's argumentative procedure in the *Metaphysical Foundations* and consequently misinterprets the import of Kant's metaphysical method in relation to his employment of the empirical concept of matter. Instead of recognizing that Kant's specification of this concept is supposed to be entirely *a priori,* Friedman's version of Kant's reconstruction of Newton presents Kant as "mounting an *a posteriori* 'boot-strap' argument . . . for the immediacy and universality of universal gravitational attraction, which Friedman calls a transcendental argument" (410). Since Friedman himself admits that there is no direct textual evidence for this kind of interpretation, he must seek to demonstrate that the metaphysical method *presupposed* by the transformation of appearances into experience is the same as the transformation itself; and he can accomplish this only by maintaining that Kant's metaphysical method brings into play an extensive body of empirical data relevant to Newton's gravitational theory. That, however, amounts to the refusal to respect the most elemental methodological restriction placed on the *Metaphysical Foundations,* namely, the fact that Kant's deductive procedure "can only explicate *a priori* the empirical *concept* of matter" (412). According to Kant's actual metaphysical method, no empirical *data* are admissible in any concept's a priori explication.

(3) Friedman rejects the approaches to the Transition problematic of the *Opus postumum* worked out in exhaustive detail by Burkhard Tuschling and Eckart Förster. Specifically, Friedman claims that Kant's recognition of the circularity in his 1786 definition of the quantity and density of matter (for details, see Förster 1987, 547–548; Tuschling 1971; Westphal 1995b, 395–404) cannot have been of great significance to Kant in the *Opus postumum*. Friedman, however, provides no substantive argument against this central pillar of Tuschling's and Förster's work on Kant's systematic intentions in the earlier fascicles of the *Opus postumum*.

(4) Friedman implausibly disregards the centrality of the dynamical theory of matter for the project of the *Metaphysical Foundations* and utterly fails to recognize its significance for Kant's thinking in the *Opus postumum*. Moreover, he is not even consistent in respecting the implications of his disregard, for at one point he claims (mistakenly) that the *Opus postumum* merely extends Kant's theory of matter by addressing points left open in the Dynamics of 1786.

(5) In attempting to offer an alternative to the type of approach to the *Opus postumum* advocated by Tuschling and Förster, Friedman proposes to treat Kant's Transition project in view of two main problems: "How can the experimental sciences of chemistry or heat be systematic and be integrated with mathematical physics? and, How can the 'top down' constitutive procedures of the Transcendental Analytic and *MAdN* be coördinated with the 'bottom up' reflective procedures of scientific investigation analyzed in the Transcendental Dialectic and Third *Critique*?" (413). Although these are certainly significant issues in the *Opus postumum*, Friedman provides no effective evidence that they are the central issues that drove Kant to open up the Transition problematic.

I have already commented on the last of these points in note 4 above. There will be occasion to return to the others in the course of this chapter.

10. See above all Adickes 1920, 207–216; 343–362, 385–397, 589–591, 669, 850–851.

11. See Tuschling 1971, 75–76, 86–87, 120–184; Westphal 1995b, 408–409. For a line of argument that is in many respects similar to Tuschling's and Westphal's, but in which the conclusions regarding the relationship between the two sets of transcendental principles are simply not drawn, see Mathieu 1958, 231–235, 253–276, 280–293, 303–304, 343–345, 445–455; Mathieu 1984, 14–22, 26–45.

12. Kenneth Westphal (1995b, 413–414) charges that Friedman's 1992 book does not seriously address the issues that are central to Tuschling's and Förster's interpretations of the Transition project of the *Opus postumum*. This charge is especially pressing in view of Friedman's assessment of Tuschling, whose work has largely determined the lay of the terrain on which debate about the *Opus postumum* has taken place over the past quarter century. Although I agree generally with Westphal's criticism, I must point out in partial defense of Friedman that he does undertake to address a feature of Kant's thinking that is also central to Tuschling's approach. I refer here to the so-called *Phoronomiekritik* from the earlier fascicles of the *Opus postumum* by which Kant in effect acknowledges that the valid content of the *Metaphysical Foundations* reduces to its chapter on phoronomy. Friedman argues against Tuschling's understanding of the phoronomy critique in a footnote (1992a, 249), and he does this in view of one of the passages (21:478.11–26) Tuschling cites to justify his reading. Friedman writes:

> The passage . . . is crucial to Tuschling's conception of "phoronomy-critique" . . . for it appears to assert that the *Metaphysical Foundations*—contrary to its own intentions—"contained no moving forces." Yet it is clear, I think, that Kant means to exclude from the *Metaphysical Foundations* "the moving forces of matter that can only be known through experience" (475.17–18), but *not* the original forces of attraction and repulsion: see, e.g., 310.24–311.6, 362.28–363.5; 22,282.12–18, 518.10–20.

There are major defects in this reading of 21:478.11–26. First of all, Friedman's reading obfuscates two essential facts about the passage: (1) Kant is referring specifically to metaphysical foundations of natural science as he understood them in the middle of 1798, *not* 1786. (2) *These* metaphysical foundations, as understood in *this* passage, contain *no* moving forces, i.e., they contain neither moving forces knowable a priori nor moving forces known empirically. These facts, of course, furnish the key to understanding Tuschling's use of the passage and others like it to support his interpretation of the phoronomy critique. (See Tuschling 1971, 90–100. Tuschling, incidentally, does not claim that all the passages composed by Kant during the phases of his thinking that embody the phoronomy critique are fully consistent with the "sharp formulation" of the critique; quite the contrary: see 95.)

The second defect in Friedman's reading and its employment against Tuschling is more serious that the first. Friedman makes no mention of the crucial background assumption of the passages that show Kant to be reducing the valid content of the *Metaphysical Foundations* of 1786 to the Phoronomy (i.e., the first main part of the *Metaphysical Foundations*). Specifically, he does not mention the fact that they all presuppose a radical revision of the Dynamics of 1786. (The results of this revision are reflected, for instance, in the lines leading up to the first supplementary passage cited by Friedman; see 21:310.3–23.) Thus, while it is true that Friedman does at least address a key feature of Tuschling's approach, he neglects to come to grips with its philosophical import for the overall interpretation of the changes that we can discern in Kant's dynamical theory of matter vis-à-vis 1786. Furthermore, he seems to miss completely the significance of these changes for Kant's conception of the relationship between his metaphysics of nature and his transcendental theory, which is what Tuschling is above all concerned to bring to light. Since I can find no other incisive critical discussion of the basis of this concern in Friedman's work, I can only conclude that he does not recognize what Tuschling's interpretation of *Opus postumum* is intended to establish about the relationship between the *Metaphysical Foundations* of 1786 and the Transition project of the *Opus postumum* as well the ramifications of this project for Kant's transcendental inquiry into the conditions of possible experience. This conclusion is confirmed by Friedman's critical references to Tuschling's account of the evolution of transcendental dynamics in the *Opus postumum* (see Friedman 1992a, 299–300 note). In taking up this account, Friedman takes pains to clarify the distinctions between "transcendental," "metaphysical," and "empirical," all of which obviously are quite relevant to questions about the connection between the *Metaphysical Foundations* and the *Opus postumum*. But he never focuses on these distinctions as they actually pertain to Tuschling's portrayal of the emergence of transcendental dynamics out of the difficulties that Kant faces in trying to determine the status of his transitional science within the architectonic scheme of his philosophy of nature.

13. By this point (see notes 4, 9, and 12 above), my disagreement with Friedman's approach to Kant's metaphysics of nature will sufficiently clear. Our differences seem to derive from two radically divergent views of the distinction between transcendental and empirical knowledge as it was articulated by Kant during the central period of his critical philosophy. Friedman's interpretation of this distinction is evident in a passage from his discussion of the aether deduc-

tion (1992a, 299–300 note; cf. note 12 above), where he reveals how the "importance of the transcendental/empirical distinction" for Kant's Transition project (and, more generally, for Kant's idea of transcendental philosophy) was first emphasized to him. But the character and the background assumptions of Friedman's interpretation are perhaps most plainly visible in a related publication (1992b). In view of the *Metaphysical Foundations* and the Transition project of the *Opus postumum*, Friedman there undertakes to solve the problem of establishing how exactly Kant's transcendental principles relate to the particular empirical causal laws that govern the interactions of substances (see 1992b, especially 83–95). But it is in fact odd that he should see this relation as presenting any problem at all, since he claims (77) that the "rule" at issue in Kant's definition of the *transcendental* schema of causality in the *Critique of Pure Reason* (see 3:138.4) is itself an *empirical* causal law. Is it not obvious that if Kant had taken this type of position in the Transcendental Analytic of the first *Critique*, then the Transition project of the *Opus postumum* (not to mention the *Metaphysical Foundations* of 1786) could never have become an issue in his theory of knowledge? For he could not possibly have drawn any kind of distinction between a priori principles of pure understanding and empirically knowable causal laws to begin with. (For related difficulties affecting Friedman's understanding of the 1787 Transcendental Deduction, see Friedman 1992a, 130–132.)

14. Regarding the fragmentary character of the manuscripts and the resulting difficulties for any systematizing interpretation of the *Opus postumum,* see Adickes 1920,36–154; Lehmann 1939, 30–40; Lehmann 1963, 491–495, 507; Tuschling 1971, 4–14.

15. On this point, especially with regard to the merely hypothetical status of the aether's existence in the earlier sketches, see Adickes 1920, 422–450; Mathieu 1958, 231–234; Tuschling 1971, 23–30, 73–75, 83–84, 131, 141, 172–175.

16. See, e.g., (in chronological order) 22:324.5–327.8, 330.6–331.31, 337.5–339.12, 346.3–350.26, 377.5–378.24, 388.2–390.30, 402.16–405.12, 459.31–462.28, 463.1–465.28, 470.15–472.8 (cf. 474.25–476.6).

17. For an attempt to determine this significance by giving the aether deduction a central role in Kant's final philosophical enterprise, see Mathieu 1958, 231–273. An opposing view is formulated by Lehmann 1963, 493–499. See also Förster 1989a, 295–302; Förster 1989b, 216–235; Förster 1991, 41–45; Friedman 1992a, 290–341.

18. Conversely, it is conceivable that we could prove a priori the existence of a universal aether without making any mention of a system of purportedly a priori concepts of moving forces and material properties. (One thinks here of the various uses to which aether concepts were put in nineteenth- and early twentieth-century physics.) But this is not an option weighed by Kant, whose interest was to establish the necessity of a priori concepts for the philosophical grounding of physics.

19. Cf. Adickes 1920, 235–238, 240–247; Förster 1989a, 298–302; Förster 1989b, 226–235; Friedman 1992a, 316–341; Hoppe 1969, 114–128; Lehmann 1953–54, 145–146; Lehmann 1963, 498.

20. See (in chronological order) 22:320.16–324.2, 343.9–345.33, 354.2–356.11, 356.25–359.13, 363.15–366.26, 370.20–372.24, 502.12–505.13.

21. Regarding the idea of an "elementary system" of moving forces, see above all Mathieu 1958, pp. XIX–XX, 209–227, 243–248; Mathieu 1989, 86–110. Mathieu undertakes to classify Kant's various attempts at providing a system of a priori concepts of moving forces and material properties in accordance with the scheme of the categories of the understanding. He also endeavors to determine the place of this system in an even more comprehensive transitional science that includes the notion of a world system, i.e., the idea of the total complex of cognizable material formations, both anorganic and organic. I think that this constructive approach is implausible (cf. Förster 1991, 38–41; Tuschling 1973, 178–179). Still, its practical value for coming to grips with the sheer mass of material contained the *Opus postumum* can hardly be denied.

22. In the rest of this paragraph, references are to two blocks of considerations in Transition 1–14 where the nerve of the aether deduction is exposed with special clarity. Both of these are taken from the system sketch contained in Transition numbers 9–11 (21:554.5–581.11; cf. 22:549.2–555.25). The first bears the formidable caption *Von der Existenz eines durch keine Erfahrung erweislichen (mithin im Erkenntnis a priori gegebenen) allverbreiteten und alldurchdringenden Weltstoffs* ("Of the existence of a universally diffused and all-penetrating cosmic matter, an existence not demonstrable through any experience [and thus given in a priori cognition]"); the second is titled *Vom specifischen Unterschiede der materie zu Körpern überhaupt* ("Of the specific difference between matter and bodies").

23. See, e.g., 21:560.10–11, 562.2/9, 563.11, 565.8, 572.6–7, 574.21.

In chapter 5, section 3 ("The Chemical Revolution") of his book (1992a), Michael Friedman discusses the *Opus postumum* in relation to developments in chemistry during the final decades of the 1700s. In particular, he shows how the Transition project, together with the aether deduction, is linked to Kant's concern with contemporary chemical theory. The discussion fits in well with a lengthy tradition of research showing that Kant was vitally concerned to integrate the latest developments in the physical sciences with his reflections on the Transition problematic. Friedman's main contribution to the extant body of this research is that he very usefully, and quite substantially, supplements our knowledge about the relationship between Kant and Lavoisier. (This relationship has been widely recognized in the literature since Adickes.) But in the next section ("The Aether-Deduction"), Friedman goes on to maintain that Kant's concern with the chemical revolution was essentially divorced from the dynamical theory of matter. This position lacks supporting evidence and credibility, especially when compared with recent scholarship offering a more balanced portrayal of Kant's attempts to come to grips with contemporary developments in physical theory against the backdrop of his dynamical theory (see Carrier 1990, 170–210; Carrier 1991, 209–230; Tuschling 1971, 30–61, 191–215; Waschkies 1991, 185–207). In general, any interpretation that ignores the centrality of the dynamical theory for the *Opus postumum* as a whole will necessarily give a highly distorted picture of Kant's considerations on aether theory as well as his attempts to link his idea of a unified system of moving forces to contemporaneous caloric theory. One indication of the weakness of Friedman's position is that the passages he cites to justify his "anti-dynamist" reading are precisely those that demonstrate clearly the centrality of the dynamical theory (see, e.g., Friedman 1992a, 317–323 and 337, where the following passages are discussed: 21:59.28–60.15, 483.24–29, 552.18–553.17; 22:359.15–360.15, 518.12–18, 521.19–21, 522.1–5 [cf. 522.5–14], 524.3–525.19, 529.27–530.12, 537.13–14 [cf. 537.15–538.6]). Another indication of the implausibility of Friedman's approach is the fact that he finds himself constrained to regard Kant's use of the concepts of attractive and repulsive forces in his late aether theory as disconnected from the considerations on the fundamental forces offered in the *Metaphysical Foundations*. In this vein, he even goes so far as to declare that Kant's use of these concepts for the explanation of chemical phenomena is "non-technical—if not metaphorical—and has no direct connection with specifically Newtonian forces (defined by the laws of motion)" (317 note). As far as I can see, this view cannot be made consistent with anything Kant says about attraction and repulsion in the *Opus postumum*. Furthermore, it conflicts with everything that Kant says about these forces from 1756 on. None of this, though, should be especially surprising in light of Friedman's propensity, apparent in the last quoted phrase, to conflate the different explanatory tasks that Kant assigns to his dynamical and mechanical accounts of force (cf. note 40 below).

24. I will use only this term when referring to Kant's universal force-continuum. Kant uses "caloric" (*Wärmestoff*) more often than "aether"; but by *A. Elem. Syst.* at the very latest, nothing essential hinges on the different names given to the material entity (cf. Tuschling 1971, 27, 39–61, 69–76, 184–189).

25. See, e.g., 21:561.7–12, 563.3–4, 565.10–15, 573.6–8, 575.12–15/24.

26. See, e.g., 21:560.1–5, 561.28–30, 562.3–10, 562.21–563.15, 564.25–27, 565.3–15, 572.3–10/20–24, 573.1–8/20–22, 573.25–574.12, 575.20–24.

27. See, e.g., 21:561.24–27, 563.11–15/21–27, 564.6–12/22–24, 571.21–24, 572.16–573.13, 574.5–12/25–26, 574.29–575.8. In the *Critique of Pure Reason* (see 3:391.1–392.9) Kant distinguishes between the "distributive unity of the understanding's experiential use" and the "collective unity of a whole of experience." The latter unity is provided, surreptitiously, by reason's dialectical procedure. It involves the "hypostization" of the "idea of the sum of all reality" (i.e., the transcendental ideal). The sum of reality at issue in the *Opus postumum*'s aether deduction is the sum of material reality underlying what Kant calls the "*one* all-encompassing experience" (see p. 157 below and 3:391.21–22). The relationship between reason and understanding in the aether deduction is a theme that lies outside the scope of this book.

28. See, e.g., 21:559.5–8/10–19, 561.22–23/28–30, 562.14–19, 563.17–564.12, 571.1–5, 571.14–572.2, 572.16–573.13, 573.25–575.8.

29. Those from the passages I am summarizing are comparatively mild. The most remarkable formulations are unquestionably those involving Kant's employment of the Transcendental Ideal's conceptual instrumentarium in order to prove the necessary existence of the cosmic matter. (On this, see 3:385.16–392.9 [especially 385.25–387.6, 388.7–20, 391.11–392.9], 401.35–402.25, 408.13–30; 21:550.11–16, 577.5–578.2, 583.20–29, 586.7–24, 600.5–8, 603.4–19. See also 22:88.30–89.12, 93.11–15, 306.5–12, 364.24–27, 449.2–11, 494.28–32, 497.20–498.11.) It is difficult to make out the ramifications of this employment. Does it supply, among other things, the groundwork for a "materialistic" approach to

transcendental philosophy (cf. 3:391.5–37, 412.4–34)? For discussion of background and related issues, see De Flaviis 1986, 104–124; Förster 1989a, 297–298; Förster 1989b, 219–228; Rohs 1978, 170–180.

30. See Adickes 1920, 389–395; Hoppe 1969, 110–114.

31. See, e.g., 21:563.14–15, 564.4–6.

32. See the references to physical aether as ground of dynamical community in note 37 below.

33. Kant is unequivocal about the subjective character of the *principle* in question, although his exploratory considerations on the connection between subjective and non-subjective transcendental conditions often strongly emphasize the seemingly paradoxical quality of the aether deduction's conclusion. For example:

> Thus, the subjective principle for the establishment [*Anstellung*] of this object [i.e., dynamical aether] is at the same time *objectively* valid for the object itself and its existence. (21:564.4–6)
> The subjective basis of experience [*das Subjective der Erfahrung*] becomes here objectively the outer object of possible experience and the basis of the latter, . . . , and is thus distributed as substance in space. (21:564.25–27)

34. See, more generally, 21:226.1–228.32, 234.36–235.16, 535.10–537.20, 539.22–541.10, 580.12–18, 584.21–586.6.

35. See Tuschling 1971, 30–34. For a highly detailed analysis of the theory of the aether subsequent to ca. 1775, I refer above all to Adickes's editorial commentary on Reflections 40, 43, 44, and 45a–54 (see 14:137–141, 233–258, 287–366, 412–456). For further analysis, see Adickes 1920, 60–65, 430–474 and Adickes 1924–25, II 173–205. Despite the philosophic defects of Adickes's approach to Kant as a "natural scientist," it is still true that no serious interpretation of the *Opus postumum*'s aether theory can afford to ignore this practically inexhaustible body of historical research.

36. See, e.g., 21:256.1–21, 340.16–24, 382.29–383.34, 515.11–19; 22:214.2–22, 215.18–30, 254.13–16, 526.26–527.25, 605.22–606.2.

37. For the characterization of the aether as a ground of community, see 21:179.11–17, 226.25–227.8, 311.26–28, 561.22–30, 562.21–563.15, 565.2–15, 575.12–24, 579.25–31, 580.12–15, 584.29–585.21, 609.2–10; 22:143.13–16, 151.17–153.14, 394.3–27. (See also 21:235.4–16, 309.6–8, 518.15–520.30, 566.7. 22:174.21–24, 178.3–21, 531.9–19.) For the highest ground of material reality in space, see 21:216.23–217.7, 228.7–23, 229.6–7, 233.5–8, 236.15–20, 253.8–10, 383.31–34, 551.4–6, 554.1–3, 562.21–27, 592.23–27; 22:195.27–196.18, 334.8–16, 360.14–15. For generative source of corporeal formation: e.g., 21:215.14–217.7, 378.19–379.6, 380.7–14, 428.14–30, 484.23–28, 542.26–543.11, 544.27–29, 547.22–548.4; 22:359.26–360.18, 378.16–24, 440.4–12, 462.18–28; 577.1–5; 607.20–608.21. (Note once again the centrality of the problem of cohesion in the dynamical theory of matter.)

38. See, e.g., 21:219.5–22, 547.22–548.4, 553.7–8, 561.3–12, 588.17–26, 593.7–11; 22:327.4–26, 330.20–331.4, 462.26–28, 471.3–8, 471.20–472.8, 474.26–476.,1, 478.26–479.13, 508.14–509.11, 525.5–526.6, 535.10–15, 577.1–5, 607.20–608.21, 614.20–615.7. Note in this context that we encounter throughout the *Opus postumum* the same heuristic view of force-centers as the one advocated

during the 1770s. On this, see jointly 21:378.19–29, 404.12, 406.22–25, 411.9–17, 412.5–9; 22:205.6–206.2, 207.3–10, 211.10–12, 428.21–429.29, 536.7–21, 537.5–538.6.

39. See, e.g., 21:216.16–217.7, 380.7–14, 428.14–30, 540.24–541.10, 544.27–29, 545.1–16; 22:211.10–15. For a more detailed treatment of this point, I refer to Adickes (1920, 402–405), who argues in favor of a complete dichotomy between the aether (or aethers) and ponderable matter. For the reasons stated in note 23 above, I do not agree with this view. Nevertheless, the substantive issue remains: why does Kant demonstrate the *propensity* to keep the aether ontologically separate from the material particulars constituted by its universal action? One reason may be traced back to Kant's preoccupation with the dominant language of the physics of imponderables during the 1770s (cf. Tuschling 1971, 39–46; cf. also Carrier 1990, 190–193). But I suggest that Kant's deeper motives have to do with the difficulties in his account of material substance discussed further on in this chapter.

40. In rejecting Burkhard Tuschling's reading of the *Phoronomiekritik* (see note 12 above), Friedman (1992a, 225–226 note) asserts that Kant's conception of dynamical moving forces needs to be understood "in the context of the eighteenth-century struggle between the corpuscular or mechanical natural philosophy and the Newtonian natural philosophy" (226). He elaborates on this claim by referring to Newton's conception of force as the cause of motion, but it soon becomes clear (226–229) that the Newtonian conception he has in mind corresponds to the concept of force at issue in Kant's descriptions of mechanics, not the dynamics of material nature. In attempting to determine the nature of the relationship between Kant's dynamical theory and Newtonian natural philosophy, Friedman thus fails to distinguish properly between the discursive levels of Kant's dynamical and mechanical accounts of moving force. That fits in with his refusal to acknowledge the centrality of the dynamical theory of matter in Kant's philosophy of nature. And we can see why both failings grow out of the inadequate conceptual framework that Friedman constructs in order to make sense of the development of eighteenth-century natural philosophy and its relation to Newton. The counterpart to the corpuscular philosophy is not (merely) Newtonian natural philosophy. It is rather the various versions of dynamical natural philosophy that ordinarily made use of Newtonian forces (or powers) of attraction and repulsion. Friedman dismisses without substantive argument (see, e.g., 138 note) the body of research relevant to this topic, and he in effect declares irrelevant the dynamistic dimensions of Newton's own philosophy that are essential to any balanced understanding of eighteenth-century natural philosophy. Historically speaking, his reading of Newton is highly selective, and indeed reductive. One indication of the degree of bias underlying Friedman's historical approach is that he cites Richard Westfall's *Force in Newton's Physics* even while he ignores how Westfall treats in detail those aspects of Newton's philosophy of nature (including Newton's aether theory) that are most directly, and obviously, pertinent to the genesis and development of eighteenth-century dynamism (see Westfall 1971, 329–332, 335–341, 363–400; cf. Westfall 1980, 301–309, 374–390, 505–512, 520–523, 638–648, 792–796).

41. See 21:165.14–16, 308.23–29, 310.3–33, 380.27–381.5, 387.15–18, 391.12–

22,409.24−27; 22:287.11−14, 373.18−21, 462.18−28, 478.26−479.13. Cf. Tuschling 1971, 60−61, 69−71, 78.

42. Besides the passages cited in note 6 above, see, e.g., 21:159.1−166.18, 170.1−174.14; 22:135.1−155.8, 267.11−276.27, 556.2−585.10.

43. Cf 1:476.6−15.

44. Certain qualifications must be placed on Tuschling's argument that the idea of Transition represents merely an "ad-hoc solution" according to which Kant attempts to furnish a radically new systematic basis for the dynamical theory while at the same time claiming that this is compatible with the Dynamics of the *Metaphysical Foundations.* (For details, see Tuschling 1971, 31−32, 61−65, 80, 84−89, 111, 122, 177−178, 180−184.) At one level, this reading is correct. But the notion of the Transition has further significance that comes to dominate the later system sketches of the *Opus postumum.* I have in mind here the conception of a "gliding transition" from the level of a priori, metaphysical principles of natural philosophy to the level of empirical concepts and the corresponding procedures of observation and experimentation. (On this, see [in chronological order] 22:320.31−321.3, 331.14−32, 354.4−24, 359.15−360.18, 367.3−369.2, 391.2−392.28, 395.4−24, 400.4−401.30, 404.10−405.12, 451.11−30.) I therefore do not agree with one of the central conclusions of Tuschling's 1971 publication. Tuschling argues that all of Kant's attempts at determining the exact nature of his transitional science end in the recognition that a continuous transition between the metaphysics of nature and physics is impossible. Since the dynamics of material nature comes to be part of Kant's transcendental theory of experience, the objects and methods of physics as an empirical science are ultimately separated from the a priori part of the doctrine of nature by a gap over which there can be "no bridge, no transition" (Tuschling 1971, 178). On my interpretation, however, a continuous transition between the two levels of our knowledge of nature—and consequently between knowledge a priori and knowledge a posteriori—is for Kant not only possible. It is also unavoidable. Thus, the main task of transcendental dynamics to show how and why it is so, and to do this in conformity with the conception of transcendental argumentation discussed in § 4 of this chapter. The difficulties inherent in the endeavor to complete this task are made manifest in Fascicle 10/11 and in Fascicle 7, where Kant repeatedly attempts to come to grips with the exigencies of an absolute idealism, on the one hand, and the collapse of the distinction between empirical and transcendental realism, on the other.

45. In the line elided Kant maintains that "otherwise it would be, as something that changes its position, an object of experience" (*sonst wäre es als stellverändernd ein Erfahrungsobjekt*). Kant obviously means to say that if we were able to represent the sum-total of the movable in space (i.e., matter) as a movable whole, then we would be representing this whole as something perceived to be moving in materially void space. That is impossible on Kant's view, since space devoid of matter (or moving forces) is no object of possible experience.

46. In this and related passages, we witness the integration of the problem of cosmogenesis with the theory of a transcendental dynamics. I cannot here explore this aspect of Kant's late aether theory, which can be traced back to the *Universal Natural History.* But see (in chronological order) 21:423.29−424.6,

378.7–379.6, 310.3–13, 256.1–19, 216.16–218.7, 579.20–580.10; 22:10.15–30; 21:38.9–11. For background, see Adickes 1920, 373–377.

47. See 14:173.1–6.

48. See 3:138.5–8. See also 3:181.19–25, 182.17–19.

49. For the foundational role played by the category of substance in Kant's metaphysics, see, above all, 3:5.20–26, 4:307.19–21, 325.25–26/31–33; Reflections 4679 (17:633.1–3), 5285, 5297. 28(1)428.10–17, 28(2):655.27–29; 29:769.15–20. But see also 3:106.25–28, 118.32–33, 200.9–15, 206.1–5, 270.17–18, 286.6–24, 359.2–12; 8:223.12–14, 224.23–225.3; Reflections 3903, 4052–4054, 4158, 4415, 4492, 4702 (cf. 3:167.2–13), 4776, 5295–5296, 5298, 5348, 5654, 6403, 6313. A detailed discussion of this role is provided by Kaulbach 1981, 182–189.

50. In other words, dynamical community is the reciprocal causality of substances not in respect of substantial permanence, which is nothing more than "the way in which we represent to ourselves the existence of things (in the appearance)" (3:165.7–9). For substantial permanence as a transcendental condition, see, generally, 3:137.30–37, 162.21–24, 163.29–32, 166.23–25; and further: 3:30.8–19, 167.2–13, 176.30–178.2, 200.6–15; Reflections 5291, 5297, 5348, 6403; 28(1):430.16–20; 28(2):563.35–564.5, 655.27–29.

51. See (jointly) 3:97.3–7, 165.10–24, 181.15–22. Cf. 1:21.35–22.5, 410.17–411.30, 415.17–416.4; 2:389.29–35, 390.15–29, 416.33–37; 28(1):433.27–434.2, 514.3–16; 28(2)639.35–640.8.

52. Cf. note 29 of chapter 2 above.

53. See 3:177.4–13, 8:224.35–38; Reflections 4762 (17:720.9–12), 5290; 28(1)431.7–25, 511.23–30; 28(2)564.11–13, 639.2–34; 29:770.24–29.

54. This kind of re-thinking would have to go beyond the standard dynamistic criticism of the corpuscular distinction between primary and secondary qualities. See § 1 of chapter 6 above.

55. See (jointly and in chronological order), 21:311.26–312.7, 338.8–11, 350.22–29, 541.20–543.11; 22:327.4–8, 346.2–10, 349.21–24, 358.1–9, 360.3–18, 360.26–361.4, 378.18–24, 402.26–403.10, 471.20–472.8, 475.26–30, 508.14–509.11, 514.21–25, 523.19–33, 535.10–15, 438.17–26, 450.14–16. The majority of these passages involve the attempt to show that what we ordinarily call substances are actually particular moving forces, while substance as such is nothing less than the collective whole of dynamical matter. Much of what Kant says is broadly consistent with the account of the relationship between physical aether and material particulars that we find already in the 1770s Reflection 44 (see pp. 126–127 above). But things get to be extremely complicated when he deals directly with the substance/accident issues raised by this kind of account:

> To classify *a priori* the moving forces of matter generally for physics towards which the metaphysical foundations have a natural (necessary) tendency. First, according to their form as attractive [force] or as repulsion. The subjects of these forces are the movable and moving *substances* themselves.
> But one can just as little speak of matters [*Materien*] as one can speak of experiences (*in plurali*), because the one, just as the other, contains a property [*Beschaffenheit*], [i.e.,] merely a qualitative and not a quantitative relation of the subject of the merely empirical representation.—The subject of motion, insofar as it is thought of as

a particular movable *substance,* as contrasted with the properties (the moving forces) adhering to it, is called a *material* [*Stoff*] (*basis materia*) and is never thought of as something self-subsistent in a certain place, but is very well thought of as something brought by something else into a certain community (*materia deferens*) or also as the originally constitutive material of an elementary matter existing apart from all community with other materials. (22:394.3–18)

If the particular subjects of attraction and repulsion are the moving and movable substances themselves, why exactly is it improper to speak of matters? And if those moving forces are regarded as adherent (and therefore accidental) properties of these particular substances, then how are we to understand their relation to the originally constitutive material of an elementary matter?

56. The passage is found in *Über eine Entdeckung, nach der alle neue Kritik der reinen Vernunft durch eine ältere entbehrlich gemacht werden soll* (On a discovery according to which any new Critique of Pure Reason has been made superfluous by an earlier one).

57. Cf. 2:90.33–91.2, 389.23–390.4, 416.33–417.3; 3:389.19–390.16; 5: 101.36–102.16, 393.11–21; 8:143.25–28, 223.20–224.7; Reflections 3781, 3907 (17:337.14–18), 3924, 4776–4777, 6050 (18:435.31–436.9); 28(1):429.13–18, 457.29–458.5, 510.28–511.9, 511.23–512.21; 28(2)563.9–35, 639.18–24, 671.18–21, 845.19–21, 1207.6–18; 29:771.2–11.

58. Cf. 3:85.17–19, 91.28–34; 4:91.3–14/29–37. "Transcendental" is generally employed by Kant to characterize some condition that makes experience possible, and that therefore provides for the possibility of a priori knowledge (see 3:145.26–29; 4:81.14–15). The expression "transcendental function" refers to such a condition insofar as it is conceived in terms of a unity of acting or action (*Einheit der Handlung* [cf. 3:85.18]). In the *Critique of Pure Reason,* this idea of function relates primarily to the unifying operations of pure understanding. The unity established through the synthetic functioning of the understanding is that unity that issues from the various acts of the understanding (*Verstandeshandlungen* [cf. 3:86.9, 92.19–20]) when these are directed to the manifold of representations given in space and time. It is the unity expressed by means of a priori concepts of the understanding insofar as these concepts furnish rules of synthesis for that manifold. Kant's problem in the aether deduction is to show how the a priori necessary function of the universal force-continuum relates to the specifically subjective functions of unity.

59. The correlativity of the unity of consciousness and the unity of the object in question here is not the same as the correlativity thematized by Henry Allison's well-known "reciprocity thesis" (see Allison 1983, 144–148, 294; and Allison 1996, 51). The thesis discussed by Allison concerns the necessary correlation that Kant establishes in the *Critique of Pure Reason* between the transcendental unity of apperception, as a purely formal unity, and an object in its "judgmental or logical sense" (Allison 1983, 146). The thesis therefore relies on the broad conception of object at issue in § 17 of the 1787 Transcendental Deduction, where Kant defines "object" as "that in the concept of which the manifold of a given intuition is *united*" (3:111.18–19). Moreover, the thesis asserts the reciprocity between the synthetic unity of apperception and the representation of an object exclusively on grounds of Kant's general argument that the pure concepts of the understanding are conditions of both the unity of apperception

and the representation of objects (on this, see Allison 1996, 51). Now Kant's physical aether can be characterized formally in terms of Kant's broad conception of object since it furnishes what Kant calls the "*one* object" of outer intuition (for the meaning of this designation see pp. 169–171 of chapter 9). Also, nothing that Kant says in the aether deduction denies that pure intellectual concepts are conditions of the unity of apperception *and* the representation of objects. Nevertheless, the reciprocity thesis that emerges from the 1787 Transcendental Deduction is not a sufficient basis for determining the aether's role in Kant's late transcendental theory. The correlativity conception of the *Opus postumum* implies that if the *one* object of all outer sensible intuition did not itself provide a condition of synthetic unity for our empirical representations, then there could be no experience of particular objects in space. Consequently, apart from the unifying function of the aether's (i.e., dynamical cosmic matter's) activity, no pure concept of the understanding could serve as a condition of unity in the representation of such objects *as* objects of experience. And if this is so, then the synthetic unity of apperception that correlates with *that* representation is not achievable apart from the unifying function of dynamical cosmic matter. In the context of the aether deduction, there is indeed complete reciprocity between the synthetic unity of apperception and the unity of an object as far as our a priori knowledge of the objects of outer intuition is concerned. But this kind of reciprocity cannot be understood in abstraction from the transcendental function of the universal continuum of moving forces. Thus, if the principle of the synthetic unity of apperception is to be based on a concept of the unity of consciousness that denotes "the point to which one must attach all employment of the understanding" (3:109.36–37), including the understanding's employment in relation to the objects of sensible intuition, then it must be linked to a principle that specifies an objective material condition of a priori synthetic unity. But the 1787 Transcendental Deduction does not provide any basis for establishing this link since it does not recognize the possibility of such a material transcendental condition.

    60. It also gives rise to new ways of approaching old problems. It is worth noting that the correlativity conception of the *Opus postumum* allows us to focus on the reasons Kant may have had for attempting the aether deduction in view of the difficulties inherent in the proof structure of the first *Critique*'s 1787 Transcendental Deduction. These well-known difficulties stem from Kant's procedure of establishing a necessary connection between the categories and the data of human sensibility (i.e., appearances) on the basis of an *analytic* principle of the synthetic unity of apperception (see 3:110.11–23, 112.7–19; cf. Allison 1996, 47–52 and Guyer 1987, 132–133, 142–143). But as long as it is true that the pure concepts of the understanding are conditions of both the unity of apperception and the representation of objects (see note 59 above), there would be no problem in establishing that connection in the context of the aether deduction. The necessary correlativity of the unity of apperception and the unity of the object at issue in the aether deduction is meant to guarantee that outer appearances will be so constituted that they can be subjected to the conditions of the understanding's unity (contrast 3:103.9–15). Interestingly, Kant insists on the analyticity of the principle that asserts the aether's existence (see, e.g., 21:559.5–14, 591.1–593.5, 600.1–601.3).

Chapter 9.   Kant's Transcendental Theory: Heterodox Considerations on Its History

1. See, e.g., 22:300.10–31, 324.5–327.20, 346.1–350.26, 359.15–361.8, 388.1–390.30, 402.15–404.9, 457.1–30, 463.1–467.18, 467.10–469.3, 483.7–484.10.

2. See the references to Aenesidemus-Schluze, Beck, Fichte, Reinhold, Schelling, and Theatetus-Tiedemann in the factual notes to Förster and Rosen's recent Cambridge edition (1993) of selections from the *Opus postumum*.

3. See, e.g., 22:325.8–326.10, 363.14–365.13, 385.3–14, 388.1–389.20, 32.5–18, 73.8–74.5, 77.11–78.14, 81.25–82.21, 82.23–89.12, 418.16–25; 21:26–13–14, 34.3–4. See also 22:333.21–334.16, 364.12–365.6, 384.9–18, 465.14–28, 484.3–10, 535.16–17, 411.26–412.2, 418.16–25, 421.7–10; 21:122.14–18, 128.3–9.

4. The theory of self-positing adumbrated in the later fascicles has a practical as well as a theoretical dimension. The subject constitutes itself not merely as determined by its relation to the general object of intuition or, in other words, in relation to the collective whole of perceptions rooted in and correlated with the causal efficacy of the moving forces of matter. It also constitutes itself as *person*. The subject posits itself as a being that knows itself to be free by virtue of its consciousness of the categorical imperative. It thereby knows itself through practical reason to be a being that has rights and duties, and that thus is necessarily motivated to act out of respect for the moral law. I discuss the ramifications of both the theoretical and practical dimensions of self-positing for Kant's idea of transcendental philosophy in Edwards 2000 (forthcoming). See also Edwards 1999 for further considerations on the relationship between Kant's transcendental theory in the *Opus postumum* and his practical philosophy.

5. On this, see pp. 1–2 of the introduction and p. 39 of chapter 2 above.

6. Not the least of these is occasioned by Kant's decision not to exclude the highest principles and concepts of morality from transcendental philosophy taken in its narrower sense, as he in fact does in the *Critique of Pure Reason*. See 3:45.13–32, 3:546.8–21.

7. For the standardly accepted account, as well as Kant's conception of the a priori anticipation of the form of possible experience, see pp. 1–4 of the introduction and pp. 55–57 of chapter 3 above.

8. See, most recently, Mathieu 1989, 268–273. For summary treatments of earlier secondary sources, see Mathieu 1958, 107–132; Tuschling 1971, 8–13. See also the exhaustive bibliography compiled by Karin Beiküfner in Blasche 1991, 233–244.

9. See, e.g., 22:425.23–426.6, 431.4–9, 440.3–15, 457.20–27, 84.5–28, 88.27–89.12, 93.11–15 (cf. 21:603.4–19), 106.20–107.21, 107.1–21, 110.9–11, 115.3–4, 117.16–19; 21:55.1–6, 55.27–56.2, 59.28–60.15, 89.2–30, 124.21–24.

10. See, e.g., 21:550.11–16, 577.16–578.2. 583.20–32, 586.7–24, 603.4–19; 22:306.5–12, 364.24–27, 494.28–32, 497.20–498.11, 449.2–20, 88.30–89.12, 93.11–15.

11. See, e.g., 22:325.8–326.14, 330.20–331.4, 332.2–14, 339.17–28, 351.1–6, 474.25–476.6, 507.12–18, 513.27–514.5, 515.19–24, 517.25–519.8, 521.11–523.29,

524.1–539.4, 18.17–19.2, 106.23–107.21, 110.9–14, 113.25–114.11, 115.3–4, 124.2–12, 420.2–421.3; 21:47.1–26, 51.23–52.3, 54.2–28, 59.28–60.15, 66.22–67.10, 124.21–25, 150.20–22. Note that when Kant refers to empty space in a number of these passages, he is referring either to mechanically empty space (i.e., to a space that offers no resistance to the motion of bodies) or else to space determined by the force of attraction but not filled by the force of repulsion (on this, see 4:496.5–23, 511.28–512.3, 512.18–32, 513.15–19, 517.4–7, 563/19–32). Although he ordinarily maintains that space is determined by both of the constitutive forces of matter, he can entertain the notion that space could be dynamically determined without thereby being materially filled. Such a space cannot, however, be a perceptible space. Michael Friedman (1992a, 320–324) recognizes this point. But since he does not acknowledge the dynamist presuppositions of Kant's late aether theory, he overlooks the problem of space generated by the aether deduction (see Friedman 1992a, 317, 324–341).

12. See, e.g., 21:219.5–10, 228.24–27, 550.28–551.6, 561.22–562.19, 573.6–9, 574.21–24; 22:325.8–327.3, 327.20–26, 338.7–339.28, 508.11–14, 517.25–518.14, 538.7–23, 431.4–24, 434.11–28, 436.14–22, 440.4–15. See also 21:59.27–60.15, 71.21–23, 124.21–24; 22:10.15–30, 107.16–21, 109.16–19, 110.9–11, 115.4–5, 117.16–19, 118.9–12.

13. For a different conception of appearance of the appearance, see (in chronological order) 22:319.24–320.2, 320.16–322.30, 328.11–16, 329.14–21, 334.20–27, 363.24–364.23, 367.3–369.2, 371.1–14. As is true of many of the central concepts of the *Opus postumum,* we must be sensitive to the specific context of their employment in order to understand the import of Kant's transcendental argumentation.

14. Kant continues by pointing out that sensible space "is not given, but is merely thought" (22:433.18–19). This reflects his concern in the later fascicles to do justice to the role of the understanding with respect to the distinction between first-order and second-order appearance. The space determined by the presence of the elementary whole of moving forces is not given in the way that individually identifiable objects occupying particular parts of space are given, for it is not the space of any "prehensible" substance. It must therefore be *thought as* the omnicomprehensive sensible or material space in which all prehensible objects are given. But it is still *sensible* space.

15. Cf. 3:65.9–16; 4.232.26–236.11.

16. Regarding this translation of *eine Größe des Mannigfaltigen außer einander,* see 3:52.23–24, 53.20.

17. The final clause (*welcher den bewegenden Kräften mit ihrer Bewegung zur Basis dient zur Möglichkeit Einer Erfahrung* [*aller zugleich möglichen*] *zusammen zu stimmen*) defies translation. The continuation of the line of argument (see 21:236.21–237.16) shows that Kant has in mind the unified material basis that makes possible the combination of the moving forces into the collective unity of experience. But my translation gives the weakest feasible interpretation of the connection between the cosmic matter and the principle of possible experience.

18. 3:111.18–19, 148.22–149.14, 152.2–24, 192.22–193.5; 4:481.2–18.

19. Cf. 4:236.1–3.

20. Cf. 4:232.26–234.29.

21. See (in chronological order) 21:221,10–13, 223.15–24, 228.6–27, 231.8–13, 235.4–8, 236.15–20, 539.27–540.12, 547.7–12, 553.6–17, 563.24–564.4, 589.27–590.9, 593.24–28/594.16–23; 22:331.23–31, 332.21–233.14, 475.3–476.1, 486.12–16, 524.1–16, 531.13–19, 538.7–25, 430.27–431.24, 440.4–15, 20.14–23, 88.30 — 89.12, 92.26–29, 117.16 19, 420.17–421.3; 21:59.28–60.15.

22. Cf. 4:232.14–20, 235.23–236.11, 241.7–25.

23. See 22:42523–426.6, 431.4–9, 440.3–15, 457.20–27, 84.5–28, 88.27–89.12, 93.11–15 (cf. 21:603.4–19), 106.20–107.21, 110.9–11, 115.3–4, 117.16–19; 21:23.27–31, 55.1–6, 55.27–56.2, 59.28–60.15, 89.2–30, 122.14–18, 124.21–24.

24. See, e.g., 22:475.1–11, 22.21–23, 22.29–23.5, 23.11–14, 25.12–21, 27.16–20, 29.16–29, 74.10–18, 80.17–81.2, 81.27–29; 21:59.28–60.4, 66.22.24.

25. See 3:51.18–57.14.

26. Cf. 3:55.9–23, 59.18–22, 61.12–24, 65.12–15; 4:236.3. According to Kant's definitional criteria (see 3:71.3–72.9, 190.24–193.24), any attempt to absorb this feature of transcendental reality into a doctrine of the transcendental ideality of space must ultimately result in a full-blown material idealism.

27. Cf. 2:403.23–404.2; 3:56.9–19, 63.24–34; 4:232.6–234.20.

28. See, e.g., (in chronological order) 21:423.29–424.6, 378.7–379.6, 310.3–13, 256.1–19, 22:194.17–195.26; 21:216.16–218.7, 579.20–580.10; 22:10.15–30; 21:38.9–11.

29. See, e.g., 3:44.24–46.17, 55.19–57.14, 71.3–72.9, 338.21–340.26.

30. See also Reflections 4144–4145, 4749; 28(2):810.31–32 (cf. Baumgarten, *Metaphysica* §§ 950–958; Wolff, *Theol. nat.* § 1051). Regarding the background of the idea of *omnipraesentia phaenomenon* and the correlative notions of the *sensorium dei* and *intima praesentia,* see Leibniz, GP VII 353–354, 358–362, 366, 386, 410–411; More, *Opera,* II(1) 165–169 and II(2) 234–235; Newton, *Opera,* IV 172–173, 238. Discussions of these and related sources are provided by Burtt 1932, 127–154, 243–299 and by Koyré 1969, 105–249.

31. 2:402.29–30.

32. 2:403.23.

33. 2:403.26–27.

34. The error on the part of the Leibnizians is, however, more serious. The particular version of the relationist account of space intrinsic to the Leibnizian position is detrimental to the a priori applicability and validity of geometry (see 2:403.23–404.20; cf. 3:63.24–64.18).

35. The most important of these relates to the term "compresence of all things [*compraesentia omnium*]" (2:410.2). Depending on emphasis, we can understand space as either (a) the sensuously cognized condition of *all things* or (b) the *sensuously cognized* condition of all things. Since the first reading blurs the distinction between *cognitio sensitiva* and *cognitio intellectualis,* it is inconsistent with the fundamental tenets of Kant's metaphysical theory in the Dissertation (see 2:395.28–31; 410.20–412.19). The second reading could be made to respect that distinction by referring *omnium* to those things that lie open to the human mind so far it is sustained by the infinite power of a single cause. Grammatically, this procedure is not without its difficulties. But the second reading has the added advantage of being compatible with the conception of

space adumbrated in § 16 (i.e., with the idea of space as *relatio omnium substantiarum intuitive spectata*). For these and related reasons, my view is that the second reading is correct. The following metaphysical fragments are directly relevant to the problematic: Reflections 4189, 4207–4208 (cf. 2:396.9–397.4), 4520. See also Reflections 3832, 4074, 4145, 4216, 4422, 4673, 4750, 5417, 5554, 5962, 6164, 6214, 6284–6285, 6317a.

36. Note Kant's concern to combine the concepts of space, divine omnipresence and Newtonian universal attraction. For access to the metaphysical problematic at issue, see the following passages from Pölitz's version of Kant's lectures on religion: 28:1107.3–1109.3. But see also 28:214.10–28, 346.25–347.30; 567.11–27, 603.16–28, 666.29–38, 797.1–11, 827.23–829.37, 888.4–10, 1209.33–1212.13, 1309.38–1310.25; 29:865.14–866.15, 1007.21–29. For Kant's earlier views on the idea of the infinite space of divine presence, see 1:24.1–30, 306.23–34, 312.23–314.36, 329.14–330.5, 481.32–36, 415.5–14; 2: 297,12–19. For a later view: 4:138.25–34.

37. Wundt 1924, 176. It is, however, interesting to note in this vein that in the letter to Herz, Kant refers indirectly to the Scholium of Section IV immediately after addressing the problem of the agreement between pure intellectual concepts and objects (see 10:131.15–25).

38. In thinking about this transformation, we should not forget that the *structural* groundwork for Kant's description of the human mind's cognitive relation to the totality of objects lies already prepared in Part 1 of the Essay on Living Forces and in Proposition 13 of the *Nova dilucidatio* (see 1:21.13–14, 24.33, 415.5–416.4).

39. Note well the distinction made in the Pölitz lectures on religion between the intimate presence of God and the immediate presence of Newtonian universal attraction as causal ground of reciprocal influence between the substances of the world:

> The omnipresence of God is furthermore the innermost presence. That is, God preserves what is substantial—the internal determinacy [*das Innere*] of substances themselves. For just this is necessary for their continued existence; and if God did not ceaselessly actuate this internal determinacy of things and what is essentially substantial in them, the things would have to cease existing. One can think of a presence that is immediate but that is not itself intimate [*innig*]. According to Newton's theorems, we have an example of this in the mutual attraction of all things in the world. These things attract each other even immediately or, as Newton expresses himself, through empty space. They therefore act on [*in*] each other reciprocally; consequently, they are one and all present to each other, though not intimately present. For there is here merely reciprocal influence, i.e., action on their states [*eine Wirkung in ihrem Zustande*], or mutual modification of their alterable determinations. But intimate presence is the actuation of the continued existence of that which is itself substantial in things. (28[2]:1107.17–31)

On the concept of empty space at issue in Newton's manner of expression, see note 11 above.

40. Cf. 2:408.13–19.

41. Cf. Stark 1984b, 345–349; Stark 1984a, 365–374.

42. Its plausibility is greatly enhanced if we also take into consideration Kant's lectures on physics. In the *Berliner Physikvorlesung*, Kant explicitly refers

to the aether as the highest cause of all derivative forces of matter. See 29:78.1–5, 79.1–10, 80.11–82.20.

43. On the Leibnizian origins of this view, see Leibniz, GP V 46–51, 141–142; VI 179, 156, 599–600, 603–604, 609–612. Wolff, *Psych. rat.* §§ 10–14, 19–23, 53–68, 81–82, 193, 257, 264–265. Cf. 2:199.28–35; 3:107.11–15.

44. See 10.131.24–25.

45. See book 3, part 2, chapter 6 of Malebranche's *De la recherche de la verité.*

46. See Reflections 4749–4750. Cf. Spinoza, *Ethica* I, Prop. 14–15, 17; II, Prop. 3–4, 40–47.

47. *Schwärmerei* is nowadays ordinarily rendered into English as "enthusiasm" (see, for example, the Guyer and Wood translation of 3:106.5 and the Förster translation of 21:19.15). My rendering is strictly technical. It conforms to the clear distinction that Kant draws between *Enthusiasmus* and *Schwärmerei* in *Beobachtungen über das Gefühl des Schönen und Erhabenen (Observations on the Feeling of the Beautiful and the Sublime)* and in the *Critique of Judgment* (see 2:251.32 and 5:271.37–272.6, 275.6–16).

48. See 18:434.10–435.6, 437.20–27.

49. See 18.435.6–11, 437.27–29; cf. 10:131.24–25. The historical referent of this view is not mentioned in either of the Reflections under consideration. According to the chronological line being laid out, the source of the view would have to be an ancient author. But it is not clear who that might be since it is not Plato. (Note, however, the reference to Plato's "mystical deduction of the Ideas" [3:246.36–37] in the *Critique of Pure Reason.*)

50. See 18:435.11–21, 437.30–438.2.

51. See 18:435.25–436.8.

52. Regarding this, see Kant's discussion of the history of pure reason in the Transcendental Doctrine of Method of the first *Critique* (3:550.33–551.29). The criteria for classifying philosophical theories specified by this discussion are consistent with what Kant says in Reflections 6051 and 6052.

53. See De Flaviis 1986, 91–242; Allison 1980, 199–22.

54. Cf. 3:72.10–28. (Paul Guyer [1987, 352–354] demonstrates the unsoundness of the corresponding argument contained in this passage from the first *Critique.*)

55. See 5:124–146, 436–461; 6:3–6.

56. See 22:55.1–2, 56.13–14, 59.21–24, 61.1–2, 64.9–11; 21:15.6–7, 19.14–25, 43.22–24, 48.26–27, 51.12–17.

57. For a comprehensive discussion, see De Flaviis 1986.

58. Kant's acquaintance with the fundamentals of Schelling's *System des transzendentalen Idealismus* is supported by his citation of a review published in April 1801 in the *Erlanger Literatur Zeitung* (see 21:97.25–26).

59. See, e.g., 22:54.23–55.3; 21:43.18–26, 51.12–52.3, 69.17–21, 55.1–6, 66.5, 69.3–21, 87.21–31, 95.27–96.11, 97.3–29, 98.12–16, 127.28–128.9, 130.13–15. For further information, see Adickes 1920, 833–845; De Flaviis 1986, 276–286.

60. Eckart Förster has argued that Kant in the *Opus postumum* does not, and cannot, uphold the distinction between transcendental and metaphysical principles, and that he therefore alters the relation between transcendental critique and metaphysical system that is characteristic of his critical philosophy

during the 1780s (see Förster 1989a, especially 296–302). He thus concludes that the conception of transcendental philosophy that Kant advocates in Fascicle 1 of the *Opus postumum* represents a "'postcritical' phase in Kant's thinking comparable to the so-called critical and precritical phases," although this does not mean that "after 1790 Kant returned to a form of metaphysical dogmatism" (285). I agree with Förster on all of these points except one. I am far more cautious than he is about describing Kant's late conception(s) of transcendental philosophy as postcritical—or even as "so-called" postcritical. I am unwilling to call this philosophic project postcritical as long as Kant still insists that it is based on an investigation of the sources of our a priori knowledge which satisfies generally his earlier accounts of what qualifies as critical philosophy (see, for example, 3:203.10–19, 460.33–461.8, 495.19–27, 543.27–544.8; 5:5.10–6.1, 167.3–10; 6:206.35–207.29; 21:7.6–27, 40.2–7, 60.60–22, 67.24–27, 73.11–16, 75.6–77.7, 79.25–80.4, 87.20–23, 104.2–12, 107.5–11, 115.23–116.3, 117.1–5, 131.14–20).

61. See, e.g., 22:59.21–24; 21:19.14–15, 48.26–27, 50.13–15.

62. In one of his factual notes to the Cambridge translation of the *Opus postumum* (see pp. 285–286), Eckart Förster takes issue with the standard reading of Kant's reference to Schelling, Spinoza, and Lichtenberg in conjunction with the three temporal dimensions of transcendental idealism (21:87.29–31). According to this reading, the three thinkers mentioned embody the past, present, and future phases of the system of transcendental idealism. Förster points to the apparent incongruity of this order, especially since it fails to assign the younger Schelling to the future dimension of the system ultimately envisaged by Kant. Förster argues that in referring to the three dimensions, Kant did not have in mind the developmental stages of his own late conception of transcendental idealism. Rather, he was alluding to the account of the subject's self-constitutive activity provided in Schelling's *System des transzendentalen Idealismus*. (This account had been analyzed in the review of Schelling's book that Kant read after April 1801. See note 58 above.) But I think there are good reasons for accepting the standard reading and, moreover, for insisting that by the middle of 1801, Kant did regard Schelling's *System* of 1800 as representing merely the current stage of transcendental philosophy. These reasons have to do with Kant's identification of his own philosophical standpoint with that of "Lichtenberg," i.e., with the symbol of transcendental idealism's future. A case can be made for the idea that this identification grows out of Kant's affirmative reception of Lichtenberg's dynamistic interpretation of Spinoza. Also, Kant was no doubt positively predisposed to Lichtenberg's critical evaluation of the type of scientific explanation that was characteristic of the Romantic philosophies of nature. (For background, see De Flaviis 1986, 276–286; Mautner 1968, 310–325, 333–340, 365–398, 436–450.)

63. For background, see Beiser 1987, especially 44–164; De Flaviis 1986, 91–143; Frigo 1977, 811–859; Tilliette 1978, 217–229; Timm 1974; Vernière 1954, especially 528–702.

64. See also, e.g., 22:18.16–19.31; 21:52.18–53.14, 54.18–55.15, 66.5, 70.23–31, 100.23–101.15, 149.29–150.5, 151.3–6. The concept of transcendental egoism (as distinguished from moral egoism [22:128.29–129.2]) at issue in these passages is consistently linked to the notion of Spinozism throughout Kant's philosophical

development. On this, see 2:389–90; 28:206–207; Reflections 3803, 5390 (cf. Reflection 6051; Wolff, *Psych. rat.* § 38; Baumgarten, *Metaphysica* §§ 392–393, 395, 348); and De Flaviis 1986, 46–50.

65. Kant is responding here to Gottlieb Ernst Schulze's *Aenesidemus, oder über die Fundamente der von dem Herrn Professor Reinhold in Jena gelieferten Elementarphilosophie,* originally published anonymously in 1792. Although Schulze's book is directed mainly against Karl Leonard Reinhold's *Elementarphilosophie,* it also contains extensive criticism of Kant. Basing himself on the Pyrrhonist arguments of the first-century thinker Aenesidemus, as well as on the skeptical dimensions of Hume's empiricist theory of knowledge, Schulze contends that the ultimate outcome of Kant's critical philosophy must be the type of skepticism that he (Schulze) advocates. Kant evidently has in mind the passages in *Aenesidemus* where Schulze finds fault with the critical theory of a priori knowledge for making everything into an "aggregate of forms and effects of the mind" and for being unable to repudiate effectively Berkeley's material idealism (see Schulze, *Aenesidemus,* 295–296 and 202–206; cf. Beiser 1987, 281–282). Kant seems to be responding to these charges first by pointing out that his theory of objective experience does indeed contain a principle of the ideality of the object as appearance, and that this principle requires an account of ideas that specify the formal determinations (*das Formale*) of possible experience. Yet according to Kant, the ideas in question make up a system (not an aggregate) of formal determinations, and this system is what makes possible all unified empirical knowledge of the external world. (This interpretation finds support in the lines elided [see 21:99.10–17]. But these are too syntactically convoluted to permit of unambiguous translation.) Second, in the second paragraph of the passage translated, Kant insists that his systematic account of the formal character of our experience of sensible objects involves a concept of realism that must be understood with reference to Spinoza's metaphysics. Apparently, Kant is countering Schulze's charge that his transcendental idealism does not prove the existence of material objects, and hence does not refute Berkeley, by appealing to the concept of realism underlying the Spinozistic theory of substance.

66. See 3:55.19–56.19, 59.19–61.32, 71.3–72.9, 190.24–191.6; 4:232.6–36, 236.33–237.31.

67. Cf. 3:59.19; 4:232.6–238.17.

68. See 3:23.19–24.42, 71.3–72.9, 191.18–193.24; 4:230.29–238.31; Reflections 6312 (18:612.23–613.8) to 6316, 6323.

69. For discussions pertinent to this issue, see Adickes 1920, 853; Daval 1951, 363–368; De Vleeschauwer 1934–37, III 598–630; Förster 1989a, 289–302; Förster 1989b, 217–235; Hübner 1973, 198–201; Lachièze-Rey 1931, 454–463; Lehmann 1939, 91–98; Lehmann 1963, 501–502, 505–506; Mathieu, 1958, 440–443; Mathieu, 1984, 41–42, 45–49; Tuschling, 1973, 188.

70. Kant gives many different formulae for transcendental idealism in the *Opus postumum.* The thread common to all of these is that "idealism" connotes an organized and comprehensive system of knowledge based on a priori principles. Beyond that, he never determines conclusively the sense of what he still calls transcendental idealism. One may want to contend that this would be im-

possible in any event, since no Kantian theory of knowledge that ascribes to the ideality of appearances can entertain seriously the notion that space is anything but transcendentally ideal. Be that as it may, my concern here is to establish that Kant does *fundamentally* throw into question his original conception of transcendental idealism. We can understand why he does so in view of the aspects of his theory of knowledge and philosophy of material nature discussed in this book.

71. We may note in this connection that Kant is one of the very first thinkers to explore systematically the epistemological ramifications of postulating the existence of a universal field entity as the material basis of interaction between objects in space. This point should be kept in mind when assessing the already well documented significance of Kant's dynamical concept of material substance for the historical origins of modern field theory, as well as for contemporary philosophic work on the ontological foundations of field theory. On this, see Berkson 1974, 21–34; Harré and Madden 1975, 181–183; Hesse 1961, 170–222; Leverre 1971, 1–102; McGuire 1974; Williams 1965, 53–94, 120–136. See also Hesse 1961, 125–137; Schaffner 1972, 3–6, 76–117.

72. See 21:87.29–31 and note 58 above. In view of the considerations on the object-relation of self-consciousness contained in the final manuscripts of the *Opus postumum,* I suspect that Kant's ultimate standpoint demonstrates greater affinity with Hegel's positions than it does with Schelling's point of departure in 1800. Kant would never be tempted to deny one critical point, viz., that the object of knowledge must be understood in terms of a subject/object *relation.*

73. Eckart Förster's introduction to the Cambridge translation of selections from the work (see pp. XXIV–XXIX) contains everything necessary to debunk factually the "mental debilitation" thesis, as applied to textual materials composed before the second half of 1801.

Bibliography

Primary Sources

Aristotle. *Aristotelis opera,* ex rec. I. Bekkeri. Berlin 1831–70. Reprint, Berlin 1960–63.

Baumgarten, Alexander Gottlieb. *Metaphysica.* Editio IV. Halae 1757. Reprint in: *Kants gesammelte Schriften.* Vol. 17. Berlin/Leipzig 1926.

Berkeley, George. *Treatise Concerning the Principles of Human Knowledge.* In: *The Works of George Berkeley.* Edited by A. A. Luce and T. E. Jessop. Vol. 2. London 1949.

Boscovich, R. J. *Theoria philosophiae naturalis ad unicam legem virium in natura existentium.* Venice 1763.

Boyle, Robert. *The Works.* Edited by Thomas Birch. London 1772. Repro., Hildesheim 1965–66.

Descartes, René. *Principia philosophiae.* In: *Oeuvres.* Edited by Ch. Adam and P. Tannéry. Vol. 7. Paris 1905.

Gassendi, Pierre. *Animadversiones in decimum librum Diogenis Laertii,* Appendix altera, quae est philosophiae Epicuri syntagma, sectio prima: De universo, seu Natura rerum. Editio IV. Lyon 1675.

Hegel, Georg Wilhelm Friedrich. *Gesammelte Werke.* Hamburg 1968–.

Hobbes, Thomas. *Elementorum philosophiae secto prima, De corpore.* In: *Opera philosophica quae latine scripsit omnia.* Edited by W. Molesworth. Vol. 1. London 1839.

Hume, David. *Enquiries concerning Human Understanding and concerning the Principles of Morals.* Edited by L. A. Selby-Bigge and P. Nidditch. Oxford 1975.

———. A Treatise *of Human Nature.* Edited by L. A. Selby-Bigge and P. Nidditch. Oxford 1978.

Kant, Immanuel. *Kants gesammelte Schriften.* Berlin 1902–.

Knutzen, Martin. *Systema causarum efficientium.* Leipzig 1745.

Leibniz, Gottfried Wilhelm. *Mathematische Schriften.* Edited by C. J. Gerhardt. Hannover 1843–63. Reproduction, Hildesheim 1962.

———. *Die philosophischen Schriften.* Edited by C. J. Gerhardt. Berlin 1875–90. Reproduction, Hildesheim 1962.

———. *Specimen dynamicum.* Translated into German, edited, introduced, and annotated by H. G. Dosch et al. Hamburg 1982.

Locke, John. *An Essay concerning Human Understanding.* Edited by P. H. Nidditch. Oxford 1975.

Malebranche, Nicholas. *De la recherche de la vérité.* Edited by G. Rodis-Lewis. In: *Oeuvres complètes de Malebranche.* Vol. 4. Paris 1958–70.

More, Henry. *Opera philosophica.* In: *Opera omnia.* Vol. 2. Hildesheim 1966.

Newton, Isaac. *Opera quae extant omnia.* Edited by S. Horsley. London 1779–85. Reimpression, Stuttgart 1962–64.

Priestley, Joseph. *The Theological and Miscellaneous Works of Joseph Priestley.* Edited by J. T. Rutt. London 1817–31. Reprint, New York 1972.

Schelling, Friedrich Wilhelm Joseph. *Schellings Werke.* Edited by M. Schröter. Munich 1927–46.

Schopenhauer, Arthur. *Sämtliche Werke.* Edited by A. Hübscher. 2d ed. Wiesbaden 1946–50.

Schulze, Gottlob Ernst. *Aenesidemus oder über die Fundamente der von dem Herrn Professor Reinhold in Jena gelieferten Elementarphilosophie: Nebst einer Verteidigung des Skeptizismus gegen die Anmassungen der Vernunftkritik.* Edited by A. Liebert. Berlin 1912.

Spinoza, Benedictus (Baruch) de. *Ethica ordine geometrico demonstrata.* In: *Opera,* im Auftrag der Heidelberger Akademie der Wissenschaften. Edited by C. Gebhardt. Vol. 2. Heidelberg 1926.

Thomas Aquinas. *Questiones disputatae de potentia.* In: *Questiones disputatae.* Edited by M. Calcattera et al. Vol. 2. Rome 1949.

———. *Summa theologica.* Latin text with English translation. Edited by T. Gilby et al. London 1963–66.

Wolff, Christian. *Cosmologia generalis.* Edited by J. École. In: *Gesammelte Werke.* Sec. 2 (Lateinische Schriften), vol. 4. Hildesheim 1962.

———. *Elementa matheseos universae,* Tomus II. Edited by J. E. Hofman. In: *Gesammelte Werke.* Sec. 2 (Lateinische Schriften), vol. 30. Hildesheim 1968.

———. *Philosophia prima, sive Ontologia.* Edited by J. École. In: *Gesammelte Werke.* Sec. 2 (Lateinische Schriften), vol. 3. Hildesheim 1977.

———. *Psychologia rationalis.* Edited by J. École. In: *Gesammelte Werke.* Sec. 2 (Lateinische Schriften), vol. 6. Hildesheim 1972.

———. *Theologia naturalis.* Edited by J. École. In: *Gesammelte Werke.* Sec. 2 (Lateinische Schriften), vol. 8. Hildesheim 1978.

———. *Vernünfftige Gedancken von Gott, der Welt und der Seele des Menschen, auch allen Dingen überhaupt* ("Deutsche Metaphysik"). Edited by Ch. Corr. In: *Gesammelte Werke.* Sec. 2 (Deutsche Schriften), vol. 2. Hildesheim 1982.

———. *Der Vernünfftige Gedancken von Gott, der Welt und der Seele des Menschen, auch allen Dingen überhaupt: Anderer Theil,* bestehend in ausführlichen Anmerckungen. Edited by Ch. Corr. In: *Gesammelte Werke*. Sec. 1 (Deutsche Schriften), vol. 3. Hildesheim 1983.

Secondary Literature

Adickes, Erich. 1920. *Kants Opus postumum, dargestellt und beurteilt*. Berlin.
———. 1922. "Zur Lehre von der Wärme von Fr. Bacon bis Kant." In: *Kant-Studien* 27:328–368.
———. 1924–25. *Kant als Naturforscher*. 2 vols. Berlin.
Allison, Henry. 1980. "Kant's Critique of Spinoza." In: *The Philosophy of Baruch Spinoza*, ed. R. Kennington. Washington. 199–222.
———. 1983. *Kant's Transcendental Idealism*. New Haven.
———. 1996. *Idealism and Freedom: Essays on Kant's Theoretical and Practical Philosophy*. Cambridge.
Ameriks, Karl. 1992. "The Critique of Metaphysics: Kant and Traditional Ontology." In: *The Cambridge Companion to Kant*, ed. P. Guyer. Cambridge. 249–279.
Anderson, Douglas. 1983. "The Neglected Analogy." In: *The Southern Journal of Philosophy* 21:481–488.
Aquila, Richard. 1989. *Matter in Mind: A Study of Kant's Transcendental Deduction*. Bloomington/Indianapolis.
Aschenbrenner, Karl. 1983. *A Companion to Kant's Critique of Pure Reason: Transcendental Aesthetic and Analytic*. Lanham, Md./New York/London.
Barié, G. E. 1951. "Du 'cogito' cartesien au moi transcendentale." In: *Revue philosophique de la France et de l'étranger* 141:211–227.
Bauch, Bruno. 1917. *Immanuel Kant*. Berlin/Leipzig.
Beck, Lewis White. 1978. *Essays on Kant and Hume*. New Haven.
Beiser, Frederick C. 1987. *The Fate of Reason*. Cambridge, Mass.
Bennett, Jonathan. 1966. *Kant's Analytic*. Cambridge.
Berkson, William. 1974. *Fields of Force: The Development of a World View from Faraday to Einstein*. New York.
Bird, Graham. 1962. *Kant's Theory of Knowledge: An Outline of One Central Argument in the Critique of Pure Reason*. London. Reprint, New York 1973.
Blasche, Siegfried, ed. 1991. *Übergang: Untersuchungen zum Spätwerk Immanuel Kants*. Franfurt am Main.
Boas, Marie. 1952. "The Establishment of the Mechanical Philosophy." In: *Osiris* 10:412–490.
Boas-Hall, Marie. 1972. "Matter in the Seventeenth Century." In: *The Concept of Matter in Modern Philosophy*, ed. E. McMullin, 76–99. 2d ed. Notre Dame/London.
Brittain, Gordon. 1978. *Kant's Philosophy of Science*. Princeton.
Broad, Charlie Dunbar. 1975. *Leibniz*. Cambridge 1975.
———. 1978. *Kant: An Introduction*. Edited by C. Levy. Cambridge.
Buchdahl, Gerd. 1988. *Metaphysics and the Philosophy of Science*. Lanham, Md.
———. 1992. *Kant and the Dynamics of Reason*. Oxford/Cambridge, Mass.

Burtt, Edwin A. 1932. *The Metaphysical Foundations of Modern Science*. 2d rev. ed. London.

Campo, Mariano. 1939. *Christiano Wolff e il razionalismo precritico*. Milan. Reprint in: Chr. Wolff, *Gesammelte Werke*. Sec. 3 (Materialien und Documente), vol. 9. Hildesheim 1980.

———. 1953. *La genesi del criticismo kantiano: Parti I–II*. Varese.

Cantor, G., and M. Hodge, eds. 1981. *Conceptions of the Ether*. Cambridge.

Capek, M. 1962. *The Philosophical Impact of Contemporary Physics*. New York.

Carrier, Martin. 1990. "Kants Theorie der Materie und ihre Wirkung auf die Zeitgenössische Chemie." In: *Kant-Studien* 81: 170–210.

———. 1991. "Kraft und Wirklichkeit: Kants späte Theorie der Materie." In: *Übergang: Untersuchungen zum Spätwerk Immanuel Kants*, ed. S. Blasche. Frankfurt am Main. 208–230.

———. 1993. "Kant's Relational Theory of Absolute Space." In: *Kant-Studien* 83: 399–416.

Cramer, Konrad. 1985. *Nicht-reine synthetische Urteile a Priori: Ein Problem der Transzendentalphilosophie Immanuel Kants*. Heidelberg 1985.

Daval, Roger. 1951. *La Metaphysique de Kant*. Paris.

De Flaviis, Giuseppe. 1986. *Kant e Spinoza*. Florence.

De Gandt, François. 1995. *Force and Geometry in Newton's Principia*. Princeton.

Delekat, Friedrich. 1969. *Immanuel Kant: Historisch-kritische Interpretation der Hauptschriften*. Heidelberg.

Dessoir, Max. 1910. *Geschichte der neueren deutschen Psychologie*. Berlin.

De Vleeschauwer, Hermann. 1934–37. *La déduction transcendental dans l'oeuvre de Kant*. Paris.

Dosch, Hans Günther, et al. 1982 (See Leibniz, *Specimen dynamicum* in list of translations.)

Edwards, Brian Jeffrey. 1987. "Dynamical Community and Dynamical 'World Matter' in Kant's Account of Material Substance." Dissertation, Universität Marburg.

Edwards, B[rian] Jeffrey. 1991. "Der Ätherbeweis des Opus postumum und Kants 3. Analogie der Erfahrung," *Übergang: Untersuchungen zum Spätwerk Immanuel Kants*, ed. S. Blasche. Frankfurt am Main. 77–104.

Edwards, Jeffrey. 1999. "Disjunktiv- und kollektiv-allgemeiner Besitz: Überlegungen zu Kants Theorie der ursprünglichen Erwerbung." In: *Recht, Staat und Völkerrecht bei Immanuel Kant*, ed. D. Hüning and B. Tuschling. Berlin. 113–134.

———. 2000 (forthcoming). "Spinoza, Freedom, and Transcendental Dynamics." In: *The Reception of Kant's Critical Philosophy: Fichte, Schelling, and Hegel*, ed. S. Sedgwick. Cambridge.

Endler, Richard. 1902. *Kants physische Monadologie im Verhältnis zur Philosophie und Naturwissenschaft*. Leipzig.

Erdmann, Benno. 1986. *Martin Knutzen und seine Zeit: Ein Beitrag zur Geschichte der Wolfischen Schule und insbesondere zur Entwicklungsgeschichte Immanuel Kants*. Leipig. Reprint, Hildesheim 1973.

Ewing, A. C. 1938. *A Short Commentary on Kant's Critique of Pure Reason*. Chicago.

Falkenstein, Lorne. 1995. *Kant's Intuitionism: A Commentary on the Transcendental Aesthetic.* Toronto.

Findlay, John N. 1981. *Kant and the Transcendental Object: A Hermeneutic Study.* Oxford.

Förster, Eckart. 1987. "Is There 'A Gap' in Kant's Critical System?" In: *Journal of the History of Philosophy* 25:536–55.

———. 1989a. "Kant's Notion of Philosophy." In: *The Monist* 72:285–304.

———. 1989b. "Kant's *Selbstsetzungslehre*." In: *Kant's Transcendental Deductions,* ed. E. Förster. Stanford, Calif. 217–284.

———. 1991. "Die Idee des Übergangs: Überlegungen zum Elementarsystem der bewegende Kräfte." In: *Übergang: Untersuchungen zum Spätwerk Immanuel Kants,* ed. S. Blasche. Frankfurt am Main. 28–48.

Friedman, Michael. 1992a. *Kant and the Exact Sciences.* Cambridge, Mass.

———. 1992b. "Regulative and Constitutive." In: *System and Teleology in Kant's "Critique of Judgment,"* ed. H. Robinson; Supplement to *The Southern Journal of Philosophy* 30:73–100.

Frigo, Gianfranco. 1977. "L'ateo di sistema: il caso di Spinoza nell storiografica tedesca dall' *Aufklärung* alla *Romantik*." *Verifiche.* 811–859.

George, Rolf. 1981. "Kant's Sensationism." In *Synthese* 47:229–255.

Gloy, Karen. 1976. *Die Kantische Theorie der Naturwissenschaft.* Berlin.

Guèroult, Michel. 1934. *Dynamique et métaphysique leibniziennes.* Paris.

Gurwitch, Aron. 1974. *Leibniz: Philosophie des Panlogismus.* New York.

Guyer, Paul. 1987. *Kant and the Claims of Knowledge.* Cambridge.

Harman, P. 1982. *Metaphysics and Natural Philosophy.* Brighton.

Harré, R. 1964. *Matter and Method.* Reseda, Calif.

———. 1970. *The Principles of Scientific Thinking.* Chicago.

———. 1972. *Philosophies of Science: An Introductory Survey.* Oxford.

Harré, R., and E. H. Madden: 1975. *Causal Powers.* Oxford.

Heimann, P. M., and J. E. McGuire. 1971. "Newtonian Forces and Lockean Powers: Concepts of Matter in Eighteenth Century Thought." In: *Historical Studies in the Physical Sciences* 5:233–306.

Hesse, Mary. 1961. *Forces and Fields: The Concept of Action at a Distance in the History of Physics.* London.

Hoppe, Hansgeorg. 1969. *Kants Theorie der Physik: Eine Untersuchung über das Opus postumum von Kant.* Frankfurt.

Hübner, Kurt. 1973. "Leib und Erfahrung in Kants Opus postumum." In: *Kant: Zur Deutung seiner Theorie von Erkennen und Handeln,* ed. G. Prauss, 192–204. Cologne.

Hund, Friedrich. 1978. *Geschichte der physikalischen Begriffe.* Mannheim/Vienna/Zürich.

Kaulbach, Friedrich. 1981a. "Der Primat der Substanzkategorie in Kants Programm einer transzendentalen Logik." In: *Beiträge zur Kritik der reinen Vernunft—1781–1981,* ed. I. Heidemann and W. Ritzel. Berlin/New York.

———. 1981b. *Philosophie als Wissenschaft: Eine Anleitung zum Studium von Kants Kritik der reinen Vernunft.* Hildesheim.

Kemp-Smith, Norman. 1923. *A Commentary to Kant's Critique of Pure Reason.* 2d ed. London.

Körner, Stephan. 1955. *Kant*. Hammondsworth, Middlesex.

Koyré, Alexandre. 1968. *Études newtoniennes*. Paris.

————. 1969. *Von der geschlossenen Welt zum unendlichen Universum*. Translated from English by R. Dornbacher. Frankfurt.

Krausser, Peter. 1981. *Kants Theorie der Erfahrung und Erfahrungswissenschaft*. Frankfurt.

Lachièze-Rey, Pierre. 1950. *L'idéalisme kantien*. 2d ed. Paris.

Laßwitz, Kurd. 1890. *Die Geschichte der Atomistik*. Hamburg/Leipzig. Reprint, Darmstadt 1963.

Laywine, Alison. 1993. *Kant's Early Metaphysics and the Origins of the Critical Philosophy*. Atascadero, Calif.

Leclerc, Ivor. 1972. *The Nature of Physical Existence*. New York.

Lehmann, Gerhard. 1939. *Kants Nachlaßwerk und die Kritik der Urteilskraft*. Neue deutsche Forschungen, no. 247. Berlin.

————. 1953–54. "Erscheinungsstufung und Realitätsproblem in Kants Opus postumum." In: *Kant-Studien* 45:140–154.

————. 1963. "Zur Frage der Spätentwicklung Kants." In: *Kant-Studien* 54: 491–507.

Levere, Travor. 1971. *Affinity and Matter*. Oxford.

Lüdtke, Franz. 1911. "Kritische Geschichte der Apperzeptionsbegriffe." In: *Zeitschrift für Philosophie und philosophische Kritik* 141:41–135.

Lütterfelds, Wilhelm. 1977. *Kants Dialektik der Erfahrung: Zur antinomischen Struktur der endlichen Erkenntnis*. Meisenheim am Glan.

Maier, Anneliese. 1949. *Die Vorläufer Galileis im 14. Jahrhundert: Studien zur Naturphilosophie der Spätscholastik*. Rome.

Mandelbaum, Maurice. 1964. *Philosophy, Science, and Sense Perception*. Baltimore.

Mathieu, Vittorio. 1958. *La filosofia transcendentale e l'Opus postumum di Kant*. Biblioteca di Filosofia 12. Turin.

————. 1984. Introduction to the same author's Italian translation of selections from Kant's *Opus postumum*. 2d rev. ed. (Biblioteca Universale Laterza.) Bari 1984.

————. 1989. *Kants Opus postumum*. Frankfurt am Main.

Mautner, Franz H. 1968. *Lichtenberg: Geschichte seines Geistes*. Berlin.

McGuire, J. E. 1970. "Atoms and the 'Analogy of Nature': Newton's Third Rule of Philosophizing." In: *Studies in the History and Philosophy of Science* 1: 3–58.

————. 1974. "Forces, Powers, Aethers and Fields." In: *Boston Studies in the Philosophy of Science* 14:119–159.

McMullin, Earnan. 1978. *Newton on Matter and Affinity*. Notre Dame.

Melnick, Arthur. 1973. *Kant's Analogies of Experience*. Chicago.

Morrison, Margaret. 1995. "Space, Time, and Reciprocity." In: *Proceedings of the Eighth International Kant Congress*, vol. 2, ed. H. Robinson. Milwaukee.

Nagel, Gordon. 1983. *The Structure of Experience in Kant's System of Principles*. Chicago.

Okruhlik, K. 1983. "Kant and the Foundations of Science." In: *Nature Mathematized*, ed. W. Shea. Dordrecht.

Parkinson, G. H. R. 1965. *Logic and Reality in Leibniz' Metaphysics*. Oxford.

Paton, H. J. 1936. *Kant's Metaphysic of Experience*. 2 vols. New York. Reprint, London 1970.

Pinder, Tillman. 1987. "Kants Begriff der transzendentalen Erkenntnis." In: *Kant-Studien* 77:1–40.

Pippin, Robert. 1981. *Kant's Theory of Form*. New Haven.

Polonoff, Irving I. 1973. *Force, Cosmos, Monads and other Themes of Kant's Early Thought*. Bonn.

Reich, Klaus. 1958. "Über das Verhältnis der Dissertation und der Kritik der reinen Vernunft und die Entstehung der kantischen Raumlehre." Introduction to the same author's edition of Kant's *De Mundi sensibilis atque intelligibilis forma e principiis*. Hamburg.

Rohs, Peter. 1976. *Transzendentale Logik*. Meisenheim am Glan.

———. 1978. "Kants Prinzip der durchgängigen Bestimmung alles Seienden." In: *Kant-Studien* 69:170–180.

Rosenberger, Ferdinand. 1882–90. *Die Geschichte der Physik in Grundzügen*. 3 vols. Braunschweig.

Rueger, Alexander. 1995. "The Art of Constructing Systems." In: *Kant-Studien* 86:26–40.

Schaffner, Kenneth F. 1972. *Nineteenth-Century Aether Theories*. Oxford.

Schofield, R. E. 1970. *Mechanism and Materialism: British Natural Philosophy in an Age of Reason*. Princeton.

Simmel, Georg. 1881. *Das Wesen der Materie nach Kants physischer Monadologie*. Berlin.

Stark, Werner. 1984a. "Bibliographie der Veröffentlichungen von Erich Adickes." In: *Kant-Studien* 75:365–374.

———. 1984b. "Mitteilung in memoriam Erich Adickes 1866–1928." In: *Kant-Studien* 75:345–349.

Strawson, Peter Frederick. 1966. *The Bounds of Sense: An Essay on Kant's Critique of Pure Reason*. London.

Strohmeyer, Ingeborg. 1980. *Transzendentalphilosophische und physikalische Raum-Zeit-Lehre: Eine Untersuchung zu Kants Begründung des Erfahrungswissens mit Berücksichtigung der speziellen Relativitätstheorie*. Mannheim/Vienna/Zürich.

Thöle, Bernhard. 1991. *Kant und das Problem der Gesetzmäßigkeit der Natur*. Berlin/New York.

Tilliette, Xavier. 1978. "Spinoza préromantique: Aspects de la première renaissance." In: *Lo Spinozismo ieri e oggi*. (Archivo di Filosofia.) Padua. 217–229.

Timm, Hermann. 1974. *Gott und die Freiheit I: Die Spinoza-renaissance*. Frankfurt am Main.

Toulmin, Stephen, and June Goodfield. 1982. *The Architecture of Matter*. 2d ed. Chicago.

Tuschling, Burkhard. 1971. *Metaphysische und transzendentale Dynamik in Kants opus postumum*. Berlin/New York.

———. 1973. "Kants Metaphysische Anfangsgründe der Naturwissenschaft und das Opus postumum." In: *Kant: Zur Deutung seiner Theorie von Erkennen und Handeln*, ed. G. Prauss. Cologne.

———. 1981. "Sind die Urteile der Logik vielleicht 'insgesamt synthetisch'?" In: *Kant-Studien* 72:304–335.

————. 1984. "Widersprüche im transzendentalen Idealismus." In: *Probleme der Kritik der reinen Vernunft*, ed. B. Tuschling. Berlin/New York 1984.

————. 1991. "Die Idee des transcendentalen Idealismus im späten Opus postumum." In: *Übergang: Untersuchungen zum Spätwerk Immanuel Kants*, ed. S. Blasche. Frankfurt am Main. 104–145.

Van Melsen, Andreas G. M. 1957. *Atom gestern und heute*. Freiburg.

Vernière, Paul. 1954. *Spinoza et la pensée française avant la révolution*. Paris.

Vogel, Karl. 1975. *Kant und die Paradoxien der Vielheit: Die Monadenlehre in Kants philosophischer Entwicklung bis zum Antinomienkapitel der Kritik der reinen Vernunft*. Meisenheim am Glan.

Vuillemin, Jules. 1955. *Physique et métaphysique kantiennes*. Paris.

Walsch, William H. 1975. *Kant's Criticism of Metaphysics*. Edinburgh.

Waschkies, Hans-Joachim. 1983. "Physik und Physikotheologie des jungen Kant: Die Vorgeschichte seiner allgemeinen Naturgeschichte und Theorie des Himmels." Habilitationsschrift, Universität Kiel.

————. 1991. "Wissenschaftliche Praxis un Erkenntnistheorie in Kant's Opus postumum." In: *Übergang: Untersuchungen zum Spätwerk Immanuel Kants*, ed. S. Blasche. Frankfurt am Main. 185–207.

Watkins, Eric. 1995. "The Development of Physical Influx in Early Eighteenth-Century Germany." In: *The Review of Metaphysics* 49:294–339.

————. 1997: "Kant's Third Analogy of Experience." In: *Kant-Studien* 88: 406–441.

Westfall, Richard. 1971. *Force in Newton's Physics*. New York.

————. 1980. *Never at Rest: A Biography of Isaac Newton*. Cambridge.

Westphal, Kenneth R. 1995a. "Does Kant's *Metaphysical Foundations of Natural Science Fill a Gap in the Critique of Pure Reason?*" In: *Synthese* 103:43–86.

————. 1995b. "Kant's Dynamic Constructions." In: *Journal of Philosophical Research* 20:382–429.

————. 1995c. "Kant's Proof of the Law of Inertia." In: *Proceedings of the Eighth International Kant Congress*, vol. 2, ed. H. Robinson. Milwaukee.

————. 1997. "Affinity, Idealism, and Naturalism: The Stability of Cinnebar and the Possibility of Experience." In: *Kant-Studien* 88:139–189.

————. 1998. "Buchdahl's Phenomenological View of Kant: A Critique." In: *Kant-Studien* 89:335–352.

Wilkerson, T. E. 1976. *Kant's Critique of Pure Reason: A Commentary for Students*. Oxford.

Williams, L. Pearce. 1965. *Michael Faraday*. London.

Wolff, Michael. 1978. *Geschichte der Impetustheorie: Untersuchungen zum Ursprung der klassischen Mechanik*. Frankfurt.

Wundt, Max. 1924. *Kant als Metaphysiker*. Stuttgart.

Translations of Individual Works and Editions Containing Translations

Boscovich, Roger Joseph. *A Theory of Natural Philosophy*. Translated by J. M. Child. Cambridge, Mass. 1966.

Kant, Immanuel. *Critique of Pure Reason.* Translated by N. Kemp-Smith. 2d ed. London 1933.

———. *Critique of Pure Reason.* Translated by W. Pluhar. Indianapolis 1996.

———. *Critique of Pure Reason.* Translated by P. Guyer and A. Wood. Cambridge 1998.

———. *De mundi sensibilis atque intelligibilis forma et principiis.* Edited with German translation by Kl. Reich. Hamburg 1958.

———. *La Forma e i principi del mondo sensibile e del mondo intelligibile.* Translated by A. Lamacchia. Padua 1967.

———. *Kant's Latin Writings: Translations, Commentaries and Notes.* Translated and edited by L. W. Beck in collaboration with M. Gregor, R. Meerbote, and J. A. Reuscher. New York / Bern / Frankfurt 1986.

———. *Opus postumum.* Translated by E. Förster and M. Rosen. Edited and Introduced by E. Förster. Cambridge 1993.

———. *The Philosophy of Material Nature: The Complete Texts of "Prolegomena to Any Future Metaphysics that Will Be Able to Come Forward as Science" and "Metaphysical Foundations of Natural Science."* Translated and introduced by J. W. Ellington. Indianapolis 1985.

———. *Theoretical Philosophy: 1755 –1770.* Translated and edited by D. Walford in collaboration with R. Meerbote. Cambridge 1992.

———. *Werkausgabe.* Edited by W. Weischedel. Vols. 1, 2, 5. Frankfurt am Main 1968.

Leibniz, Gottfried Wilhelm. *Hauptschriften zur Grundlegung der Philosophie.* Translated by A. Buchenau. Selected, introduced, and annotated by E. Cassirer. 3d ed. Hamburg 1966.

———. *Philosophical Essays.* Translated by R. Ariew and D. Garber. Indianapolis 1981.

———. *Philosophical Papers and Letters.* Translated by L. Loemker. Dordrecht 1969.

———. *Specimen dynamicum.* Translated into German, edited, introduced, and annotated by H. G. Dosch et al. Hamburg 1982.

Index

Action: in corpuscularianism, 98–99; fatalism of, 185; Leibniz's laws of, 67, 211n14, 213n31; reciprocal causal, 8, 37, 52–53, 202n29

Adickes, Erich, 176, 180, 227n53, 241n39; on the Reflections, 240n35; on substance, 226n35

Aenesidemus, 252n65

Aether, 8; a priori proof of, 144, 237n18; Cartesian assumption of, 115, 224n9; in *De igne*, 112, 117–18, 123; in determination of substance, 129; as generative source, 113, 143, 148, 159; as ground of community, 158, 240nn32,37; as ground of material reality, 127; hypothetical status of, 237n15; and *Inaugural Dissertation*, 174–82; in interplanetary space, 225n14; as *materia lucis*, 117, 118, 233n2; in *Monadologia physica*, 227n60; Newton's concept of, 102–3, 241n40; in objective experience, 158, 167; in *Opus postumum*, 145, 152–58, 165, 169, 171, 182, 239n27, 240n35; repulsive force in, 141; role in cosmogenesis, 174–75; as self-subsistent material, 174; in Transition 1-14, 155–58, 238n22; and unity of experience, 165–66; in *Universal Natural History*, 114–18; in void-space argument, 143

Aether, cosmic, 126; a priori proof of, 154; dynamical, 124, 150; in dynamical theory of matter, 158; in transcendental theory, 151, 245n59; and universal causal influence, 9, 163–64

Aether, dynamical theory of, 123, 127–29, 132–44, 233n1, 237n17; attractive and repulsive force in, 103, 239n23; Friedman on, 236n13; origins of, 227n49; space in, 146, 247n11; substance in, 128–29, 131, 134, 159; transcendental conditions in, 240n33

Aether, physical, 152–53; as continuum of forces, 145, 155, 158; as cosmic matter, 148; dynamical conception of, 9, 93, 240n32; in the Dynamics, 134; as elastic matter, 112, 113, 123, 227n60; light as function of, 233n2; and material particulars, 243n55; Newton's concept of, 227n53; in the Reflections, 125–29, 148, 159, 181; as source of physical bodies, 125–26; in Third Analogy, 145; as transcendental condition, 186

Agent and patient, reciprocal action between, 13

Allison, Henry, 210n26, 244n59

Amphiboly of the Concepts of Reflection (*Critique of Pure Reason*), 48, 49–51

Analogies of Experience (*Critique of Pure Reason*), 194n7; commentaries on, 11; and elucidation 2, 22; influence in, 200n8; mutuality among, 29, 30, 42, 196n21, 202n28; transcendental principles of, 22, 202n27

265

Analytic of Pure Practical Reason (*Critique of Pure Reason*), 185

Anticipations of Perception, 3–4, 144, 232n110; empty space in, 30–34; magnitude of appearances in, 32–33; natural philosophy in, 34; sensation in, 194n7

Appearance: of the appearance, 170, 247n13; perduring, 208n6

Appearances: affinity of, 208n96; coexistence of, 27; delimitation of space by, 31–32; in experience, 157; field of, 2, 4; first- and second-order, 130, 247n14; intensive magnitude of, 32–34, 204n49; knowledge of, 129; objects as, 190, 191; real of, 203n45; relation of, 35–36; sequence of, 27–28, 29; synthesis of, 197n8

Apperception, 16; community of, 22, 43–46, 207nn90,96; critical theory of, 21–22, 146; in *Critique of Pure Reason,* 244n59; empirical unity of, 22; pure, 207n96. *See also* Unity, of apperception

Apprehension: sequence of, 28; synthesis of imagination in, 17, 18–19, 198nn19–20, 201n19

A priori knowledge: aether proof from, 152; critical theory of, 144, 158, 189, 192; in *Critique of Pure Reason,* xi, 1–10; development of theory, 57; dynamical community and, 91; of empty space, 31; experience in, 153, 197n7; material transcendental conditions in, xi, 1–10, 49; and monadology, 138; role of influence in, 38; in Third Analogy, 7, 158

Aristotelianism: concept of force, 8, 61; concept of form, 66, 97, 101, 221n14; concept of properties, 221n14; concept of substance, 66, 75, 210n11, 221n14; and corpuscular philosophy, 220nn8,14; doctrine of elements, 221n16; and dynamism, 65–68; entelechy in, 74; scheme of nature, 109

Aristotle, *De generatione et corruptione,* 221n14, 222n16

Art, mechanical laws of, 227n46

Atomism. *See* Corpuscularianism

Attraction: in account of cohesion, 125, 137, 142; collective and distributive, 126, 142, 227n55; in cosmogenesis, 227n56; in *De igne,* 118; function of, 124; and object of sensation, 133; as principle of form, 227n59; true versus apparent, 232n108; in *Universal Natural History,* 116

Attraction, Newtonian, 80, 105, 116, 182; and cohesion, 137; and divine omnipresence, 249n36; effect on cosmic aether, 126; empirical data for, 234n9; as fundamental force, 143; influence on British dynamism, 100; as primitive law of nature, 224n11; reciprocal influence in, 249n39

Attractive and repulsive force, 229n80; in aether theory, 239n23; Boscovich on, 103–5; as condition of community, 124; in constitution of substance, 91; and continuum of influences, 54, 93; in *Critique of Pure Reason,* 151; in dynamical philosophy, 99, 124–25, 131, 139; in the Dynamics, 132, 137; Friedman on, 241n40; influence as, 50–51, 149; interaction between, 155, 224n12, 225n25; in isolation of substances, 91; in knowledge of substance, 50–51; in metaphysics of corporeal nature, 137–38; in *Monadologia physica,* 120, 122, 127, 132; and monadological concept of matter, 112; Newton on, 101–3; in *Opus postumum,* 158, 239n23; Priestley on, 107–9; as reciprocal influences, 160; in the Reflections, 148; transeunt, 148–49; universal conflict of, 126; in *Universal Natural History,* 114. *See also* Moving forces; Repulsion

Bennett, Allison, 196n3

Berkeley, George, 105

Boscovich, R. J., 100, 103–5, 131; dynamism of, 109; law of force-interaction, 224n68, 226n42; point-center theory of, 108; *Theoria,* 104, 224n69

Boyle, Robert, 220n5

Buchdahl, Gerd, 195n12

Caloric theory, 155, 238nn23–24

Causality: category of, 200n7; in corpuscular theories, 110; of determinations, 20, 25; divine, 79–80; empirically knowable, 237n13; Hume on, 105–6; of substances, 14–15, 24, 30, 200n5; in temporal sequence, 29

Chemical solvency, 231n106

Chemistry: Kant's concern with, 238n23; nineteenth-century, 220n3

Coexistence, 197n16; of appearances, 27; basic meaning of, 17–18; empirical cognition of, 15; empirical representation of, 19–20, 36; ground of, 199n21; knowledge of, 18, 198n20, 206n82; and objective sequence, 27–30; perceptual conditions and, 18–19; principle of, 79, 81; relation of, 43; in world-space, 157. *See also* Community; Substances, coexistent

Cognition: a priori material basis of, 156, 183; in *Critique of Pure Reason*, 3, 182; formal determinacy of, 186; intellectual and sensible, 129, 228n60, 248n35; objective, 168; perceptual, 107–9; role of light in, 16; theoretical, 169

Cohesion: in dynamical theory of matter, 240n37; ground of, 142; in *Metaphysical Foundations*, 138, 141–42; as property of matter, 125, 137; and solidity, 225n16

Community: attraction and repulsion in, 124; category of, 37, 46–47, 56, 197nn3,5, 202n27; as *commercium*, 20, 21, 22; as condition of experience, 45; in core argument 1, 25–26, 27, 233n1; in *Critique of Pure Reason*, 16, 161, 196n21; influence in, 25; mechanical concept of, 52; mediate, 206n79; objective ground of, 43; occasionalist account of, 218n27; principle of, 46, 197nn7–8, 200n7; proof of principle, 22, 23; reciprocal causal action in, 52–53; as reciprocal causality of substances, 14–15, 46; relation of, 25–26, 232n1; in Third Law of Mechanics, 48; transcendental principle of, 11, 28, 29, 30, 42, 53, 54; and world-whole, 13–16, 46–47. *See also* Dynamical community

Compositum reale, 22, 199n28

Conatus, Leibniz's concept of, 66, 212n21

Concept acquisition, 219n44

Concepts of Reflection, Amphiboly of, 48, 49–51

Consciousness: of coexistent objects, 45. *See also* Self-consciousness; Unity, of consciousness

Consequence, relation of, 22

Continual creation, 210n3

Continuity, Leibnizian law of, 223n46

Core argument 1 (Third Analogy of Experience): community in, 25–26, 27, 233n1; influence in, 24–25

Core argument 2 (Third Analogy of Experience), 29; dynamical community in, 27; void-space argument in, 26, 35

Corpuscles, 96; and formation of bodies,

224n12; perception of, 97–98; in solar system, 115; in *Universal Natural History*, 114–18

Corpuscularianism, 203n47, 220n3; and Aristotelianism, 220nn8,14; causation in, 110; conception of substance, 110; fundamentals of, 96–99; imponderables in, 222n20; Leibniz on, 100–101; and natural philosophy, 241n40; physical action in, 98–99; seventeenth-century, 66

Cosmogenesis: aether's role in, 174–75; attraction in, 227n56; Newton's, 114–17; in transcendental dynamics, 242n46; in *Universal Natural History*, 112, 118, 242n46

Cosmology: Kant's, 126, 197n16; Wolff's, 68, 69–72, 214n37, 217n21

Cramer, Konrad, 195n12

Density, 231n106

Descartes, René: on aether, 115, 224n9; Leibniz on, 210n1; metaphysics of, 89; *Principia philosophiae*, 65, 224n9; view of matter, 220n5

Determinations: causality of, 20, 25; ground of, 200n10; reciprocal sequence of, 17–18, 25

Dispositions: seventeenth-century concept of, 98, 220n13

Divine intellect: and particular substances, 79; representational activity of, 80, 217n20

Dogmatism, metaphysical, 251n60

Dynamical community: aether theory in, 159, 240n32; a priori function of, 91, 165; in core argument 2, 27; development of theory, 86, 89–90, 148; and dynamical theory of matter, 182; in Elementary System 1-7, 160; ground of, 146; history of, 61; in the *Inaugural Dissertation*, 9, 82–86, 88–89, 146, 149–50; influence in, 148–49; and the intelligible world, 82; isolation of substances in, 149; in *Opus postumum*, 9; perceptual experience in, 147; precritical accounts of, 161; as reciprocal causality, 161; relation of, 59; as relation of physical influence, 73, 81, 163; role in perceptions, 21, 29, 46; and spatial community, 20, 82; and Spinozistic definition of substance, 158–63; in Third Analogy, 8; in Transcendental Analytic, 162; transcendental theory of, 144, 145–

Dynamical community (*continued*) 46. *See also* Substance, dynamical account of

Dynamical continuum: aether as, 103, 123, 158; and conception of matter, 41; epistemic function of, 42; of material forces, 174; as object of outer experience, 173

Dynamical plenum, 1; in *Critique of Pure Reason*, 151; in knowledge of nature, 42; in *Metaphysical Foundations*, 5–6; in objective experience, 167; in space, 3–4; and theory of experience, 10, 58, 150

Dynamics: corporeal, 67–68; Leibniz on, 211n15; science of, 65; transcendental, 145–46

Dynamics (*Metaphysical Foundations*), 132–44, 230n100, 242n44; attractive and repulsive force in, 132, 137; empty space in, 142; matter in, 138–44; metaphysics of, 139; physical aether in, 134; substance in, 144; Theorem 8, 137, 141, 144; transition problematic of, 151; void-space argument in, 151

Dynamism: after physical monadology, 123; a priori proof for, 145; Aristotelian, 65–68; attractive and repulsive force in, 99, 124–25; Boscovich's, 109; British, 99, 100, 105; eighteenth century, 110; and empiricism, 100; and mechanical principles, 214n35; in *Metaphysical Foundations*, 143; nature under, 109–11; prior to *Metaphysical Foundations*, 136; rationalist interpretations of, 99–109; Wolff's, 68–72, 100, 222n22

École, Jean, 215n51

Elasticity, 231n106; of aether, 112, 113, 123, 227n60; of monads, 228n60

Elementary System 1-7 (*Opus postumum*), 159–60

Elements, Aristotelian doctrine of, 221n16

Ellington, J. W., 209n17

Elucidation 1 (*Critique of Pure Reason*), 16, 20–21, 29; empty space in, 37–38, 58–59, 209n22; experience in, 39, 56, 59; light in, 206n76; matter in, 16, 40–42, 47, 48, 55

Elucidation 2 (*Critique of Pure Reason*), 21–22; transcendental unity in, 46, 207n96; unity of apperception in, 59

Empirical laws, and transcendental laws, 4–6, 195nn11,16

Empiricism: British, 106; and dynamism, 100

Empty space. *See* Space, empty; Void-space argument

Endler, Richard, 226n35

Ens extra mundanum, 85

Entelechy, Aristotelian, 74

Existence: a priori proof of, 55–56, 194n5; relation of, 39

Experience: appearances in, 157; conditions of, 39–40, 47, 205n73; of cosmic matter, 173; formal determinations of, 252n65; light as condition of, 39; material conditions of, 163; one all-encompassing, 157, 163; outer, 23, 169, 171; transcendental conditions of, 2, 7; transcendental theory of, xii, 54, 93, 151, 192

Experience, objective, 23, 30, 252n65; causal conditions of, 38; dynamical plenum in, 167; in elucidation 1, 59; formal conditions of, 3; in *Opus postumum*, xi, xii, 166, 167; possibility conditions of, 168; role of aether in, 158, 167; transcendental principles in, 232; unity of, 55

Experience, unity of, 5, 163–66, 239n27; moving forces in, 247n17; synthetic unity of, 175; in Third Analogy, 55, 156, 175, 189

Falkenstein, Lorne, 194n7

Fanaticism, philosophic, 183, 188, 250n47

Fatalism, of actions, 185

Field theory, modern, 253n71

First Analogy of Experience (*Critique of Pure Reason*), 24; independent status of, 28

First Antinomy (*Critique of Pure Reason*), empty space in, 31, 32

Fluids: imponderable, 222n20; ponderable, 225n16

Force: as active material principle, 99; in the Amphiboly of the Concepts of Reflection, 48; Aristotelian concept of, 8; Berkeley on, 105; as cause of influence, 90; as cause of motion, 241n40; derivative, 67, 71, 72; in dynamical community of substances, 61; dynamical concept of, 52; in *Essay on Living Forces*, 73–78; fundamental, 143; Hume on, 105; in interaction of substances, 74,

224n68, 226n42; Leibniz on, 101, 212nn20–21, 213n25; Locke on, 222n19; mechanistic explanation of, 109; monistic conception of, 127–28; ontologically primitive, 101; passive, 67, 68, 70, 213n30, 214n35; as *potentia agendi*, 66; Priestley on, 107–9; primitive, 66–67, 71, 72, 102; in Third Analogy, 147; and Third Law of Mechanics, 51–55; in Transcendental Analytic, 52; in *Universal Natural History*, 114–18; Wolff on, 68–72. *See also* Attractive and repulsive force; Moving forces; Substantial force; Transeunt substantial force

Force, active, 68, 99, 213n12; derivative, 67; in *Essay on Living Forces*, 89; Leibniz on, 75–76, 216n5; Newton on, 101; versus passive force, 214n35; Wolff on, 70, 87

Force-centers: as model of matter, 104; in *Opus postumum*, 240n38

Force continuum: aether as, 145, 155, 158; transcendental function of, 163

Form: Aristotelian concept of, 66, 97, 101, 221n14; essential, 219n35; hierarchy of, 221n14; matter as correlate of, 97

Formalism: epistemological, 56; exceptions to, 193n5; of intuition, 39; transcendental, 57, 151, 205n64; of understanding, 2, 39

Förster, Eckart, 234n9, 235n12, 250n60, 251n62; on Kant's mental debilitation, 253n73

Freedom, transcendental, 185–86

Friedman, Michael, 195n12, 216n5, 228n66; on the Dynamics, 230n100; on empty space, 247n111; on Kant's metaphysics, 236n13; on *Opus postumum*, 233n4, 234n9, 238n23; on the Phenomenology, 231n107; on Tuschling, 235n12, 241n40

Gassendi, Pierre, 220n5

Generation, Aristotelian view of, 221n16

Geometry: metaphysics and, 119, 225n25, 226n34; validity of, 248n34

God: causality of, 185; as ground of existents, 79, 85, 217n19; phenomenal omnipresence of, 121, 179, 249nn36,39; representational activity of, 87

Gravitation, 119, 232n107; aether in, 155; mechanical explanation of, 223n45. *See also* Attraction, Newtonian

Guyer, Paul, 196n21, 199n26, 202n28, 250n54

Harmony: of monads, 49, 63; and problem of other worlds, 216n4. *See also* Substances, harmony of

Heat: dynamical explanation of, 99; as material entity or quality, 35

Hegel, Georg Wilhelm Friedrich, 253n72

Heimann, P. M., 220n14

Herz, Marcus, 179, 180, 182, 249n37

Hinske, Norbert, 225n28

Hume, David: on causation, 105–6; theory of knowledge, 252n65

Idealism: absolute, 242n44; formal, 191; material, 190. *See also* Transcendental idealism

Imagination: productive, 205n66; synthesis functions of, 208n99; synthesis in apprehension, 17, 18–19, 198nn19–20, 201n19

Imponderables: in corpuscularianism, 222n20; physics of, 241n39; theories of, 225n17

Influence: in Analogies of Experience, 200n8; as attractive and repulsive force, 50–51, 149; in cognition of entities, 16; in community, 25; as condition of experience, 39–40; continuum of, 48, 53, 149, 150, 206n82; in core argument 1, 24–25; definition of, 24; in dynamical community of substances, 61; and empty space, 30–37; and material force, 50–51; and matter, 40–42, 53, 148–51, 160; in non-empty space, 36–37; reciprocal causal, 41, 55, 160; relation of, 24–25, 37, 149, 200n10; role in a priori knowledge, 38; role of light in, 38; role of transeunt force in, 87–89; in space, 1, 21, 38, 205n59; in Third Analogy, 145, 147, 148–49, 161; and Third Law of Mechanics, 91–95; in Transcendental Analytic, 52, 200n8; in transcendental theory of experience, 151; understanding of, 25; in void-space argument, 23, 149, 201n14. *See also* Physical influence

Inherence, relation of, 22

Intuition: of all things in God, 180, 183, 184, 186–87; and appearance, 228n64; a priori forms of, 165; in doctrine of self-positing, 246n4; empirical, 197n15,

Intuition (*continued*)
199n23; formalism of, 39, 175; manifold of, 172, 193n5; outer, 171, 172, 190, 245n59; of space, 33, 171, 176, 178
Isolationism, ontological, 74, 79, 86–87. *See also* Substance, monadological theory of; Substances, isolation of

Judgment: disjunctive, 13; Leibniz's theory of, 213n31

Kant, Immanuel: apperception theory of, 16; Copernican Revolution of, 193n4; cosmology of, 126, 197n16; criticism of Leibniz, 149, 208n1; late manuscripts of, 169, 188; late philosophy of, xi–xii; and Lavoisier, 238n23; letter to Herz, 179, 180, 183, 247n37; mental debilitation of, xi, 188, 191, 253n73; as natural scientist, 240n35; on Newton, 231n100, 232n107; philosophy of material nature, xii, 181; physical monadology of, 118–23; polemics against Eberhard, 162; postcritical thinking of, 251n60; precritical metaphysics, xii; theory of knowledge, xii, 154, 194n6, 230n90. Works: *Critique of Pure Reason:* Amphiboly of the Concepts of Reflection, 48, 49–51; —, Analytic of Principles, 194n7, 205n63; —, a priori knowledge in, xi, 1–10; —, apperception in, 244n59; —, cognition in, 3, 182; —, community in, 16, 161; —, dynamical plenum in, 151; —, empirical concepts in, 195n13; —, empty space in, 30–32, 204n57; —, experience in, 57, 168; —, formalism in, 39; —, pure understanding in, 244n58; —, Transcendental Aesthetic of, 171, 172; —, Transcendental Deduction, 193n5, 207n96, 208n96, 245n59; —, Transcendental Doctrine of Method, 250n52; —, transcendental function in, 244n58; —, transcendental idealism of, 169, 175; —, transcendental knowledge in, 2 (*see also* Analogies of Experience; Elucidation 1–2; Third Analogy of Experience; Transcendental Analytic); *De igne,* 112, 117, 118, 123; *Essay on Living Forces,* 61, 249n38; —, isolationism in, 82; —, part I, 79; —, scientific content of, 73–78; —, substance in, 120; —, world in, 215n2; Fragments on Physics, 133; *Inaugural Dissertation,* 61, 82–86; —,

aether in, 174–82; —, a priori knowledge in, 189; —, dynamical community in, 9, 88–89, 146, 149–50; —, influence in, 90; —, isolationism in, 82, 87; —, knowledge theory after, 180; —, metaphysical theory in, 248n35; —, phenomenal omnipresence in, 174–82; —, Scholium of, 85, 176, 177–82, 219n46, 249n37; —, space in, 174–82; *Mechanics,* 234n9; —, *Metaphysical Foundations of Natural Science,* 5–6; —, argumentative procedure in, 234n9; —, celestial bodies in, 199n23; —, cohesion in, 138; —, corporeal nature in, 51; —, dynamical theory of, 113, 231n100, 235n9; —, empty space in, 143; —, matter in, 51–55, 133, 229n66; —, Phenomenology of, 142, 143, 231n107; —, phoronomy chapter of, 235n12; —, and Reflections on Physics, 124; —, scholarship on, 195n12; —, substance in, 144; —, and Third Analogy, 48; —, transcendental philosophy in, 229n66 (*see also* Dynamics); *Monadologia physica,* 112, 118–23; —, aether in, 227n60; —, attractive and repulsive force in, 120, 122, 127, 132; —, dynamical theory of, 130; —, matter in, 122; —, Proposition 2, 119; —, Proposition 11-13, 122–23, 124; —, theory of matter after, 226n42; *Nova dilucidatio,* 61, 78–82; —, force in, 87; —, Proposition 13, 78–79, 85, 86–87, 217n18, 249n38; —, substance in, 120; *Opus postumum,* 234n9; —, aether in, 145, 152–58, 165, 169, 171, 182, 239n27, 240n35; —, attraction and repulsion in, 158, 239n23; —, continuum of forces in, 154; —, correlativity conception of, 245n60; —, dynamical theory in, 9, 238n23; —, early fascicles of, 113, 114, 123; —, experience in, xi, xii, 166, 167; —, final fascicles of, 176, 189; —, force-centers in, 240n38; —, knowing subject in, 168; —, knowledge in, xi; —, matter in, 158, 238n23; —, relation to Third Analogy, 9–10, 147–66; —, sensation in, 194n9; —, space in, 82, 164, 173–74, 181; —, Spinozism in, 180, 186–90; —, substance in, 162; —, synthetic unity in, 166; —, time in, 174; —, transcendental dynamics of, 153, 236n12; —, transcendental theory before, 180; —, transcendental theory in, 146, 169, 176, 186, 246n4, 250n60,

252n70; —, transition problematic of, 156, 158, 234n9, 235n12; —, Transitions 1-14, 154–58, 163, 172–74, 233n5, 237n13, 238nn22–23; Reflections on Physics, 123–30, 138–39, 183, 240n35; —, aether in, 125–29, 148, 159, 181; —, attractive and repulsive force in, 148; —, continuum of matter in, 127–28; *Reflexionen zur Metaphysik*, 176; *Träume eines Geistersehers*, 226n34; *Universal Natural History:* celestial bodies in, 199n23; —, corpuscular concept in, 226n42; —, cosmogenesis in, 112, 118, 242n46; —, cosmology of, 126; —, matter in, 114–18
Kaulbach, Friedrich, 243n49
Kemp-Smith, N., 199nn2,26, 200n5
Knowledge: of coexistence, 18, 198n20, 206n82; empirical, 236n13, 252n65; in *Opus postumum,* xi; perceptual, 168; transcendental, 2, 60, 236n13. *See also* A priori knowledge

Lehmann, Gerhard, 237n17
Leibniz, Gottfried Wilhelm: Aristotelian dynamism of, 65–68; Boscovich on, 104; general ontology of, 63–65; Kant's criticism of, 149, 208n1; laws of action, 67, 69, 213n31; metaphysics of, xii, 8, 61, 72; monadological theory of substance, 63–65, 133, 148, 210n11, 216n3, 222n23, 230n90; and "other worlds," 216n4; philosophy of nature, 100–101; on physical inflence, 87; theory of judgment, 213n31. Works: *Animadversiones in partem generalem Principiorum Cartesianorum,* 65; *De ipsa natura,* 64; *Specimen dynamicum,* 66, 74
Lichtenberg, Georg Christoph, 187, 251n62
Light: in cognition of entities, 16; as condition of experience, 39, 40; dynamical explanation of, 99; in elucidation 1, 206n76; as function of physical aether, 233n2; and mediate community, 20, 21, 38; in space, 1, 46; in void-space argument, 38
Locke, John, 222n19

Malebranche, Nicholas, 178, 179, 182–83, 184; Leibniz on, 210n1
Mass: and dynamical theory of matter, 228n64; mechanical concept of, 209n22, 228n64

Material nature: constructive hypotheses about, 149; dynamics of, 189; Kant's philosophy of, xii, 181; monadological theory of, 130–32, 226n34; and transcendental theory, 4–6
Material transcendental conditions: and empty space, 1; in a priori knowledge, xi, 1–10; in Third Analogy, 48
Mathieu, Vittorio, 238n21
Matter: a priori concepts of, 154, 159; Berkeley on, 105; Boscovich on, 103–5; causal efficacy of, 99; and community principle, 53–54; as condition of experience, 39, 40; constitutive forces of, 232n1, 247n11; as continuous magnitude, 135–36; corpuscular concept of, 93, 96–99, 112, 117–18, 139; as correlate for form, 97; Descartes's view of, 220n5; divisibility of, 228n64; in the Dynamics, 138–44; in elucidation 1, 16, 40–42, 47, 48; empirical concept of, 5, 204n56, 229n66; extensive magnitude of, 32–33, 122, 203n45; fluid states of, 117; force-center model of, 104; Hume on, 105; impenetrability of, 109, 122–23, 132, 140, 181, 228n64; inertness of, 213n23; and influence, 40–42, 53, 148–51, 160; internal structure of, 109; Leibniz on, 101; as material substance, 93, 133, 135; mechanical definition of, 209n16; metaphysical definition of, 83; in *Metaphysical Foundations of Natural Science,* 51–55, 133, 229n66; "metaphysico-dynamical" explanation of, 140, 230nn98,100; in *Monadologia physica,* 122; monadological concept of, 112–13, 126, 161, 229n76; non-mechanistic theory of, 34; as observable objects, 41; in *Opus postumum,* 158; particulate, 108; perception of, 150; Priestley on, 106; primary affections of, 97; properties of, 122–23; reciprocal influence of, 41; and sensation, 3; as sensible space, 172; in space, 1, 21, 40, 46, 194n9; as substance, 110; and *substantia noumenon,* 130; in Third Analogy, 112, 145, 147–51, 175; in Transcendental Analytic, 52; in transcendental idealism, 49; in Transition 1-14, 233n4; unity of, 163–66; as universal continuum of forces, 127; in void-space argument, 23, 38
Matter, cosmic: experience of, 173, 247n17; transcendental function of, 162, 175; and

Matter, cosmic (*continued*)
unity of apperception, 55–60; in void-
space argument, 55

Matter, dynamical theory of, 35, 53–55,
73, 91, 152–53; aether in, 158; and chemistry, 238n23; cohesion in, 240n36; and
dynamical community, 182; in eighteenth century, 93; influences in, 48;
and mass, 228n64; material forces in,
150; in *Metaphysical Foundations*, 113,
231n100, 235n9; Priestley on, 106, 108;
self-subsistence in, 109; space in, 82,
204n48, 205n59; transcendental principle of, 51

McGuire, J. E., 220n14

Mechanical philosophy. *See* Corpuscularianism

Mechanics: as metaphysical discipline,
209n22; rational, 52, 216n5; science
of, 96

Metaphysical dogmatism, 183, 184, 188

Metaphysics: and geometry, 119, 225n25,
226n34; Leibnizian, xii, 8, 61, 72; of
morals, 185; of nature, 228n62; and physical monadology, 118; post-Scholastic,
90; rationalist, 184; transition from,
65–68, 159

Monadology, physical, 118–23; in the Reflections, 125. *See also* Substance, monadological theory of

Monads: effect of repulsion on, 126–27;
elasticity of, 228n60; force of, 213n25;
harmony of, 49, 63; as mathematical
point, 226n34; occupation of space
by, 226n32; perception of, 72; physical
unity of, 119; relations between, 127;
spheres of activity of, 121, 122–23, 135;
Wolff on, 68, 69–70, 214n44

Morality, in transcendental philosophy,
246n6

Motion: absolute versus relative, 231n100;
communication by impact, 99, 222n17;
mechanical communication of, 209n17,
213n23; as object of external sense,
229n67; perception of, 38; as property
of matter, 195n15; Wolff's rules of, 71

Moving forces: causal efficacy of, 246n4;
as cause of sensation, 129; cognitive
function of, 168; in definition of substance, 109, 243n55; eighteenth-century
concept of, 99; elementary system of,
155, 238n21; formal determinations of,

164; mechanical account of, 241n40; in
Monadologia physica, 120; and the soul,
77; in space, 242n45; unified system of,
238n23; in unity of experience, 247n17;
universal continuum of, 171, 245n59;
Wolff's, 216n4. *See also* Attractive and
repulsive force

Nagel, Gordon, 206n79

Natural philosophy: Boscovich's, 103–5;
and corpuscularianism, 241n40; Leibnizian approach to, 230n100; mathematical foundations of, 76; Newtonian,
76, 101–3, 241n40; physical aether in,
112; seventeenth-eighteenth century, 93,
95, 148, 221n14, 241n40; *vis inertiae* in,
222n18

Natural science: epistemology of, 10; general, 204n56; metaphysical foundations
for, 128–29, 236n12. *See also* Kant, Immanuel: *Metaphysical Foundations of
Natural Science*

Nature: Aristotelian scheme of, 109;
causal uniformity of, 54; continuity
in, 224n69; corpuscular account of, 97;
dynamist view of, 109–11, 128; formal
unity of, 5, 6; mechanical scheme of,
96; metaphysics of, 152, 228n62, 230n90,
233n4, 236n12; Romantic philosophies
of, 251n62; sensible, 4; transcendental
law of, 15, 54

Nature, corporeal: attractive and repulsive force in, 137; Boscovich's system of,
103–5; force in, 75; general doctrine of,
204n56; lawfulness of, 80, 195n10; laws
of, 65; Leibniz's, 68, 72; in *Metaphysical
Foundations*, 51; metaphysics of, 55, 134,
136, 144, 153, 159; transition to, 65–68,
159; in void-space argument, 54

Neoplatonism, 183

Newton, Isaac: cosmogenesis of, 114–17;
Kant on, 231n100, 232n107; "moon
test" of, 232n107; natural philosophy
of, 101–3, 221n16; *Opticks*, 102–3, 104;
Principia, 114, 231n100, 232n107; *regulae philosophandi*, 221n15. *See also* Attraction, Newtonian

Objects: as appearances, 190, 191; a priori knowledge of, 4, 39, 157, 165; empirically knowable, 41, 143; experience of,
2–3, 58–60, 194n5, 252n65; intuition

of, 245n59; perceptual cognition of, 161; perceptual experience of, 56; representation of, 245nn59–60; and transcendental principles, 32; unperceived, 197n16. *See also* Substances

Occasionalism, Malebranchean, 86

Omnipresence, divine, 179, 180, 249nn36,39. *See also* Phenomenal omnipresence

Paralogisms of Pure Reason, 210n26

Paton, H. J., 44, 197n9

Perception: reality in, 33–34; role of dynamical community in, 21, 46, 147; sense, 97–98, 106

Perceptions: of material particulars, 150; reciprocal determinability of, 43, 207n88; reversibility of, 17, 18, 201n14; sequence of, 19, 30, 36; synthesis of, 21, 60, 165

Permanence: principle of, 28, 29, 201n24; substantial, 243n50

Phenomenal omnipresence, 167–74; of God, 121; in *Inaugural Dissertation*, 174–82; Newtonian idea of, 176, 181; space as, 178

Physical bodies: internal composition of, 35; and isolationist concept of substance, 130; Wolff's account of the composition of, 68, 213n34

Physical influence: dynamical community and, 73, 81, 163; finite substances in, 87; and harmony of substances, 81–82, 86; in *Inaugural Disseration*, 82; and isolation of substances, 148; mind/body problem in, 77–78, 81; in *Nova dilucidatio*, 78–82

Physics: Cartesian, 230n99; corpuscular explanations in, 140; empirical, 144, 152–53, 195n16; of imponderables, 241n39; Kant's lectures on, 249n42; metaphysical foundations for, 93; philosophical grounding of, 237n18; and transcendental laws, 5

Plato, 250n49

Platonism, Cambridge, 192

Pluhar, W., 199n26

Potentia, Scholastic idea of, 66, 75, 212n20

Priestley, J. B., 100, 106–9, 131; *Disquisitions Relating to Matter and Spirit*, 106, 108; theory of knowledge, 106, 230n90

Properties: Aristotelian concept of,

221n14; cohesion as, 125, 137; corpuscular doctrine of, 97–98, 107–9; fundamental, 132; of matter, 122–23; Priestley on, 107–9; primary and secondary, 98, 110, 224n68, 243n54; special, 141

Rationalism: Cartesian, 210n11; Spinozistic, 64, 210n11; Wolff's, 68–72

Realia, absolute, 34

Realism: empirical, 190; in transcendental idealism, 182–92, 242n44

Reason: dialectical procedure of, 239n27; opposing principles of, 31; perfect, 212n18; "task of," 150

Reinhold, Karl Leonard, 252n65

Repulsion: in corporeal formation, 224n12; in definition of matter, 132–33; effect on monads, 126–27; efficacy of, 205n59; expansive force of, 141; in Kant's monadology, 122, 123; as material ground, 227n59; Newton on, 103; role in impenetrability, 124; role of aether in, 125–26; in Third Analogy, 147. *See also* Attractive and repulsive force

Schelling, Friedrich Wilhelm Joseph, 187, 202n29, 250n58, 251n62, 253n72

Schulze, Gottlieb Ernst, 252n65

Science: of dynamics, 65; natural, 10, 128–29, 204n56, 236n12

Science, transitional, 152–58, 195n16, 236n12, 238n21; Tuschling on, 242n44

Second Analogy of Experience (*Critique of Pure Reason*), 16; relation to Third Analogy, 27–28, 29; substances in, 202n25

Self-affection, doctrine of, 154, 168–70

Self-consciousness: object-relation of, 253n72; transcendental unity of, 22, 43–47

Self-positing, doctrine of, 154, 168–70; cognitive activity in, 190; intuition in, 246n4; space in, 182; subject in, 191, 246n4; transcendental idealism in, 186

Self-subsistence: of aether, 174; in corpuscular theory, 220n10; and dynamical theory, 109

Sensation, 194n5; in Anticipations of Perception, 194n7; and appearance, 228n64; intensive magnitude of, 194n7; matter of, 3, 194n9; Priestley on, 108; production of, 228n64; real of, 4, 32–

Sensation (*continued*)
35, 195n9, 204n49; and repulsion, 122; as subjective representation, 32–33

Sense perception: in corpuscular doctrine, 97–98; British philosophers on, 106

Sensibility: formal conditions of, 39, 42, 205n63; Leibniz's concept of, 208n1

Sequence: reciprocal, 17–18, 25; singularity in, 27

Simmel, Georg, 226n35

Solar system: lawfulness of, 115; relative motions in, 232n107; in *Universal Natural History*, 114–17

Soul, moving force of, 77

Space: absolute versus relative, 231n100; coexistent objects in, 40; as conceivable (*spatium cogitabile*), 172; and corpuscular theory, 140; and divine omnipresence, 249n36; and dynamical aether theory, 146; as dynamical field, 37; dynamically undetermined, 36; dynamical plenum in, 3–4, 175; dynamical relations of, 76; in *Essay on Living Forces*, 73–78; as form of intuition, 171, 176, 178, 190; hypostatically conceived, 171–72, 174; and impenetrability of matter, 181; in *Inaugural Dissertation*, 174–82; influence in, 1, 21, 38, 205n59; intuition of, 33; Leibnizian account of, 176–77, 178; light in, 1, 21; material, 167–74; material reality in, 159; matter in, 1, 21, 40, 194n9; moving force in, 242n45; Newtonian account of, 176–77, 178; in *Nova dilucidatio*, 78–82; one object in, 170; in *Opus postumum*, 82, 164, 173–74, 181; as phenomenal omnipresence, 178; real in, 203n45; reality of, 176–77; relationist view of, 76, 225n14, 248n34; relation of influence in, 37; sensible, 247n14; sensuously cognized, 248n35; substance in, 90; in transcendental idealism, 175, 185, 189, 190, 253n70; transcendental reality of, 31, 174; in Transition 1-14, 172–74; tri-dimensionality of, 78, 217n17

Space, dynamically determined. *See* Space, non-empty

Space, empty: a posteriori proof for, 116; and community, 21; in *Critique of Pure Reason*, 30–31; in the Dynamics, 142; in elucidation 1, 58–59, 209n24; experience of, 157; and influence, 30–37; interstitial, 33, 34–36, 139; mechanical

concept of, 247n11; and primitive matter, 140; in *Universal Natural History*, 115–17; in the world, 232n108. *See also* Void-space argument

Space, non-empty, 1–2, 189–90; causal agencies in, 38; influence in, 36–37, 46; matter in, 46

Spatial relations, origin of, 80

Spinoza, Benedictus: Leibniz on, 210n1; Lichtenberg on, 251n62; non-critical metaphysical theory of, 184; on substance, 83, 89, 158–63, 183, 185, 192

Spinozism, xii, 83, 251n64; in Analytic of Pure Practical Reason, 185; in *Opus postumum*, 180, 186–90; as philosophic fanaticism, 183; space and time in, 185; as transcendental idealism, 167, 175–76, 182–92

Subject: knowing, 168, 169; percipient, 164–65; self-affecting, 168; self-constitutive activity of, 251n62; self-positing, 191, 246n4

Subject/object relation, 165

Substance: and aether theory, 159; a priori representation of, 170; Aristotelian concept of, 66, 75, 210n11, 221n14; causality of, 14–15, 24, 30, 200n5, 201n14; community of, 8, 42, 64–65, 131, 211n12, 217n19; as complex of relations, 49; in corpuscular philosophy, 97; in the Dynamics, 144; in *Essay on Living Forces*, 73–78, 120; external relations of, 74, 121; and internal relations, 50; metaphysical definition of, 83; metaphysics of, 68, 230n90, 243n49; non-isolationist view of, 91; non-monadological theory of, 136, 208n6; in *Nova dilucidatio*, 120; in *Opus postumum*, 162; permanence of, 11, 28; prehensible, 247n14; Priestley on, 107; real community of, 22; secondary literature on, 226n34; self-contained, 64; Spinozistic account of, 83, 89, 158–63, 183, 185, 192; Wolff on, 68–72, 119, 120, 148, 219n39

Substance, as appearance, 19, 55–60, 170, 208n6; in aether theory, 129, 131, 134; attractive and repulsive force in, 50; divisibility of, 133

Substance, dynamical account of, 95, 110–11, 131, 177, 204n57; force in, 61; intelligible world in, 82; and Leibniz's universal community, 149; reciprocal causality in, 243n50; in Third Analogy, 232n1; and universal harmony, 217n21; Wolff's, 43, 46, 69, 214n43

Substance, monadological theory of, 6, 8; aether in, 128–29, 148; and dynamical philosophy, 100, 105, 111; in Fragments on Physics, 133; Kant's repudiation of, 130–31, 134–35, 149; Leibniz's, 63–65, 133, 148, 210n11, 216n3, 222n23, 230n90; in material nature, 130–32, 226n34. *See also* Monadology, physical

Substances: causal reciprocity between, 37, 243n50; *commercium* of, 43, 45, 61, 68, 78–82, 217n20; consensus of, 218n27; co-ordination of, 83, 177, 178; determinations of, 202n25; dynamical field of, 206n82; in empirical intuition, 37; infinite multitude of, 63, 210n1; internal determinations of, 176, 226n34, 249n39; mediate community of, 206n79; mutual determinations of, 80; Newtonian law of interaction of, 76; non-empty space between, 36; in *Nova dilucidatio*, 78–82; objective simultaneity of, 201n14; ontological independence of, 215n2; perception of, 26, 27, 207n88; permanence of, 28; reciprocal causality of, 14–15, 25, 29–30; in relation of influence, 200n10; in Second Analogy, 202n25; space between, 26; universal connection of, 215n49; wholes of, 84. *See also* Objects

Substances, coexistent, 15, 26–37, 197n3; consciousness of, 45; dynamical whole of, 208n96; experience of, 16, 202n27, 206n82; multiplicity of, 84–85; in *Novo dilucidatio*, 78–79, 217n19; relation of appearances as, 35–36; in space, 18, 40; totality of, 38. *See also* Coexistence

Substances, communication of, 61, 63, 73, 89, 90, 148, 210n11; post-Scholastic problem of, 149

Substances, corporeal: Cartesian account of, 66, 68, 210n11, 214n35; interaction between, 76, 80, 237n13; Leibniz on, 212n19

Substances, finite. *See* Monads

Substances, harmony of, 8, 61, 63, 64, 65, 69, 149; and dynamical community, 89; and ontological isolationism, 86; and physical influence, 81–82, 86; in Proposition 13, 86; "task of reason" and, 150

Substances, isolation of, 82, 122, 161, 216n3; and attractive and repulsive force, 91; in dynamical community, 149; in empty space, 28; physical influence in, 148; and reciprocal action, 74, 79; in theory of matter, 93

Substances, reciprocal action of, 1, 58–59, 74, 84; and coexistence, 217n21; and divine causation, 79–80; and dynamical community, 87, 89; in perception of objects, 60; transcendental source of, 82

Substantial force, 68, 74–75; Aristotelian concept of, 61; Leibniz's account of, 65, 80, 100–101, 119, 211n14, 213n31, 222n23; monistic conception of, 77; and principle of coexistence, 80; Wolff on, 72, 75. *See also* Force, active

Substantia phaenomenon, 49, 129–30, 228n64; non-monadological interpretation of, 144

Temporal sequence according to the law of causality, transcendental principle of, 28, 29

Theosophy, through intuition, 183

Thing, concept of, 201n12

Third Analogy of Experience (*Critique of Pure Reason*), xii, 144; apperception in, 23, 47, 207n96; a priori knowledge in, 7, 158; community principle in, 8, 232n1; core argument 1, 16–18, 24–26, 233n1; core argument 2, 18–20, 27; epistemology of, 166; exegesis of, 11; existence proof in, 57, 151–52; force in, 145; influence in, 145, 147, 148–49, 161; material conditions in, 48; matter in, 112, 145, 147–51, 175; and *Metaphysical Foundations*, 48; objective experience in, 23, 55; physical aether in, 145; preeminence of, 46, 202nn27,29; priority of, 22; proof structure of, 16–22; relation to *Opus postumum*, 9–10, 147–66; relation to Second Analogy, 16, 27–28, 29; repulsion in, 147; scholarship on, 196n1; "task of reason" in, 150; and Transcendental Analytic, 7–10; transcendental argument of, 2, 6–10, 9, 151, 165; and transcendental knowledge, 4; unity of experience in, 156. *See also* Analogies of Experience; Void-space argument

Third Law of Mechanics: community principle in, 48; First Remark to, 52–53

Time: intuition of, 33; non-perceivability of, 57, 58, 198n18, 202n27; in *Opus postumum*, 174; perception of, 17, 19; transcendental idealism of, 185, 190; transcendental reality of, 184

Transcendental affinity, 193n5, 208n96

Transcendental Analytic (*Critique of Pure Reason*), 2, 4; Amphiboly chapter of, 8, 150; Appendix to, 49; constitutive procedures of, 235n9; dynamical community in, 162; force in, 91; and formalism, 193n5; influence in, 52, 200n8; substance in, 91; *substantia phaenomenon* in, 129; and Third Analogy, 7–10; twentieth-century commentaries on, 11, 196n1; understanding in, 39; void-space argument in, 57

Transcendental Deduction (*Critique of Pure Reason*), 193n5, 207n96, 208n96, 245n59

Transcendental egoism, 251n64

Transcendental idealism, xii; conceptual instrumentarium of, 239n29; of *Critique of Pure Reason*, 169, 175; as formal idealism, 191; as form of Spinozism, 167, 175–76, 182–92; of later works, 170; matter in, 49, 133, 252n65; in *Opus postumum*, 146, 186; realism in, 182–92; of space, 185, 190; space in, 175, 189, 253n70; temporal dimensions of, 251n62; of time, 185, 190; transcendental reality and, 248n26

Transcendental laws: conflict among, 31; and empirical laws, 4–6, 195nn11,16; of nature, 15; of pure understanding, 234n9

Transcendental philosophy, xii; a priori argument in, 1; argumentative procedures of, 1–2, 7; causal reciprocity in, 60; dynamical matter in, 145; formalism in, 205n63; materialistic approach to, 239n29; in *Metaphysical Foundations*, 229n66; morality in, 246n6; in *Opus postumum*, 146, 169, 176; origins of, 180; void-space argument in, 23

Transcendental proof, aim of, 33–34

Transeunt causal influences, 1, 193n; in community of substances, 81; and cosmic aether, 9, 163–64; in form of world, 86; Leibnitz on, 63–64; and matter of sensation, 194n9; and physical influence, 76, 148; and the soul, 78; in space, 4; and world matter, 8

Transeunt substantial force: as cause of influence, 87–89, 161; in connection of substances, 82; in form of world, 84; in *Inaugural Disseration*, 8; and physical influence, 73. *See also* Substantial force

Transition: in Leibniz, 65–68, 138; in Kant, 33, 138, 144, 152–159, 195n16, 233n4, 235n12, 238n21, 242n44

Tuschling, Burkhard, 234n9, 235nn11–12, 241n40; on idea of Transition, 242n44

Understanding: formalism of, 2, 39; synthesis functions of, 208n99

Understanding, pure, 13, 165, 203n45; a priori principles of, 237n13; constitutive cognitive accomplishments of, 43; in *Critique of Pure Reason*, 244n58; functions of, 39; Leibniz's concept of, 208n1; and productive imagination, 205n66; transcendental laws of, 234n9; and unity of apperception, 245n60

Unity: of experience, 5, 55, 156, 163–66, 175, 180; of matter, 163–66; of monads, 119; of nature, 5, 6; of self-consciousness, 22, 43–47; synthetic, 166, 169; transcendental, 207n96; of world-whole, 15–16, 86

Unity, of apperception, 22, 55–60, 245n60; in *Critique of Pure Reason*, 244n59; and synthesis functions of understanding, 208n99; in Third Analogy, 43; transcendental, 44–45; and unity of matter, 163–66

Unity, of consciousness, 22, 165, 207n89, 244n58, 245n59; in *Opus postumum*, 182; pure understanding in, 45; subjective, 44; in relation to world-whole, 60

Vogel, Karl, 216n3, 226n35

Void-space argument, 1, 3, 16, 26–37; aether in, 143; in Anticipations of Perception, 30–34; a priori proof of, 147; in core argument 2, 26, 35; corporeal nature in, 54; developmental background of, 60; dynamical explanations in, 141; and Dynamics, 151; in elucidation 1, 37–38; influence in, 23, 149, 201n14; light in, 38; material conditions in, 233n2; matter in, 38, 55, 150; in *Metaphysical Foundations*, 5–6; in Third Analogy, 7, 9–10, 32, 57–59, 145,

204n57; in Transcendental Analytic, 57. *See also* Space, empty
Volume, corporeal, 231n106
Voluntarism, metaphysical, 218n24

Watkins, Eric, 201n14, 204n57, 206n82
Westphal, Kenneth, 193n5, 202n28, 233n4; on the *Metaphysical Foundations,* 195n12, 234n9; on Newton, 241n40; on the *Opus postumum,* 235n12; on transcendental affinity, 208n96
Wolff, Christian: agnosticism of, 70, 120; account of composition of physical bodies, 68, 213n34; *Cosmologia generalis,* 68, 69–72, 216n5; dynamism of, 68–72, 100, 222n22; metaphysics of, 8, 61; rules of motion, 71; transcendental cosmology of, 68–72, 217n21; *Vernüftige Gedanken,* 68–69

World: egoistic, 218n28; empirically determinate features of, 209n24; empty space in, 232n108; in *Essay on Living Forces,* 215n2; essential form of, 84–85; form of, 82, 88–89; intelligible, 82, 85, 219n35; reciprocal action between substances in essential form of, 84; and representational totality, 83–84; substances composing, 85; succession of states of, 83, 218nn29,33
World-bodies, 199n23; empirically knowable, 16; mediate community of, 20, 21
World matter: subjective aspect of, 164; and transeunt causal influences, 8
Worlds: multiplicity of, 84; other, 216n4, 218n24
World-whole: community and, 13–16, 46–47; interacting substances in, 60; unity of, 15–16, 86

Text:	10/13 Galliard
Display:	Galliard
Composition:	G & S Typesetters, Inc.
Printing and binding:	Thomson-Shore
Index:	Roberta Engleman